Central Asian Ismailis

The Institute of Ismaili Studies
Ismaili Heritage Series, 15
General Editor: Farhad Daftary

Previously published titles:
1. Paul E. Walker, *Abū Yaʿqūb al-Sijistānī: Intellectual Missionary* (1996)
2. Heinz Halm, *The Fatimids and their Traditions of Learning* (1997)
3. Paul E. Walker, *Ḥamīd al-Dīn al-Kirmānī: Ismaili Thought in the Age of al-Ḥākim* (1999)
4. Alice C. Hunsberger, *Nasir Khusraw, The Ruby of Badakhshan: A Portrait of the Persian Poet, Traveller and Philosopher* (2000)
5. Farouk Mitha, *Al-Ghazālī and the Ismailis: A Debate in Medieval Islam* (2001)
6. Ali S. Asani, *Ecstasy and Enlightenment: The Ismaili Devotional Literature of South Asia* (2002)
7. Paul E. Walker, *Exploring an Islamic Empire: Fatimid History and its Sources* (2002)
8. Nadia Eboo Jamal, *Surviving the Mongols: Nizārī Quhistānī and the Continuity of Ismaili Tradition in Persia* (2002)
9. Verena Klemm, *Memoirs of a Mission: The Ismaili Scholar, Statesman and Poet al-Muʾayyad fiʾl-Dīn al-Shīrāzī* (2003)
10. Peter Willey, *Eagle's Nest: Ismaili Castles in Iran and Syria* (2005)
11. Sumaiya A. Hamdani, *Between Revolution and State: The Path to Fatimid Statehood* (2006)
12. Farhad Daftary, *Ismailis in Medieval Muslim Societies* (2005)
13. Farhad Daftary, ed., *A Modern History of the Ismailis* (2011)
14. Farhad Daftary and Shainool Jiwa, ed., *The Fatimid Caliphate: Diversity of Traditions* (2018)

Central Asian Ismailis
An Annotated Bibliography of Russian, Tajik and Other Sources

Dagikhudo Dagiev

I.B. TAURIS
LONDON • NEW YORK • OXFORD • NEW DELHI • SYDNEY
in association with
THE INSTITUTE OF ISMAILI STUDIES
LONDON, 2022

I.B. TAURIS
Bloomsbury Publishing Plc
50 Bedford Square, London, WC1B 3DP, UK
1385 Broadway, New York, NY 10018, USA
29 Earlsfort Terrace, Dublin 2, Ireland

In association with The Institute of Ismaili Studies
Aga Khan Centre of 10 Handyside Street, London N1C 4DN
www.iis.ac.uk

BLOOMSBURY, I.B. TAURIS and the I.B. Tauris logo are trademarks of Bloomsbury Publishing Plc

First published in Great Britain 2022

Copyright © Islamic Publications Ltd, 2022

Dagikhudo Dagiev has asserted his right under the Copyright, Designs and Patents Act, 1988, to be identified as Author of this work.

For legal purposes the Acknowledgements on p. xiv constitute an extension of this copyright page.

Cover image: Restored mausoleum of Nāṣir-i Khusraw in Yumgān. Image courtesy of the Aga Khan Trust for Culture 169914 © Aga Khan Trust for Culture / Aga Khan Cultural Service, Afghanistan

This work is published open access subject to a Creative Commons Attribution-NonCommercial-NoDerivatives 3.0 licence (CC BY-NC-ND 3.0, https://creativecommons.org/licenses/by-nc-nd/3.0/). You may re-use, distribute, and reproduce this work in any medium for non-commercial purposes, provided you give attribution to the copyright holder and the publisher and provide a link to the Creative Commons licence.

Bloomsbury Publishing Plc does not have any control over, or responsibility for, any third-party websites referred to or in this book. All internet addresses given in this book were correct at the time of going to press. The author and publisher regret any inconvenience caused if addresses have changed or sites have ceased to exist, but can accept no responsibility for any such changes.

A catalogue record for this book is available from the British Library.

A catalog record for this book is available from the Library of Congress.

ISBN: HB: 978-0-7556-4496-4
PB: 978-0-7556-4495-7
ePDF: 978-0-7556-4497-1
eBook: 978-0-7556-4498-8

Series: Ismaili Heritage Series

Typeset by RefineCatch Limited, Bungay, Suffolk

To find out more about our authors and books visit www.bloomsbury.com and sign up for our newsletters.

The Institute of Ismaili Studies

The Institute of Ismaili Studies was established in 1977 with the object of promoting scholarship and learning on Islam, in the historical as well as contemporary contexts, and a better understanding of its relationship with other societies and faiths.

The Institute's programmes encourage a perspective which is not confined to the theological and religious heritage of Islam, but which seeks to explore the relationship of religious ideas to broader dimensions of society and culture. The programmes thus encourage an interdisciplinary approach to the materials of Islamic history and thought. Particular attention is also given to issues of modernity that arise as Muslims seek to relate their heritage to the contemporary situation.

Within the Islamic tradition, the Institute's programmes promote research on those areas which have, to date, received relatively little attention from scholars. These include the intellectual and literary expressions of Shi'ism in general, and Ismailism in particular.

In the context of Islamic societies, the Institute's programmes are informed by the full range and diversity of cultures in which Islam is practised today, from the Middle East, South and Central Asia, and Africa to the industrialized societies of the West, thus taking into consideration the variety of contexts which shape the ideals, beliefs and practices of the faith.

These objectives are realised through concrete programmes and activities organized and implemented by various departments of the Institute. The Institute also collaborates periodically, on a programme-specific basis, with other institutions of learning in the United Kingdom and abroad.

The Institute's academic publications fall into a number of inter-related categories:

1. Occasional papers or essays addressing broad themes of the relationship between religion and society, with special reference to Islam.
2. Monographs exploring specific aspects of Islamic faith and culture, or the contributions of individual Muslim thinkers or writers.
3. Editions or translations of significant primary or secondary texts.
4. Translations of poetic or literary texts which illustrate the rich heritage of spiritual, devotional and symbolic expressions in Muslim history.
5. Works on Ismaili history and thought, and the relationship of the Ismailis to other traditions, communities and schools of thought in Islam.
6. Proceedings of conferences and seminars sponsored by the Institute.
7. Bibliographical works and catalogues which document manuscripts, printed texts and other source materials.

This book falls into categories five and seven listed above.

In facilitating these and other publications, the Institute's sole aim is to encourage original research and analysis of relevant issues. While every effort is made to ensure that the publications are of a high academic standard, there is naturally bound to be a diversity of views, ideas and interpretations. As such, the opinions expressed in these publications must be understood as belonging to their authors alone.

Ismaili Heritage Series

A major Shi'i Muslim community, the Ismailis have had a long and eventful history. Scattered in many regions of the world, in Asia, Africa, and now also in Europe and North America, the Ismailis have elaborated diverse intellectual and literary traditions in different languages. On two occasions they had states of their own, the Fatimid caliphate and the Nizari state of Iran and Syria during the Alamut period. While pursuing particular religio-political aims, the leaders of these Ismaili states also variously encouraged intellectual, scientific, artistic and commercial activities.

Until recently, the Ismailis were studied and judged almost exclusively on the basis of the evidence collected or fabricated by their detractors, including the bulk of the medieval heresiographers and polemicists who were hostile towards the Shi'is in general and the Ismailis among them in particular. These authors in fact treated the Shi'i interpretations of Islam as expressions of heterodoxy or even heresy. As a result, a 'black legend' was gradually developed and put into circulation in the Muslim world to discredit the Ismailis and their interpretation of Islam. The Crusaders and their occidental chroniclers, who remained almost completely ignorant of Islam and its internal divisions, disseminated their own myths of the Ismailis, which came to be accepted in Europe as true descriptions of Ismaili teachings and practices. Modern orientalists, too, studied the Ismailis on the basis of these hostile sources and fanciful accounts of medieval times. Thus, legends and misconceptions have continued to surround the Ismailis through the 20th century.

In more recent decades, however, the field of Ismaili studies has been revolutionized due to the recovery and study of genuine Ismaili sources on a large scale – manuscript materials which in different ways survived the destruction of the Fatimid and Nizari Ismaili libraries. These sources, representing diverse literary traditions produced in Arabic, Persian and Indic languages, had hitherto been secretly preserved in private collections in India, Central Asia, Iran, Afghanistan, Syria and the Yemen.

Modern progress in Ismaili studies has already necessitated a complete re-writing of the history of the Ismailis and their contributions to Islamic civilization. It has now become clear that the Ismailis founded important libraries and institutions of learning such as al-Azhar and the Dar al-'Ilm in Cairo, while some of their learned *da'i*s or missionaries developed unique intellectual traditions amalgamating their theological doctrine with a diversity of philosophical traditions in complex metaphysical systems. The Ismaili patronage of learning and extension of hospitality to non-Ismaili scholars was maintained even in such difficult times as the Alamut period, when the community was preoccupied with its survival in an extremely hostile milieu.

The Ismaili Heritage Series, published under the auspices of the Department of Academic Research and Publications of the Institute of Ismaili Studies, aims to make available to wide audiences the results of modern scholarship on the Ismailis and their rich intellectual and cultural heritage, as well as certain aspects of their more recent history and achievements.

To the memory of my mother
Navruzova Majlis (1938–2013)

Contents

	Preface	xiii
	Acknowledgements	xv
	Abbreviations	xvii
	Note on Transliteration	xxii
	Illustrations	xxiv
	Maps and Tables	xxvi
1.	Ismaili History in Central Asia	1
	Early Ismaili History in Central Asia	1
	Toponyms of Badakhshān/Pamir	3
	The Ismaili *Daʿwa* in Central Asia	12
	Nāṣir-i Khusraw and the Ismailis of Badakhshān	15
	The Badakhshānī Ismailis during the Alamūt period	23
	Taqiyya and the Ismailis in the Post-Alamūt Era	30
	The *Ḥudūd al-Dīn* in the Context of Central Asia	32
	Pīr and *Pīrship* in Central Asia	36
	The Political History of Badakhshān	39
	The Russian Revolution and the Panjebhai Movement	54
	The Ismaili Community in the Soviet Era	57
	The Ismaili Community in the Post-Soviet Era	60

2.	Ismaili Studies by Russian, Soviet and Post-Soviet Scholars	63
	The Ismailis under Russian and Soviet Rule	63
	The Ismailis in Soviet Studies	67
	Review of the Literature on the Ismailis in Soviet Scholarship	71
	Manuscripts Discovered in Badakhshān	90
	Review of the Literature on the Ismailis in Post-Soviet Scholarship	102
	Outline of the Activities and Projects Conducted by the Manuscript Office	105
	Post-Soviet Scholarship on the Ismailis	108
3.	Bibliography of Works by Imperial Russian, Soviet and Post-Soviet Scholars	117
	References	253
	Index	267

Preface

This bibliographical study focuses primarily on the Ismaili literature produced by Russian, Soviet and post-Soviet scholars in the constituent countries of the former Soviet Union and, in particular, in Central Asia. Works on Ismaili literature such as those by Louis Massignon (1883–1962) and Asaf A. A. Fyzee (1899–1981) represent pioneering attempts to collect and catalogue literature on the Ismailis and their doctrines in the broader sense. Further progress in the field of Ismaili studies was made in the middle of the twentieth century, and advances in research and publications are reflected in the pages of the *Index Islamicus* edited by James D. Pearson (1911–1997), and by its continuation, the *Quarterly Index Islamicus*.

Research on Ismailism includes work on recently discovered Ismaili manuscripts which have been preserved privately especially by members of Ismaili communities from Syria to Yemen and from Central Asia to India. These hitherto unknown manuscript sources have become available to a wider audience thanks to the intensive field work carried out by modern scholars, who include Wladimir Ivanow (1886–1970), author of *Ismaili Literature: A Bibliographical Survey* (1963) *inter alia*, and Ismail K. Poonawala who compiled the *Biobibliography of Ismāʿīlī Literature* (1977). Thanks to their endeavours, approximately 1300 titles attributed to more than 200 authors were identified and classified.

The most recent and most comprehensive bibliography on Ismaili sources is by Farhad Daftary and is entitled *Ismaili Literature* (2004). This is a detailed history of the scholarship in the field of Ismaili studies and is among the first of such studies to include a number of major works on the Ismailis written by Russian and Soviet scholars.

The bibliographic study presented here focuses primarily on the written materials produced by Russian scholars from the era of the expansion of Russian imperial rule in Central Asia (then known as Turkestan) in the mid-nineteenth century to the period after 1917 by Soviet and then post-Soviet scholars. Moreover, this bibliographical study includes other studies on Nāṣir-i Khusraw and the Ismailis of Central Asia. In addition, this study aims to show the trajectory of the development of Ismaili studies in the regions under Russian influence. Initially, research in Ismaili studies in Central Asia was carried out by Russian intelligence and military officers, and only later by scholars of oriental studies. Even though the October Revolution of 1917 did not completely change the imperialist attitude towards the peoples of Central Asia found amongst these scholars, the approach to the study of religion was formulated in terms of Marxism and Communist party ideology.

This study first presents the historical background of the Central Asian region in three periods: the Russian, Soviet and post-Soviet eras. Then the second part of this study consists of an annotated bibliography of published books and articles, recorded materials, unpublished manuscripts, theses and documents in the main by Russian, Soviet and post-Soviet scholars on the Ismailis of Central Asia, a field in which relatively little has been published in the West.

Thus, innovatively, this work focuses mainly on Central Asia, which includes Badakhshān, a mountainous district that is the home of one of the earliest established Ismaili communities. Known also as Transoxania, or Mā warā' al-nahr in Arabic, Central Asia is more appropriately designated by the term Greater Khurāsān. It was in fact in the region (*jazīra*) of Khurāsān that the Ismaili mission (*daʿwa*) and the activities of its *dāʿī*s (missionaries) found great success in spreading Ismaili teachings, particularly in the province of Badakhshān.

Throughout this study, where English quotations of works in Russian, Persian or Tajik are provided, the English translations are by the author unless otherwise stated.

Acknowledgements

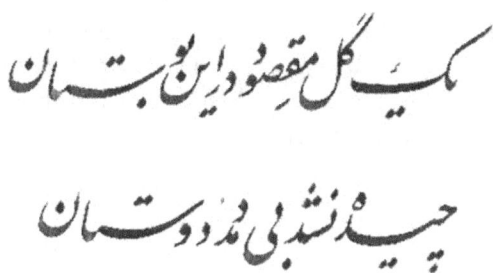

Not a single flower was picked in this garden
Without the help of friends
(Saʿdī d. 691/1292)

The most satisfying part of the present work for me is being able to express my thanks to the people who embarked with me on this journey and to acknowledge their support. Without them this work would never have been completed. To begin with, I would like to express my sincere gratitude to Qudratbek Ėl'chibekov and Hokim Qalandarov who have been very generous, allowing me to use their private libraries and offering tremendous assistance in identifying the relevant literature.

In addition, I wish to thank my friends and colleagues Bobomullo Bobomulloev, Muzaffar Zoolshoev, Abdulmamad Iloliev, Otambek Mastibekov and Nourmamadcho Nourmamadchoev for all their help with the materials related to this project.

Several other people at the IIS have assisted me with the project, and I am truly grateful to them for their comments and suggestions: Dr Farhad Daftary, the late Kutub Kassam, Dr Gurdofarid Miskinzoda and Dr Maria De Cillis. I wish also to thank Leila Dodykhudoeva for her assistance with the Russian and Tajik sources, Dr Isabel Miller, Russell Harris and

Marjan Afsharian whose editorial suggestions have contributed to the realisation of the final version of this work.

Last but not least, I must thank my wife Nargis for her love and understanding and our beautiful children who are the true joy and inspiration in my life.

Even though this project has not been an easy journey, it has enabled me to understand more deeply the history of the region, its earliest inhabitants, the Zoroastrian religion and tradition, pre-Islamic and Islamic beliefs and rituals, and the eras from the Achaemenids to Alexander the Great, the Sasanians to the Arab conquest, the Sāmānids to the Turkic and Mongol invasions, the Tīmūrids to the Uzbeks, and that of the Great Game during the time of Russo-British imperial rivalry in the late nineteenth and early twentieth centuries.

Abbreviations

AAF (RSST)	*Akhboroti Akademiĭa Fanho. Respublikai Sovetii Sotsialistii (Tojikiston)*
AAS	*Aziĭa i Afrika Segodniĭa*
AIT	*Akademiĭai Ilmhoi Tojikiston*
AKDN	Aga Khan Development Network
AKF	Aga Khan Foundation
AME	*Anthropology of the Middle East*
AN SSSR	Akademiĭa Nauk (Soĭuz Sovetskikh Sotsialisticheskikh Respublik)
ANRT	Akademii Nauk Respubliki Tadzhikistana
ANT (SSR)	Akademii Nauk Tadzhikskoĭ (Sovetskoĭ Sotsialisticheskoĭ Respubliki)
ANT (SSR)	Akademii Nauk Tadzhikskoĭ (Sovetskoĭ Sotsialisticheskoĭ Respubliki)
AS	*Adabiët va san'at*
BAISR	*Bulletin de l'Académie Impériale des Sciences de Russie*
BSE	*Bol'shaĭa Sovetskaĭa Ėntsiklopediĭa*, ed. A.M. Prokhorov et al. 3rd edition, Moscow: Sovetskaĭa Ėntsiklopediĭa, 1969–1978; translated as *The Great Soviet Encyclopedia*. New York and London: Macmillan and Collier Macmillan, 1973–1982.
CAC	*Central Asia and the Caucasus*
CAS	*Central Asian Survey*
DIFM	Darülfünun Ilâhiyat Fakültesi Mecmausi (Istanbul)

EAST	*Ėntsiklopediiai Adabiët va San'ati Tojik*, ed. A.K. Qurbonov. Dushanbe: Sarredaktsiiai Ilmii Ėntsiklopediia Sovetii Tojik, 1986–1989.
EB	Ėlektronnaia biblioteka
EES	*Ėtika: Ėntsiklopedicheskiĭ slovar'*, ed. P.G. Apresiana and A.A. Guseĭnova. Moscow: Gardariki, 2001.
EI	*The Encyclopaedia of Islam*, ed. M.T. Houtsma et al. 1st edition, Leiden: E.J. Brill; London: Luzac, 1913–1938; reprinted, Leiden: E.J. Brill, 1987.
EI2	*The Encyclopaedia of Islam*, ed. H.A.R. Gibb et al. New edition, Leiden: E.J. Brill, 1960–2004.
EIAK	*Ėtnologiia, Istoriia, Arkheologiia, Kul'turologiia*
EIF	*Ezhegodnik Islamskoĭ Filosofii*
EIR	*Encyclopædia Iranica*, ed. E. Yarshater. London-New York: Columbia University, 1985—. Also available online at: http://www.iranicaonline.org/
EIS	*Encyclopaedia Islamica*, ed. Wilferd Madelung and Farhad Daftary. London: Brill, 2008—. Also available online at: https://referenceworks.brillonline.com/browse/encyclopaedia-islamica
EMA	*Encyclopedia of Modern Asia*, ed. David Levinson and Karen Christensen. New York: Charles Scribner's Sons, 2002.
EO	*Ėtnograficheskoe obozrenie*
ER	*The Encyclopedia of Religion*, ed. Mircea Eliade. New York: Macmillan, 1987.
ERE	*Encyclopaedia of Religion and Ethics*, ed. J. Hastings. Edinburgh: T. and T. Clark, 1908–1926.
ES	*Ėntsiklopedicheskiĭ slovar'*, ed. B.A. Vvedenskiĭ. Moscow: Bol'shaia Sovetskaia Ėntsiklopediia, 1953–1955.
ESBE	*Ėntsiklopedicheskiĭ Slovar'*, ed. Brokgauz-Efron, F.A. Brokgauz and I.A. Efron. St Petersburg, 1890–1907.
EST	*Ėntsiklopediiai Sovetii Tojik*, ed. M. Osimī and M. Dinorshoev. Dushanbe: Sarredaktsiiai Ilmii Ėntsiklopediia Sovetii Tojik, 1978–1988.
FE	*Filosofskaia Ėntsiklopediia*, ed. F.V. Konstantinova. Moscow: Sovetskaia Ėntsiklopediia, 1960–1970.
FES	*Filosofskiĭ Ėntsiklopedicheskiĭ Slovar'*, ed. S.S. Averintsev, Ė.A. Arab-Ogly and L.F. Il'ichev. Moscow: Sovetskaia Ėntsiklopediia, 1989.

FHAAIJT	*Falsafa va Huquq, Akhbori akademiiai ilmhoi Jumhurii Tojikiston*
FISZAA	*Filologiia i istoriia stran zarubezhnoĭ Azii i Afriki*
FS	*Filosofiia i sovremennost'*
GBAO	Gorno-Badakhshān Autonomous Oblast'
GSE	*The Great Soviet Encyclopedia*
HI	*Handwörterbuch des Islam*, ed. A.J. Wensinck and J.H. Kramers. Leiden: E.J. Brill, 1941.
IAN (TSSR)	Izvestiia Akademii Nauk (Tadzhikskoĭ Sovetskoĭ Sotsialisticheskoĭ Respubliki)
IAN SSSR	Izdatel'stvo Akademii Nauk, Soiuz Sovetskikh Sotsialisticheskikh Respublik
IANRT	Izvestiia Akademii Nauk Respubliki Tadzhikistan
IC	*Islamic Culture*
IEA RAN	Institut Ėtnologii i Antropologii. Rossiĭskaia Akademiia Nauk
IES	*Islam: Ėntsiklopedicheskiĭ Slovar'*, ed. G.B. Miloslavskiĭ, U.A. Petrosian, M.B. Piotrovskiĭ and S.M. Prozorov. Moscow: Nauka, 1991.
IF	*Iranskaia Filologiia*
IFKA	*Istoriko-filosofskie i kul'turnye aspekty*
IFZ	*Istoriko-Filologicheskiĭ Zhurnal*
IH	*Ilm va haët*
IIS	The Institute of Ismaili Studies, London
IJHM	*IRAN: Istoriia i Sovremennost'*
INA AN	Instituta Narodov Azii. Akademii Nauk. USSR
ISCU	Ismaili Special Collections Unit
ITREB	Ismaili Tariqa and Religious Education Board
ITREC	Ismaili Tariqa and Religious Education Committee
IVRAN	Institut Vostokovedeniia Rossiĭskoĭ Akademii Nauk
JA	*Journal Asiatique*
JASB	*Journal and Proceedings of the Asiatic Society of Bengal*
JBBRAS	*Journal of the Bombay Branch of the Royal Asiatic Society*
JRAS	*Journal of the Royal Asiatic Society*
JSIS	*Journal of Shi'a Islamic Studies*
KLE	*Kratkaia Literaturnaia Ėntsiklopediia*, ed. A.A. Surkov. Moscow: Sovetskaia Ėntsiklopediia, 1962–1978.
KPSS	Kommunisticheskaia Partiia Sovetskogo Soiuza (Communist Party of the Soviet Union)
KSINA	*Kratkie soobshcheniia Instituta Narodov Azii*

KSIV	*Kratkie soobshcheniia Instituta vostokovedeniia*
LGU	Leningradskiĭ gosudarstvennyĭ universitet
MGU	Moskovskiĭ gosudarstvennyĭ universitet
MI	*Mir Islama*
MS	*Maktabi Sovetī*
NAA	*Narody Azii i Afriki*
NFE	*Novaia Filosofskaia Ėntsiklopediia*, ed. B.S. Stepin, A.A. Guseĭnov, G.U. Semigin, A.P. Ogurtsov. Moscow: Mysl', 2019.
NP	*Nomai Pazhouhishgoh*
NR	*Nauka i Religiia*
NZ	*Nauchnyĭ Zhurnal*
OF	*Otdel filosofii*
PIKFSA	*Problemy istorii, kul'tury, filologii stran Azii*
PV	*Peterburgskoe vostokovedenie*
RAN	Rossiĭskaia Akademiia Nauk
REI	*Revue des Études Islamiques*
ROMSV	*Religiia i obshchestvennaia mysl' stran Vostoka*
SE	*Sovetskaia Ėntsiklopediia*, see, Bol'shaia Sovetskaia Ėntsiklopediia
SEI	*Shorter Encyclopaedia of Islam*, ed. H.A.R. Gibb and J.H. Kramers. Leiden: E.J. Brill, 1953.
SET	*Sovetskaia ėtnografiia*
SFH	*Seriiai falsafa va huquq*
SFIH	*Seriiai falsafa, iqtisodiët va huquqshinosī*
SGE	*Soobshcheniia Gosudarstvennogo Ėrmitazha*
SIE	*Sovetskaia Istoricheskaia Ėntsiklopediia*, ed. E.M. Zhukov. Moscow: Sovetskaia Ėntsiklopediia, 1961–1976.
SNAA	*Strany i narody Azii i Afriki*
SS	*Sadoi Sharq*
SSA	*Simvol, Syriaca & Arabica*
TASSR	Turkestan Autonomous Soviet Socialist Republic
TIKO	*Tadzhiks: Istoriia, kul'tura, obshchestvo*
TV	*Turkestanskie vedomosti*
UCA	University of Central Asia
UZIKU	*Uchënye zapiski Imperatorskogo Kazanskogo universiteta*
UZLGU	*Uchënye zapiski Leningradskogo gosudarstvennogo universiteta*
VI	*Voprosy istorii*
VII	*Vestnik instituta iazykov*

Abbreviations

VISA	Voprosy istorii stran Azii
VKU	Vestnik Khorogskogo universiteta
VL	Vostochnai͡a literatura
VLGU	Vestnik Leningradskogo gosudarstvennogo universiteta
VPU	Vestnik pedagogocheskogo universiteta
VTNU SFN	Vestnik Tadzhikskogo Nat͡sional'nogo Universiteta. Serii͡a filologicheskikh Nauk
VTTU	Vestnik Tadzhikskogo tekhnicheskogo universiteta
VU (RTSU)	Vestnik universiteta (Rossiĭsko-Tadzhikskiĭ slavi͡anskiĭ universitet)
ZKV	Zapiski Kollegii Vostokovedov
ZV	Zvezda Vostoka
ZVORAO	Zapiski Vostochnogo otdelenii͡a Russkogo arkheologicheskogo obshchestva

Note on Transliteration

The material used for this work is mainly in Russian and Tajik. Modifications have been introduced to the ALA-LC Romanisation tables for Slavic alphabets, which is a set of standards for the Romanisation of texts in various writing systems used by the American Library Association and the Library of Congress for the transliteration of Russian (Cyrillic) into English. The exceptions are: 'й' as (ĭ); 'я' as (i̯a); 'ю' as (i̯u); 'ё' as (ë); 'ц' as (t̂s); 'ы' as (y); 'щ' as (shch); 'э' as (ė); 'ъ' as (″); 'ь' as (').

To transcribe the Cyrillic Tajik alphabet, the *World's Writing System* has been used, as it represents Tajik letters more satisfactorily. The Cyrillic Tajik alphabet differs from the Russian alphabet in the five following letters: 'ғ' as (gh); 'қ' as (q); 'ӯ' as (ū); 'ъ' as ('). Since the Tajik Cyrillic alphabet does not differentiate between the letters (ح) and (ه), this study transliterates both letters as (h).

Note on Transliteration

The transliteration system for Arabic and Persian characters is the one used by the *Encyclopaedia Islamica*.

Consonants						**Short Vowels**	
ء	ʾ	ز	z	ک	k	‒	a
ب	b	ژ	zh	گ	g	‒	u
پ	p	س	s	ل	l	‒	i
ت	t	ش	sh	م	m		
ث	th	ص	ṣ	ن	n	**Long Vowels**	
ج	j	ض	ḍ	ه	h	آ	ā
چ	ch	ط	ṭ	و	w/v	و	ū
ح	ḥ	ظ	ẓ	ی	y	ي	ī
خ	kh	ع	ʿ				
د	d	غ	gh			**Diphthongs**	
ذ	dh	ف	f			‒و	aw
ر	r	ق	q			‒ي	ay
ة	a; at (construct state)						
ال	al- (article)						

Illustrations

1. The restored mausoleum of Nāṣir-i Khusraw in Yumgān. Image courtesy of the Aga Khan Trust for Culture 169914 © Aga Khan Trust for Culture / Aga Khan Cultural Service – Afghanistan — 16
2. Fayḍābād, the capital of historical Badakhshān and present capital of Badakhshān of Afghanistan. Photo credit: Khwahan, https://commons.wikimedia.org/wiki/File:Fayzabad_City_of_Badakhshan.jpg#file, licensed under CC-BY-SA-3.0 — 40
3. The Panj River (Amū Daryā) which divides Tajik Badakhshān from Afghan Badakhshān as a result of Anglo-Russian rivalry in Central Asia in the late 13th/19th century. Image courtesy of Dmitriĭ Buevich, Russia — 49
4. Khārūgh, the capital of Badakhshān of Tajikistan. Image courtesy of Mikhail Romanyuk — 61
5. The Aga Khan addressing members of the Ismaili community during his visit to Badakhshān in 1998. Photo credit: AKDN / Zahur Ramji — 62
6. Bobojon Ghafurov (1908–1977). Photo credit: unknown, https://tg.wikipedia.org/wiki/Акс:Академик_Бобоҷон_Ғафуров.jpg, licensed under CC-BY-SA-3.0 — 74
7. Aleksandr Aleksandrovich Semënov (1887–1958). Courtesy of the Institute History, Archaeology and Ethnography, Academy of Science, Tajikistan — 77
8. Wladimir Alekseevich Ivanow (1886–1970). Courtesy of F. Daftary — 78

Illustrations

9. Mikhail Stepanovich Andreev (1873–1948). Photo credit: unknown, https://ru.wikipedia.org/wiki/Файл:Andreev_MS_1939.jpg , licensed under CC-BY-SA-3.0   80
10. Evgeniĭ Ėduardovich Bertel's (1890–1957). Photo credit: unknown, https://az.wikipedia.org/wiki/Fayl:Yevgeni_Bertels.gif , licensed under CC-BY-SA-3.0   81
11. *Hājat va Munājāt-i Mubārak-i Wakhānī*. Courtesy of Abdulmamad Iloliev   93
12. Ivan Ivanovich Zarubin (1887–1964). Courtesy of the Institute of Humanities named after Academician B. Iskandarov, the Academy of the Sciences of the Republic of Tajikistan   95
13. *Kulliyat-i Mubārak-i Wakhānī*. Courtesy of Abdulmamad Iloliev   96

Maps and Tables

Map of Badakhshan. Courtesy of Russell Harris   48

Table of the ranks of the Ismaili religious hierarchy at various historical periods   34

1

Ismaili History in Central Asia

Early Ismaili History in Central Asia

This book is a study of Russian, Soviet and post-Soviet scholarship in Ismaili studies and particularly regarding Ismailis in the region presently known as Central Asia, which in modern contexts has been mainly defined as incorporating the five former Soviet republics of Kazakhstan, Kyrgyzstan, Tajikistan, Turkmenistan and Uzbekistan. Historically, the term Central Asia could also take in other areas, such as those in present-day Afghanistan, northern and western Pakistan, north-eastern Iran, Kashmir and Xinjiang in western China.[1] Central Asia has also been identified by other names such as Khurāsān or more precisely Greater Khurāsān which included the current province of Khurāsān in Iran,[2] Afghanistan, Turkmenistan, Uzbekistan, Tajikistan, most of Kyrgyzstan, the southern territories of Kazakhstan, and northern and western Pakistan. Khurāsān in its narrow sense comprised the cities of Nīshāpūr and Ṭūs (now in Iran), Balkh and Herat (now in Afghanistan), Marv (now in Turkmenistan), Samarqand and

---

[1] Yuri Bregel, *An Historical Atlas of Central Asia* (Leiden, 2003), p. vii. See also James A. Millward, 'Positioning Xinjiang in Eurasian and Chinese History: Differing visions of the "Silk Road"', in Colin Mackerras and Michael Clark, ed., *China, Xinjian and Central Asia: History, Transition and Crossborder Interaction into the 21st Century* (London: Routledge, 2009), pp. 55–74; F. Mayor, 'Foreword', in A.H. Dani and B.A. Litvinsky, ed., *History of Civilizations of Central Asia*, vol. 3, *The Crossroads of Civilizations, A.D. 250 to 750* (Paris: UNESCO, 1992–2005), p. 8.

[2] 'in pre-Islamic and early Islamic times, the term "Khurāsān" frequently had a much wider denotation, covering also parts of what are now Soviet Central Asia and Afghanistan; early Islamic usage often regarded everywhere east of western Persia, *Djibal* or what was subsequently termed "Irak" *'Adjami*, as being included in a vast and ill-defined region of Khurasan, which might even extend to the Indus Valley and Sind', C.E. Bosworth, 'Khurāsān', *EI2*, vol. 5, pp. 55–59. See also Mir Ghulam Muhammad Ghubar, *Khurasan* (Kabul, 1937), pp. 5–6.

Bukhāra (now in Uzbekistan), and Khujand and Panjakent (now in Tajikistan). However, the name Khurāsān was used to designate an even larger region that encompassed most of Transoxania (Farā-rūd[3] in Persian and in Arabic, Mā warā' al-nahr, meaning 'beyond the river') and Sogdiana[4] in the north, that extended westward to the Caspian Sea, southward to include the Sīstān desert, and eastward to the Hindu Kush mountains in Afghanistan. The toponym Transoxania is also used for the portion of Central Asia that corresponds approximately to modern-day Uzbekistan, Tajikistan, southern Kyrgyzstan and south-west Kazakhstan – in essence the region between the Amū Daryā and the Syr Daryā (the Oxus and Jaxartes rivers of the ancient Greeks).

Thus, some uncertainty exists when it comes to defining the precise borders of this region since this was not an issue in earlier times. However, it is not essential for this study. Firstly, Central Asia has historically been closely tied to its people, both nomadic and settled, and to the Silk Road.[5] It acted as a crossroads in the movement of people, goods and ideas, and as a conduit for the spread of religions between Europe, West Asia, South Asia and East Asia. During pre-Islamic and early Islamic times, this region was mainly dominated by Iranic peoples including sedentary Sogdians, Khwārazmians, Bactrians, semi-nomadic Scythians (Saka) and Alans.[6] The ancient sedentary population played an important role in the history of Central Asia. After the expansion of Turkic peoples into these territories in the early medieval era,[7] Central Asia also became the homeland of many Turkic peoples who, much later, as a result of Soviet

---

[3] Dehkhoda, *Lughat Nāma-i Dihkhudā*, Online Reference. Available online at: http://parsi.wiki/dehkhodaworddetail-cbe368c6fbcf43b68107af29bc35fb45-fa.html [Last accessed, 21 December 2015].

[4] André Wink, *Al-Hind: The Making of the Indo-Islamic World, vol. I: Early Medieval India and the Expansion of Islam Seventh to Eleventh Centuries* (Delhi, 1990), p. 109.

[5] The Silk Road or Silk Route was a network of trade routes that for centuries was central to cultural interactions throughout Asia, connecting China to the Mediterranean region and beyond. See, Vadime Elisseeff, *The Silk Roads: Highways of Culture and Commerce* (New York, 2001).

[6] V.I. Abaev and H.W. Bailey, 'Alans', *EI*, vol. 1, pp. 801–803; Also, Walter Pohl, 'Conceptions of Ethnicity in Early Medieval Studies', in Lester K. Little and Barbara H. Rosenwein, ed., *Debating the Middle Ages: Issues and Readings* (Malden, MA, 1998), pp. 13–24.

[7] Richard N. Frye, tr. with commentary, *Ibn Fadlan's Journey to Russia: A Tenth-Century Traveler from Baghdad to the Volga River* (Princeton, NJ, 2005).

national-territorial delimitation policies, emerged with new titular names such as Kazakh, Uzbek, Turkmen, Kyrgyz and Uyghur. From this point of view, Central Asia can be defined as the western, Turko-Iranian, part of the inner-Asian heartland, whose indigenous population comprised various Iranic peoples, most of whom had been Turkicised, and a growing Turkic population who to varying degrees adopted elements of the indigenous Iranian culture.[8]

Toponyms of Badakhshān/Pamir

The earliest surviving designation of Badakhshān as a geopolitical entity dates to late antiquity.[9] 'The name Badakhshān occurs first in Hüan ts'ang's narrative, about 630' (as the kingdom of Po-to-chang-na).[10] It was attested in the travelogue of the Chinese Buddhist monk and scholar Xuanzang (玄奘, d. 664).[11] The area described is small and appeared to have consisted of the lower basin of the Kokcha river and left bank of the upper Oxus. However, the Arabic sources of the classical period designated wider areas as Badakhshān, the extension of which reached to areas east of Balkh generally ending in Ṭokhāristān, thus corresponding to the modern province of Qaṭaghan and districts of Kholm and Baghlān.[12] The Venetian traveller Marco Polo (1254–1324), who passed through these areas on his journey to the court of the Mongol emperor Kublai Khān (r. 1260–1294), employed the toponym Badakhshān in various forms (i.e. Balascian, Baulascia, Baudascia).[13] There is a difference of opinion

---

[8] Yuri Bregel, *An Historical Atlas of Central Asia* (Leiden, 2003), p. vii.

[9] E. Bretschneider, *Mediaeval Researches from Eastern Asiatic Sources: Fragments towards the Knowledge of the Geography and History of Central and Western Asia from the 13th to the 17th Century* (London, 1888), vol. 2, p. 66.

[10] Samuel Beal, *Si-Yu-Ki. Buddhist Records of the Western World. Tr. from the Chinese of Hiuen Tsiang (A.D. 629)* (London, 1884), vol. II, p. 291.

[11] Ibid.

[12] X. de Planhol, D. Balland, W. Eilers, 'Badakšān', *EIR*, 1988. Available online at: https://iranicaonline.org/articles/badaksan [Last accessed, 11 October 2020]; G. Le Strange, *The Lands of the Eastern Caliphate: Mesopotamia, Persia and Central Asia; from the Moslem Conquest to the time of Timur* (London, 1966), p. 432; also V. Minorsky, *Ḥudūd al-'Ālam, 'The Regions of the World': A Persian Geography 372 AH – 982 AD* (London, 1937), p. 439.

[13] Sir Henry Yule, ed., *The Book of Ser Marco Polo, the Venetian, Concerning the Kingdoms of Marvels of the East* (London, 1871), vol. 1, p. 152.

regarding the meaning of the toponym. Historically, Marco Polo claimed that *Baulacia* referred to *Laʻl* (ruby or lapis lazuli). Modern scholars, such as the late C.E. Bosworth, have argued that the term *Badakhsh* originally denoted the region, and that only later did it come to mean ruby.[14] On the other hand, the Russian scholar, T.N. Pakhalina, looking at the word from a linguistic perspective, argues that the term originally consisted of two components, *Badakhsh* and *ān*, meaning 'Land of Kings'.[15] The historical region of Badakhshān lies across north-eastern Afghanistan and south-eastern Tajikistan, with some portions now in western regions of China and in northern Pakistan. Badakhshān contains diverse ethno-linguistic and religious communities, the majority being the Farsi-speaking Tajiks and Pamiri-speaking Tajiks along with significant Kyrgyz and Uzbek minorities. The region is also called the Pamir (or Pamirs) after its high mountain range. Although the precise extent of the Pamir range is debatable, it is commonly argued that it largely lies within the Gorno-Badakhshān Autonomous Oblast' (GBAO) of Tajikistan. Since the beginning of the last century Russian and Soviet scholars carrying out research on the region have used the term Pamiri to refer to the Tajik people of Gorno-Badakhshān, identifying as Pamiris those who speak East Iranian languages such as Shughnī, Rūshānī, Wakhī, Sarikūlī, Ishkāshimī and Yazgulāmī.[16] The fact that Russian and Soviet academic works referred to the Tajiks of the Pamir region as Pamiri eventually led to the development of a new identity: the Pamiri people of Gorno-Badakhshān.[17]

The Pamir range of mountains became known in Persian as 'Bām-i dunyā' ('the Roof of the World') and 'Pā-yi Mihr' ('Feet of the Sun'). A recent study has suggested that in Afghanistan people still write 'Pamir',

---

[14] V.V. Bartol'd, 'Badakhshan', *EI*, vol. 1, pp. 552–554. [Reprint in *EI2*, vol. 1, pp. 851–855]; C.E. Bosworth, 'Pamirs,' *EI2*, vol. 8, p. 245.

[15] T.N. Pakhalina, *Pamirskie Yazyki* [Pamiri Languages] (Moscow, 1969), pp. 5–11. See, Nourmamadcho Nourmamadchoev, *The Ismāʻīlīs of Badakhshan: History, Politics and Religion from 1500 to 1750* (PhD dissertation, SOAS, University of London, 2015), pp. 34–35.

[16] Antje Wendtland, 'The Position of the Pamir Languages within East Iranian', *Orientalia Suecana*, 58 (2009), pp. 172–188.

[17] Dagikhudo Dagiev, 'Pamiri Ethnic Identity and Its Evolution in post-Soviet Tajikistan', in Dagikhudo Dagiev and Carole Faucher, ed., *Identity, History and Trans-Nationality in Central Asia: The Mountain Communities of Pamir* (London, 2018), pp. 23–44.

as 'Pā-yi Mihr' or 'Mitr' ('Mithra').[18] Meanwhile, a local scholar, Abusaid Shokhumorov, in his book *Pamir–Strana Ariev* (Pamir: Land of the Aryan people)[19] disputes the definition of 'Pamir' suggested by previous scholars and argues that the term is a highly complex one, consisting of two parts: the first – 'Pām' or 'Bām', the second – 'Er' or 'Ir'. Both syllables are independent and bear specific meanings. Hence, 'Pām' ('Bām') is translated as 'country', 'habitat', and 'Ir' ('Er') as the self-referential name of those ancient peoples known as the Aryans (later known as the Iranians), which reflects the idea that the name is purely geographical, indicating a certain locality. Therefore, the use of the term Pamiri is problematic, as many of the people covered by this definition consider themselves Tajik, or prefer other local identities, such as Shughnī, Rūshānī, Wakhī, Sarikūlī and Yazgulāmī, instead.[20] However, its use has become commonplace and it has been welcomed quite generally as a new and specific reference to the Pamiri-speaking people and the Ismailis of Tajikistan, although this has led scholars sometimes to conflate the terms Pamiri and Ismaili.[21]

In the early 2nd/8th century, Central Asia became gradually incorporated into the expanding Islamic world. This was also the time when, as a result of the Arab conquests, the spread of Islam was accompanied by a simultaneous wave of Arabisation. Then, following the demise of the Umayyad dynasty in 132/750, the Iranian lands came under the rule of the Abbasids who legitimised the use of Persian and Iranian customs within the framework of the religion of Islam. As part of the Islamic lands, the region shared many cultural features with its Muslim neighbours in the south and the west, but combined them with the certain features it shared with the world of the inner-Asian nomads. However, it

---

[18] Mithra was the second-most important deity for the Zoroastrians and may even have occupied a position of parity with Ahura Mazda. He was associated with the Sun, and in time, the name Mithra [Mihr] became a common word for 'Sun', whilst the expression 'Pa-i Mihr' – meaning 'the foot of the sun or sun god' – indicated a mountainous land in the east where the sun rises. See, Mina Mingaleeva, ed., *Pamir – Krysha Mira. Sbornik proizvedeniĭ o Pamire* (n.p., 2011). Available online at: https://skitalets.ru/information/books/pamir-krysha-mira-2410_4723/ [Last accessed, 11 June 2020].

[19] Abusaid Shokhumorov, *Pamir – Strana Ariev* [Pamir: Land of the Aryan people] (Dushanbe, 1997).

[20] Dagiev, 'Pamiri Ethnic Identity', p. 25.

[21] Ibid.

was the Sāmānids in particular, semi-independent governors of Transoxania for the Abbasids between 261 and 395/819 and 999, who promoted the revival of the Persian language, while also continuing to patronise Arabic to a significant degree.[22] Indeed they can be said to have done more in this regard than other Persian dynasties of the age, such as the Ṣaffārids (247–393/861–1003) or the Būyids (334–447/945–1055), who also ruled over parts of the Iranian plateau. It can be argued that the Sāmānid dynasty established the first state after the Arab invasion that was ruled over by indigenous rulers and furthermore brought virtually all of Greater Khurāsān under a unified government. For this reason, it has been judged one of the most effective dynasties in the history of the region and a factor in the renaissance of Persian culture and identity during the Islamic era.[23] Samarqand and Bukhārā, capital cities under the Sāmānids, flourished as centres of the study of poetry, astronomy, mathematics, philosophy, Qur'an, *ḥadīth* and many other disciplines. It was also during Sāmānid rule that the first Ismaili *dāʿī*s reached the area which is now called Central Asia.[24]

The Ismailis are one of the main branches of Shiʿi Islam. They emerged in the middle of the 2nd/8th century when the Shiʿi Muslim community split over the question of the succession to Imam Jaʿfar al-Ṣādiq (d. 148/765). Those Shiʿis who continued to give allegiance to the line of Jaʿfar al-Ṣādiq through his son Ismāʿīl became known as the Ismailis. In this they differ from the Ithnā ʿasharīs (Twelver Shiʿi) who traced their imamate in the progeny of Mūsā al-Kāẓim (d. 183/799), a younger half-brother of Ismāʿīl b. Jaʿfar.

Following the death of Ismāʿīl b. Jaʿfar's son, Muḥammad b. Ismāʿīl, around 179/795, the Ismailis bifurcated. Representatives of one branch, known as the Qarmaṭīs, believed that Muḥammad b. Ismāʿīl would return as the Mahdī (or *qāʾim*). Adherents of the other branch, who became known as the Ismailis, engaged in promoting their own cause while maintaining anonymity to avoid persecution. In the 3rd/9th century they finally surfaced with a sophisticated political and doctrinal structure by which they were able to gain widespread support and political success. As

---

[22] Elton L. Daniel, *The History of Iran* (London, 2001), p. 74.

[23] Richard Foltz, *A History of the Tajiks: Iranians of the East* (London: I.B. Tauris, 2019), p. 1.

[24] The term *dāʿī* (pl., *duʿāt*) refers to a religio-political missionary or propagandist responsible for spreading the Ismaili doctrine and winning followers for the imam. See, F. Daftary, 'Dāʿī', *EIS*, vol. 5, pp. 871–878.

a result, the Fatimid caliphate under the leadership of Imam ʿAbd Allāh al-Mahdī was established in Ifrīqiya (present-day Tunisia and Algeria) in 297/909. After the Fatimids moved to Egypt, they established their capital at the newly-founded city on the Nile, which they named al-Qāhira (Cairo), and the influence of Ismaili doctrines spread considerably. The Fatimid empire at its height exerted its influence, through the work of the Ismaili *daʿwa*, far beyond Egypt and North Africa, to lands such as Yemen, Iran, Central Asia and Sind. The Ismailis represented one of the largest branches of Shiʿism at the time, with the characteristics of an independent religious community, establishing an extensive network of *dāʿī*s who travelled as far as India and the remoter regions of Central Asia.

By the 260s/870s, the *daʿwa* had reached the Jibāl in western Persia during the time of the *dāʿī* Khalaf al-Ḥallāj, who established Rayy as his local headquarters. His successors extended the activities of the *daʿwa* to Qumm, Iṣfahān, Hamadān and other cities in the region. Ghiyāth, the third *dāʿī* of the Jibāl, succeeded in extending the *daʿwa*'s activities even further to Khurāsān on his own initiative. However, the Ismaili *daʿwa* was not officially established in Khurāsān until the last decade of the 3rd/early 10th century by the *dāʿī* Abū ʿAbd Allāh al-Khādim, who based the mission's headquarters at Nīshāpūr.[25] Later Abū Saʿīd al-Shaʿrānī, the successor of Abū ʿAbd Allāh al-Khādim in Nīshāpūr, managed to convert several of the province's notable military men. The next local head of the *daʿwa*, al-Ḥusayn b. ʿAlī al-Marvazī, who was converted by Ghiyāth, had commanded the Sāmānid military forces in Sīstān. Al-Marvazī extended the *daʿwa*'s activities to Herat, Ghūr, Maymana and other adjacent areas of Badakhshān in eastern Khurāsān, presently located in western Afghanistan. Apparently, there is a shrine in the village of Turbat (*turbat* means 'grave' and the village is named after the shrine) in Ishkāshim of modern Afghanistan that some people associate with al-Ḥusayn b. ʿAlī al-Marvazī. The shrine is called Mazār-i Sayyid Amīr Ḥusayn Sadād.[26] According to some beliefs amongst the Badakhshānī Ismailis, Amīr Ḥusayn was a preacher (*dāʿī*) who came to the region before the 5th/11th century. Although it is not certain whether al-Marvazī sought to promote the *daʿwa* in Badakhshān, the association of his name with a shrine would seem to indicate that the earliest activities of the *daʿwa* in the region took

---

[25] Farhad Daftary, *The Ismāʿīlīs: Their History and Doctrines* (2nd ed., Cambridge, 2007), pp. 112–113.

[26] Mir Baiz Khan, 'Living Traditions of Nasir Khusraw: A Study of Ismāʿīlī practices in Afghan Badakhshān' (Unpublished Fieldwork Report for the IIS, 2004), pp. 215–217.

place around his lifetime.²⁷ However, what is certain is that, despite rebelling against the Sāmānids and being defeated by them in 306/918, al-Marvazī was able to return to Khurāsān and in fact was made chief *dāʿī* of Khurāsān, and later was succeeded by al-Nasafī.

Meanwhile, the Ismaili *daʿwa* was already spreading through Kirmān, Sīstān, Multan, Baluchistān, Gurgān, Ṭabaristān, Rayy and Khwārazm.²⁸ The Sāmānid epoch (3rd–4th/9th–10th centuries), is thus known as the time when the Ismaili *daʿwa* spread across Greater Khurāsān. Under the Sāmānids, who were able to create a stong centralised state, trade and commerce developed and flourished, connecting the most important cities and regions of Asia, such as China and India, with the Middle East and Europe. The fact that the Silk Road lay across the region eventually led to the further development of trading centres, a synthesis of cultures and various religions, the flowering of science, music, poetry and the expansion and enhancement of the cities of Khurāsān. The Sāmānids instigated the growth and development of the modern Persian language in the cities of Balkh, Bukhārā and Samarqand, and the language later on spread throughout the lands of what is now Central Asia, Afghanistan, Iran, Iraq and Azerbaijan. Later, it spread yet further afield into the Indian subcontinent, from about the 5th/11th century onwards.²⁹ As for the province of Badakhshān, one should not forget that it lies between major cities such as Samarqand, Bukhārā, Balkh and Herat which were centres of classical Persian language and culture in the 3rd/9th and 4th/10th centuries.³⁰ The cradle of the Persian literary renaissance lay in the eastern regions of Greater Iran, another term often used to refer to Greater Khurāsān and Transoxiana,³¹ and so the literary traditions of Badakhshān were a part of this. The first poems written in Persian, also known as Darī,

---

²⁷ Shaftolu Gulamadov, *The Hagiography of Nāṣir-i Khusraw and the Ismāʿīlīs of Badakhshān* (PhD dissertation, University of Toronto, 2018), p. 65.

²⁸ Farhad Daftary, *The Ismāʿīlīs Their History and Doctrines* (2nd ed., Cambridge, 2007), pp. 111–113.

²⁹ Lars Johanson and Christiane Bulut, ed., *Turkic-Iranian Contact Areas: Historical and Linguistic Aspects* (Wiesbaden, 2006), pp. 165–208; Muzaffar Alam, 'The Pursuit of Persian: Language in Mughal Politics', *Modern Asian Studies*, 32 (1998), pp. 317–349.

³⁰ Behrooz Mahmoodi-Bakhtiari, 'Planning the Persian Language in the Samanid Period', *Iran and the Caucasus*, 7 (2003), pp. 251–260.

³¹ Richard N. Frye, *The Heritage of Persia* (London, 1976), pp. 286–289; A.V. Williams Jackson, *Early Persian poetry, from the beginnings down to the time of Firdausi* (New York: The Macmillan Company, 1920), pp. 17–19.

were composed in Central Asia. The first significant Persian poet was Abū ʿAbd Allāh Rūdakī (d. 330/941), who flourished in the 4th/10th century, when the Sāmānids were at the height of their power.[32] By this time, the Persian language was already widespread in the major cities of the province of Badakhshān and even those people who preserved their own eastern Iranian dialects in the most remote valleys of Badakhshān still used Persian as a lingua franca: a language for literature, poetry and science.

It was during the time of the Sāmānid *amīr* Naṣr b. Aḥmad (r. 301–331/914–943) that, as a result of the activities of Ismaili *dāʿī*s, the Ismaili Shiʿi faith was remarkably successful in Khurāsān. According to Ibn al-Nadīm,[33] Naṣr b. Aḥmad himself was converted to Ismaili Islam by the *dāʿī* Muḥammad b. Aḥmad al-Nasafī (also known as Nakhshabī, d. 332/943). According to this same source, the Sāmānid *amīr* also recognised the imamate of the Fatimid Imam-caliph al-Qāʾim bi-Amr Allāh (r. 322–334/934–946) and paid dues to him.[34] As mentioned, Daftary argues that the *daʿwa* was officially taken to Khurāsān during the last decade of the 3th/9th century by Abū ʿAbd Allāh al-Khādim, who based himself in Nīshāpūr.[35] As Khurāsān's chief *dāʿī*, al-Nasafī was one of the first to introduce Neoplatonic philosophy into his thought. His major work, *Kitāb al-Maḥṣūl*, written around 300/912 and summarising his views on prophecy, and no longer extant, was widely circulated and acquired much popularity in Qarmaṭī circles.[36] However, al-Nasafī's views were criticised by Abū Ḥātim al-Rāzī (d. 322/934) al-Nasafī's contemporary

---

[32] A. Mirzoev, *Abūabdullo Rūdakī* (Dushanbe, 1958), p. 23; A. Afsahzod, *Odamushshuʾaro Rūdakī* (2nd ed., Dushanbe: 'Adib', 2008), p. 20; Hokim Qalandarov, *Rūdakī va Ismoiliīa* [Rūdakī and the Ismailis] (Dushanbe, 2012).

[33] Abu'l-Faraj Muḥammad b. Isḥāq al-Nadīm (d. 385/995) was a bibliophile of Baghdad and compiler of the Arabic encyclopaedic bibliographic catalogue known as the *Kitāb al-Fihrist*.

[34] A. Sameev, *Somoniën dar oinai taʾrīkh* [Sāmānids in the Mirror of History] (Khujand, 1998), vol. 2, p. 165. F. Daftary, *The Ismāʿīlīs: Their History and Doctrines* (2nd ed., Cambridge, 2007), pp. 111–113.

[35] Ibid., p. 113.

[36] On al-Nasafī and his work, see Daftary, *The Ismāʿīlīs* (2nd ed., Cambridge, 2007), p. 29, and the introduction to Abū Tammām, *The "Bāb al-shayṭān" from Abū Tammām's Kitāb al-shajara*, ed. Wilferd Madelung and Paul E. Walker (Leiden, 1998). Al-Nasafī's *Kitāb al-Maḥṣūl* can be partly reconstructed through citations in al-Rāzī's *Kitāb al-Iṣlāḥ*, al-Bustī's *Kashf asrār al-Bāṭiniyya*, and al-Kirmānī's *Kitāb al-Riyāḍ*.

dāʿī from Rayy, who in his *Kitāb al-Iṣlāḥ* sought to correct certain aspects of al-Nasafī's teachings.[37] Al-Rāzī's corrections were criticised, in due course, by Abū Yaʿqūb al-Sijistānī (d. after 361/971), al-Nasafī's student and successor in Khurāsān.[38] Al-Nasafī and other early *dāʿī*s of the Iranian lands, such as al-Rāzī and al-Sijistānī, through their highly sophisticated works, aimed at attracting the ruling elite and the educated classes to the teachings of the *daʿwa*. Their works on *kalām* (speculative theology), revolving around the central Shiʿi doctrine of the imamate, used the most advanced and intellectually fashionable philosophical terminology of the time, without compromising the essence of their religious message.[39]

Daftary further argues that it was in such circumstances that al-Nasafī, al-Rāzī, and most importantly al-Sijistānī, drawing on a type of Neoplatonism then widespread among the educated circles of Khurāsān, wrote on various philosophical themes that are generally absent in the writings of al-Qāḍī al-Nuʿmān (d. 363/974) and other contemporary Ismaili authors living in the Arab lands and North Africa. The Iranian *dāʿī*s elaborated complex metaphysical systems of thought with a distinct Neoplatonic emanational cosmology, representing the earliest tradition of philosophical theology in Shiʿi Islam.[40]

When Naṣr b. Aḥmad, under the influence of the *dāʿī* al-Nasafī, became an Ismaili he sent dues to the value of 119,000 (Fatimid) *dīnar*s to the Fatimid Imam-caliph al-Qāʾim, as compensation for the death of al-Nasafī's teacher, the *dāʿī* al-Ḥusayn b. ʿAlī al-Marvazī (who lived between the second half of the 3th/9th to the first half of the 4th/10th century), and who had been executed by the Sāmānids.[41] According to

---

[37] Abū Ḥātim al-Rāzī, *Kitāb al-Iṣlāḥ*, ed. Ḥasan Mīnūchihr and Mahdī Muḥaqqiq (Tehran, 1377 Sh./1998), with an English introduction by Shin Nomoto, pp. 1–34. For al-Rāzī's other work on prophetology, *Aʿlām al-nubuwwa*, which is a record of an open debate with the philosopher Abū Bakr al-Rāzī.

[38] Eva-Maria Lika, *Proof of Prophecy and the Refutation of the Ismāʿīliyya: The Kitāb Ithbāt Nubuwwat al-Nabī by the Zaydī al-Muʾayyad bi-llāh al-Hārūnī (d. 411/1020)* (Berlin, 2017), p. 68.

[39] Farhad Daftary, 'The Iranian School of Philosophical Ismailism', *Ishrāk* [Illumination], *EIF*, vol. 4, pp. 15–16.

[40] Ibid., p. 16.

[41] B. Dodge, tr., *The Fihrist of al-Nadīm: A Tenth-Century Survey of Muslim Culture*, vol. 2 (New York, 1970), p. 467; also translated in Samuel Stern, 'The Early Ismāʿīlī Missionaries in North-West Persia and in Khurāsān and Transoxania', *BSOAS*, 23 (1960), pp. 56–90; Patricia Crone and Luke Treadwell, 'A New Text on Ismailism at the Samanid Court', pp. 238–261, in Patricia Crone, *The Iranian Reception of Islam: The Non-Traditionalist Strands* (Leiden, 2016), p. 238.

Ibn al-Nadīm, the Fatimid imam-caliph wrote a letter offering blessings and support for the reign of Naṣr b. Aḥmad Sāmānī. However, the sudden conversion of the Sāmānid *amīr* worried the Sunni *ʿulamā*' (religious scholars) and the Sunni establishment as a whole, and they responded quickly by instigating his son Nūḥ to rise up against him. The plot against Naṣr b. Aḥmad, hatched by Nūḥ with the support of the Sunni *ʿulamā*' and the Turkish soldiery, brought an end to his reign.[42] The accession of Nūḥ (r. 331–343/943–954) led to the execution of al-Nasafī and most of his associates, which opened the way for the Turkish *amīr*s in the Sāmānid army, backed by the Sunni *ʿulamā*', to take over the running of the Sāmānid state.[43] However, this military coup not only ended the reign of Naṣr b. Aḥmad, but eventually weakened the Sāmānid state itself and led to the fall of the most successful Persian/Tajik state in Greater Khurāsān since the Arab invasions.

Regarding these events Abusaid Shokhumorov (1955–1999), a leading Tajik scholar in the study of the Central Asian Ismailis, says that following the massacre of Ismailis during the reign of the later Sāmānid *amīr*s, the creative movement of the Tajik (Iranian) people, which had developed within the framework of Ismaili Islam, was suppressed in Central Asia and control of the Sāmānid state was seized by *amīr*s such as Sebüktigin (r. 367–387/977–997), the founder of the Ghaznavid dynasty.[44] This was a period of dramatic change in the history of the region. Previously, movements such as those of the Qarmaṭīs, the

---

[42] Nūḥ I (r. 331–343/943–954), called for a *jihād* (or religious war) against the Qarmaṭī 'heretics' and many Ismailis were persecuted all over eastern Khurāsān and Transoxania. Nevertheless, there is some evidence that neither Ismaili propaganda nor the *daʿwa* disappeared as the Ismailis changed from promoting the *daʿwa* overtly and made it a covert activity. *Daʿwa* activities continued in Khurāsān under the leadership of *dāʿī*s such as al-Nasafī's son Masʿūd, nicknamed 'Dihqān' (landowner), and Abū Yaʿqūb Isḥāq b. Aḥmad al-Sijistānī (d. after 361/971). Daftary, *The Ismāʿīlīs* (2nd ed., Cambridge, 2007), p. 113. Also Stern, 'The Early Ismāʿīlī Missionaries, pp. 59–60; reprinted in his *Studies in Early Ismāʿīlism* (Jerusalem and Leiden, 1983), pp. 189–233.

[43] Rashīd al-Dīn Faḍl Allāh Hamadānī, *Jāmiʿ al-tawārīkh: qismat-i Ismāʿīliyan*, ed. Muḥammad Taqī Dānishpazhūh and Muḥammad Mudarrisī Zanjānī (Tehran, 1338 Sh./1959), p. 13.

[44] Abusaid Shokhumorov, 'Somoniën va junbishi Ismoiliiā' [The Sāmānids and the Ismaili Movement], in A. Muhammadkhojaev and M. Mahmadjonov ed., *Falsafa dar ahdi Somoniën* [Philosophy during the Sāmānid Era] (Dushanbe, 1999), p. 168.

Shuʿūbiyya[45] and the Muʿtazila had enjoyed considerable success.[46] Reasoning and rational thought, incorporating Greek philosophy, became fused with and synthesised by these new movements. Now, the Ismaili *daʿwa* was considered a direct threat to the Sunni establishment and their protectors the Ghaznavid sultans, since the Ismaili *dāʿī*s and their sympathisers were supported by the Fatimids in Egypt, whose spiritual authority they acknowledged rather than that of the Abbasid caliph and the Sunni establishment.

The Ismaili *Daʿwa* in Central Asia

However, with regard to the spread of the Ismaili *daʿwa* in Central Asia, Daftary says that in fact it seems to have met with greater success there after the demise of the Sāmānids.[47] Nonetheless, it could still face tough resistance from the authorities. As such the Ismailis, who were leaning towards rational thought and philosophy and had endeavoured to bring both intellectual traditions into religious discourse, were accused by Sunni *ʿulamā'* of being *kāfir*s (unbelievers) and *thānāwiyyūn* (dualists).[48]

However, since the Ismaili *daʿwa* was propagated in Khurāsān by *dāʿī*s who were well-informed people, religious activists, poets, philosophers and writers such as al-Nasafī, Abū Ḥātim al-Rāzī, al-Sijistānī and Nāṣir-i Khusraw, a large volume of literature was produced on Ismaili theology and philosophy.[49] Hence one can say that the Ismaili *daʿwa* never diminished completely but continued through many agencies including *dāʿī*s and the newly converted Ismailis who had fled from the Sāmānid

---

[45] The Shuʿūbiyya was a movement in early Muslim society which rejected the privileged status that the Arabs had hitherto enjoyed. Most of the Shuʿūbīs were Persians, although references to Aramaeans, Copts and Berbers, among others, are also found in the literature. See, S. Enderwitz, 'Shuʿūbiyya', *EI2*, vol. 9, pp. 513–516.

[46] Muʿtazila is the name given to a religious movement founded in Basra in the first half of the 2nd/8th century by Wāṣib b. ʿAṭāʾ (d. 131/748), subsequently becoming one of the most important theological schools of Islam. See, D. Gimaret, 'Muʿtazila', *EI2*, vol. 7, pp. 783–793.

[47] Daftary, *The Ismāʿīlīs* (2nd ed. Cambridge, 2007), p. 203.

[48] Muḥammad Riḍā Nājī, *Farhang va tamadduni Islāmī dar Qalamru-yi Sāmāniyān* (Tehran, 1342 Sh./1963), p. 77; Daftary, *The Ismāʿīlīs* (2nd ed., Cambridge, 2007), pp. 112–113.

[49] Muḥammad Riḍā Nājī, *Farhang va tamadduni Islāmī dar Qalamru-yi Sāmāniyān*, p. 77; Daftary, *The Ismāʿīlīs* (2nd ed., Cambridge, 2007), pp. 112–113.

court to the mountainous areas of Khurāsān where they were able to maintain their religious life.

One such region was Badakhshān, which is characterised by its high mountains and harsh environment, making this region a safe haven for the Ismailis in times of turmoil, as when they fled from persecution in the cities of the Sāmānid state.[50] Even though some scholars have argued that Shi'i and Ismaili ideas and teachings spread into Khurāsān and its mountainous regions such as Badakhshān long before the establishment of the Sāmānid state,[51] others are of the opinion that the Ismaili *da'wa* initially reached Badakhshān during the Sāmānid period, since the Ismaili *dā'ī*s were operating more or less openly in the territories under Sāmānid control.

The region of Badakhshān, and, in particular, the far-flung mountainous districts, became vital for the survival of the Ismailis and people associated with them, acting as a shield against persecution instigated by the Sunni Ghaznavids who brought the reign of the Sāmānids to an end, and then by their sucessors, the Saljūqs (5th–6th/11th–12th centuries). The persecution of the Ismailis continued, however. In 436/1044–1045, a large number of Ismailis, who had recognised the imamate of the Fatimid Imam-caliph al-Mustanṣir bi'llāh (r. 427–487/1036–1094) as a result of the activities of the Fatimid *dā'ī*s, were massacred in Khurāsān on the orders of the local Qarakhānid ruler, Bughrā Khān (r. 409–423/1018–1051). Conversely, despite such events, the Ismailis in the region survived, and in 488/1095 Aḥmad b. Khiḍr, another Qarakhānid who ruled over Bukhārā, Samarqand and western Farghāna,[52] was accused by the local Sunni *'ulamā'* of having converted to Ismailism and was executed.[53]

This persecution is reflected in the poetry of Nāṣir-i Khusraw where he mentions the Turkic rulers in general, and the Saljūqs in particular, who

---

[50] Abusaid Shokhumorov, *Razdelenie Badakhshana i sud'by Ismailizma* [The Delimitation of Badakhshān and the Fate of Ismailism] (Dushanbe, 2008), p. 26.

[51] Yahia Baiza, 'The Shi'a Isma'ili *Da'wat* in Khurasan: From its Early Beginning to the Ghaznawid Era', *Journal of Shi'a Islamic Studies*, 8 (2015), pp. 37–59; David Morgan, *Medieval Persia, 1040–1797* (London, 1988), pp. 19–20; Elton L. Daniel, *The History of Iran* (London, 2001), pp. 73–75.

[52] On the history and topography of Farghāna, see M. Zoolshoev, 'Farghāna', *EIS*, vol. 5, pp. 748–782.

[53] Ibn al-Athīr, *al-Kāmil*, vol. 9, pp. 180–181 and vol. 10, pp. 58–59; al-Maqrīzī, *Itti'āz*, vol. 2, pp. 191–192; and V.V. Barthold, *Turkestan: Down to the Mongol Invasion* (London, 1928), pp. 251, 304–305 and 316–318. In Daftary, *The Ismā'īlīs* (2nd ed., Cambridge, 2007), p. 203.

dominated the eastern Islamic lands and persecuted the Ismailis of Khurāsān. For Nāṣir-i Khusraw, Khurāsān was the land in which the *āzādmard*, the free-spirited and creative men, lived and built wonderful cities and culture, giving rise to science, religion, poetry and philosophy. However, with the rule of the foreign invaders, the Saljūqs, all these achievements were destroyed:

> The land of Khurāsān, once the home of culture,
> Has now become a mine rich in barbarian demons.
> Wisdom once had a home in Balkh, but its house
> Now lies in ruins, its fortune overturned.
> If the kingdom of Khurāsān was once like Solomon's,
> How has it now become the kingdom of the cursed devil?
> The land of Khurāsān once feasted on religion,
> Now religion has become the companion of avaricious Qarun.
> The house of Qarun has now made all Khurāsān
> A model for the world entire of how sinister fate unfolds.
> Their slaves at one time were the Turks.
> But sometimes things turn this way and sometimes that,
> So now they themselves are slaves to the Turks.
> Has not that star of Khurāsān turned sinister and dark?
> Even the servant of the Qipchāq is now a lord
> And the free-born wife willingly a handmaid.
> Consequently, if the deficient man becomes a lord,
> Learning declines and vice increases.
> I shall not give my heart to the slaves of the world,
> Even though you have pledged your heart to Fate,
> You might place your trust in the sinister wolf,
> But the wise consider the wolf as not to be trusted.[54]
>
> (Nāṣir-i Khusraw, *Dīvān*, 37: 16–26)

While in exile in Badakhshān as a result of the persecution of the Saljūqs, Nāṣir-i Khusraw recalled his homeland of Khurāsān with nostalgia, sorrow and bitterness:

> Pass by, sweet breeze of Khurāsān,
> To one imprisoned deep in the valley of Yumgān,

---

[54] Cited and tr., in Alice C. Hunsberger, *Nasir Khusraw, The Ruby of Badakhshan: A Portrait of the Persian Poet, Traveller and Philosopher* (London, 2000), pp. 44–45. For the original Persian version see Nāṣir-i Khusraw, *Dīvān*, ed. M. Mīnuvī and M. Muḥaqqiq (Tehran, 1388 Sh./2009).

Who sits huddled in comfortless tight straits,
Robbed of all wealth, all goods, all hope.
Cruel fate has rudely stolen away by force
All peace from his heart, all rest from his body.
His heart swells more full of sorrow than a pomegranate
bursting with seed,
His body shrinks, more consumed than a shrivelled winter reed.
That beautiful face and that handsome figure
Are now fallen into weakness, ugliness and ruin.
That face, once bright as spring's anemones,
Crackles now like autumn leaves from exile's miseries.
Even family turn away from him like strangers.
None can help him now, save the mercy of God.[55]

(Nāṣir-i Khusraw, *Dīvān*, 208: 1–7)

Nāṣir-i Khusraw and the Ismailis of Badakhshān

The revival of the Ismaili *daʿwa* in Khurāsān after the fall of the Sāmānids is associated with the activities of the most famous Ismaili *dāʿī*, poet, traveller and philosopher, Nāṣir-i Khusraw. As he says in his *Safar-nāma* (Travelogue), Abū Muʿīn Nāṣir b. Khusraw b. Ḥārith al-Qubādiyānī was born in 394/1004 in the Marv district of north-eastern Khurāsān, modern-day Qubādiyān in present Tajikistan. In the past, it lay in the province of Balkh whose capital is now in Afghanistan. Little is known of his childhood and early years except for a few references in his own poems, and other works. Although his works clearly show that he became an Ismaili, it is not quite clear how and when this happened. With reference to his *Safar-nāma* where he describes his conversion symbolically as an 'awakening dream' or 'mid-life crisis', it seems that perhaps sometime after his 'dream', which is regarded as his spiritual journey, he set out on the *ḥājj* (pilgrimage) and ultimately reaching Cairo the capital of the Fatimid caliphate and the centre of their *daʿwa*. Daftary states that '[d]espite the opinion of earlier scholars, it is almost certain, as Ivanow and Corbin had perviously argued, that Nāṣir-i Khusraw had already become an Ismaili, probably having previously been an adherent of Twelver Shiʿism, prior to his departure for Egypt.'[56]

Nāṣir thus embarked on a seven-year journey, intending to make the pilgrimage to Mecca, going from Marv towards Nīshāpūr, which at the

---

[55] Hunsberger, *Nasir Khusraw*, pp. 228–229.
[56] Daftary, *The Ismāʿīlīs* (2nd ed., Cambridge, 2007), p. 206.

time was one of the cultural centres of Khurāsān. However, he took a less direct route for the pilgrimage, as he then headed towards the Caspian coast in northern Iran, into eastern Anatolia, and down through Syria and Palestine. Although he did make the pilgrimage to Mecca from Jerusalem, he did not go back to his native Khurāsān but on returning to Jerusalem made his way to Cairo. On the return journey from Egypt, he made his way to the Hijaz, across the Arabian Peninsula, and through Iran, some seven years after his departure, to his home in Balkh. Throughout his travels he kept a detailed journal, on which the *Safar-nāma* is based.

In the *Safar-nāma*, we are informed that he visited the Fatimid court in Cairo and from his *Dīvān* of poetry we learn that there he met and studied with the important Fatimid *dāʿī* al-Muʾayyad fiʾl-Dīn al-Shīrāzī (d. 470/1078).[57]

The restored mausoleum of Nāṣir-i Khusraw in Yumgān

---

[57] Al-Muʾayyad fiʾl-Dīn al-Shīrāzī was a prominent *dāʿī*, who belonged to an Ismaili family from Daylam. Al-Muʾayyad's growing influence in Fārs resulted in court intrigues and Sunni reaction against him. In 438/1046, he was obliged to leave for Cairo, where he arrived in 439/1047. In 450/1058, he was appointed *dāʿī al-duʿāt*, a post he held for almost 20 years until shortly before his death in 470/1078. As chief *dāʿī*, al-Muʾayyad delivered the weekly lectures, known as the *majālis al-ḥikma*; these lectures, entitled *al-Majālis al-Muʾayyadiyya*, were compiled in due course. See, Daftary, *Historical Dictionary*, p. 177.

He became thoroughly imbued with the Shiʿi Ismaili doctrine of the Fatimids, and was appointed as the *ḥujja* or chief *dāʿī* of Khurāsān by the Fatimid Imam-caliph al-Mustanṣir bi'llāh (r. 427–487/1036–1094). On returning to his native Khurāsān, Nāṣir was confronted with enormous challenges, as recounted in his *Dīvān*, facing danger and death threats while trying to spread the Ismaili *daʿwa* in Balkh and in Māzandarān in northern Iran. In due course, Nāṣir was subjected to yet more severe persecution by the Sunni authorities, being accused as irreligious (Persian, *baddīn*), heretic (*mulḥid*), Qarmaṭī and Rāfiḍī.[58] His house was destroyed, and there was even an attempt on his life, forcing him to flee.[59] Nāṣir-i Khusraw eventually ended up living in exile in the valley of Yumgān, a district which is now in modern-day Badakhshān of Afghanistan. There, he found refuge in a land ruled by an Ismaili *amīr*, Abu'l-Maʿālī ʿAlī b. al-Asad, whom he praised in his *Jāmiʿ al-ḥikmatayn*:

> Because these would-be scholars have branded anyone who studies the science of creation as a *kāfir*, those who do seek out the 'how' and the 'why' have been struck dumb. Those who expound this knowledge have fallen speechless; ignorance has taken over people's minds, and especially the people of our land of Khurāsān and the realms of the East. The *amīr* of Badakhshān ʿAyn al-Dawla wa'l-Dīn, Zayn al-Milla, Shams al-Aʿlā, Abu'l-Maʿālī ʿAlī b. al-Asad,[60] says in this sense:
>
>> The learned man's glory lies in his knowledge and culture.
>> The ignorant man's glory lies in gowns and stolen finery.
>> The learning and refinement of the scholar have now become
>> Contemptible – how many men possess culture today?
>> Nobodies are at the forefront while the delighting
>> Superior men are shoved to a far remove – an astonishment!
>> No one knows the cause of this, apart from Him
>> Who is the cause of all causes.

---

[58] Nāṣir-i Khusraw, *Zād al-musāfirīn*, pp. 3, 402, also his *Dīvān*, ed. Taqavī, pp. 110, 217, 430, 448; ed. Mīnuvī, pp. 162, 234, 287, 436; tr. Wilson and Aavani, pp. 73, 113. See, Daftary, *The Ismāʿīlīs* (2nd ed., Cambridge, 2007), p. 206.

[59] Nāṣir-i Khusraw refers to these unhappy events in many of his odes; see his *Dīvān*, ed. Taqavī, pp. 110, 217, 430, 448; ed. Mīnuvī, pp. 162, 234, 287, 436; tr. Wilson and Aavani, pp. 73, 113. See, Daftary, *The Ismāʿīlīs* (2nd ed., Cambridge, 2007), p. 206.

[60] Little is known of this Ismaili ruler; cf. Daftary, *The Ismāʿīlīs* (2nd ed., Cambridge, 2007), pp. 206–207, where he is described as 'the autonomous *amīr* of Badakhshān'.

'Alī b. al-Asad says so: From top to bottom
The world is pain and toilsomeness (ta'ab).[61]

Thus, it appears that 'Alī b. al-Asad, the *amīr* of Badakhshān, was an educated man, and a poet who wrote in Persian, some of his verses being cited in the *Jāmi' al-ḥikmatayn*. He also asked Nāṣir-i Khusraw to elucidate a long philosophical poem written in Persian a century earlier by Abu'l-Haytham Aḥmad b. al-Ḥasan al-Jurjānī (4th/10th century).[62] The evidence in *Jāmi' al-ḥikmatayn* indicates that 'Alī b. al-Asad either was an Ismaili himself or had a strong interest in Ismaili beliefs, which clearly shows not only the spread of Ismailism in Badakhshān prior to Nāṣir-i Khusraw's arrival, but also the pervasiveness of the Persian language and admiration for the Persian language and poetry in the region. 'Alī b. al-Asad was also an independent ruler whose dynasty survived in Khurāsān under Saljūq dominion, doubtless due in part to the inhospitable mountain terrain of his kingdom making it difficult to invade. Nāṣir-i Khusraw called him 'vigilant, astute, brilliant, incisive of intellect, far-sighted, subtle in reflection, correct in his opinions, possessed of a powerful memory, pure of heart, utterly praiseworth and yet, alongside all these virtues and merits, a religious man'.[63] Beben says that despite the fact that 'there is no documented evidence', '[i]t is [still] possible that one of 'Alī b. al-Asad ancestors may have been among the converts at the Sāmānid court in the previous century and that the remote corner of Badakhshān could have served as a place of refuge for Ismaili sympathisers fleeing from the persecution unleashed by the Amīr Nūḥ and his successors.'[64] Certainly the fact that Nāṣir-i Khusraw sought refuge in Badakhshān would seem to corroborate the idea that it was known as a haven for Ismailis.

Nāṣir spent the rest of his life in exile in Badakhshān, championing the Ismaili cause and teachings. There he acheived some peace and tranquility and produced some of his major philosophical and theological works. He was also successful in spreading the Ismaili *da'wa* and gaining supporters and followers, both among the ordinary people and the ruling elite. The success of his work in Badakhshān can still be seen in his legacy

---

[61] Nāṣir-i Khusraw, *Kitāb-i jāmi' al-ḥikmatayn*, tr. Ormsby, *Between Reason and Revelation*, pp. 30–31.
[62] Ibid., p. 1.
[63] Ibid., p. 32.
[64] Beben, *The Legendary Biographies*, p. 68.

there where he is regarded as a *sayyid, pīr, shāh, ḥaḍrat* and *ḥujjat*.⁶⁵ As Eric Ormsby puts it: 'Though his work proved influential, often in surreptitious ways, Nāṣir himself remained a puzzle to later writers, and legends, often fabulous, sprouted up about his name'.⁶⁶ However, there were also people who branded him a 'heretic'. For example, a little-known heresiographer Ibn al-Dāʿī al-Rāzī regarded Nāṣir-i Khusraw as the founder of a heretical sect known as 'the Nāṣīriyya', also stating that 'he was a cursed poet who led many people astray'.⁶⁷

As regards his poetry, Wladimir Ivanow, a pioneer of modern Ismaili studies, wrote: 'A tall, robust, rustic looking man, Nasir brings into his works the rustic, primitive atmosphere ... Nasir was not a pioneer in writing on philosophical matters in Persian, but his style is extremely unartistic, dull, full of unnecessary repetitions ...'.⁶⁸ However the general consensus, both among Persian as well as Western scholars, is that Nāṣir-i Khusraw is a vital figure in the history of Persian literature, a master of both poetry and prose and a profound thinker. Shiblī Nuʿmānī, a 20th-century scholar of Persian literature who wrote a history of poets and literature of Iran, stated: 'Before everyone else, Nāṣir-i Khusraw inserted philosophical ideas and concepts into poetry'.⁶⁹ Further, Badīʿ al-Zamān Furūzānfar asserts that 'Nāṣir-i Khusraw is a master with a powerful poetic nature and a rare style. His poetry is profound and meaningful, and his manner of expression reaches the highest degree of solidity and strength. The versification of scientific laws and arguments that Khusrawī Sarakhsī initiated, Nāṣir-i Khusraw carried to its perfection'.⁷⁰ Eric Ormsby also points out that, 'As his works have been

---

⁶⁵ All these titles are discussed in the section on the Ismaili history in Badakhshān.

⁶⁶ Nāṣir-i Khusraw, *Kitāb-i jāmiʿ al-ḥikmatayn*, tr. Eric Ormsby as *Between Reason and Revelation: Twin Wisdoms Reconciled* (London, 2012), p. 6.

⁶⁷ Ibn al-Dāʿī, *Kitāb Tabṣirat al-ʿawāmm*, ed. A. Iqbāl (Tehran, 1313 Sh./1934), p. 184. In, Ormsby, *Between Reason and Revelation*, p. 6.

⁶⁸ W. Ivanow, *Nasir-i Khusraw and Ismailism* (Bombay, 1948), p. 11, in Ormsby, *Between Reason and Revelation*, p. 7.

⁶⁹ Shiblī Nuʿmānī, *Shiʿr al-ʿajam ya tārīkh-i shiʿr va adabiyāt-i Īrān*, tr. Muḥammad Taqī Fakhr Dāʿī Gīlānī (2nd ed., Tehran, 1365 Sh./1986), vol. 5, pp. 177–179. See also, Alice C. Hunsberger, ed., *Pearls of Persia: Philosophical Poetry of Nāṣir-i Khusraw* (London, 2012), p. xviii.

⁷⁰ Badīʿ al-Zamān Furūzānfar, *Sukhan va sukhanvarān* (4th ed., Tehran, 1369 Sh./1990), p. 154, note 1. Quoted in Hunsberger, *Pearls of Persia*, p. xxi.

published and studied, his originality as a thinker as well as an early master of Persian prose and poetry has been recognised and acclaimed.'[71]

While in exile, Nāṣir-i Khusraw completed a number of treatises including *Gushāyish va rahāyish*, *Khwān al-ikhwān*, the *Shish faṣl*, *Wajh-i dīn*, and *Zād al-musāfirīn*, probably his greatest philosophical and theological works, as well as a portion of his *Dīvān* of poetry, while also spreading the *daʿwa* and the Ismaili interpretation of Shiʿi Islam among the inhabitants of Badakhshān and surrounding areas. However, in this context, one should not forget that the philosophical works written by Nāṣir-i Khusraw and other Ismaili *dāʿī*s were never meant to be understood by the majority in any age, and it was always the case that only a minority of educated individuals (later designated by terms such as *pīr* and *khalīfa*) were able to read and understand this literature, and so interpret it for ordinary believers, the *mustajīb*s. But it is unlikely that someone such as Nāṣir-i Khusraw, who had committed his life to the Ismaili *daʿwa*, having gone to Badakhshān would not have sought to propagate the faith there.

> Whether Nāṣir-i Khusraw was the first to convert the local people is unknown, but as an ardent Ismaili missionary he certainly preached and taught Ismailism in the region. According to his own testimony, he sent one book with missionary purposes (*yakī kitāb-i daʿwat*) to all parts of the world (*aṭrāf-i jahān*) every year and was the commander of the *shīʿat* in Yumgān.[72]

One of the most important of the works Nāṣir-i Khusraw wrote in Badakhshān is his *Wajh-i dīn*, a masterpiece of *taʾwīl*, remarkable for its succinctness and clarity, which was evidently designed to address certain matters concerning Ismaili beliefs in the Persian language and which served subsequently as the main source of religious knowledge for the Ismaili *khalīfa*s in Badakhshān. As Daftary puts it, 'Nāṣir simply and masterfully applies his esoteric exegesis to the system of ideas, concepts, doctrines and methods of interpretation propounded in the Ismāʿīlī works

---

[71] Nāṣir-i Khusraw, *Kitāb-i jāmiʿ al-ḥikmatayn*, tr. Ormsby as *Between Reason and Revelation*, p. 7.

[72] Gulamadov, *The Hagiography of Nāṣir-i Khusraw*, p. 7. 'Gratitude to God because of Whose grace I have become the commander over the soul and property of the Shīʿat in Yamgān' (*shukr an khudāy-ra kih bih Yumgān zi faẓl-ī ū, bar jān-u māl-i shīʿat farmān ravā shudam*) in Ḥakīm Abū Muʿīn Nāṣir-i Khusraw, *Dīvān*, ed. Naṣr Allāh Taqavī (Tehran: Kitābkhānah-i Tihrān, 1304-7/1925-28), p. 283, line 19. *Dīvān-i ashʿār*, ed. Mujtabā Mīnuvī and Mahdī Muḥaqqiq (Tehran, 1353 Sh./1974), p. 140, line 36.

of an earlier period, works that the exile in Yumgān took as a representation of the ideally valid and sacred truth'.[73]

The date of Nāṣir-i Khusraw's death is not known, but some sources indicate that it occurred in the year 470/1077, while other accounts mention the year 481/1088, and that it happened in Yumgān, where his tomb is still a popular place for pilgrimage, as that of a great Ismaili philosopher or indeed as a Sufi master whose fame has spread throughout the region.[74] Over the years Nāṣir-i Khusraw acquired the reputation of a miracle-worker. Many stories have been narrated and recorded about him and some of these have been published.[75] Abdulmamad Iloliev has argued that one cannot underestimate their importance for the study of Ismailism in Badakhshān: 'where the gap between the oral and written traditions was not filled until the 19th and early 20th century, oral materials are considerably important in understanding and interpretation of the events in the past.'[76] What is more, the sorts of legends that came to surround his persona were of the kind that have always been associated with famous persons, historical figures, religious authorities or heroes. They come to form part of the biographies of these prominent individuals and play an important part in the life, history and beliefs of a given group of people, a community or nation, and the legacies of these religious and heroical persons live on in the memories of the people who honour and revere them. So, fabrications and narrations of legends once again exhibit Nāṣir-i Khusraw's significant role in the history of the Ismaili religious community, as well as the identity and traditions of the Ismailis of Central Asia. Alice Hunsberger in her biography of Nāṣir-i Khusraw concluded that these narratives, 'reveal clues of the popular conception of this man; that is, what is remembered of the man can give us an inkling of the powerful effect he had on the public consciousness'.[77]

As regards the later medieval history of the Ismailis in Iran, after the establishment of the Nizārī Ismaili *daʿwa* at Alamūt in the late 5th/11th

---

[73] Daftary, *The Ismāʿīlīs* (2nd ed., Cambridge, 2007), p. 209.

[74] Mehdi Aminrazvi, 'Nāṣir-i Khusraw', *The Oxford Encyclopedia of Philosophy, Science, and Technology in Islam*, vol. 1 (Oxford, 2014), pp. 71–74.

[75] Saidjalol Badakhshi, *Bahr ul-akhbor: silsilai hikoiatho doir ba haëti Nosiri Khusraw va saëhati u ba Badakhshonzamin* [Ocean of News: A Sequence of Legends about the Life and the Journey of Nāṣir-i Khusraw in Badakhshān] (Khārūgh, 1992).

[76] Abdulmamad Iloliev, *The Ismāʿīlī-Ṣūfī Sage of Pamir: Mubarak-i Wakhani and the Esoteric Tradition of the Pamir Muslims* (Amherst, NY: Cambria Press, 2008), p. 31.

[77] Hunsberger, *Nasir Khusraw*, p. 18.

century, it might be argued that they knew nothing of Nāṣir-i Khusraw and his writings.⁷⁸ One might potentially agree with Daniel Beben's statement that this is the case since there is no direct reference to Nāṣir-i Khusraw or his work in known Nizārī writings.⁷⁹ However, there are several studies that present evidence to show that the Nizārī Ismailis were aware of Nāṣir-i Khusraw. One such by Daryoush Mohammad Poor has identified a particular tradition attributed to the Prophet, cited by Nāṣir-i Khusraw in the *Jāmiʿ al-ḥikmatayn*, and later to be found in the works of two important Ismaili thinkers, al-Shahrastānī's *Majlis* written in the 6th/12th century and in al-Ṭūsī's *Rawḍa-yi taslīm* written in the 7th/13th century.⁸⁰ 'God the Exalted established His religion on the analogy with His creation of the world so that one might be guided from His creation to His religion and from there be led to His Oneness (*yegānegī*)'.⁸¹ It is possible that all three scholars had access to the same source which is yet unknown but equally that al-Shahrastānī had read Nāṣir-i Khusraw's *Jāmiʿ al-ḥikmatayn*, and possibly al-Ṭūsī also, which would indicate the continuity of an intellectual tradition. In addition, both Hermann Landolt and Daryoush Mohammad Poor have pointed out that the Sufi ʿAyn al-Quḍāt Hamadānī (492–526/1098–1131) is held to have cited verses from one of Nāṣir-i Khusraw's poems;⁸² he lived at the height of the Alamūt era and was aware of Ismaili beliefs, examining the Nizārī doctrine of *taʿlīm* and challenging al-Ghazālī's polemical account of their thinking.⁸³ If

---

⁷⁸ Beben, *The Legendary Biographies*, p. 114.

⁷⁹ Apparently, it was in the tradition of philosophy to not follow a strict regime of referencing.

⁸⁰ Daryoush Mohammad Poor, 'Extra-Ismaili Sources and a Shift of Paradigm in Nizārī Ismailism', in Orkhan Mir-Kasimov ed., *Intellectual Interactions in the Islamic World: the Ismaili Thread* (London, 2020), p. 235.

⁸¹ Nāṣir-i Khusraw, *Kitāb-i jāmiʿ al-ḥikmatayn*, tr. Ormsby, *Between Reason and Revelation*, p. 145.

⁸² 'In this short notice on Nāṣir-i Khusraw, Jāmī (d. 898/1492) cites six verses which, he says, were quoted by ʿAyn al-Quḍāt in his *Zubdat al-ḥaqāʾiq* from a poem by Nāṣir-i Khusraw', in Hermann Landolt, 'Early Evidence for the Reception of Nāṣir-i Khusraw's Poetry in Sufism: ʿAyn al-Quḍāt's Letter on the Taʿlīmīs', in Omar Alí-de-Unzaga, ed., *Fortresses of the Intellect: Ismaili and other Islamic Studies in Honour of Farhad Daftary* (London, 2011), pp. 369–386.

⁸³ Daryoush Mohammad Poor, 'Extra-Ismaili Sources and a Shift of Paradigm in Nizārī Ismailism', pp. 219–245. See also his *Command and Creation: A Cosmological Treatise*, a Persian edition and English translation of Muḥammad al-Shahrastānī's *Majlis-i maktūb* (London, 2021), Introduction.

Nāṣir-i Khusraw was known to other people who lived and wrote at the time when Nizārī Ismailis had their state in the land of Iran then surely, with their admiration for knowledge and science, and their use of Persian as opposed to Arabic, the Nizārīs would have been aware of the existence of Nāṣir-i Khusraw, the only Ismaili *dāʿī* of Fatimid times who wrote his works, prose and poetry, in Persian.

The Badakhshānī Ismailis during the Alamūt period

Following the death of the Fatimid Imam-caliph al-Mustanṣir in 487/1094, the dispute over his succession led to a major split in the Ismaili community, dividing the Ismailis into Nizārī and Mustaʿlī branches. Al-Mustanṣir had initially designated his eldest son Abū Manṣūr Nizār (437–488/1045–1095) as his successor. However, al-Afḍal as the all-powerful vizier and 'commander of the armies', whose sister was married to Nizār's younger half-brother Abu'l-Qāsim Aḥmad (467–495/1074–1101), moved swiftly and placed Aḥmad on the Fatimid throne with the title of al-Mustaʿlī bi'llāh.[84] There is little in the literature regarding this particular period of the Ismaili *daʿwa* in Badakhshān, and indeed it is one of the most obscure periods in the history of the Ismailis of that region. However, according to oral tradition, being devoted to Nāṣir-i Khusraw's *daʿwa* they continued with his teaching until contact was made with the Nizārī Ismailis during the late Alamūt period. Meanwhile, only a few sources have been identified from the Alamūt period, such as *Haft bāb-i Bābā Sayyidnā*, by Ḥasan-i Maḥmūd-i Kātib, wrongly attributed to Ḥasan-i Ṣabbāḥ, who was designated as Bābā and Sayyidnā (our master) by the contemporary Nizārīs. The treatise was composed around 596/1200 and contains an account of the declaration of the *qiyāma* in 559/1164 at Alamūt[85] by Ḥasan II *ʿalā dhikrihi al-salām*, acknowledged as the 23rd Nizārī Ismaili imam. The treatise generally deals with the Nizārī teachings of the Alamūt period after the declaration of the *qiyāma*. With the recent publication of Ḥasan-i Maḥmūd-i Kātib's

---

[84] Daftary, *The Ismāʿīlīs* (2nd ed., Cambridge, 2007), p. 241.

[85] *Qiyāma* or resurrection, in Islamic eschatology is used as a reference to the Last Day or Day of Judgment. However, in Ismaili thought, *qiyāma* is used in reference to the end of any partial cycle (*dawr*) in the history of mankind, and the declaration of *qiyāma* at Alamūt for the Nizārī community was understood spiritually and symbolically to mean the manifestation of the unveiled truth, or *ḥaqīqa*. See, Daftary, *Historical Dictionary*, p. 140.

Dīvān-i Qā'imiyyāt, which consists of Ismaili religious poems from the 7th/13th century, new light has been shed on the *Haft bāb* and the analysis of this treatise, which has a remarkable value from historical, social, political and religious perspectives. As a result, it has been suggested that Ḥasan-i Maḥmūd-i Kātib also wrote *Haft bāb-i Bābā Sayyidnā*,[86] one of the few surviving books from the Alamūt period discovered in Badakhshān. Ḥasan-i Maḥmūd-i Kātib was also known as Ḥasan-i Ṣalāḥ-i Munshī and was a contemporary of four imams of the Alamūt period, from Ḥasan II *'alā dhikrihi al-salām* (d. 561/1166) to 'Alā' al-Dīn Muḥammad (d. 653/1255). It is almost certain that he witnessed the declaration of the *qiyāma* as he refers to this in the *Haft Bāb*.[87] Therefore, one can assume that he was born at the end of the 6th/12th century. As Badakhchani says, Ḥasan-i Maḥmūd-i Kātib was probably born in northwestern Iran, in the region of Qazwīn and joined the Ismaili community at a young age. For a long period, he acted as a scribe in the court of the Ismaili rulers of Quhistān in south-eastern Khurāsān. He moved to Alamūt, the centre of the Nizārī Ismaili state, around 637/1240 and died there in 644/1247.[88]

The author of a later Ismaili treatise, *Sīlk-i gawhar-rīz*, records among the Ismaili religious authorities in Badakhshān a certain Shaykh Zayd, who went to the court of Imam Ḥasan II *'alā dhikrihi al-salām*. He remained there for seven years and received a *farmān* of appointment as a religious authority for the Ismaili community of Badakhshān.[89] However, there is little other evidence about Shaykh Zayd. In this regard Marshall

---

[86] Hasan-i Mahmud Kotib [Ḥasan-i Maḥmūd-i Kātib], *Devoni Qoimiët* [*Dīvān-i Qā'imiyyāt*], ed. Jalal Badakhchani and Ato Mirkhoja (Dushanbe, 2015). Also Ḥasan-i Maḥmūd-i Kātib, *Dīvān-i Qā'imiyyāt*, intr. M.R. Shafī'ī Kadkanī, Persian ed. and English intr. Jalal Badakhchani (Tehran, 2011).

[87] Ḥasan-i Maḥmūd-i Kātib, *Haft bāb*, ed. and tr. S.J. Badakhchani as *Spiritual Resurrection in Shi'i Islam: An Early Ismaili Treatise on the Doctrine of Qiyāmat* (London, 2017), p. 68, n. 194. Also Ḥasan-i Maḥmūd-i Kātib, *Dīvān-i Qā'imiyyāt*, intr. M.R. Shafī'ī Kadkanī, Persian ed. and English intr. Jalal Badakhchani (Tehran, 2011), Persian text, introd. p. 107, n. 1, English tr., p. 11.

[88] Ibid., p. 2.

[89] Kuchāk [Gawhar Rīz], *Sīlk-i gawhar-rīz*, ed. K. Ėl'chibekov, Photostat version (Dushanbe, n.d.), p. 36. Also, Kudratbek Ėl'chibekov, *Ierarkhiía Dukhovenstva v Ismailizme Badakhshana (na osnove rukopisi 'Sīlk-i gawhar-riz')* [The Religious Hierarchy among the Ismailis of Badakhshān (based on the manuscript *Sīlk-i gawhar-rīz*)] (Dushanbe, 2016), p. 168.

Hodgson has also argued that '[t]he Ismāʿīlīs of the upper Oxus valleys, beyond the Saljūq presence, had, at least at one time, a local *dāʿī* independently responsible to Cairo; at any rate they do not seem to have been involved, at least at first, in the movements which took place among the Ismāʿīlīs in the Saljūq lands'.[90] Similarly Daftary says, '[i]t was much later, in the Alamūt period of Nizārī history, that the Ismāʿīlīs of Badakhshān and adjacent regions accorded their allegiance to the Nizārī *daʿwa*'.[91] But he maintains that by the 7th/13th century the Nizārī Ismailis were actively propagating their *daʿwa* in Badakhshān.[92] Maryam Muʿizzī in a recent work argues that the Nizārīs of Quhistān apparently remained in contact with their co-religionists in Badakhshān following the destruction of Alamūt.[93] When the Nizārī Ismaili poet Nizārī Quhistānī (645–720/1247–1320) refers in one of his poems to 'the provinces that are under the authority of the imam', and lists Tūrān, Āmu [Daryā], the Orient and China it seems that he is referring to Badakhshān.

---

[90] Marshall Hodgson, 'The Ismāʿīlī State', in J.A. Boyle, ed., *The Cambridge History of Iran*: vol. 5 (Cambridge, 1968), pp. 427–428.

[91] Daftary, *The Ismāʿīlīs* (2nd ed., Cambridge, 2007), p. 243.

[92] Daftary, 'The Medieval Ismāʿīlīs of the Iranian Lands', in C. Hillenbrand, ed., *Studies in Honour of Clifford Edmund Bosworth, vol. II: The Sultan's Turret: Studies in Persian and Turkish Culture* (Leiden, 2000), pp. 43–81.

[93] Maryam Muʿizzī, *Ismāʿīliyya-yi Badakhshān* (Tehran, 1395 Sh./2017), p. 148.

> [No wonder there are], so many sweet countries under the dominion of the Friends of God (*awliyā'*); [namely] an Egypt of sufficiency, a Rome of renunciation, and a Baghdad of security.
>
> The Iranian provinces represent love, while the Tūrānian provinces represent intellect; and in between them, the Oxus of wisdom flows beseemingly.
>
> Prosperous Khurāsān and blissful 'Irāq are both [in this dominion]; the latter is a house of contentment, and the former a home of convalescence.
>
> Do you know what lies within the Orient of insolvency? It is the China of justice, peace, equity, splendour, dignity and purity.
>
> In the presence of the King of the beneficent men, the dominion of all seven climes of the world and the totality of the universe, are all like the poor child (*ṭufayl*) of a beggar.
>
> Well, to put it in a nutshell, His Command is the jewel of the seal of Unity; and to make this story short, the land of Gnosis is, indeed, in our hands.[94]

In this poem the 'Āmū' of Nizārī Quhistānī is clearly the Āmū Daryā, which rises in the mountains of Badakhshān and flows throughout the region, a region which borders China. Tūrān was an ancient name for the region which encompasses Badakhshān and the poet regards Tūrān as a place of joy, love, justice, peace and harmony which is significant for Ismailis. In fact, these kinds of allusions are common in Ismaili poetry, particularly when they refer to places where their imam or his followers reside.[95] This shows that Badakhshān, like the Alamūt mountain fortresses, had become a haven for the Ismailis over several centuries.

However, in the post-Alamūt period, another schism occurred following the death of the Nizārī Imam Shams al-Dīn Muḥammad (d. ca. 710/1310) that split the community once again, into the Muḥammad-Shāhī and Qāsim-Shāhī branches. There is very little information regarding this event but what is clear is that the succession was disputed by Shams al-Dīn's sons, 'Alā' al-Dīn Mu'min-Shāh and Qāsim-Shāh. The Muḥammad-Shāhī (or Mu'minī) imams, who were engaged in religious and political life, initially seem to have acquired numerous followers in certain regions, notably northern Persia, Badakhshān and Syria.[96] However, this line became extinct by the end of the 12th/18th century.

---

[94] The poem has been kindly translated from Persian into English for this work by Rahim Ghulami.

[95] Mu'izzī, *Ismā'īliyya-yi Badakhshān*, p. 148.

[96] Daftary, *The Ismā'īlīs* (2nd ed., Cambridge, 2007), p. 414.

The Qāsim-Shāhī imams, who were mainly based in Iran, lived a clandestine life, mostly in hiding, although they made systematic efforts to extend their influence over the various Nizārī communities.[97] Maryam Muʿizzī argues that it was only at the end of the 9th/15th and the beginning of the 10th/16th century that the Qāsim-Shāhī imams re-established contact with their followers in Badakhshān and were able to bring the Ismaili community there under their authority.[98] One of the sources regarding the Muḥammad-Shāhī and the Qāsim-Shāh split is an early 10th/16th-century text from Badakhshān entitled *Irshād al-ṭālibīn fī dhikr aʾimmat al-Ismāʿīliyya*. Even though the work advocates the Muḥammad-Shāhī lineage, it is the most complete account available of this schism.[99]

At any event, according to both oral tradition and certain historical sources, *dāʿī*s were sent to Badakhshān during the late Alamūt period by the Nizārī imams.[100] Mīrzā Sang Muḥammad Badakhshī, in his *Tārīkh-i Badakhshān* (13th/19th and early 14th/20th centuries), using oral traditions, provides some details about the arrival of Persian *dāʿī*s, suggesting that as early as 481/1088 and 490/1096,[101] a *darvīsh* arrived in Shughnān, Badakhshān, but does not refer to him as a Nizārī Ismaili *dāʿī* sent from Alamūt. Professors Bosworth and Madelung name two persons, Shāh Khāmūsh and Shāh Malang, as *dāʿī*s who were sent by the Nizārī imams.[102] The former, initially called Sayyid Mīr Ḥasan Shāh, later became known as Sayyid Shāh Khāmūsh. He was a Ḥusaynid ʿAlid, tracing his descent to Mūsā al-Kāẓim (d. 183/799), the seventh imam of the Twelver Shiʿis. Much later, in the 10th/16th century, he was followed by Shāh

---

[97] Ibid.

[98] Muʿizzī, *Ismāʿīliyya-yi Badakhshān*, p. 205.

[99] Daniel Beben, 'The Ismaili of Central Asia', *Oxford Research Encyclopedia of Asian History*, Online Publication Date: Apr 2018. Available online at: http://oxfordre.com/asianhistory/view/10.1093/acrefore/9780190277727.001.0001/acrefore-9780190277727-e-316 [last accessed, 11 June 2019].

[100] Daftary, *The Ismāʿīlīs* (2nd ed., Cambridge, 2007), pp. 451–452.

[101] However, Daftary dates the first arrival of Nizārī *dāʿī*s to the late Alamūt period, and Bosworth and Madelung say Shāh Malang and Shāh Khāmūsh arrived in Badakhshān in the 7th/13th century. See, Daftary, *The Ismāʿīlīs* (2nd ed., Cambridge, 2007), p. 452; Bosworth, 'Shughnān', *EI2*, vol. 9, pp. 459–460 and Madelung, 'Ismāʿīliya', *EI2*, vol. 4, pp. 198–206. For more details see, Gulamadov, *The Hagiography of Nāṣir-i Khusraw*, p. 134.

[102] Madelung, 'Ismāʿīliya', *EI2*, vol. 4, p. 198. Bosworth, 'Shughnān', *EI2*, vol. 9, pp. 495–496.

Malang. Daftary writes that according to the tradition preserved in Badakhshān, the first of these Nizārī *dāʿīs* was a certain Sayyid Shāh Malang, who was followed by a second Nizārī *dāʿī*, Mīr Sayyid Ḥasan Shāh Khāmūsh. However, it has to be noted that the historical sources and oral tradition with regard to the arrival of the Nizārī *dāʿīs* in Badakhshān contradict each other. Shaftalou Gulamadov has identified five versions of the Badakhshānī tradition about the identity, place of origin and time of arrival of these *dāʿīs*.[103]

Both Mīrzā Sang Muḥammad Badakhshī in his *Tārīkh-i Badakhshān* and Sayyid Ḥaydar Shāh Mubārak Shāhzāda (d. 1363/1943) in his *Tārīkh-i Mulk-i Shughnān* indicate that Sayyid Shāh Khāmūsh and Shāh Malang came from the province of Khurāsān in present-day Iran although they give different cities there as their points of origin or departure,[104] and they go on to say that these *dāʿīs* were the ancestors of dynasties of *pīrs* and *mīrs* who ruled in Badakhshān for centuries. However, although the Nizārī state in Iran had been destroyed by the Mongols, protected by the mountains of the Pamir and the Hindu Kush, Badakhshān largely escaped the cataclysm of the Mongol invasions.[105] Indeed, Bartol'd argued that 'Badakhshān was not affected by the Mongol conquests and remained till the 9th/15th century under the rule of [a local] dynasty'.[106] Nevertheless, a recent study by A.B. Petrov has shown that the Badakhshān region did not completely escape the Mongol assault, but it had not been conquered when Chingiz Khan laid siege to Tirmiz in 617/1220-21.[107]

However, he further concludes that:

---

[103] Daftary, *The Ismāʿīlīs* (2nd ed., Cambridge, 2007), p. 452; however, see Shaftolu Gulamadov, *The Hagiography of Nāṣir-i Khusraw* (PhD dissertation, University of Toronto, 2018), pp. 129–142.

[104] Sayyid Haĭdarshoh Muborakshohzoda, *Taʾrīkh-i Mulki Shughnān* (Khārūgh, 1992), pp. 6–9.

[105] Haĭdarsho S. Pirumshoev, 'The Pamirs and Badakhshan', in Chahryar Adle, Irfan Habib and Karl M. Baipakov, ed., *History of Civilizations of Central Asia, vol. 5: Development in Contrast: from the Sixteenth to the mid-Nineteenth century* (Paris, 2003), pp. 225–228.

[106] V.V. Bartol'd, 'Badakhshan', *EI*, vol. 1, pp. 552–554. [Reprint in *EI2*, vol. 1, pp. 851–855].

[107] A.B. Petrov, 'Badakhshan XIII–XIV vv. pod Vlast'iû Mongol'skikh Khanov' [Badakhshān 13th–14th Centuries under the Rule of the Mongol Khans], *ZVORAO*, 2 (2006), p. 528.

i) Badakhshān was not subjected to a barbaric destruction of the population like, for example, the cities and regions of *Mā warā' al-nahr*.
ii) even the conquest of this region was carried out by Chingiz Khan, either by force or on occasion negotiation.
iii) more often the Mongols preferred to negotiate with the rulers of Badakhshān rather than seize the region and bleed it.
iv) the position of the local rulers was special. They enjoyed greater privileges and rights than the rulers of other conquered territories, which is clearly seen from the analysis of numismatic material and written sources.
v) the region was rich in both precious stones and, apparently, working silver mines.
vi) during the 8th/14th century the rulers of the Chaghatay state, one of the Mongol successor states, tenaciously kept this area under their control even under the most difficult conditions of civil strife.[108]

So it would appear that the local *amīrs* of Badakhshān continued to rule over the region in a semi-independent fashion during the Mongol period, and that Wakhān, Ishkāshim, Shughnān and Darvāz escaped the Mongol invasions:

At the beginning of the 7th/13th century, on the eve of the Mongol invasions, Badakhshān, Wakhān, Ishkāshim and Shughnān were subject to the ruler of Khwārazm, Muḥammad Khwārazm-Shāh, whose empire encompassed the greater part of Central Asia. There is no direct evidence that these people were conquered by the Mongols, though the conquest of both Xinjiang and the bulk of Afghanistan makes this is highly probable. Their subjugation by Tīmūr and the Timurids has, however, been abundantly demonstrated.[109]

In fact it was Tīmūr's great-grandson, Abū Sa'īd (r. 855–873/1451–1469), who wanted to incorporate Badakhshān into his realm, and succeeded in conquering it after a number of punitive expedtions.[110] Later the region was conquered in 993/1584 by the Uzbeks, although they were persistently resisted by different local dynasties, including the Ismaili *mīrs* of Shughnān.[111] The region was then ruled by various dynasties,

---

[108] Ibid., p. 539.
[109] Pirumshoev, 'The Pamirs and Badakhshan', p. 225.
[110] Nourmamadchoev, *The Ismā'īlīs of Badakhshan*, p. 60.
[111] Daftary, *The Ismā'īlīs* (2nd ed., Cambridge, 2007), p. 452.

including local Tajik, as well as Turkic and Afghan ones. These dynasties were headed by *murīd*s, *mīr*s or *bek*s, wealthy landlords whose authority depended very much on the political situation, external as well as internal.[112]

Taqiyya and the Ismailis in the Post-Alamūt Era

With the fall of Alamūt in 654/1256 the Ismailis moved from the Caspian provinces to other parts of Iran and the neighbouring regions. This period is one of the most obscure in Ismaili history not only in Iran but elsewhere. Although historians of the time, such as ʿAṭā'-Malik Juwaynī (d. 681/1283), say that the Ismailis were totally extinguished, the community in fact survived and developed in a different form on the peripheries of Muslim states. Thus, it becomes apparent that communities like those in Badakhshān, as well as northern areas of Pakistan, in common with other Ismaili communities in the Middle East and the Indian subcontinent, continued in isolation, which allowed each community to develop a distinctive tradition of its own.

The structure of the Ismaili *daʿwa* institutions in the Nizārī Ismaili state in Iran had not remained the same as that under the Fatimids in Egypt. The Nizārī *daʿwa* had become simpler, reflecting the changed circumstances of the Ismailis in Iran confronting the Saljūq sultans. As a result, it was referred to as the *daʿwat-i jadīda*, that is, 'the new preaching', by contrast to *daʿwat-i qadīma* or the 'old preaching'. The idea behind the *daʿwat-i jadīda* was a modification of the doctrine of the imamate, which was called the doctrine of *taʿlīm* (teaching). However, it has been argued that this 'new teaching' did not mean a change of doctrine, but rather the reformulation of an old Shiʿi doctrine that the Ismailis had long been acquainted with, the Shiʿi doctrine of *taʿlīm*, or authoritative teaching by the imam,[113] and this provided the basis for the Nizārī Ismaili teachings of the later Alamūt times and subsequent periods. Following the destruction of the Nizārī Ismaili state, centred at the mountain fortress of Alamūt in northern Iran, in 654/1256[114] and of other Ismaili fortresses, as well as the news of the execution of Rukn al-Dīn Khurshāh (d. 655/1257), the last lord of Alamūt and the 27th Nizārī imam, the Nizārī

---

[112] Bakhodur I. Iskandarov, *Vostochnaia Bukhara i Pamir v period presoedineniia Srednei Azii k Rossii* (Stalinabad, 1960), pp. 36–37.
[113] Daftary, *The Ismāʿīlīs* (2nd ed., Cambridge, 2007), p. 339.
[114] Ibid., p. 396.

Ismailis became isolated in different areas of Iran. Many of them became assimilated into other communities, mainly the dominant Sunni community.[115] But they also moved to areas in Central Asia, Sind, the Punjab and various other parts of the Indian subcontinent, where there already were Ismaili communities.[116] Under these circumstances, the scattered Nizārī communities in the Persian-speaking world resorted once again to the strict observance of *taqiyya*.[117] It is important to bear in mind that the observance of *taqiyya* in this period, marked by the absence of a viable central *daʿwa* organisation and leadership, was not imposed on the community.[118] The Nizārīs had become experienced in adopting external guises to safeguard themselves. For a while during the Alamūt period, they had even adopted the *sharīʿa* in its Sunni form.[119]

Thus, when after the fall of Alamūt, rulers and religious scholars again attacked the Ismailis as *kāfir* (infidel) or *mulḥid* (heretic), and they were threatened again with persecution,[120] they developed ways to secure and safeguard themselves. They started to conceal themselves under Sunni, Sufi or Twelver Shiʿi guises, elements of which, with the passage of time, came to be included in their diverse traditions. When the Ismailis of Badakhshān concealed their true religious beliefs the result was the amalgamation of various Sufi and Twelver Shiʿi elements in their beliefs and practices.[121] The practice of *taqiyya* also continued in other areas where the Ismailis used Sufi terminology, such as *khānaqāh*, *darvīsh* (dervish), *ʿārif* (gnostic), *qalandar* (wandering dervish) as well as *pīr* and *murshid* to refer to elements of their organisation and their people.[122] It was during this period that the

---

[115] Ibid., p. 410.

[116] Fidāʾī Khurāsānī, *Kitāb-i Hidāyat al-muʾminīn al-ṭālibīn*, ed. A.A. Semënov (Moscow, 1959), p. 20. Daftary, *The Ismāʿīlīs* (2nd ed., Cambridge, 2007), p. 410.

[117] *Taqiyya* is an Arabic word that in the Ismaili context means the precautionary dissimulation of one's true religious beliefs, especially in time of danger. The Nizārī Ismailis have been obliged to dissimulate rather strictly to protect themselves against widespread persecution. See, Daftary, *Historical Dictionary*, p. 165.

[118] Daftary, *The Ismāʿīlīs* (2nd ed., Cambridge, 2007), p. 410.

[119] Ibid.

[120] Farhad Daftary, 'Assassins', *EIS*, vol. 3, pp. 911–914.

[121] Hafizullah Emadi, 'Praxis of *Taqiyya*: Perseverance of Pashaye Ismāʿīlī Enclave, Nangarhar, Afghanistan', *Central Asian Survey*, 19 (2000), pp. 253–264.

[122] Daftary, *The Ismāʿīlīs* (2nd ed., Cambridge, 2007), p. 412. See also, Nizārī Quhistānī, *Dīvān*, ed. M. Muṣaffā (Tehran, 1371–1373 Sh./1992–1994), vol. 1; L. Lewisohn, 'Sufism and Ismāʿīlī Doctrine in the Persian Poetry of Nizārī Quhistānī (645–721/1247–1321)', *Iran, Journal of the British Institute of Persian Studies*, 41 (2003), pp. 229–251.

institution of the *pīr* or *pīrship*, another example of the deployment of Sufi terminology, was introduced as a central element in the religious hierarchy (*ḥudūd al-dīn*) of the Nizārī Ismailis of Central Asia, and this usage survived throughout the Soviet period.

The *Ḥudūd al-Dīn* in the Context of Central Asia

One aspect of studying the Ismailis, as carried out by pre-Soviet Russian and Soviet scholars, concerned the role of religious leaders, and specifically, the hierarchy of religious authorities. The Ismaili hierarchy served as a means of maintaining the community and providing it with guidance on religious and socio-political issues. However, due to the risk of persecution, religious leaders and their associates were frequently compelled to hide their true identity, revealing their status to only a few loyal Ismailis. So study of the *ḥudūd al-dīn* is limited by the lack of written sources and reliance solely on oral testimony, which has acted as an impediment to any profound analysis of the topic in the context of Central Asia. One of the exceptions to this dearth of primary sources is Nāṣir-i Khusraw's introduction to his *Jāmiʿ al-ḥikmatayn*,[123] where he provides a short but precise explanation of the concepts of *ḥudūd al-dīn*, *ḥadd-i jismānī* and *ḥadd-i rūḥānī*. But this only refers to the state of affairs in the 5th/11th century and is not necessarily valid for later centuries.[124]

Publications in the secondary literature on the theme of the *ḥudūd al-dīn* include a brief study by Wladimir Ivanow,[125] the relevant sections in Henry Corbin's *History of Islamic Philosophy*[126] and Farhad Daftary's monograph, *The Ismāʿīlīs*.[127] Soviet studies on the subject included, notably, A.E. Bertel's' *Nāṣir-i Khusraw and Ismailism* which paid particular attention to the spiritual realm of the Ismaili hierarchy. In

---

[123] Nosir Khusrav [Nāṣir-i Khusraw], *Jome'-ul-hikmataĭn* [Jāmiʿ al-ḥikmatayn], ed. K. Olimov, K. Askardaev and A. Sharipov (Dushanbe, 2011). See also Eric Ormsby, tr., *Between Reason and Revelation, Twin Wisdoms Reconciled*, an annotated English translation of Nāṣir-i Khusraw's *Kitāb Jāmiʿ al-ḥikmatayn* (London, 2012).

[124] Dagikhudo Dagiev, 'The Ismāʿīlī Hierarchy - *Ḥudūd al-Dīn* - in the Context of Central Asia', *JSIS*, 10 (2019), p. 344.

[125] In Wladimir Ivanow, 'The Organisation of the Fatimid Propaganda', *JBBRAS*, NS, 15 (1939), pp. 1–35; reprinted in Bryan S. Turner, ed., *Orientalism: Early Sources*, vol. 1, *Readings in Orientalism* (London, 2000), pp. 531–571.

[126] See, Henry Corbin, *History of Islamic Philosophy*, tr. L. Sherrard (London, 1993), pp. 86–93.

[127] Daftary, *The Ismāʿīlīs* (2nd ed., Cambridge, 2007), pp. 211–223.

addition, fieldwork in Badakhshān (1959–1963) led to the collection of primary material, such as *Bāb dar bayān-i dānistan-i ʿālam-i dīn*; *Risāla dar bāb-i haft ḥudūd-i dīn*, and *Dawāzdah faṣl* which also speak about the concept of the *ḥudūd al-dīn* and the role and influence of the Ismaili religious authorities. These original works are preserved at the Rudaki Institute of Oriental Studies and Written Heritage in the Academy of the Sciences of the Republic of Tajikistan, and it is hoped will provide fruitful material for further studies on this important subject.

The establishment of the Ismaili spiritual hierarchy dates back to the mid-4th/10th century, but it originally did not have an elaborate structure or organisation until the Fatimids had established themselves in Egypt.[128] The *daʿwa* organisation acquired its definite shape during the reign of al-Ḥākim (r. 386–411/996–1021), the sixth Fatimid Imam-caliph, as reflected in the work of Ḥamīd al-Dīn al-Kirmānī.[129] Paul Walker argues that the theme of *ḥudūd* is vital to the Ismaili cause. In Fatimid times, it consisted of twelve office-holders called either *lāḥiq* or *ḥujja* or even *naqīb*, each of whom was in charge of one of the twelve districts or territories (s. *jazīra*) of the known world.[130] Each *jazīra* represented an independent region for the purpose of propagating the *daʿwa*.[131] In the writings of the Ismaili jurist al-Qāḍī al-Nuʿmān[132] produced earlier in the 4th/10th century, the twelve *jazāʾir* are listed as al-ʿArab (Arabs), al-Rūm (Byzantines), al-Ṣaqāliba (Slavs, i.e. Eastern Europeans), al-Nūb (Nubians), al-Khazar (Khazars), al-Hind (India), al-Sind, al-Zanj (East Africans), al-Ḥabash (Abyssinians), al-Ṣīn (China), al-Daylam (the Persians), and al-Barbar (the Berbers). Interestingly enough Khurāsān, of which Nāṣir-i Khusraw claimed to be the *ḥujjat* in the second half of the 5th/11th century, is not included as a *jazīra* in al-Nuʿmān's list.[133] However, Daftary points out that 'al-Nuʿmān's well-informed and possibly Ismāʿīlī

---

[128] Nadia Eboo Jamal, *Surviving the Mongols: The Continuity of Ismaili Tradition in Iran* (London, 2002), p. 28.

[129] H. Corbin, *History of Islamic Philosophy*, p. 89.

[130] Paul E. Walker, 'The Ismaili *Daʿwa* in the Reign of the Fatimid Caliph Al-Ḥākim', *Journal of the American Research Center in Egypt*, 30 (1993), pp. 161–182.

[131] Daftary, *The Ismāʿīlīs* (2nd ed., Cambridge, 2007), p. 217.

[132] Al-Qāḍī al-Nuʿmān b. Muḥammad, *Taʾwīl al-daʿāʾim*, ed. M.Ḥ. al-Aʿẓamī (Cairo, 1968–1972), vol. 2, p. 74. See also, Abū Yaʿqūb al-Sijistānī, *Ithbāt al-nubuwwāt*, ed. W. Madelung and P. Walker (Tehran, 1395/2016), p. 268, where seven of these *jazāʾir* are named, together with al-Turk.

[133] Daftary, *The Ismāʿīlīs* (2nd ed., Cambridge, 2007), p. 218.

The ranks of the Ismaili religious hierarchy at various historical periods[1]

Fatimid period[2] (909–1171)	Alamūt period[3] (1090–1256)	Post-Alamūt period[4]	According to Sayyid Ḥaydar Shāh's text[5]
al-nāṭiq	Imām	Imām	Imām
al-Asās/al-waṣī	mutaʿalim	ḥujjat/Pīr	ḥujjat (Nāṣir-i Khusraw)
al-Imām/al-mutimm	muʿallim	dāʿī	dāʿī
al-lāḥiq	māʾī/Bāb-i bāṭin	muʿallim	maʾdhūn-i akbar
al-yadd	zabān-i ʿilm	maʾdhūn-i akbar	muʿallim-i ṣādiq
al-janāḥ	ḥujjat-i aʿẓam	maʾdhūn-i aṣghar	(ishāns)
al-maʾdhūn	dast-i qudrat		maʾdhūl-i aṣghar (khalīfas)
al-mustajīb/al-muʾmin			other believers

[1] For more details on the table and the Ismaili religious hierarchy see Muzaffar Zoolshoev, 'The Soviet State and a Religious Movement: A Socio-Historical Study of the Ismaʿīlī Panjebhai Movement in Soviet Tajik Badakhshan (early 1920s late 1930s)' (Unpublished Report for the IIS, 2015), p. 108.

[2] Abū Yaʿqūb al-Sijistānī, *Kitāb al-maqālid al-malakūtiyya*, ed. I.K. Poonawala (Tunis, 2011), p. 437.

[3] Naṣīr al-Dīn Ṭūsī, *Rawḍa-yi taslīm*, ed. and tr. S.J. Badakhchani as *Paradise of Submission: A Medieval Treatise on Ismaili Thought* (London, 2005), pp. 122–123.

[4] Khayr-khwāh-i Harātī, *Taṣnīfāt*, ed. W. Ivanow (Tehran, 1961), pp. 2–3.

[5] A.V. Stanishevskiĭ, 'Sbornik arkhivnykh documentov i materialov po istorii Pamira i ismailizma', vol. 2, 1923, pp. 175–262 (Unpublished Report), pp. 179–184. Haydar Shāh was a local scholar who wrote a History of Shughnān in the request of A.A. Semënov.

contemporary, Ibn Ḥawqal, who himself travelled through eastern Persia and Transoxania around 358/969, does mention Khurāsān as a *jazīra* of the Fatimid *daʿwa*'.[134] One of the Ismaili manuscripts discovered in Badakhshān in 1967, gives the names of only two *ḥujjas* of the Fatimid period, Nāṣir-i Khusraw in Khurāsān and Bābā Sayyidnā (Ḥasan-i Ṣabbāḥ) in Persia.[135] They were, of course, the two most prominent ones, at least in historical terms. At the time of Nāṣir-i Khusraw's arrival in Badakhshān, the term *dāʿī* was used to refer to a religious rank, and later on, other terms such as *maʾdhūn* and *muʿallim* were introduced. These terms are not unique to the Ismailis of Badakhshān, as they were used in other areas where the Ismaili *daʿwa* was active.

The table above shows that there were either seven or nine main ranks, described slightly differently by various authors and covering various historical periods,[136] however, the core assumption that the Ismaili teaching is in accordance with the imam's guidance never changed.

In the case of the Badakhshān community, the hierarchy continued unchanged from the post-Alamūt period when the role of the *pīr* was introduced until the late 14th/20th century when new Imamat institutions were introduced by the present Ismaili imam. Thus the ranks below that of the imam were *ḥujja*, *pīr*, *muʿallim* (teacher) and finally *khalīfa* (the deputy of a *pīr*).[137] The Ismaili hierarchy, through its religious dimension or *ḥudūd al-dīn*, sought to demonstrate an understanding of the realms of spiritual and material existence. The study and analysis of the Ismaili sources allow us to better understand the Ismaili hierarchy and its role in preserving and sustaining the integrity of the Ismaili community and the continuity of its religious practice.

---

[134] Ibn Ḥawqal, *Ṣūrat al-arḍ*, p. 310; tr. Kramers and Wiet, vol. 2, p. 304. In Daftary, *The Ismāʿīlīs* (2nd ed., Cambridge, 2007), p. 218.

[135] *Sīlk-i gawhar-rīz*, ed. Qudratbek Elchibekov (retyped version of a manuscript in the Ismaili Special Collections Unit, The Institute of Ismaili Studies, London), p. 91; Ėlʹchibekov, *Ierarkhiía Dukhovenstva*, p. 73.

[136] See W. Ivanow, 'The Organisation of the Fatimid Propaganda', *JBBRAS, NS*, 15 (1939), pp. 1–35; Ėlʹchibekov, *Ierarkhiía Dukhovenstva*, pp. 45–54; S. Virani, *The Ismailis in the Middle Ages*, pp. 71–83.

[137] Hakim Elnazarov and Sultonbek Aksakolov, 'The Nizari Ismailis of Central Asia in Modern Times', in Farhad Daftary, ed., *A Modern History of the Ismailis: Continuity and Change in a Muslim Community* (London, 2011), p. 68.

Pīr and *Pīrship* in Central Asia

In Central Asia the Ismailis are mainly concentrated in Badakhshān. As mentioned above, Nāṣir-i Khusraw is regarded as the founder of this community in Badakhshān, although there is evidence of earlier *dāʿīs* travelling to the Pamirs. In its external structure, Badakhshānī Ismailism differs only in terms of certain aspects of its tradition and rituals from other expressions of Ismaili beliefs found elsewhere. Followers of the tradition of Nāṣir-i Khusraw in Central Asia are now spread across parts of four modern states: Badakhshān of Tajikistan, Badakhshān of Afghanistan, the Xinjiang region of China, and the Gilgit, Hunza and Chitrāl areas of northern Pakistan. With regard to the context of Central Asia, it was Ivanow who first demonstrated that in the post-Alamūt period Persian terms borrowed from Sufism, such as *pīr* and *murīd*, replaced Arabic terms such as *ḥujja*, *dāʿī* and *maʾdhūn* in the *ḥudūd al-dīn*.[138] This was part of the form of *taqiyya* adopted in this period similar to that used by Ismailis in other parts of the Iranian world. The term *pīr* is derived from Persian meaning an 'older person', the equivalent of the Arabic word *shaykh*. In the religious context, *pīr* refers to a 'spiritual master' or 'spiritual guide'. In Badakhshān, besides the terms *pīr* and *murīd*, the term *khalīfa* (successor, vicegerent),[139] was also introduced.

The religious hierarchy remained mainly three-tiered, with the *pīr* as the spiritual guide in the absence of the imam, the *khalīfa* as the *pīr*'s deputy, and the *murīd* as his disciple.[140] In the religious hierarchy, one *pīr* could have several *khalīfa*s. The *khalīfa* performed all the religious duties under the instruction of his *pīr*. Historically, the *pīr*s were responsible for the organisation of the *daʿwa* in their areas of jurisdiction and this included the provision of religious instruction, ensuring the correct practice of the faith and the development and sustaining of a healthy relationship with rulers, and with non-Ismaili communities amongst or alongside whom the Ismailis lived. The position of the *pīr* was regarded as one of the highest; the *pīr* could be replaced by his son or, in the absence of a son, by a very close relative. This hereditary succession of religious authority is one of the

---

[138] Wladimir Ivanow, *Brief Survey of the Evolution of Ismailism* (Leiden, 1952), p. 67.

[139] For details on the origins and application of this term, see, A. Pakatchi, 'Khalīfa', *EIS*, vol. 5, pp. 407–464.

[140] Najima N. Susumu, 'Pir, Waiz and Imam: The Transformation of Socio-Religious Leadership among the Ismailis in Northern Pakistan', *Area Studies Working Paper Series*, 23 (Tokyo, 2001), p. 7.

important characteristics of the Ismaili tradition in Badakhshān, where families of *pīrs* and *khalīfas* remained in charge of religious matters for centuries. This enabled them to maintain the practice of religious duties independently from whoever was in charge of the political establishment over the region, whether local rulers, outsiders, Sunnis or Communists. The religious hierarchy was also a stronger marker of identity than any political authority by virtue of its role as protector and preserver of Ismaili religious belief and ritual practice from the time of Nāṣir-i Khusraw onwards. In this regard the *Sīlk-i gawhar-rīz* is of great significance in identifying the genealogy of the Ismaili imams and the religious hierarchy in the context of Badakhshān and the role of the *pīrs* there.

The Russian ethnographer and archaeologist Alekseĭ A. Bobrinskoĭ (1861–1938), during his visit to Badakhshān in 1901, after conversations with the local *pīrs* and *murīds*, concluded that, 'the *pīr* is the complete ruler of the heart and soul of the *murīd*, and has rights over the moral, family and civil duties of the *murīds*.'[141] *Pīrs* were directly appointed by the imams as it was their prerogative to bestow the title of *pīr* upon a *murīd*, and in order to be appointed a *pīr* it was not necessary to be a *sayyid* (a descendant of the Prophet's family).[142] However, in most cases *pīrs* and their *khalīfas* belonged to either a *sayyid* family or a *khwāja* clan.[143]

In his recent study, 'Pirship in Badakhshān', Abdulmamad Iloliev details the significant role played by the *pīrs* in organising and maintaining the socio-religious and socio-political affairs of the community in the late 13th/19th and early 14th/20th centuries.[144] Iloliev defines the role of the *pīrs*' network, referred to as the *pirship*, 'as an institution of social control and organisation that not only provides religious guidance, but also collects and distributes the religious dues, and responds actively to the immediate political and social environment of its time.'[145] Over time the role and the authority of the *pīrs* increased and they became very powerful; they represented and negotiated on behalf of the community with the rulers of the area or the neighbouring *amīrs* regarding political and social issues.

---

[141] A.A. Bobrinksoĭ, 'Sekta ismail'ī͡a v russkikh i bukharskikh predelakh Sredneĭ Azii' [The Ismaili Sect in Russian and Bukharan Central Asia], *EO*, 2 (1902), pp. 1–20.

[142] Ibid., p. 10.

[143] *Khwājas* usually marry someone from their own social rank, the daughter of a *sayyid* or of another *khwāja*. See also, Abdulmamad Iloliev, 'Pirship in Badakhshan: The Role and Significance of the Institute of the Religious Masters (*Pirs*) in Nineteenth and Twentieth Century Wakhan and Shughnan', *Journal of Shiʿa Islamic Studies*, 6 (2013), p. 169.

[144] Ibid., p. 156.

[145] Ibid.

As a result of the rivalry between the amirates of Bukhārā and Afghanistan in the 13th/19th century, the Ismaili community found itself under enormous pressure from these Sunni *amīrs* who raided the region, treating the local Ismailis brutally and imposing heavy taxes on the population on the pretext that being Ismaili they were not fully Muslim. When the Ismaili *pīrs* became important agents during the 'Great Game' (the rivalry between the British and the Russian empires over Central Asia in the late 19th and early 20th centuries), and negotiated on behalf of the community with the Russian representatives, asking for their region to be annexed to the Russian empire, their aim was to avoid the privations and suffering imposed upon the population by the Afghan and Bukharan *amīrs*.[146]

There is also a considerable body of literature on Ismaili doctrines produced by the *pīrs* between the 8th/14th and the 12th/18th centuries. This includes the *Ṣaḥīfat al-nāẓirīn* (also known as *Sī va shish ṣaḥīfa*, composed in 857/1453). The text exists in two versions: one attributed to Pīr Ghiyāth al-Dīn Iṣfahānī, and a second attributed to Pīr Sayyid Suhrāb Valī.[147] Another *pīr* of the early 10th/16th century was Khayrkhwāh-i Haratī, who was regarded as the head of the *daʿwa* in Khurāsān, including Badakhshān.[148]

However, gradually the role of the *pīrs* were reduced and in particular from the middle of the 20th century, with the establishment of new

---

[146] B.I. Iskandarov, *Iz istorii dorevoluts̄ionnogo Tadzhikistana* [On the History of Pre-Revolutionary Tajikistan] (Dushanbe, 1974), pp. 41–71; Ėl'bon Hojibekov, *Ismailitskie dukhovnye nastavniki (piry), ikh rol' v obshchestvennoĭ zhizni Shugnana (vtoraīa polovina XIX - 30-e gody XX vv.)* [Ismaili Spiritual Mentors (*pīrs*) and their Role in the Social Life of Shughnan: the Second half of the 19th Century – 1930s] (Dushanbe: 'Bukhoro', 2015), pp. 50–119; Otambek Mastibekov, *Leadership and Authority in Central Asia: the Ismaili Community in Tajikistan* (London, 2014), pp. 52–55.

[147] A detailed discussion on Ghiyāth al-Dīn Iṣfahānī and Sayyid Suhrāb Valī will be provided later on in this study.

[148] Khayrkhwāh-i Haratī was a Nizārī Ismaili *dāʿī* and poet, who was born in Ghūriyān near Herat. His life and activities coincided with the early Anjudān period in Nizārī history (i.e. mid 9th–early 10th/15th–16th centuries), when the Nizārī *daʿwa* activities were revived under the direct leadership of the Qāsim-Shāhī Nizārī imams themselves. He was appointed as the chief *dāʿī* or *ḥujja* and as *pīr* of Khurāsān and Badakhshān. See Daftary, *Historical Dictionary*, p. 127. His collected works were edited and published by Wladimir Ivanow as *Taṣnīfāt-i Khayrkhwāh Haratī* (Tehran, 1961). See also, Beben, 'The Ismaili of Central Asia', p. 6.

imamate institutions, and the development of modern technology, which improved direct communications between the Ismaili imam and his *murīd*s all over the world, reduced the role of the *pīr*s. Then the need for an institutional restructuring of the Ismaili community in modern times resulted in the ending of the role of the *pīr* and its institutions.

Structurally the institution of *pīrship* was an extension of the Ismaili religious hierarchy, i.e. *ḥudūd al-dīn*, but on a much smaller scale. The religious terminology and dimension were defined by, and adapted to, the local environment of the post-Alamūt era. The Ismailis of Badakhshān upheld the belief that the religious authority of the institution of *pīrship* had always been based upon Ismaili religious doctrines, as the directions were given by the imam, who directly or indirectly appointed the *pīr*s. However, in the post-Alamūt era in Badakhshān until 13th/19th century there was very little evidence available to confirm direct contact with the higher ranks of the Ismaili *daʿwa* and therefore, there is not much evidence of *pīr*s being directly appointed by the Ismaili imam, although some *pīr*s were appointed by agents of the imam, who had been given the authority to do so. However, *Sīlk-i gawhar-rīz* mentions several instances of Ismaili *pīr*s who visited the Ismaili imams' headquarters, first in Persia and later in India and received *farmān*s about their appointments. For instance, individuals such as Shāh Gadā, Shāh ʿAbd al-Raḥīm and Faqīr Shāh visited the court of the Imām Khalīl Allāh ʿAlī where they were appointed as *pīr*s over different areas of Badakhshān.[149] During the reign of Ḥasan ʿAlī Shāh, Aga Khan I, the Ismailis of Badakhshān established even closer contact with the imamate. A series of *farmān*s and documents confirm this conection. The study by Kawahara Yayoi and Umed Mamadsherzodshoev of 164 historical documents collected from private collections of the Ismailis of Badakhshān includes Imām Ḥasan ʿAlī Shāh's decrees and rescripts.[150]

The Political History of Badakhshān

This study focuses mainly on the Ismailis of Badakhshān, a region of present-day Tajikistan and historically part of Greater Khurāsān. The

---

[149] Kuchāk [Gawhar Rīz], *Sīlk-i gawhar-rīz*, p. 185; Ėlʼchibekov, *Sīlk-i gawhar-rīz*, p. 131.

[150] Kawahara Yayoi and Umed Mamadsherzodshoev, *Documents from Private Archives in Right-Bank Badakhshan (Fascimiles)*, TIAS Central Eurasian Research Series 8 (Tokyo: Department of Islamic Area Studies, Centre for Evolving Humanities, Graduate School of Humanities of Sociology, University of Tokyo, 2013). For more see, Gulamadov, *The Hagiography of Nāṣir-i Khusraw*, pp. 109–110.

region of Badakhshān was divided into four sectors as a result of Russian and British colonial policies. A large part of Badakhshān now lies within Tajikistan and another section, with its historical capital city of Fayḍābād lies in Afghanistan. Two other parts of historical Badakhshān fall within the borders of present-day Pakistan and China. Similarly, the Ismaili community which observes the Nāṣir-i Khusraw tradition is also spread across these four countries. The focus here is primarily on the Ismailis of Badakhshān in present-day Tajikistan with some reference to the other parts of Badakhshān now lying within Afghanistan, China and Pakistan.

The political history of Badakhshān over the last millennium is undeniably connected with the existence and spread of Ismaili Islam in the region. The harsh topography and remoteness of the area have played a major role in maintaining and preserving the Ismaili community's rituals and traditions. The power struggle between local and foreign rulers continued until the late 13th/19th century, when Britain and Russia, the colonial powers, effectively stoked religious feuds in order to further their respective imperial policies in the region.

Fayḍābād, the capital of historical Badakhshān and present capital of Badakhshān of Afghanistan

Long before the Achaemenids,[151] the Iranian people developed the principle of what we call now local autonomy. This means that the *shāhanshāh* (supreme king) recognised the autonomy of each *kishwar* (country), as part of a vast empire. Petty rulers were then called *shāh*, and were subservient to the *shāhinshāh* (King of Kings).[152] Based on this principle, the Sāsānid empire (224–651) and later in the Islamic period, the Sāmānid state,[153] included Badakhshān, Shughnān, Wakhān and Darvāz, as independent *kishwar*s. As already mentioned, after the fall of the Sāmānids in the late 4th/10th century and the movement of Turkic nomadic tribes into their domains, Badakhshān remained outside the lands of subsequent states, such as those of the Ghaznawid and Saljūq Turks and retained its independence until the beginning of the 8th/14th century, when the Tīmūrids (771–913/1370–1507) annexed various parts of it.[154]

The last local independent *shāh* of Badakhshān, Shāh Sulṭān Muḥammad, was executed by the Tīmūrid sultan Abū Saʿīd in 780/1466–67. According to the sources he claimed descent, like all his predecessors, from the Achaemenid Dāryūsh I (Darius the Great, r. 522–486 BCE) and Alexander the Great (336–323 BCE).[155] The founder of the Mughal empire, Bābur, refers to the Alexander lineage of Shāh Sulṭān Muḥammad.[156] There is scant evidence available regarding the local rulers of Badakhshān, apart from some coins minted in the name of ʿAlī Shāh and dating to 690/1291. Other evidence is provided by coins (dating to the years 690–691/1290–1292) in the name of his son Dawlat Shāh b. ʿAlī Shāh minted with the title of 'al-Sulṭān al-ʿĀẓim'.[157] This indicates that ʿAlī Shāh

---

[151] The Achaemenid Empire (ca. 550–330 BCE), also called the First Persian Empire, was founded by Cyrus the Great and based in Western Asia, though it covered an area from the Aral sea to North Africa. See also, Gareth C. Sampson, *The Defeat of Rome: Crassus, Carrhae and the Invasion of the East* (Barnsley, 2008).

[152] Shokhumorov, *Razdelenie Badakhshana*, pp. 25–26.

[153] The Sāmānids, the first local dynasty after the Arab domination, ruled from the 3rd/9th to 4th/10th centuries.

[154] Shokhumorov, *Razdelenie Badakhshana*, p. 26.

[155] Ibid., p. 26.

[156] Ẓahīr al-Dīn Muḥammad Bābur, *The Baburnama: Memoirs of Babur, Prince and Emperor*, tr. W.M. Thackston (Washington, DC, 1996), p. 15.

[157] D. Dovudi and L. Ilish, 'Manety Badakhshana v sobranii Tiubingenskogo universiteta FRG' [Coins of Badakhshān in the Collection of Tübingen University FRG], *Soobchshenie natsionalʾnogo muzeīa respubliki Tadzhikistana, imeni Kamoliddina Bekhzoda*, vol. 8 (2009), p. 101; A.B. Petrov, 'Badakhshan XIII–XIV vv. pod Vlastʾiu Mongolʾskikh Khanov' [Badakhshān 13th–15th Centuries under the Rule of the Mongol Khans], *ZVORAO*, 2 (2006), pp. 496–540. Muʿizzī, *Ismāʿīliyya-yi Badakhshān*, p. 153.

was an independent ruler. However, these coins do not show any traces of Shi'i or Sunni Islam and nor do they show whether these rulers had any connection to Abu'l-Ma'ālī 'Alī b. al-Asad, the *amīr* of Badakhshan in the time of Nāṣir-i Khusraw.[158] Nevertheless, there is a possibility that Shāh Sulṭān Muḥammad was a descendant of 'Alī b. al-Asad given that, at the time when the Tīmūrid Abū Sa'īd (d. 926/1520–21) sought to eliminate him, many writers and historians, including Marco Polo, Dawlatshāh Samarqandī and Bābur, wrote that Shāh Sulṭān Muḥammad was of the lineage of Alexander the Great.[159] Nevertheless, there is no evidence to substantiate this claim and scholars believe that it was part of the legends fabricated by historians on the orders of Shāh Sulṭān Muḥammad to provide legitimacy for his rule. But Marco Polo referred to this claim in his travelogue written in the early 8th/14th century, so even if it is considered only myth, there can be no doubt that it was a long-standing claim.[160]

According to some scholars, most notably Abusaid Shokhumorov, by the time of Shāh Sulṭān Muḥammad, the majority of the population in Badakhshān openly practiced Ismailism.[161] He himself was a poet and had a *Dīvān* of poetry and there were a number of renowned poets including Mawlānā Ṣāḥib Balkhī and Khwāja Maḥmūd Bursa,[162] philosophers and Ismaili scholars at his court. One of them may have been the philosopher, scientist and poet, Ghiyāth al-Dīn 'Alī b. Amīrān Sayyid al-Ḥusaynī al-Iṣfahānī, who most probably arrived in Badakhshān during the reign of Shāh Sulṭān Muḥammad.[163] He was a prolific writer on mathematics as well as religion and his *Dānish-nāma-yi jahān* was allegedly written in response to the *Dānish-nāma* of Ibn Sīnā. There are other treatises attributed to Ghiyāth al-Dīn and preserved by the Ismaili community in

---

[158] Mu'izzī, *Ismā'īliyya-yi Badakhshān*, p. 153.

[159] Sir Henry Yule, ed., *The Book of Ser Marco Polo, the Venetian*, vol. 1, p. 149; Dawlatshāh b. 'Alā' al-Dawla, *Tadhkirat al-shu'arā*, ed. Fāṭima 'Alāqah (Tehran, 1385 Sh./2007), pp. 819–820; Ẓahīr al-Dīn Muḥammad Bābur, *The Baburnama: Memoirs of Babur, Prince and Emperor*, tr. W.M. Thackston (Washington, 1996), p. 15.

[160] Yule, ed., *The Book of Ser Marco Polo*, vol. 1, p. 149. See also Mu'izzī, *Ismā'īliyya-yi Badakhshān*, p. 148.

[161] Shokhumorov, *Razdelenie Badakhshana*, p. 27; Beben, 'The Ismaili of Central Asia', p. 8. See, Mīrzā Muḥammad Ḥaydar Dūghlāt, *Tārīkh-i Rashīdī*, ed. 'Abbāsqulī Ghaffārī Fard (Tehran, 1383 Sh./2004), pp. 346–347 (quoted in Beben, 'The Ismaili of Central Asia').

[162] Samarqandī, *Tadhkirat al-shu'arā*, pp. 817–820, 851–853.

[163] Ghiësud al-Din Alii Iṣfahānī [Ghiyāth al-Dīn Iṣfahānī], *Nujūm*, ed. Umed Shohzodamuhammad (Khārūgh, 1995).

Badakhshān. However, until now the attribution of these treatises to any particular Ismaili figure has not been verified, despite being included in Andreï Bertel's and Muhammadvafo Bakaev's *Catalogue*.[164]

The Tīmūrids were Sunnis and adopted punitive measures against the Ismailis in their domains. The Tīmūrid governor, Sulṭān Ways Mīrzā, violently suppressed an Ismaili uprising in Badakhshān which was led by the Muḥammad-Shāhī Imam Rāḍī al-Dīn ʿAlī in 915/1509. Tīmūrid rule in Badakhshān came to an end when the Shaybānid Uzbek ruler ʿAbdullāh Khān II seized most of Badakhshān in 992/1584, although he also faced revolts by the Ismailis there.[165]

In the mid 11th/17th century, Badakhshān fell under the control of Mīr Yārībeg Khān (r. 1067–1119/1657–1707), who succeeded in establishing a dynasty which ruled over most of the region for almost two centuries. Like his predecessors the Shaybānids and the Tīmūrids, Mīr Yārībeg Khān professed Sunni Islam and was strongly opposed to the Ismailis. His descendents continued to oppress and attack the Ismailis, for instance, in the mid 12th/18th century raiding Chitrāl.[166] The religious hostility and intolerance of the Yarids resulted in the Ismailis being declared adherants of a heretic creed and was one of the main reasons for the sharp socio-political and cultural decline of Badakhshān.[167] Moreover, prior to this, there are numerous documents dating to the beginning of the 11th/17th century which provide information about the condemnation of the Ismailis by the ruling authorities. These documents which were discovered and published by Khalīlallāh Khalīlī in Kabul in 1959 include a series of *waqf* (endowment) deeds whose wording contains anti-Ismaili sentiments.[168]

---

[164] A.E. Bertel's and Mamadvafo Bakaev, *Alfavitnyĭ katalog rukopiseĭ obnaruzhennykh v Gorno-Badakhshanskoĭ avtonomnoĭ oblasti ėkspeditsieĭ 1959–1963 gg.* [Alphabetical Catalogue of Manuscripts found by the 1959–1963 Expedition to the GBAO], ed. B.G. Ghafurov and A.M. Mirzoev (Moscow, 1967), pp. 78–119.

[165] Beben, 'The Ismaili of Central Asia', p. 8. See, Mīrzā Muḥammad Ḥaydar Dūghlāt, *Tārīkh-i Rashīdī*, ed. ʿAbbāsqulī Ghaffārī Fard (Tehran, 1383 Sh./2004), pp. 346–347, referenced by Beben in 'The Ismaili of Central Asia'.

[166] Mirzo Sangmuhammadi Badakhshī and Mirzo Fazlalibeki Surkhafsar, *Tārīkh-i Badakhshon*, pp. 32–33; Beben, 'The Ismaili of Central Asia', p. 8.

[167] Ibid. Also see, Gabrielle van den Berg, 'Keeping Religion Alive: Performing Pamiri Identity in Central Asia', *International Institute for Asian Studies*, 74 (Summer 2016), p. 37.

[168] Khalīlallāh Khalīlī, *Yumgān* (Kabul, 1959), pp. 2–15. See also, Shokhumorov, *Razdelenie Badakhshana*, p. 27.

The *waqf* deeds specifically state that the lands around the tomb of Nāṣir-i Khusraw were granted as *waqf* administered by the *shaykh* of the *mazār* (mausoleum or shrine). Nāṣir-i Khusraw was declared a Sunni saint, and a shrine was built over his grave. Another anti-Ismaili campaign occurred with the rise to power in Kabul of Aḥmad Shāh Durrānī (r. 1160–1186/1747–1772), who fought a devastating campaign against the Yārid dynasty and the Ismailis of Badakhshān. The weakening of Yārid rule over Badakhshān allowed for the emergence of a semi-independent Shughnān region. In this regard Shaftolu Gulamadov writes that:

> In the second half of the 11th/17th century, the Ismāʿīlīs seem to have established closer contacts with their Imams, who, as demonstrated were generally practicing pious circumspection under Twelver Shīʿism. Still later, in the second half of the 12th/18th century, other, more significant, socio-political developments in Ismāʿīlism and in Badakhshān took place, making this period different from the immediate preceding centuries. First, the power of later Yārids, who were clearly anti-Ismāʿīlī, weakened due to internecine wars and the constant struggles with other external dynasties. Second, the Ismāʿīlī imamate in Iran and subsequently in India came to operate openly, which seems to have encouraged the Ismāʿīlīs of Badakhshān to follow suit and carry out their religious activities more publicly. The Imam authorized the *pīr* to establish the Ismāʿīlī *daʿvah* in Badakhshān. From the mid-18th century until the time of the composition of the *Sīlk-i gawhar-rīz* (completed in the 1830s) and until the beginning of the 20th century the Ismāʿīlī *daʿvah* operated actively in Badakhshān.[169]

As regards Shughnān, even though local sources indicate that the ruling dynasty was not Ismaili, the sources confirm that in the course of the 12th/18th century it developed a close relationship with the heads of the Ismaili *daʿwa*. One such Shugnānī ruler was Shāh Vanjī, who became the disciple of a prominent Ismaili *pīr*, Khwāja Muḥammad Ṣāliḥ. According to *Sīlk-i gawhar-rīz*, a work written by Khwāja Ṣāliḥ's grandson, Shāh Vanjī sponsored the efforts of a number of missionaries to spread the *daʿwa* in other parts of the region.[170] But this should be seen as an interlude since from then on there was a constant struggle between Sunni rulers on the one hand, and the Ismaili population and the *pīrs* on the other. Indeed, from the 10th/16th century onwards, after the Tīmūrid conquests,

---

[169] Gulamadov, *The Hagiography of Nāṣir-i Khusraw*, pp. 84–85. See also, Ėl'chibekov, *Ierarkhiĩa Dukhovenstva*, p. 269.

[170] Beben, *The Legendary Biographies*, p. 287.

Badkhshān was no longer a place of refuge for Ismailis and instead considered as unbelievers the Ismailis of Badakhshān had to practise *taqiyya*.[171]

This study will now narrow its focus to the areas where Ismailis have been the majority or dominant group. The Ismailis of this region, often referred to as Pamiri or Pamiri-Tajik people, have been studied by a number of scholars, such as the historian Bahodur Iskandarov (1912–2004). He provided a thorough examination of the history of the late medieval and modern periods even though, like his contemporaries, he was subject to Soviet ideological constraints on his scholarship. However, by focusing on a reconstruction of the past, Iskandarov was able to sidestep the Russian-Soviet political and ideological understanding and interpretation of the literature on the Ismailis.

Until the early 11th/17th century, the remote regions of Badakhshān, that is Wakhān, Shughnān, Rūshān and Darvāz, had enjoyed virtual independence under the rule of indigenous dynasties. Throughout the 12th/18th century, Rūshān, Shughnān and Wakhān fought for political independence from the rulers of Badakhshān, Qundūz and Darvāz, and eventually became semi-independent satellite kingdoms under the sovereign rulers of Darvāz, who levied taxes on them. In 1829, an Uzbek khan called Murād Beg who ruled over Qunduz to the east of Badakhshān invaded the region.[172] Like previous external rulers he targeted the Ismaili population of the region in slave raids, forcing many Ismailis to flee to the inaccessible gorges of Shughnān and the surrounding areas. As a result of this persecution, the only Ismaili communities in Badakhshān that were able to preserve their beliefs and practice were those living in isolated mountain gorges such as those in the districts of Wakhān, Shughnān and Darvāz.

Thus in the first half of the 13th/19th century, Shughnān (including Rūshān) and Wakhān while preserving a degree of independent rule, varying in degree and length, acknowledged also the authority of more powerful neighbours such as the *amīr* of Badakhshān, although Murād Beg, the ruler of the local feudal state of Qunduz, was able to maintain his independence.

---

[171] Shokhumorov, *Razdelenie Badakhshana*, p. 27.

[172] Murād Beg mounted several devastating invasions of Wakhān (in which he killed the ruler of Wakhān) and Shughnān (leading to a significant reduction in population). See, John Wood, *A Journay to the Source of the River Oxus* (London: John Murray, 1872), pp. 159–160.

Throughout the 13th/19th century there seem to have been a series of wars between the rulers of Shughnān and Wakhān for control of Ishkāshim, and other areas such as Ghārān (known for its ruby mines), Shākhdara and Ghund. Likewise, there were frequent wars between the Kyrgyz of the Eastern Pamir and Darvāz and Shughnān over Rūshān and Bartang.[173]

Around 1295/1878, the Khanate of Bukhārā incorporated Darvāz along with Qalʿa-yi Khumb and the valley of Vanj and Yazghulām into its territories as Eastern Bukhārā. But the end of the 13th/19th century saw increasing rivalry between Russia and Britain for influence in this part of Central Asia. This resulted in an Afghan army under Amīr ʿAbd al-Raḥmān Khān (r. 1299–1319/1880–1901) invading Wakhān, Shughnān and Rūshān. The expansionist policies of ʿAbd al-Raḥmān Khān prompted an immediate response from Tsarist Russia.

As a result of this situation, the British and Russian colonial powers decided to hold a special conference on the Pamir question, which took place in St Petersburg in April 1309/1892. The conference considered two main issues: (i) sending Russian armed forces to the Pamir region; and (ii) demarcating the territory of the Pamir region and marking the borders of China, Afghanistan and British India. The conference also decided to send an Anglo-Russian commission to this region to study the topography of the northern and eastern borders of Afghanistan.[174]

This arbitrary demarcation of the borders, agreed between Great Britain and Russia on 25 February 1313/1895, put an end to a series of protracted border disputes.[175] On 29 August 1313/1895, the commission finalised the border demarcation. Britain and Russia signed an agreement in London defining 'the spheres of influence of the two countries in the region of the Pamirs' to which both Afghanistan and Bukhārā had

---

[173] N. Elias, 'Report of a Mission to Chinese Turkistan and Badakhshan 1885-1886', in M. Ewan, ed., *Britain and Russia in Central Asia, 1880-1907* (London, 2008), vol. 5, pp. 47–48.

[174] *Illustrated London News*, 14 June, 1884, p. 574. The *Times* carried a similar notice entitled 'The Northen and North-Western Frontiers of Afghanistan' on 9 June 1884, p. 5, in Neil K. Moran. *Kipling and Afghanistan: A Study of the Young Author as Journalist Writing on the Afghan Border Crisis of 1884–1885* (London, 2005), p. 13.

[175] The Earl of Kimberley to M. de Staal, Foreign Office March 2, 1895. 'Agreement between the governments of Great Britain and Russia with regard to the spheres of influence of the two countries in the region of the Pamirs. 1894', in Martin Ewans, ed., *Britain and Russia in Central Asia, 1880–1907* (London, 2008), pp. 252–254.

consented in advance.¹⁷⁶ According to this treaty, Darvāz, and parts of Rūshān, Shughnān and Wakhān on the left bank of the Panj River, became part of Afghanistan. Furthermore, under the same agreement the administration of Wakhān, Shughnān and Rūshān on the right bank of the Panj River was nominally transferred to the *amīr* of Bukhārā as compensation for his loss of territories in Darvāz. The outcome of the 1313/1895 establishment of the frontier between the Emirate of Bukhārā (which had become a Russian protectorate), and Afghanistan, which was under the tutelage of British India, was that the lion's share of historical Badakhshān now became part of Afghanistan.¹⁷⁷

Following the demarcation of the borders, the Russians set up permanent military headquarters in Khārūgh, now the capital of Gorno-Badakhshān, and expelled the Afghan forces installed there. Having already made the *amīr* of Bukhārā and the Khan of Khoqand their vassals in 1285/1868 and 1293/1876, respectively, the Russians now established their sovereignty over the whole Pamir region.¹⁷⁸ However, the demarcation of the region of Badakhshān did not put an end to the suffering of the local people at the hands of the Afghan and Bukharan *amīr*s. While the British had 'granted' the districts of Wakhān, Shughnān and Rūshān on the left bank of the Panj River, to the Afghan *amīr*, the Russians had left the territories on the right bank of the Panj in the hands the *amīr* of Bukhārā. Having received these districts from the Russians, the *amīr* of Bukhārā appointed his viceroy governor there. In fact, the rule of the *amīr* of Bukhārā lasted only nine years (1313–1321/1895–1904), during which he continued with the same anti-Ismaili policy he had pursued previously.

The main reason for the unwillingness of the Ismaili population of the Pamirs to accept the *amīr*'s rule was their religious differences.¹⁷⁹ The local people under the leadership of the Ismaili *pīr*s vented their frustration at the Russian decision that left them in the hands of the Bukharan *amīr*. Following a request from the Russian military garrison in Khārūgh to include the

---

¹⁷⁶ Seymour Becker, *Russia's Protectorates in Central Asia: Bukhara and Khiva, 1865–1924* (London, 2004), p. 124.

¹⁷⁷ Haĭdarsho S. Pirumshoev, *Ta'rīkh-i Darvoz* [The History of Darvāz] (Dushanbe, 2008), p. 108; Dagikhudo Dagiev, *Regime Transition in Central Asia: Stateness, Nationalism and Political Change in Tajikistan and Uzbekistan* (London, 2013), pp. 93–94.

¹⁷⁸ L.N. Khariukov, *Anglo-russkoe sopernichestvo v TSentral'noĭ Azii i ismailizm* [Anglo-Russian Rivalry in Central Asia and Ismailism] (Moscow, 1995), pp. 100–113.

¹⁷⁹ Shokhumorov, *Razdelenie Badakhshana*, p. 62.

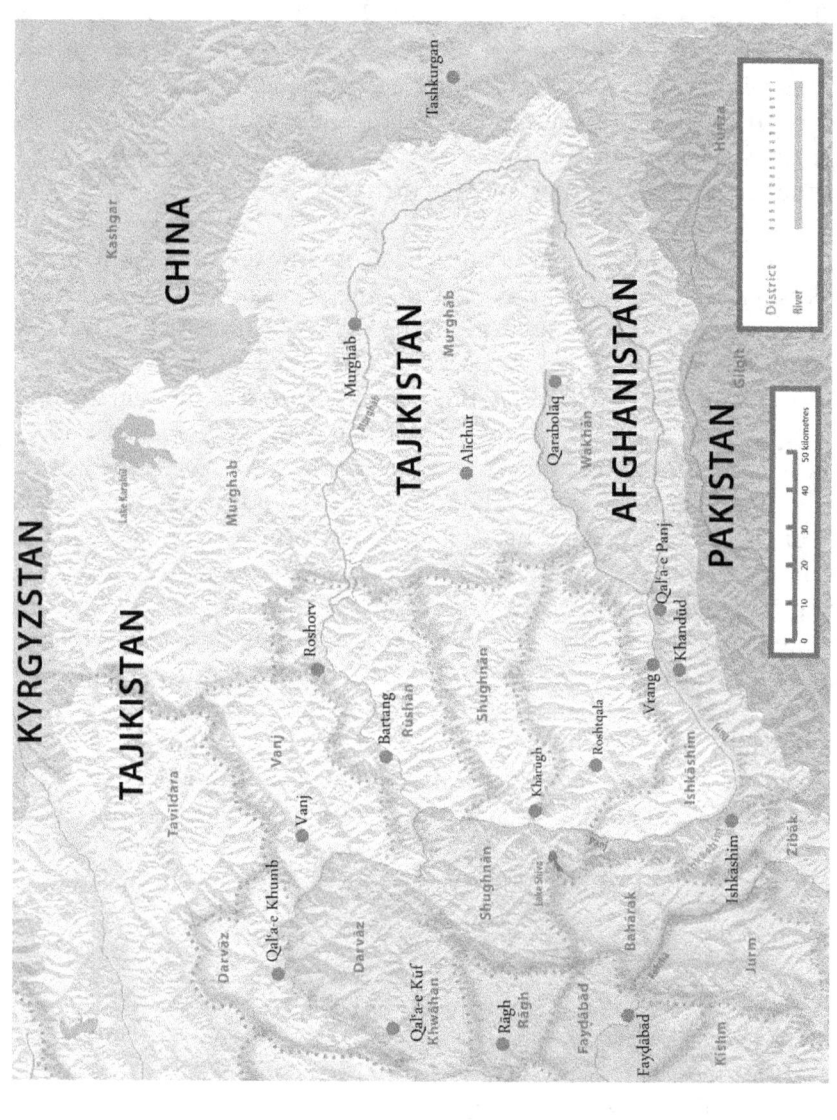

Map of Badakhshan

The Panj River (Amū Daryā) which divides Tajik Badakhshān from Afghan Badakhshān as a result of Anglo-Russian rivalry in Central Asia in the late 13th/19th century

Pamir region under the direct control of the Russian governor-general of Turkestan, several uprisings against the *amīr* of Bukhārā broke out.

The representatives of the *amīr* of Bukhārā ʿAbd al-Aḥad Khān (r. 1303–1328/1885–1911) regarded the Ismailis as 'infidels' and so their treatment of them was inhuman. In this regard, the Russian officer L.N. Khariukov wrote, 'after the establishment of a new border in the Pamir (and the Pamir's transfer to Bukharan administration) at the behest of the great powers, without taking into account the vital interests of the Pamir nationalities, life became even harder for the Ismaili populations.'[180] As a result several letters were sent to the Russians on behalf of the Ismaili community under the leadership of the *pīr*s, such as the one from Yūsuf ʿAlī Shāh (d. 1932) who played a critical role at this point in the history of the Pamīr region. The Russians also felt some responsibility for the fate of the people whose territory they had transferred to Bukhārā, and began to create obstacles for the Bukharan officials in pursuing their anti-Ismaili policy in the region. T.G. Tukhtametov wrote, 'During the anti-Bukharan

---

[180] Khariukov, *Anglo-russkoe sopernichestvo*, p. 63.

uprising of 1314/1896, the Tsarist authorities began intensively intervening in the affairs of the Bukharan authorities over Shughnān, Rūshān and Wakhān, and this undermined the authority of Bukharan officials in the eyes of the local inhabitants.'[181]

In 1905, upon being apprised of several of the grievances of the Ismailis, the *pīrs* appealed to the Russian authorities. This situation forced the Russians to take a decisive step in terms of changing the status and the socio-political situation of the western Pamir, and the region was taken out of Bukharan control and handed over to the Russian governor-general of Turkestan.[182] As a result, there was for a time some kind of certainty and stability in the social life of the communities in Wakhān, Shughnān and Rūshān. Beside protecting them from the depredations of the Afghans and Bukharans, the newly arrived Russians began road building, encouraged the use of horses[183] and gradually a minimum of basic health care was established through the Russian *feldsher* system.[184] A public school was opened in Khārūgh in 1914, and the commitment of the local Ismaili community to educate both boys and girls is recorded in late 13th/19th century reports by explorers.[185] A road between Osh (now in Kyrgyzstan) and the Murghāb district (now in Gorno-Badakhshān) was opened in 1315/1897 and connected to Khārūgh a few years later. However, stability

---

[181] T.G. Tukhtametov, 'Antirusskie poiski inostrantsev v Bukhare i na Pamire. Politicheskie techeniia v emirate Bukhara' [The Anti-Russian Search for Foreigners in Bukhara and the Pamirs. Political Trends in the Emirate of Bukhara], *Voprosy istorii Tadzhikistana. Uchenye zapiski* [Questions on the History of Tajikistan. Scholarly Notes], vol. 26. Seriia obshchest. nauk, 4 (Stalinabad, 1961), pp. 140–177.

[182] Shokhumorov, *Razdelenie Badakhshana*, p. 78. We might also note here than the Russian annexation of Turkestan as a whole increased the size of the Russian empire by approximately 11 per cent.

[183] O. Olufsen, *Through The Unknown Pamirs – The Second Danish Pamir Expedition, 1898–99* (London, 1904), p. 117: 'When I passed from Langarkish to Khorok the first time in 1896, there were no horses to be seen. But of late years the province has made much progress under Russian protection, and now the little horses of Kirghiz and Badakhshān have been imported. These horses are small, persevering, sagacious, and well adapted to mountain use, and they are highly prized by the people.'

[184] *Feldsher* is the Russian term for a health care professional who provides various medical services, mainly in rural areas. *Feldshers* provide primary, obstetrical and surgical care services in many rural medical centres and ambulatory care across Russia.

[185] Hermann Kreutzmann and Teiji Watanable, ed., *Mapping Transition in the Pamirs: Changing Human-Environmental Landscapes* (Cham, 2016), p. 248.

and progress for the Pamirs was short lived, as it was interrupted by the revolutions and upheavals in Russia starting at the end of the 1917 and continuing in 1918.

As noted above, Russian imperial interest in Badakhshān was strategic and formed an integral part of Russian strategy in the Great Game. In addition to competition with British imperial rule in the end of the 13th/19th and the beginning of the 20th century, it intersected with an anti-Ismaili strategy that was being unfolded by Russian military forces in Bukhārā, Afghanistan and China.

In 1902 the Consulate of Russia in Kashgar reported to the Tsar Nicholas II that the Ismaili faith had spread in Kashgar (eastern China) and Osh. This expansionist trend was perceived as a threat to Russian interests in the region. Therefore, the Russians decided to block communications between the Ismailis of Central Asia and their spiritual leader, Sulṭān Muḥammad Shāh, Aga Khan III (r. 1885–1957), the Nizārī Ismaili imam. The Russian Consulate, thus, viewed the Ismailis as agents of British imperial interests, who could work against Russian interests in the region.[186]

According to Bobrinskoĭ, writing in the early years of the 20th century, and in contrast to the state of affairs in the 11th/17th and 12th/18th centuries, the Ismaili faith had now spread throughout Badakhshān and neighbouring regions and prevailed in the Wakhān valley, the Zībāk and Mundjān areas of Chitrāl, Kandjut (now in Afghanistan and Pakistan), Ishkāshim, Ghārān, Shughnān on both sides of the Panj River, Rūshān and Sarikūl (now in China). Furthermore, Bobrinskoĭ propounded, in Afghan Darvāz, Ismailis were found in villages such as Jārf, Ghūmaĭ, Āmurd and Jāmarj, and below Qalʿa-yi Khumb (the centre of Darvāz), and on the Afghan side in villages such as Khādara and Zingiria. In the village of Yāgīd, on the other side of the Panj River, most of the population were Ismaili, with a minority being Ithnāʿasharī. In the Katagan village of Guria, there were a few Ismaili families, while the majority were Sunni. Furthermore, the Hazāra communities near Kabul were mostly Ismaili with only a small portion being Ithnāʿasharī. In Bukhārā, Qoqand and Osh, the residents who were natives of Shughnān and Wakhān were all Ismaili.[187]

---

[186] Stanishevskiĭ, *Ismailizm na Pamire* (1902–1931) [Ismailism in the Pamirs (1902–1931)], p. 108. Also, Kharīukov, *Anglo-russkoe sopernichestvo*, pp. 100–113.

[187] Bobrinskoĭ, 'Sekta ismailʾīa', p. 18.

Tsarist colonial policy and imperial interests resulted in the marginalisation of the broader Tajik religious communities, a process which continued into the Soviet era. Communities were isolated by the establishment of borders that were political rather than geographic, making conditions difficult for the Ismailis in parts of Badakhshān in both Tajikistan and Afghanistan, the western regions of China and northern India (now northern Pakistan).[188] Until then, the Ismailis of the region had been united in their common faith, culture and history, as well as through the Persian language, which was used as a lingua franca throughout Central Asia, Afghanistan, in the north of the Indian sub-continent and in Kashgar in the west of China.[189] However, in the course of the 13th/19th century, with British control of India and the Russian advance in Central Asia, Farsi ultimately lost its status and other languages became dominant. Since then, the Tajik Ismaili communities in the north of Pakistan have adopted Urdu, and those in western China used Uyghur, as their functioning languages.[190]

Meanwhile, once the Pamir region had been subjugated in 1905–1906 and placed under the direct rule of the Russian Tsar, the situation gradually stabilised, and until the October Revolution in Russia in 1917, supreme power remained with the Russian military forces (the governor-general of Turkestan). In the Pamir region, this was implemented by the Russian Pamir military detachment in Khārūgh. Over time, the Tajik Ismailis came to be recognised by the Russians and to a certain extent the attitude towards the Ismailis and their spiritual leader, Sulṭān Muḥammad Shāh, Aga Khan III, in the early decades of the 20th century improved:

> In 1912, at the invitation of His Majesty, the Emperor of Russia Nicholas II, the spiritual leader of the Ismailis – His Highness Sulṭān Muḥammad Shāh [Aga Khan III] visited St Petersburg. He was in amicable relations with the Tsar of Russia. Subsequently, the Aga Khan was highly appreciative of the accord for the voluntary joining of the Pamirs to the Russian Imperial Rule. Already in 1913, the first delegation of the Pamirs visited St Petersburg to

---

[188] Karl Jettmar, *Religii Hindukusha*, tr. from German by K.D. Tsivina (Moscow, 1986).

[189] Edward A. Allworth, *The Modern Uzbeks. From the Fourteenth Century to the Present* (Stanford, 1990), p. 104.

[190] Linda Tsung, *Language Power and Hierarchy: Multilingual Education in China* (London, 2014).

celebrate the 300th anniversary of the House of Romanov. Among them there were ʿAzīz Khān, the ruler of Shākhdara, a resident of Bartang-Mastalī, and a resident of Alay-Tahur Bek.[191]

Compared to the rulers of Bukhārā and the Afghans, the Russian evinced a much more humane attitude towards the local people, especially the Ismailis. In addition, as has been said, they helped to develop education by establishing modern schools, which later on embarked on teaching local culture and tradition, and by teaching sciences and modern languages significantly contributed to the future development of the region. Correspondingly, a Russian scholar of oriental studies, Bobrinskoĭ, expressed an influential opinion in this regard:

> In conclusion, I must express my opinion about our relationship with Islam in Central Asia. Currently, we support only Sunnis, ignoring not only the small minorities (Ismailis, Babis), but even the Shiʿa, as if our goal is the unification of Islam and the absorption of all its ramifications by Sunnism, which, I think, does not fully coincide with our interests. I think that our direct political calculation should be to recognise that all the branches of Islam have the right to an official and independent life, and, as a consequence of this recognition, I would consider it obligatory for us to protect this right, given to everyone, from the encroachments of the stronger sides or more militant confession.[192]

Bobrinskoĭ visited the local *pīr*s and discussed the Ismaili Weltanschauung with them. According to him they displayed a liberal and tolerant interpretation of Islam. He believed that the Pamiri *pīr*s should be acknowledged for the crucial role they played in the modern history of the region. This was probably the case as it was the tremendous efforts of the local *pīr*s, local political leaders and certain intellectuals in the Pamirs that had preserved and maintained the cultural heritage of the community down the centuries and helped it to flourish.

---

[191] *Istoriia Pamira*, available online at: http://www.pamir-spb.ru/istoriya.html [Last accessed, 16 April 2017]. Also see, Sunatullo Jonboboev, 'Geography, ethnicity and cultural heritage in interplay in the context of the Tajik Pamiri identity', in Dagikhudo Dagiev and Carole Faucher, ed. *Identity, History and Trans-Nationality in Central Asia: The Mountain Communities of Pamir* (London, 2018), pp. 11–22.

[192] A.A. Bobrinskoĭ, 'Sekta ismailʾiā', p. 18.

The Russian Revolution and the Panjebhai Movement

The Russian Revolution put an end to Tsarist rule and revolutionary committees were established in every corner of the empire, eventually taking initiatives and establishing the new social order, or as it was labelled later on, Sovetskaĩa Vlast' (Soviet power), which was also known locally as the Hukūmat-e Shūravī. In the Pamir, until December 1918, power remained in the hands of the Pamir border detachment of the Provisional Government, headed by Colonel V.V. Fenin (1875–1933). But when the Council of Peoples' Commissars of the Turkestan Autonomous Soviet Socialist Republic (TASSR) sent a detachment of Revolutionary Guards headed by P. Volovik to the Pamirs in November 1918; however before they reached the Pamirs in December, Fenin and his collaborators fled to India.[193] The fall of Tsarism in Russia was received with pleasure by the *amīr* of Bukhārā, Mīr Muḥammad 'Alīm Khān (r. 1911–1920), who immediately endeavoured to take advantage of the situation, with the help of local officials, in order to regain control over the western Pamir region. But the people of Shughnān rose against the Bukharan soldiers in support of the new Soviet authorities,[194] and as a result the *amīr* of Bukhārā's attempt at a take-over proved abortive. Another failed attempt was made by an anti-Bolshevik group known as the Basmachi,[195] who sought to restore traditional rule over these territories and implemented harsh measures against the local Ismailis.

In 1921, the Pamir Revolutionary Committee was established; it began to organise the Hukūmat-e Shūravī in the villages and the mountain districts. After the Hukūmat-e Shūravī was established in the Pamirs, daily life and protection of the state's borders were administered by a military-political Troĭka consisting of T.M. D'iakov, T. Khuseĭnbaev and S. Shotemur, who have been recorded by history as the organisers of Hukūmat-e Shūravī in the Pamirs.[196] A study of archival documents

---

[193] Diplomba: *Tadzhikskiĭ narod v period mezhdu dvukh revolutsiĭ (fevral'-oktiabr' 1917 goda)*. Available online at: http://diplomba.ru/work/84575 [Last accessed, 20 May 2019].

[194] Hakim Elnazarov and Sultanbek Aksakolov, 'The Nizari Ismailis of Central Asia in Modern Times', in Farhad Daftary, ed., *A Modern History of the Ismailis: Continuity and Changes in a Muslim Community* (London, 2011), pp. 45–75, 53.

[195] The Basmachi were anti-Soviet rebels in Turkestan between the Russian Revolution and the early 1930s. The term, derived from the Turkic word *basmak* (to attack or raid), connotes banditry and was originally a pejorative term used by the Russians.

[196] M. Nazarshoev, *Muborizi rohi haqiqat* [Fighter for Justice] (Dushanbe, 1993), pp. 10–11. Shokhumorov, *Razdelenie Badakhshana*, p. 87.

reveals that until 1922 the attitude of the new government towards the Ismailis was completely neutral and there were no repressive measures against either *pīr*s or ordinary Ismailis. In the first years of Soviet rule, despite the fact that the Communist Party and its ideology were fundamentally hostile to religion, attempts were made to maintain good relations with religious figures and their *murīds*.[197]

Following the establishment of Soviet rule in the Pamirs, the region was transferred to the Farghāna Oblast of TASSR in 1923, becoming part of the Turkestan region. Two years later, in 1925, with the demarcation of national borders, the Pamir region was promoted to the status of 'Autonomous Oblast [region] of Gorno-Badakhshān'. It was then transferred to the Tajik Autonomous Soviet Socialist Republic, which became known as the Soviet Socialist Republic of Tajikistan in 1929.[198] According to the Soviet authorities, the incorporation of the Pamir region was carried out on the basis of common geographic, linguistic, cultural and ethnic features. Some historical sources of the 19th and early 20th century, including ethnographic studies by the Russians, argued that the people of the Pamir region, regardless of certain differences such as linguistic diversity and divergence of belief from the lowland Tajiks, referred to themselves as 'mountain Tajiks'.[199] In fact, several Tajik Ismailis played a vital role in the formation and the establishment of the autonomous region of Badakhshān and the national republic of Tajikistan. One of these was Shirinsho Shohtemur (1899–1937). Originally from Shughnān, he received his secondary education at a Russian school and played an instrumental role in the formation of modern Tajikistan. For this reason he was declared a national hero of Tajikistan in 2006.[200]

However, the voluntary submission of the Pamir region to Russian imperial rule, on the one hand, and the Bolshevik Revolution in Russia, on the other, led to divisions in the Ismaili religious hierarchy in the region. The dramatic changes in the socio-political life of the Ismaili

---

[197] Ibid., p. 87.

[198] Dagiev, *Regime Transition in Central Asia*, p. 26.

[199] A.M. D'iakov, *īazyki sovetskogo Pamira. Kul'tura i pis'mennost' Vostoka* [Languages of the Soviet Pamirs. Culture and Writing of the East], vol. 10 (Moscow, 1931); A.S. Davydov, *Ėtnicheskaīa prinadlezhnost' korennogo naseleniīa Gornogo Badakhshana (Pamir)* [Ethnicity of the Indigenous Population of Gorno-Badakhshān (Pamir)] (Dushanbe, 2005); Dagiev, 'Pamiri Ethnic Identity', pp. 23–44.

[200] Dagiev, *Regime Transition in Central Asia*, p. 28.

community engendered reforms to religious traditions and rituals in order to modernise the community so that it could face of the challenges of the modern era. The Panjebhai was one such movement, headed by a group of Ismaili community leaders, which attempted to rise to the challenge.

The term Panjebhai is a compound of two nouns: *panj* 'five' and *bhai* 'brother', both components of which appear in a variety of South Asian languages (such as Hindi, Gujarati, Punjabi, etc.). The first component, *panj*, means five in Persian and Sanskrit, while the second component, *bhai*, means brother in a variety of modern South Asian languages.[201] According to Paul Bergne, the Ismaili reform movement in the Pamirs became known as the Panjebhai movement in the 1920s.[202] The movement initially spread among the Ismailis of South Asia in the second half of the 19th century. It spread in Soviet Badakhshān, predominantly in Shughān and Rūshān, during the early 1920s and its activities coincided with the visit of a high-profile Ismaili emissary of the Imam Sulṭān Muḥammad Shāh, Pīr Sabzalī Ramḍān ʿAlī (1871–1938) in 1923.[203] During these years, advocates of the movement in Badakhshān introduced changes to both the religious and social life of the community. For instance, they sought to introduce religious education throughout the community and attempted to simplify some religious rituals. However the introduction of initiatives such as the new *panj tasbīḥ ʿAlī-i Zamān* funeral ceremony instead of the old *Charāgh-i rawshan*[204] funeral rite and the establishment of the 'trusted groups' or *anjuman*s who would be

---

[201] Muzaffar Zoolshoev, 'Forgotten Figures of Badakhshan – Sayyid Munir al-Din Badakhshani and Sayyid Haydar Shah Mubarakshahzada', in Dagiev and Faucher, ed., *Identity, History and Trans-Nationality in Central Asia*, pp. 143–172. For more details, see also Zoolshoev, 'The Soviet State and a Religious Movement'.

[202] Paul Bergne, *The Birth of Tajikistan: National Identity and the Origins of the Republic* (London, 2007), p. 97.

[203] Zoolshoev, 'Forgotten Figures of Badakhshan'; Zoolshoev, 'The Soviet State and a Religious Movement'.

[204] *Charāgh-i rawshan*: a religious funeral ceremony conducted by the family of the deceased. The ceremony is ascribed to Nāṣir-i Khusraw and known also as *daʿwat-i Nāṣir*. There are two types of *daʿwat* ceremony in Badakhshān; the first is *daʿwat-i fanā*, performed for the soul of the deceased; and the second, is *daʿwat-i baqā*, performed for the eternal life of the soul. See also, H. Elnazarov, 'Chirāgh-i Rawshan', *EIS*, vol. 5, pp. 676–681.

responsible for the collection and sending of religious dues known as *zakāt* to Bombay, to the Ismaili Imam Sulṭān Muḥammad Shāh, Aga Khan III, met with strong opposition from some influential *pīr*s and *khalīfa*s, who then began an active campaign against the movement.

Another significant element of the movement's history is the fact that its emergence coincided with the establishment of Soviet power which became distinctly hostile towards religion in the interwar years. By the late 1930s, and as a result of the Soviet anti-religion campaign, the leading Panjebhais, as well as the *pīr*s who opposed them, had all been either imprisoned or eliminated by the state authorities. Only a small number of the Panjebhai groups continued practising their new *panj tasbīḥ 'Alī-i Zamān* funeral ceremony in some villages in Shugnān and Rūshān.[205]

The movement's aim to introduce reforms and bring modernity to the Ismaili community in the Pamir region coincided with the development of modern schools, hospitals, cultural centres, power stations, roads and airports in all major areas of the region brought under Soviet rule, which dramatically changed the living standards of the local Ismaili community.

The Ismaili Community in the Soviet Era

During the Soviet era, the Badakhshān region had the highest proportion of individuals with higher education qualifications in the Soviet Union. It produced a great number of highly educated professionals who made valuable contributions to the Tajik state and society. Improved health, education, social welfare and security resulted in rapid demographic changes and greater mobility, which prompted many Ismailis to migrate to the lowlands of Tajikistan and to other parts of the Soviet Union. However the Ismailis, like the rest of the Soviet peoples, also experienced the collectivisation of agriculture, when land was nationalised and the cultivation of certain cash crops (e.g. tobacco and cotton) was forced upon the people. Furthermore, 'beginning in the 1930s and continuing intermittently until the late 1960s, the Soviet authorities forcibly transferred people from the central and eastern zones of Tajikistan to provide labour for new industries and, especially, for intensive agricultural projects.'[206]

---

[205] Zoolshoev, 'Forgotten Figures of Badakhshan', pp. 143–172.

[206] Shirin Akiner and Catherine Barnes, 'The Tajik Civil War: Causes and Dynamics', in Kamoludin Abdullaev and Catherine Barnes, ed., *Politics of Compromise: The Tajikistan Peace Process*, Accord Issue 10 (London, 2001), pp. 16-21.

The forced migration of the mountain people, including Ismailis, to the southern lowlands of Tajikistan with their very hot summers resulted in many deaths. In 1937–1938 the 'great purges' of Soviet intelligentsia and intellectuals who displayed any opposition to Soviet rule, or who might possibly present an obstacle to the realisation of the Hukūmat-e Shūravī, included a great many of the Ismaili political, intellectual and cultural elite. Furthermore, the local youth were encouraged to move to other parts of the Soviet Union to meet the deficit in labour elsewhere.[207]

By the end of the 1920s, the Soviet authorities had started placing restrictions on religious freedom and the activities of the religious communities and their leaders. Taking a Marxist perspective, the Soviet government regarded any religious belief, ceremonies and functionaries as the means of manipulating uneducated people in order to disturb them or distract them from building the new Soviet society and creating the new Soviet man (*Homo Sovieticus*).[208] In the history of the Ismailis of Soviet Tajikistan the year 1936 marked a turning point. A particular concern for the Hukūmat-e Shūravī and the Communist Party was the border issue between Tajikistan, China and Afghanistan, given the number of Tajik Ismailis residing in these countries. Moscow decided to seal the borders of Tajikistan with Afghanistan and China, which resulted in the complete isolation of the Ismailis of Tajikistan from their co-religionists in those countries. Above all, the sealing of the borders was intended to prevent any future contacts with the Ismaili imam and his representatives. The Hukūmat-e Shūravī launched a new propaganda campaign, accusing the *pīrs* and other religious officials of being class enemies and disloyal to the Soviet system. Moreover, the strengthening of the Hukūmat-e Shūravī all over the country and the consolidation of centralised power led to the imposition of a strict atheist ideology, which gradually forced prominent religious authorities such as *pīrs* to flee the country, and if they did not they were either jailed or executed.[209]

Thus, during the Soviet era religious life and the practice of the faith became restricted in every aspect and in some areas it was almost

---

[207] Sarfaroz Niyozov, 'Shi'a Ismaili Tradition in Central Asia: Evolution, Continuities and Changes', *Central Asia and the Caucasus*, 24 (2003), pp. 39–46. Available online at: http://www.ca-c.org/journal/eng-06-2003/05.niyprimen.shtml [Last accessed, 7 May 2019].

[208] Alexander Zinoviev, *Homo Sovieticus* (Paladin Grafton Book, 1986).

[209] Shokhumorov, *Razdelenie Badakhshana*, pp. 72–76.

impossible for religious communities to maintain and observe their traditions and rituals. The Hukūmat-e Shūravī considered any religion or religious ritual as outdated myths, superstitions and expressions of fanaticism, and membership in religious communities was suppressed.[210] Therefore the clerics, or *khalīfa*s, had to 'hand over all religious matters to local officials', as refusal could have led to imprisonment or even the death penalty. Government officials or representatives of the state institutions, including whistle-blowers, were present during religious ceremonies with the result that the *khalīfa*s could not perform their religious duties.[211] However, some *khalīfa*s did manage to perform rituals as they regarded it their duty to do so, even though the consequences could be dire.[212] The *khalīfa*s went underground and some ordinary members of the community also risked their lives and, in private, maintained their devotional practices, in particular, the funeral ceremony. The oppressive measures of the Soviet authorities could not prevent the performance of these religious obligations, and this led to the practice of a 'parallel Islam', where religious rites were performed informally and secretly.[213] However, a shift in the official approach occurred during the Second World War, particularly in 1943, when the Soviet authorities desperately needed the support of the entire Soviet population in the war effort against Nazi Germany. They finally relaxed state repression and restrictions on religion, allowing people to perform their religious duties and ceremonies and re-opening many mosques, churches, synagogues and other places of worship.

A similar policy of détente towards religion occurred in the 1960s when the Soviet authorities realised the impossibility of imposing atheism on the population and decided to change their policy and keep religion under their control, creating official religious structures. As far as the Ismailis were concerned, henceforth, *khalīfa*s were appointed by the state,

---

[210] Frank Bliss, *Social and Economic Change in the Pamirs (Gorno-Badakhshan, Tajikistan)*, tr. from German by Nicola Pacult and Sonia Guss (London, 2005), p. 62.

[211] Valentin Bushkov and Tokhin Kalandarov, 'Ismaility Tadzhikistana: Traditsii i Sovremennost', *Central Asia and the Caucasus*, 6 (2002), pp. 130–135. Available online at: http://www.ca-c.org/journal/2002/journal_rus/cac-06/15.busrus.shtml [Last accessed, 9 Nov. 2014].

[212] Ibid.

[213] A. Matveeva, 'The Perils of Emerging Statehood: Civil War and State Reconstruction in Tajikistan an Analytical Narrative on State-making', *Crisis States Research Centre* (March, 2009), p. 8.

but nonetheless the observance of religious practices continued to be a highly private and concealed domain of life.[214]

The Ismaili Community in the Post-Soviet Era

In 1986, Mikhail Gorbachev introduced the policy of *perestroĭka* (reconstruction) and *glasnost'* (openness) in the Soviet Union, and the attitude of the state towards religion underwent a complete change, as a process of political, cultural and religious renaissance took place throughout the USSR. The Soviet state's monolithic atheist policy could not survive the renaissance of its multi-ethnic and multi-religious society, and the year 1991 saw the dissolution of the Soviet Union.

Like other Soviet National Republics, Tajikistan declared its independence on 9 September 1991, and the Ismaili community of Badakhshān remained an integral part of it. Tajik Ismailis, like many other people in the newly independent Tajikistan, actively participated in the political developments of the early 1990s, which ultimately led to a civil war (1992–1997). Some Ismaili activists founded a movement called *La'l-i Badakhshān*, with the aim of achieving greater autonomy for the GBAO.[215] In the early stages of the civil war in 1992–1993, many Ismailis took refuge in Badakhshān, which the war had isolated from the outside world. The inflow of refugees from other war-zones in Tajikistan resulted in food shortages and the conflict caused a complete implosion of the economy and a humanitarian catastrophe of enormous proportions. But, from 1993 on, the Aga Khan Foundation (AKF)'s rural development interventions in Tajikistan coordinated relief and humanitarian assistance. Subsequently, with the change in political climate and the restoration of stability, the AKDN has grown extensively in Tajikistan to become a major force for improving the quality of life in the country.

In addition to this, the re-establishment of connections with their current Imam, Shah Karim al-Husayni, Aga Khan IV, as well as with the global Ismaili community, brought about a new climate of hope for the Tajik Ismailis. Various institutions began working in varying capacities in the region, including grassroots initiatives with local businesses and education, and working towards the development of civil society in the post-Soviet era.

---

[214] Niyozov, 'Shi'a Ismaili Tradition in Central Asia', pp. 39–46.
[215] Dagiev, *Regime Transition in Central Asia*, p. 115.

Khārūgh, the capital of Badakhshān of Tajikistan

Moreover, three visits by Aga Khan IV to Tajikistan in 1995, 1998 and 2008 generated a new spirit in all the people of the region. For the first time in centuries, the Ismailis and their fellow Muslims in Badakhshān joined in recognising their common aspirations. In each of his visits, the Ismaili imam stressed the importance of peaceful co-existence, education and ethics for the development of the economy and civil society in Central Asia. These visits substantially raised the self-confidence of the people, sparked hope in many of them, and contributed to the peace process. The people of the Pamirs now face the future as a revitalised and confident community that hopes to play a constructive role within the gobal Ismaili community in general and in Central Asia in particular.[216]

In October 2009, an Ismaili Centre in Dushanbe was opened by Aga Khan IV and the President of Tajikistan Emomali Rahmon. The Ismaili Centre was built in the heart of the capital city with the purpose of encouraging a 'spirit of peace and dialogue and in the search for knowledge and human dignity'. The Ismaili Centre offers the Ismaili community's own outlook and understanding of Islam as 'a thinking, spiritual faith'.[217]

Earlier, in 2000, the University of Central Asia (UCA) was founded. The Presidents of the Kyrgyz Republic, Tajikistan, and Kazakhstan, along

---

[216] Niyozov, 'Shi'a Ismaili Tradition in Central Asia', pp. 39–46.
[217] Fayaz S. Alibhai, 'An Architectural Manifestation of the Continuity between Tradition and Modernity', *The Middle East in London*, 6 (2009), p. 8.

The Aga Khan addressing members of the Ismaili community during his visit to Badakhshān in 1998

with Aga Khan IV, signed the International Treaty and Charter establishing this secular, private, not-for-profit university, which was ratified by the relevant parliaments and registered with the United Nations. The UCA's Tekeli Town campus in Kazakhstan was officially opened in 2003, the Naryn campus was inaugurated in September 2016 in the Kyrgyz Republic, and the second residential campus in Tajikistan, in Khārūgh, opened in September 2017. The UCA brings with it the commitment and partnership of the broader AKDN by offering an internationally recognised standard of higher education in Central Asia. The UCA's mission is to promote the social and economic development of Central Asia, particularly its mountain communities, while at the same time helping the different peoples of the region to preserve and draw upon their rich cultural heritage and diverse traditions as assets for the future.

2

Ismaili Studies by Russian, Soviet and Post-Soviet Scholars

توانا بود هر که دانا بود   ز دانش دل پیر برنا بود

Thy source of might is knowledge
Thus old hearts grow young again[1]

The Ismailis under Russian and Soviet Rule

The maxim that 'knowledge is power' was demonstrated by the campaigns of the imperial powers of Britain and Russia to document and research the areas now under their control. Once any territorial disputes had been settled between them, they embarked on studying and exploring both the region of Central Asia and the people under their colonial rule. Russia's interest in Ismaili studies is believed to have been provoked by the colonial policies of British India. Earlier in the 13th/19th century, Afghanistan had lost a great part of eastern Pashtunistān to British India. The accession of ʿAbd al-Raḥmān Khān to the throne of Afghanistan in 1880 saw him expand his territory to include Kāfiristān, Qaṭaghān, Badakhshān and Chahār-wilāyat. Much of the present northern Afghanistan had already been subdued and his expansionism was certainly a response to British military involvement in his country's affairs. At the same time, the Russian military presence in Turkestan (present Central Asia) highlighted the region's geo-political importance, which lay between territories under the effective control of the two imperial powers. As a result, the Pamir region became an area of rivalry between the British and Russian empires, in the struggle referred to as the Great Game. For the Russians this was an

---

[1] Abulqosim Firdawsī, *Shohnoma*, ed. Kamol Aĭynī and Zohir Ahrorī (Dushanbe, 2007), vol. 1, p. 24.

imperial expansionist policy aimed at gaining control over the new territories, while the British lent support to ʿAbd al-Raḥmān Khān, *amīr* of Afghanistan, in order to compensate him for the loss of eastern Pashtunistān. Due to this colonial rivalry there was a need for knowledge about the area, people, culture, religion and geography of the territories occupied.[2]

Accordingly, the Russian empire, in the British fashion, ordered scholars to begin studying the people and countries of Russian Turkestan.[3] This was a time when scholars were given the task of defining priorities in the study of new regions. In this regard Serebrennikov, a Russian explorer of the Pamir region, noted, 'It is precisely this mountainous country ... that represents the sources of the Amū Daryā flowing through the whole of Central Asia from the heights of the Pamirs to the Aral Sea and known since ancient times under the name of Oxus.'[4] Almost in the same manner, M.S. Andreev later wrote in 1905, 'The pre-Pamiri countries have similarities with the Caucasus in terms of their multitude of ethnographic units. Here, in every valley one can see a distinct dialect and authentic custom that has no analogy even in the most nearby village.'[5] During the second half of the 19th century and the beginning of the 20th century, a number of archaeological monuments were studied, but the greater

---

[2] B. Lashkarbekov, S. Yusufbekov and S. Khodjaniyazov, 'Ismailism and Central Asian Ismailis in the Russian and Soviet Studies' (Unpublished Report for the IIS, 2000), p. 11.

[3] The first study of this kind was undertaken by Konstantin von Kaufmann (1818–1882), the first Governor-General of Russian Turkestan (1867–1882). *Turkestanskiĭ Alʾbom* (The Turkestan Album) is a unique photographic survey dedicated to the history, ethnography, geography, economy and culture of Central Asia.

The Russian Orientalist A.L. Kun (also spelled Kuhn) compiled the first three parts, and the album was formerly referred to as the Kun Collection. Other compilers included M.T. Brodovskiĭ, M.A. Terentyev, N.V. Bogaevskiĭ and the photographer N.N. Nekhoroshev. The Military-Topographic Department, Military District of Tashkent printed the lithographic parts of each plate. The production work was primarily done in St Petersburg and Tashkent in 1871–72. Available online at: https://www.loc.gov/rr/print/coll/287_turkestan.html [last accessed, 7 May 2019]

[4] A. Serebrennikov, 'Ocherki Shugnana' [Sketch of Shugnan], *Voennyĭ sbornik*, 226 (1896), pp. 1–52; A. Serebrennikov, *Ocherk o Pamire* [Sketch of Pamir] (St Petersburg, 1900), p. 1.

[5] M.S. Andreev, 'Bliny v pripamirskikh stranakh' [Oral Epic in the Pamir Countries], in *TV*, 32 (1905), pp. 3–33.

successes of Russian orientalism were in the fields of historical geography, history, irrigation and numismatics. The pioneering contribution of the eminent Russian Orientalist Vasiliĭ Vladimirovich Bartol'd (1869–1930) to the study of the history of Central Asian peoples has been generally acknowledged by specialists in this field.[6]

Material on the beliefs, culture, way of life, languages and dialects of the Ismaili areas, as well as on the history, political and socio-economic problems faced by the Ismailis, were primarily collected by amateur scholars during secret missions, as military envoys, adventurers from all walks of life, naturalists and officers in the Russian army. A characteristic feature of these studies was a non-differential approach to integrated knowledge. In the 20th century, the salient feature of Soviet scholarship was its ideological focus; a disciplinary approach in studying the Pamir area and the Pamiri people took the general form of a survey that only took account of certain cultural aspects of Ismailism. Soviet ethnographic research began to be shaped along national republic lines and categorised according to the numerous ethnic minorities living in the vast area of the Soviet Union. Along with the Russian scholars, indigenous cadres of various nationalities, including Tajik specialists and a number of Ismailis, participated in these ethnographic surveys.

Under the Soviet regime, the Ismaili-populated areas were studied with reference to the disciplines of archaeology, ethnography, anthropology, linguistics and history. Having identified the cultural peculiarities of the economically and culturally backward peoples in the peripheral areas of Tsarist Russia, Soviet ethnography aimed at defining the specific form of non-capitalist methods to be used in order to develop these peoples along the socialist model. The experience of the first generations of Soviet ethnographers, who began their studies during the pre-revolutionary period, has provided indispensable information. Collecting research material, ethnographic methods, observation, and a scientific approach to material and cultural evidence in pre-Soviet scholarship were the major features in the study of the way of life and culture of these peoples.

Interest in Ismaili studies can be said to have appeared in Russian scholarship during the course of the Russian annexation of Turkestan in the second half of the 19th century, and in connection with the Ismaili

---

[6] V.V. Bartol'd, *Four Studies on the History of Central Asia*, tr. V and T. Minorsky, 3 vols (Leiden, Brill: vol. 1, 1956; vol. 2, 1958; vol. 3, 1962).

areas in the region. On the one hand, British colonial rule in India where the Ismaili imams had resided since the 1840s, and on the other hand, the expansionist policy of the Russian empire that had incorporated Ismaili-populated regions, caused the Russians to view the Ismaili imam as an agent of the British imperialists, who could work against Russian interests.[7] First of all, the Russian consulates in Bombay and Kashgar indicated their alarm and sent reports to the Turkestan Governor-Generalship on the apparently pro-British stance of the Ismaili Imam Sulṭān Muḥammad Shāh, Aga Khan III (d. 1957).[8] In addition to this, Baron Cherkasov, the Head of the Russian Political Agency in the Turkestan Governor-Generalship, also provided some information on the Tajik Ismailis. In his account, Baron Cherkasov shows little knowledge of Islam, though he was allegedly conversant in Persian. In this reports, he claims that the religion of *Panjtanī* among the Mountain Tajiks, which is how he refers to Ismailism in his report, neglected the usual precepts of Islamic religious duties and obligations.[9] He added that there was little in terms of religious hierarchy but much worship of saints and sanctuaries.

Alekseĭ Bobrinskoĭ, who met three Ismaili *pīr*s in various areas during an expedition in the Pamirs, published a booklet called *Sekta ismail'ia v russkikh i bukharskikh predelakh Sredneĭ Azii* (The Ismaili Sect in Russian and Bukharan Central Asia), which is distinct from his ethnographic study of the Ishkāshimīs and Wakhānīs. This booklet consists of interviews with Sayyid Yūsuf ʿAlī Shāh, Sayyid Kāẓim and ʿAlī Mardān Shāh, well-known Ismaili *pīr*s in the Western Pamirs at the turn of the 20th century. The booklet is not an academic work and is most subjective in relation to the people with whom he spoke and with regard to their beliefs. Despite that, as a result of its publication, Bobrinskoĭ was considered an authority on the religion of the mountain Tajiks. Either due to his poor Persian, a deficient interpreter, or reluctance on the part of the *pīr*s to initiate an open discussion with an outsider on matters of faith, Bobrinskoĭ describes the main religious authorities of the Ismailis as illiterate people, who neither understand nor follow Islamic tenets.

---

[7] A.V. Stanishevskiĭ, *Ismailizm na Pamire* (1902–1931). *Sbornik dokumentov*, Academiia Nauk USSR, Glavnoe Archivnoe Upravlenie pri-Sovete Ministrov Uzbekskoĭ SSR: Institute Vostokovedeniia (Tashkent, 1933).

[8] On this point see, p. 70 above.

[9] Baron A. Cherkasov, 'Otchët', in N.A. Khalfin, *Rossiia i Bukharskiĭ ėmirat na Zapadnom Pamire (konets XIX – nachalo XX v.)* (Moscow, 1975), pp. 104–105.

However, it seems that Bobrinskoĭ's main issue of concern was the genealogies of the *pīrs*, the number of their followers and the procedure of paying the *zakāt*.[10] Paradoxically, many years later the well-known Russian scholar, Aleksandr A. Semënov, recalled with admiration his meetings with lay Ismailis whom he regarded as 'peasant-philosophers' due to their knowledge of Greek philosophy.[11]

On the whole, pre-Soviet scholarship did not produce significant works on the Ismailis, and even the reports of the Russian political, military and diplomatic missions generally dealt with the political aspects of the life of the community. The dearth of robust academic literature and the lack of accurate knowledge on the Ismailis and their religious beliefs, history and philosophy as well as the role of their imams, frequently led to misunderstandings about them on the part of other religious groups. However, the archival material collected from diplomatic missions, military service and clandestine documents is still very useful as the historical record of a given era and its ideas, and for the statistical data it provides.

The Ismailis in Soviet Studies

Most studies on the Ismailis during the Soviet era were carried out on the basis of Marxist-Leninist ideology. The aim of Marxism was, in fact, to fight for the transformation of society on a national and international scale, and it considered religion as a factor leading to class division in human society.[12] Religious studies were to be approached in the light of historical Marxism, which, by nature stands in contradiction to religious ideas and teachings.[13] Meanwhile, the Soviet government initiated a scrupulous study of religion 'per se'. These measures can be said, in the broader sense of the word, to have been undertaken as part of an atheist campaign to eradicate religion, 'the opium of the masses', as well as part

---

[10] Bobrinskoĭ, 'Sekta ismail'i͡a', pp. 1–20.

[11] A.A. Semënov, 'Iz oblasti religioznykh verovaniĭ shugnanskikh ismailitov' [On the Realm of the Religious Belief of the Shugnani Ismailis], *MI*, 1 (1912), p. 523.

[12] Georgi Plekhanov, *Selected Philosophical Works*, vol. 3 (Moscow, 1976), pp. 117–183.

[13] Dimitry V. Pospielovsky, *A History of Marxist-Leninist Atheism and Soviet Anti-Religious Policies*, vol. 1: *A History of Soviet Atheism in Theory, and Practice, and the Believer* (New York, 1987), p. 11.

of the implementation of the grand project to reinterpret the past along the lines of Marxist theory. Communist agitators argued that religion being reactionary was the instrument of class enemies and a remnant of imperialism.[14] The study of Islam materialised in this hostile environment. A book by a leading Soviet scholar on Islamic studies, Nikolaï Smirnov, reflects this policy. Smirnov's book[15] begins with a reference to Marx and Lenin's critique of religion and the religious Weltanschauung; it pays great attention to presenting the social function of religion as an instrument of a class-ridden society, and exposing the class character of the activities of religious organisations which were aimed at protecting the interests of the oppressor class.[16] The book, which was regarded as a major work on the study of Islam, is in two parts: (i) from the first encounters of the *Kievan Rus'* (East Slavic tribes) with Muslims in the 7th/13th to the early 20th century; (ii) from the period following the October Revolution up to the early 1950s. The work analyses various aspects of Islam such as the religion and culture of Muslims from historical, social and political perspectives, from the early days of Islam through its development and expansion into different lands. It also provides different studies of the Russian people, in particular their intellectual perception of Islam over the course of history. However, as the author argues, 'the study [...] of Islam and the religious organisations in the history of the East and of modern life, in particular, shows up the role of Islam as an instrument of imperialist policy used for the colonial enslavement of the people of the East; [this] is the most important task for Soviet historians.'[17]

Following these premises, Ismailism, alongside all other religious traditions, came under attack in several studies written during the Soviet era. As regards the Ismailis, the prejudices were twofold: not only did Soviet scholars engage in Ismaili studies from a Marxist ideological perspective, but they were also victims of the bias in the historical sources which they used when writing about the Ismailis. These anti-Ismaili sources had been influenced by the polemical writings of earlier Sunni authors such as Abū ʿAbd Allāh Muḥammad b. ʿAlī b. Rizām al-Kūfī, better known as Ibn Rizām, who lived in Baghdad during the first half of

---

[14] Vladimir Lenin, 'Novaĭa Zhizn'', in *Lenin: Collected Works*, vol. 10 (Moscow, 1965), pp. 83–87.

[15] N.A. Smirnov, *Ocherki Istorii Izucheniĭa Islama v SSSR* (Moscow, 1954).

[16] Ibid., p. 3.

[17] Ibid., p. 263.

the 4th/10th century and Abū Manṣūr ʿAbd al-Qāhir b. Ṭāhir al-Baghdādī (d. 429/1037). F. Daftary, in his studies, has demonstrated that the Sunni polemicists and heresiographers often deliberately incorporated or fabricated anti-Ismaili accounts in their writings.[18] Also the establishment of an Ismaili state centered at the fortress of Alamūt under the leadership of Ḥasan-i Ṣabbāḥ (d. 518/1124), and Ismaili opposition to the Saljūq Turks, who ruled the eastern Islamic lands of Iran and Central Asia and who supported the Abbasid caliphs, led to further Sunni reaction against the Ismailis in general, and the Nizārī Ismailis of Persia and Syria in particular. The new literary campaign was initiated and led by Niẓām al-Mulk, vizier of the Saljūq sultan Malik-Shāh (r. 465–485/1072–1092). He was one of the most fervent opponents of the Ismailis and of their daʿwa, and his Siyāsat-nāma, a work in the Mirror for Princes genre, has been regarded as one of the important sources, albeit from the viewpoint of a staunch opponent, on early Ismaili daʿwa activity in Persia and Khurāsān.[19] He devoted a chapter in the Siyāsat-nāma to condemnation of the Ismailis and an account as he saw it of their history to date. However, the earliest polemical treatise against the Persian Ismailis and their doctrine of taʿlīm (the authoritative teaching in religion of an imam in every age after the Prophet Muhammad) was written by al-Ghazālī (450–505/1058–1111).[20] He was, in fact, commissioned by the Abbasid caliph al-Mustaẓhir (487–512/1094–1118) to produce a major treatise in refutation of the Bāṭinīs, a demeaning designation meaning 'esotericists' coined for the Ismailis by their adversaries.[21] He completed this task in the Niẓāmiyya madrasa in Baghdad in 488/1095.

These were the kinds of primary sources by Muslim writers that were examined by Russian and Soviet scholars who also used a number of medieval European works based on the distorted images derived from the Crusaders who, despite military and diplomatic encounters with the Fatimids in Egypt and the Nizārī Ismailis in Syria, had remained unversed in the teachings of Islam and notably Ismaili beliefs, and engaged in

---

[18] Farhad Daftary, 'Sunni Perceptions of the Ismailis: Medieval Perspectives' in Orkhan Mir-Kasimov, ed., Intellectual Interactions in the Islamic World: The Ismaili Thread (London, 2020), pp. 13–26.

[19] Daftary, The Ismāʿīlīs (2nd ed., Cambridge, 2007), p. 209.

[20] See Farouk Mitha, Al-Ghazālī and the Ismailis: A Debate on Reason and Authority in Medieval Islam (London, 2003).

[21] Ibid., pp. 26–27. Daftary, The Ismāʿīlīs (2nd ed., Cambridge, 2007), pp. 10–11.

fanciful speculations and the fabrication of legends developing the stories of the Ismailis' Muslim opponents yet further.[22]

Defamation of the Ismailis of Badakhshān and their leader, the Aga Khan, was not a Soviet invention, but dated back to the time of the Russian empire and the rivalry between the colonial powers. At that time, the Russian colonial rulers erroneously considered Aga Khan III a British agent.[23] Soviet Communist scholars continued with the same imperial misperception. This is demonstrated by Maĭskiĭ's 1935 statement, 'Ismailism is the ideology of the feudal aristocracy, and it is clear that the ideology of the class could not be the enemy of the same class. The modern Ismaili caliph – Sulṭān Muḥammad Shāh, Aga Khan III – is a major bourgeois politician and a staunch supporter of the British Raj in India.'[24]

It was this alleged support for the British in India that was the reason for the Communist government in Moscow clinging on to the pre-Soviet vision of Aga Khan III. The Aga Khan had appealed to his *murīd*s (his followers) in India and Central Asia to lend their support to the British during the Second World War. The hardening of Soviet policy vis-à-vis the Ismailis, as mentioned, justified and encouraged Soviet scholars in taking a more aggressive stance in their works. The writings of these scholars are sometimes not far short of prejudice due to their continuous reliance on the medieval sources. G. Ashurov (1930–2020), E. Bertel's (1890–1957), A. Bertel's (1926–1995), A. Bogoutdinov (1911–1970), E. Braginskiĭ (1905–1989), B. Ghafurov (1908–1977), A. Zakuev (1988–1968), L. Klimovich (1907–1989), A. Semënov (1873–1958), L. Stroeva (1910–1993) and Kh. Dodikhudoev (1936–2021), were all Soviet scholars who directly or indirectly studied the Ismailis. The scholars who dealt more strictly with the philosophical aspect of the Ismailis were A. Bogoutdinov, S. Grigorian (1920–1974), A. Sagadeyev (1931–1997) and O. Trakhtenberg

---

[22] Farhad Daftary, 'Wladimir Ivanow and Modern Ismaili Studies', in Stanislav M. Prozorov and Hakim Elnazarov, ed., *Russian Scholars on Ismailism* (St Petersburg, 2014), pp. 24–37. Also, Farhad Daftary, *The Assassin Legends: Myths of the Isma'ilis* (London, 1994), pp. 62–64.

[23] Khaëlbek Dodikhudoev, *Mazhabi Ismoiliīa va mohiīati ijtimoii on. Rohhoi bartaraf namudani boqimondai din* [Ismaili Belief and its Social Aspects. Ways to Eliminate a Religious Remnant] (Dushanbe, 1967), pp. 38–41.

[24] P.M. Maĭskiĭ, 'Sledy drevnikh verovaniĭ v pamirskom ismailizme' [Traces of Ancient Beliefs in Pamiri Ismailism], *Sovetskaīa ėtnografiīa*, 3 (1935), pp. 48–58, especially p. 58.

(1889–1959).²⁵ Soviet studies were diametrically opposed to what came to be identified as 'bourgeois orientalist scholarship'. The ideological tendentiousness and consequences of the myopia of Soviet scholarship becomes more obvious in the work of these scholars, as for example, in the work of Dodikhudoev, who has produced several books, numerous articles and delivered countless lectures on Ismaili philosophy.²⁶

Review of the Literature on the Ismailis in Soviet Scholarship

Khaëlbek Dodikhudoev is an important and interesting case for this study as well as for the further development of Ismaili studies in the post-Soviet era. Firstly, Dodikhudoev was regarded as a major scholar in the field of Ismaili studies, during both the Soviet and post-Soviet periods; secondly, even though he was a product of Soviet schooling, Dodikhudoev also had the advantage of being born into an Ismaili family in Badakhshān of Tajikistan. Thirdly, as a dynamic scholar during both the Soviet and post-Soviet eras, his scholarship will also be examined in terms of the shift in Ismaili studies since the disintegration of the Soviet Union in the section below entitled 'Review of the Literature on the Ismailis in Post-Soviet Scholarship'.²⁷ During the Soviet period, Dodikhudoev's views about the origins of the Ismaili movement were in line with the Marxist understanding of religion. While this view was shared by the above-mentioned colleagues and scholars, Dodikhudoev argued that an analysis of the secondary literature shows two opposing attitudes towards the medieval Ismaili movement:

> According to the one, held mainly by the bourgeois orientalists, the intellectual speculations of the Ismailis not only did not go beyond the

---

²⁵ O.B. Trakhtenberg, *Ocherki po istorii zapandno-evropeĭskoĭ srednevekovoĭ filosofii* [Essays on the History of Western European Medieval Philosophy] (Moscow, 1957); A.V. Sagadeev and S.N. Grigorian, tr., *Iz istorii filosofii Sredneĭ Azii i Iran VII–XII vv.* [On the History of the Philosophy of Central Asia and Iran, VII–XII Century] (Moscow, 1960); A.M. Bogoutdinov, ed., *Istoriĭa filosofii* [The History of Philosophy], vol. 1 (Moscow, 1957), pp. 239–249.

²⁶ In a recent publication Dodikhudoev admitted that ideological restrictions were in place in Ismaili studies during the Soviet period. Dodikhudoev, *Filosofskiĭ ismailizm* [Philosophical Ismailism] (Dushanbe, 2014), pp. 6–7.

²⁷ For more discussion on Dodikhudoev see, pp. 108–115.

framework of Islamic dogmas, but, on the contrary, refined them. Therefore, the accusations against the Ismailis of heresy, atheism and allegations of socialist inclinations are groundless. W.A. Ivanow, A. Ismail, H. Corbin, A. Nanji, S.H. Naṣr and others hold this viewpoint.[28]

At the same time, Dodikhudoev, like his Soviet contemporaries, adopted the second interpretation with regard to the emergence of the Ismaili movement which is in line with the official Marxist approach to the study of religion:

> ... Ismailism initially emerged from contradictions within the Shiʿi Imamate. With a series of doctrinal changes in virtually all aspects, including theological, philosophical and socio-political ones, the movement grew into a powerful counter-weight to the Sunni orthodoxy and to Shiʿism itself, while it invariably bore an implicit mark of popular aspirations. This point of view has been promoted by a number of scholars and students of the history and doctrine of Ismailism, including A.M. Bogoutdinov, B.G. Ghafurov, L.V. Stroeva, Alessandro Bausani, H. Enayat, K. Keshawarz, Hermann Ley, Bernard Lewis and Ehsan Tabari.[29]

Moreover, the excessive reliance of Soviet scholars on medieval sources that were opposed to the Ismailis was not incidental since it conformed to the Marxist understanding of the emergence of religions as a part of the class struggle between different groups in society. The medieval sectarian discourse provided evidence for the analysis of the social system because, in the Marxist view, orthodox and heterodox schools have often corresponded to the respective ideologies of the antagonistic classes. Within this framework, Dodikhudoev assumed a pragmatic stance, perhaps on the basis that the dominant Marxist ideology allowed for a reinterpretation of Ismaili philosophy as one of rebellion and as a form of medieval freethinking, with this reinterpretation disguised as atheist propaganda and as essentially founded on anti-Islamic agendas. Therefore, Dodikhudoev may have viewed Ismailism as a medieval sectarian discourse on political philosophy, a theory initially laid out by Soviet

---

[28] Khaëlbek Dodikhudoev, *Filosofiiā krestʼiānskogo bunta: O roli srednevekovogo ismailizma v razvitii svobodomysliiā na musulʼmanskom Vostoke* [The Philosophy of a Peasant Revolt: The Role of Medieval Ismailism in the Development of Thought in the Muslim East] (Dushanbe, 1987), p. 6.

[29] Ibid., p. 7.

Oriental Studies and by the Soviet Tajik scholar Bobojon Gharufov. The latter's main work *Tadzhiki* (The Tajiks) traces the history of the Tajiks from ancient times. The sections of the book on the Ismailis and Qarmaṭīs during the Sāmānid era best illustrate partisan scholarship with reference to medieval Sunni sources. Ghafurov argued that the rise of the Qarmaṭīs was related to the internal weaknesses of the Sāmānid state, relying on the material in *al-Kāmil fī'l-ta'rīkh* by Ibn al-Athīr (555–630/1160–1233), a Sunni historian of the medieval era, to develop his argument. He also linked the Qarmaṭī movement to the major uprisings that occurred under the leadership of the Ismaili *dāʿī* al-Marvazī who was defeated in 306/918, first in Herat and then in Nīshāpūr.[30]

Equally, Ghafurov could not, or intentionally did not, draw a distinction between the Qarmaṭīs and the Ismailis, as was the case with many Soviet and post-Soviet scholars.[31] He uses the taxonyms Qarmaṭī and Ismaili interchangeably, apparently with the meaning of an anti-bourgeois community. In his analysis, the bourgeois class confronted a rival utilitarian aristocracy who skilfully manipulated mass discontent to their own advantage. In this manner, underlying religious sensitivities prevailed over ideological commitment. Ghafurov cleverly embarks on speculation about the dualist nature of the Qarmaṭī movement in which the peasants are again betrayed by their masters. Further in the same work, when discussing the Saljūqs and the era of the Khwārazm-Shāhs from the 5th/11th to the 7th/13th century, Ghafurov defines Ismaili doctrine as distinct from the beliefs of the Qarmaṭīs, but nonetheless considers the Ismaili *daʿwa* as an extension of the early Qarmaṭī movement: 'The movement, now renamed Ismailism, came to be used by local feudal rulers in their struggle against the Saljūqs. The Ismaili sect with its new programme of action, transformed itself into a clandestine terrorist organisation'.[32] Every now and then Ghafurov moves back and forth between class and ethnic differentiation by writing of the natural anti-Turk and pro-Tajik (Persian) stance of the Ismailis.

---

[30] B. Ghafurov, *Istoriīa Tadzhikskogo Naroda v Kratkom Izlozhenii. S Drevneĭshikh vremien do velikoĭ Oktīabrskoĭ Revolīutsii 1917* [The History of the Tajik People in Summary. From Ancient Times to the Great October Revolution in 1917], vol. 1. (Moscow, 1952), pp. 201–203. For the *dāʿī* al-Marvazī, see also Chapter 1 of this work, pp. 7–8, and 10.

[31] This point will be further illustrated in the section 'Review of the Literature on the Ismailis in Soviet Scholarship', pp. 71–90.

[32] Ghafurov, *Istoriīa Tadzhikskogo Naroda*, p. 202.

Bobojon Ghafurov (1908–1977)

Ghafurov was not alone in his claims, as the same view was supported by a range of Soviet scholars, including Bertel's and Stroeva who regarded the Ismailis and their ideology as a 'class struggle in feudal societies of the Middle East'.[33] The Ismailis have been described as an extreme religious group who from the early days of their religious formation up to the Fatimid and later Alamūt periods terrorised their political and religious opponents in order to achieve their ultimate goals. Furthering his argument, Ghafurov also accused Aga Khan III of being a lackey of the British monarchy.[34]

However, to be fair, not all scholarly works were composed in line with Marxist ideology and neither did all academics succumb to bias in their pursuit of Ismaili studies. During the Second World War, particularly after 1943, there was a positive shift in Soviet policy towards religion and

---

[33] A.E. Bertel's, *Nasir-i Khosrov i ismailizm* [Nāṣir-i Khusraw and Ismailism] (Moscow, 1959). Liūdmila V. Stroeva, 'Ismailiti Irana i Sirii v zarubezhnoĭ i sovetskoĭ literature' [Soviet and Foreign Historiographical Literature on the Ismailis of Iran and Syria v XI–XII Centuries], in *Istoriografiiā i istochnikovedenie istorii stran Azii* (Leningrad, 1965), pp. 138–148.

[34] B. Ghafurov, 'Aga Khan', *Journal Bezbozhnik* [The Atheist], 10–11 (1940), pp. 8–9.

religious ceremonies.³⁵ The reasons for this are to be found in the Soviet authorities' general effort to acquire the maximum support of the Soviet people in the 'patriotic war' against Nazi Germany. They eventually eased some of the restrictions on religious authorities performing religious duties and ceremonies. This also created opportunities for academics to carry on with their work freely. Certainly, this policy played a positive role in the study of religion, and consequently the lion's share of academic literature on the Ismailis was produced at that time. The Soviet government became more tolerant towards religion, and even though the relatively short-lived rule of the Soviet leader, Nikita S. Khrushchev (r. 1953–1964), brought back some restrictions, it was a time when a new generation of scholars emerged who were more disposed towards academic success and achievement in contrast to the first generations of military officers or government agents who were commissioned for the service of Imperial Russia and the Communist Party. There are indeed exceptions in terms of impartial scholarship which did not necessarily yield to strict ideological demands and state-sponsored interpretations. Many studies regarding the study of Ismaili history, philosophy, rituals and beliefs were conducted to a high academic standard and these have been held in considerable respect by modern scholars studying the Ismailis of Badakhshān.

Badakhshān, as mentioned earlier, is a land-locked region surrounded by the high Pamir Mountains which have protected and preserved not only the community but also ancient rituals, cultural traditions and linguistic diversity. Persian has served as a lingua franca between speakers of the various Pamiri languages, and between them and the rest of the Persian-speaking world. Moreover in Badakhshān, Persian is the language used for most works of religious literature as well as other literature, notably poetry. It was the beauty of the manuscripts and a fascination with calligraphy that attracted Russian scholars to Ismaili studies and the study of Ismaili rituals, traditions and practices. One of the most dynamic scholars in the field of Ismaili studies was Aleksandr A. Semënov, whose output included more than twenty articles along with the partial translation of Nāṣir-i Khusraw's *Wajh-i dīn* into Russian, and encompassed

---

³⁵ Ro'i Yaacov, *Islam in the Soviet Union: From the Second World War to Gorbachev* (New York, 2000). Also, Timur Dadabaev, 'Religiosity and Soviet "Modernisation" in Central Asia: Locating Religious Traditions and Rituals in Recollections of Antireligious Policies in Uzbekistan', *Religion, State and Society*, 32, 4 (2014), p. 331.

an edition of the work of Fidā'ī Khurāsānī's *Kitāb Hidāyat al-mu'minīn al-ṭālibīn* with an extensive introduction. Futhermore, he also devoted several articles to Ismaili studies. One of these was 'Iz oblasti religioznykh verovaniĭ shugnanskikh ismailitov' (On the Realm of the Religious Beliefs of the Ismailis of Shughnān); Semënov collected the material for this article in 1912 as a scholar, while still in the service of the colonial administration. The article describes many aspects of Shughnānī Nizārī Ismaili doctrine on the concept of God and the creation of the world. He argued that even though a thousand years had passed since the spread of Islam amongst the mountain Tajiks, people were still able to maintain ancient beliefs, and Islam had not be able to completely supercede the primitive beliefs of the people including the role of the *pīr*s who played an important part in the daily lives of the mountain Tajiks. 'Ismailitskaiā oda, posviāshchennaiā voploshcheniiū Aliiā v boga' (An Ismaili Ode Dedicated to the Incarnation of God in 'Alī) is concerned with an Ismaili ode, the *qaṣīda-i-Dhurriya* by Raqqāmī Khurāsānī, which Semënov understood as dedicated to the incarnations of what he referred to as 'Alī-God. In the article he argued that in what he termed 'classical Ismailism' there is no special concept such as *sharī'a, ma'rifa* and *haqīqa*, as in Sufism. However, beginning from 7th–8th/13th–14th centuries after the fall of the Nizārī state, Ismaili approaches assimiliated Sufi ones to some extent. Hence Sufi religious concepts and terms are visible in some of the Ismaili writings of this period which are influenced by Sufism, and therefore the studies of individual Ismaili scholars were compiled in the spirit of Sufism. In 'Nasyri Khosrov o mire dukhovnom i material'nom' (Nāṣir-i Khusraw on the Spiritual and Material Worlds), Semënov says that, according to Nāṣir-i Khusraw, the spiritual world was first created, and then the natural world appeared from it.

Nāṣir-i Khusraw believed the spiritual world to be absolute, wise, graceful, scientific, majestic and revered. The cause of the material world is the imperfection of the Universal Soul, by virtue of which it is considered lower in degree and rank than the Universal Intellect. This world belongs to the Universal Soul, as it serves as the main source through which the Universal Soul corrects its imperfections. 'Protivorechiiā vo vzgliādakh na pereselenie dush u pamirskikh ismailitov i u Nasyr-i Khosrova' (Contradictions in the Views on Metempsychosis in the Works of Nāṣir-i Khusraw and Pamiri Ismailis), is a study on the highest degree of accomplishments of the human soul which can only be achieved with a knowledge of the meaning and value of this material world. 'Sheĭkh Dzhelal-ud-Din-Rumi po predstavleniiām shugnanskikh ismailitov' (The

Aleksandr Aleksandrovich Semënov (1873–1958)

Shughnānī Ismailis' View of Shaykh Jalāl al-Dīn Rūmī), is an article which begins with an introduction by Semënov and was written on the basis of recorded conversations with a resident of the Shughnān district whose name, for some reason, was not given. It deals with the meetings and conversations between Jalāl al-Dīn Rūmī and Shams-i Tabrīzī. In 'Vzgli͡ad na Koran v vostochnom ismailizme' (The Qur'an from the Viewpoint of Oriental Ismailism), Semënov expressed his personal fascination with the Ismaili philosophical interpretation of the Qur'an. In particular, Nāṣir-i Khusraw's arguments and interpretation of Qur'anic verses and in *Wajh-i dīn* appeared to Semënov so far advanced from the ossified forms of Islamic orthodoxy that it could be easily modified to the needs of time and environment.[36] These works and others are saturated with creative ideas reflecting the historical reality of the Ismailis of Central Asia.

---

[36] For further details on all these works see Chapter 3.

Wladimir Alekseevich Ivanow (1886–1970)

It is unarguable that Wladimir Ivanow, who also worked for the Asiatic Museum of the (Imperial) Russian Academy of Sciences as well as later on for the Asiatic Society of Bengal in Calcutta in the 1920s, made great contributions to Ismaili studies.[37] Since he was commissioned in 1931 by the Ismaili Imam Aga Khan III, to research the manuscripts and literature related to the history and doctrines of the Ismailis, it has often been thought that he evinced great sympathy for Ismaili doctrines. However, more to the point, he had unprecedented access to sources in India and later Pakistan, Iran and Central Asia. He also spent much time at the seat of Aga Khan III in Bombay. As a result, besides the publication of Ismaili manuscripts, he also published numerous articles on Ismaili doctrines and philosophy. Being at the heart of the Ismaili community, he had access to archives and other privately owned materials and documents and so he was in a far better position to tackle issues related to Ismaili studies than other scholars. Meanwhile, he was troubled by how some historical sources were full of contradictions and biases against the Ismailis, whereas he saw the Ismailis as a purely defensive community

---

[37] Farhad Daftary, *Fifty Years in the East: The Memoirs of Wladimir Ivanow* (London, 2015), p. 70.

struggling against fanatical persecution. This view differed from that of his contemporaries, who considered Ismailism a 'class struggle', and identified Ismaili *dāʿī*s as 'secret agents', 'troublemakers' and 'assassins'. Ivanow did not regard these writers as scholars but rather as rumour-pedlars. For him the Ismaili *dāʿī*s were 'prominent public and political figures' who occupied a special place not only in the history of the Ismaili community, but in the Muslim *umma* as a whole due to their extensive knowledge and contributions in various fields of learning such as philosophy and theology.[38]

Another important scholar in the field of Ismaili Studies was the great ethnographer, Mikhail Stepanovich Andreev, author of the book *Tadzhiki Doliny Khuf* (The Tajiks of the Khuf Valley). He was a pioneer in the study of the rituals and ceremonies of the Ismaili Tajiks of the Khuf Valley, situated in the present-day Rūshān district of the GBAO. This work is considered to be the most valuable ethnographical study written on the Ismaili inhabitants of Badakhshān.[39] However, Andreev's study displays the influence of the pre-revolutionary Russian ethnographer-collectors, who limited themselves to describing certain aspects of the life and culture of the people under study. As a result, Andreev's scholarly interpretation of the material presented in the work cannot fully satisfy the reader. A number of important social occurrences of the time are not given an accurate explanation. For example, the book says very little about the representatives of the privileged class in Shughnān and Rūshān and about their relationship with the *al-fuqarāʾ* tax-paying class. The author does not disclose the presence of slave labour in the Pamir region, in particular in Khuf itself. He explains the local rulers practice of selling local people they ruled over exclusively on the basis of religious beliefs. Andreev writes that the Shughnān *shāh*s could 'without disturbing their religious conscience, calmly enslave and sell in bondage their own subjects, infidels for them (the Ismailis), which they could not do according to their religious beliefs, if these subjects were Sunni.' The Shughnān *shāh*s were mostly Sunnis of foreign origin, it is true. However, this practice of theirs was not only engaged in for religious motives, but

---

[38] For a full bibliography of Ivanow's works see, *Fifty Years in the East: The Memoirs of Wladimir Ivanow*, edited with annotations by Farhad Daftary (London, 2015).

[39] M.S. Andreev, *Tadzhiki Doliny Khuf* (*Verkhov'ia Amu Dar' ia*) [The Tajiks of the Khuf Valley (The Upper Reaches of the Amū Daryā)] (Stalinabad, Part 1, 1953; Part 2, 1958).

Mikhail Stepanovich Andreev (1873–1948)

was the result of social attitudes and conditions. Put briefly, the rulers of the Pamir countries were vassals of Badakhshān, and they were obliged to include a number of slaves for the *amīr* of Badakhshān in the tribute they sent to him.[40]

Another prominent Russian-Soviet scholar was Andreĭ Evgen'evich Bertel's, who dedicated his life to textual studies. Like his father Evgeniĭ Ėduardovich Bertel's, a scholar of remarkably high stature, outstanding scholarship and erudition, he was also a prolific writer.

His extensive studies covered a wide range of themes in classical Persian and Tajik literature. In particular, his elegant translations of Ḥāfiẓ, Rūmī and other famous Persian poets into Russian with commentaries, and numerous works and articles written in perfect Persian, brought him deserved fame even in Iran. His father, Evgeniĭ Bertel's, wrote the entry on Nāṣir-i Khusraw in the *Encyclopedia of Islam*[41] as well as the Russian translation of Nāṣir-i Khusraw's *Safar-nāma*. He was one of the first Soviet scholars to regard Nāṣir-i Khusraw as an

---

[40] Ibid., p. 29.
[41] Evgeniĭ Bertel's, 'Nāṣir Khusraw', *EI2*, pp. 869–870.

Evgeniĭ Ėduardovich Bertel's (1890–1957)

advocate of the rights of the peasants in their struggle against the ruling class. In the preface to the *Safar-nāma*, he emphasises Nāṣir-i Khusraw's important role in teaching and spreading the Ismaili *daʿwa* among the Pamiri Tajiks. However, according to Evgeniĭ Bertel's, in his time Ismailism was no longer fighting against feudalism, but rather had become an instrument of British imperialism.[42]

His son, Andreĭ Bertel's, wrote *Nasir-i Khosrov i Ismailizm* (Nāṣir-i Khusraw and Ismailism),[43] a serious pioneering study in Soviet scholarship, and maintained the same standard for subsequent studies. Andreĭ Bertel's addressed the development of Ismailism during the time of Nāṣir-i Khusraw against the backdrop of contemporary social life. He explored Nāṣir's role, which he analysed through an examination of his philosophical treatises and poetry. He also organised a number of field expeditions to Badakhshān, including one in 1959–1963 under the aegis

---

[42] Evgeniĭ Bertel's, 'Vstuplenie', in *Safar-namė*, p. 17.
[43] Andreĭ Bertel's, *Nasir-i Khosrov i ismailizm* [Nāṣir-i Khusraw and Ismailism]. AN USSR, IV (Moscow, 1959).

of the Academy of Sciences of the USSR and the Institute of Oriental Studies of the Academy of Sciences of the Republic of Tajikistan. The expedition headed by Bertel's discovered many rare manuscripts, which are now preserved in the Rudaki Institute of Oriental Studies and the Written Heritage in Dushanbe. In 1959-1960, he discovered a highly significant Ismaili manuscript which consisted of five philosophical epistles and critically edited the text under the title *Piat' filosofskikh traktatov na temu Āfāq va Anfus* (On the Relationship Between Man and the Universe) providing an extensive commentary.[44] The epistles deal with various aspects of Ismaili doctrine, such as the relationship between microcosm and macrocosm, and between Man and Universe. On the basis of these field trips and the materials discovered, in 1971 and 1972 a local scholar, Amirbek Habibov (1916-1998), produced two monographs entitled *On the History of Tajik Literature in Badakhshān* and *The Treasures of Badakhshān*.[45] Also as a result of these expeditions, Bahodur Iskandarov published his edition of a work by two local scholars, Qurbān Muḥammad-zāda (aka Ākhūnd Sulaymān, d. 1953) and Muḥabbat Shāh-zāda (aka Shāh Fitūr, d. 1959), *Istoriĩa Badakhshana*, in Moscow in 1973 with an extensive introduction.

Perhaps the best example of Ismaili studies in the Soviet period is provided by the writings of Liŭdmila V. Stroeva (1910-1993). Her major works are: *Dvizhenie Ismailitov v Isfakhane v 1100-1107 gg.* (The Ismaili Movement in Isfahan in 1101-1107) and *K Voprosu O Soĩsial'noĭ Prirode Ismailitskogo Dvizheniĩa v Irane v XI-XIII vv.* (On the Problem of the Social Nature of the Ismaili Movement in Iran in the 11th-13th Centuries). Even within the ideological constraints of the time, in her studies Stroeva managed to draw a realistic picture of the last years of the Ismaili state of Alamūt. *Gosudarstvo Ismailitov v Irane v 11-13vv.*, leaving aside some compulsory ideological 'embellishment', may be the least biased study of Ismaili history in Russian. Here is an extract from her writings:

> From the beginning of the 13th century, the Ismaili state received a large number of Muslims who emigrated there from various feudal estates.

---

[44] The published edition contains five philosophical treatises written in Persian in the 5th/11th to 7th/13th centuries: – [Maḥmūd b. 'Abd al-Karīm Shabistarī] *Mir'āt al-muḥaqqiqīn*, ['Azīz al-Dīn Nasafī] *Zubdat al-haqā'iq*, *Umm al-Kitāb*, *Uṣūl al-ādāb* and *Āfāq-nāma*.

[45] For more details about these publications, see Chapter 3.

This seems to have been due to the conducive policy of Jalāl al-Dīn Ḥasan – *Naw-Musulmān* (New Muslim). Even later, the Ismaili state began to attract many people because of its economic prosperity... the attraction being that in the Ismaili lands any people, even enemies of the Ismailis, could find refuge and political asylum. This tradition was never violated and was known far and wide.[46]

In her work, Stroeva expounded upon the Ismaili movement in Iran and Syria between the 3rd and 7th/9th and 13th centuries, presenting it as a popular movement of the masses aimed at social emancipation and liberation under the leadership of Ḥasan-i Ṣabbāḥ (440s–518/1050s–1124) and his disciples.[47] As for the methods of 'individual terror' attributed to them, Stroeva contended that it was a class war waged against the stratum of exploiters.[48] Class-consciousness, according to Stroeva, was their central motive because:

> The overwhelming majority of the population, the rank and file Ismailis, were occupied in agriculture, cattle breeding and handicrafts. From among them personnel for military raids were recruited, and likewise from among them came forth the *fidā'īs*. They carried on their shoulders the burden of public welfare (construction, irrigation and repair, etc.). Freedom from the political domination of the [Turks] gave them a deep sense of satisfaction. *Al-daʿwa al-jadīda* (the new preaching) became a profound articulation of this victory, of complete independence, and of state-building. In it they found their faith in the Imam, who, in their minds, was, in some ways, connected with the establishment of social justice and material equality in the future.[49]

Through this modern interpretation of the religious state, Stroeva attempted to define the role of the *daʿwa* in the political life of Alamūt: 'Striving for material equality, the ordinary Ismailis have maintained through the history of their state, respect for, and faith in their leaders whose lifestyles were not in any way dissimilar to theirs'.[50] As Stroeva put it regarding the local non-Turkic elite: 'The Iranian feudals mobilised all

---

[46] Liūdmila Stroeva, *Gosudarstvo Ismailitov v Irane v 11–13 vv.* [The Ismaili State in Iran in the 11th-13th Centuries] (Moscow, 1978), p. 219.
[47] Ibid., pp. 104–136.
[48] Ibid., p. 158.
[49] Ibid., p. 168.
[50] Ibid.

their forces against the Ismailis in the life-and-death struggle. In spite of everything, however, the Ismaili state survived for the simple reason that the Ismailis knew what they stood for'.[51] Thus in academic circles the stories of the Assassin legends were replaced by a new scholarly view of the Ismailis and the impact of their doctrines on the development of feudal society and culture, one which gradually began to gain acceptance.[52] In conclusion Stroeva declared:

> In the Ismaili state they demolished the political power of the Saljūqs, ousted the Saljūq administration; a traditional form of governing, hereditary monarchy, was substituted by the rulership of Ḥasan-i Ṣabbāḥ and his disciples who expressed the interests of the popular masses – the artisans, urban poor and peasants. This was a significant achievement of the rebels.[53]

Unlike the medieval heresiographers and indeed some modern scholars, Stroeva refrained from attacking Ḥasan-i Ṣabbāḥ. For Stroeva, Ḥasan-i Ṣabbāḥ was not a 'shrewd man' with devious schemes and sinister plots, nor did he claim the imamate for himself and his progeny. Rather, she writes, 'on its dogmatic level *al-daʿwa al-jadīda* was no different from *al-daʿwa al-qadīma* [the old preaching]. Ḥasan-i Ṣabbāḥ did not proclaim himself imam, but preached in the name of the imam.'[54] Stroeva, nonetheless, tended to see *al-daʿwa al-jadīda* as a deviation from *al-daʿwa al-qadīma* brought about by social factors. The circumstances that led to the split of the Ismailis into Mustaʿlī and Nizārī branches, she contended, were identical to those entailing the formation of similar groups. As was always the case, this schism is explained in terms of controversies about the person of the imam. Thus, her understanding of the split following the death of the Imam-caliph al-Mustanṣir biʾllāh (d. 487/1094) is not watertight and her claim that Ḥasan-i Ṣabbāḥ was dissatisfied with *al-daʿwa al-qadīma* is not substantiated.

On the whole, and in contrast to some of her colleagues, Stroeva took a balanced approach to the treatment of Ismaili history. It is unfortunate that her contemporaries in Soviet academia often showed an outright hostility to the Ismailis. Thus, the academician Bogoutdinov, while

---

[51] Ibid., p. 170.
[52] Ibid., p. 168.
[53] Ibid., p. 108.
[54] Ibid., p. 107.

'defending' Rūdakī, 'implicated', as he put it, for his explicit ties with the Ismailis at the Sāmānid court, writes, 'However, it is more likely that Rūdakī sometimes articulated the political orders of aristocratic circles connected with the Fatimids in his poetry... Moreover, even many "leftist" Ismaili preachers of the 4th/10th century were known for their religious fanaticism.'[55] Likewise, a Soviet historian of philosophy, A.K. Zakuev, who wrote on the doctrinal affinity of the Ikhwān al-Ṣafā' and the Ismailis, concluded that 'undoubtedly, there are many similarities between the teachings and methods of the Ikhwān al-Ṣafā' and the Ismailis. Nevertheless, the peaceful, liberal and humanistic teaching of Ikhwān al-Ṣafā', which propagates love, equality and good disposition towards other people, is, in its essence, at odds with the aggressive intolerant views of the Ismailis.'[56]

Another important figure in the field of Ismaili studies was Lidiĩa Semënova (1925–2005). One of her works, *Iz Istorii Fatimidskogo Egipta* (On the History of the Fatimids in Egypt), covers the period from the second half of the 4th/10th century to the first half of the 6th/12th century when the Ismaili imams were ruling over a great empire. Written from a Marxist perspective, it interprets the Ismaili movement in terms of a 'class struggle' in which the Fatimids promised social justice for those people who had become disappointed with the Abbasids. The Fatimid empire in Egypt is characterised as a feudal state, with a very high level of development in agriculture, crafts and trade. However, according to Lidiĩa Semënova '...excessive centralisation over time began to have a negative impact on the life of the country',[57] while the 'strengthening the power of the military class and the intensification of the struggle within the army, and the weakening of the Ismaili religious hierarchy...'[58] ultimately led to the disintegration of the empire. In spite of the fact that the book was written in the spirit of Marxist ideology, it displays a scholarly standard in examining and analysing historical sources without preconceptions or doctrinal biases.

---

[55] A.M. Bogoutdinov, *Ocherki po istorii tadzhikskoĭ filosofii* [Essays on the History of Tajik Philosophy] (Dushanbe, 1961), p. 58.

[56] A.K. Zakuev, *Filosofiĩa 'Brat'ev chistoty'* [Philosophy of the 'Brethren of Purity'] (Baku, 1961), p. 8.

[57] Lidiĩa Semënova, *Iz istorii Fatimidskogo Egipta. Ocherki i materialy* [On the History of the Fatimids in Egypt. Essays and Sources] (Moscow, 1974), p. 152.

[58] Ibid.

The Ismailis in Soviet Badakhshān were also studied in terms of ethnography, cultural anthropology, modern history and politics. Lidiiā Fedorovna Monogarova's (1921–2011) ethnographic survey contains references to Ismailism in the Pamirs. Her outline of its origins is a slightly modified version of the orientalist definition common at the time:

> Ismailism, rooted in the divination of ʿAlī, the son-in-law of the Prophet Muhammad, is one of the two major ramifications in the Shiʿi branch of Islam. The emergence of the denomination in the middle of 2nd/8th century is believed to have been connected to a dispute over the right to succession to the imamate after the sixth Shiʿi Imam Jaʿfar al-Ṣādiq, who allegedly deprived his elder son Ismāʿīl of hereditary rights. Some of Jaʿfar's followers, however, did not accept his decision and declared Ismāʿīl the rightful seventh imam, and thereafter the Ismaili sectarians defected.[59]

However, Monogarova, similar to many of her colleagues of the Soviet era, instantly finds a social explanation for a religio-political development:

> The denial of Ismāʿīl's right to the succession was a pretext for the formation of the new sect, as the genuine reason behind the split was 'the struggle between feudalism' and incipient capitalist relations, especially [since] many Ismaili followers were among the wealthy and educated classes of the urban and provincial bourgeoisie ... the propagators of Ismailism penetrated far into the depths of the lower social level.[60]

Monogarova further argued that the Ismailis in the Western Pamirs, who regard Nāṣir-i Khusraw as the first propagator of the Ismaili *daʿwa* there, were different from their fellow Muslims.[61] In her view, which is in line with Marxism, the Ismaili system was formed under the influence of the Indo-Iranian and Zoroastrian religious perspectives on Islam and, therefore, it had a deep impact, particularly because the population of Pamiri lands adopted the Ismaili faith while they were still in a patriarchal and feudal stage of development, maintaining their ancient animistic beliefs.[62]

There are a few studies that have argued that Soviet and post-Soviet scholarship has referred back to the pre-Islamic era to explain rituals and

---

[59] L.F. Monogarova, *Preobrazovaniiā v bytu i kulʾture pripamirskikh narodnosteĭ* [Transformations in the Life and Culture of the Pamiri Nationalities] (Moscow, 1972), p. 63.
[60] Ibid.
[61] Ibid.
[62] Ibid., pp. 63–64.

traditions that they felt did not readily fit with Islam. One such is Daniel Beben's PhD thesis, in which he said that 'Soviet and post-Soviet scholarship on the Badakhshāni Ismāʿīlī tradition has often invoked a supposed Zoroastrian past as a means of explaining the presence of pre-Islamic "survivals" in the beliefs and practices of Ismāʿīlīs, particularly observances that were perceived as reflecting a veneration of light or fire'.[63] However, this is a somewhat generalised statement with regard to Soviet and post-Soviet scholarship and the significance of 'a supposed Zoroastrian past' for Soviet and post-Soviet scholars deserves some investigation. What is more, Soviet and post-Soviet scholars and archaeologists were among the first to provide detailed information on Buddhist castles and temples in the Wakhān region.[64] And indeed, before the studies of Soviet scholars, it was Western Europeans visiting the region who made claims about the survival of Zoroastrian beliefs and traditions in Badakhshān, which were reiterated later by Western scholars during the Soviet and then the post-Soviet periods.[65] Soviet scholars, working under an official stance of atheism, naturally adopted a neutral approach to the question of the pre-Islamic

---

[63] Beben, *The Legendary Biographies*, p. 48.

[64] B. Ghafurov, *Tadjiki. Drevneĭshaia̅, drevnai̅a i srednevekovai̅a istorii̅a* [The Tajiks. Earliest, Ancient and Medieval History], *Kniga pervai̅a* [Book One] (Dushanbe, 1989), pp. 188–191, 214–217; Aktam Babaev, *Kreposti Drevnego Wakhana* [Fortresses of Ancient Wakhān] (Dushanbe, 1973); M.A. Bubnova, *Gorno-Badakhshanskai̅a Avtonomnai̅a Oblast' Zapadnyĭ Pamir (pami̅atniki II tys. do n. ė. - XIX v.)* [Gorno-Badakhshān Autonomous Region of Western Pamir (monuments of the 2nd millennium BC – xix c.) (Dushanbe, 1997). Abdulmamad Iloliev, 'The Silk Road castles and temples: ancient Wakhan in legends and history', in Dagikhudo Dagiev and Carole Faucher ed., *Identity, History and Trans-Nationality in Central Asia: The Mountain Communities of Pamir* (London, 2018), pp. 91–105.

[65] 'The Oxus valley having been the cradle of the religion of Zoroaster, the valleys south of the Hindoo Koosh are not likely to have escaped its influence. In Wakhan there are many towers and structures which are still ascribed to the worshippers of fire, and the tradition of this worship still lingers in Yassin. The secluded easily defensible valleys of Yassin and Gilgit are so eminently suited to afford shelter from persecution of the followers of a dying faith, that fire-worship probably existed in them long after it had been driven out of neighbouring, more accessible, valleys'. John Biddulph, *Tribes of the Hindoo Khoosh* (Calcutta: office of the superintendent of government printing, 1880), p. 108. See also, Ole Olusen, *Through the Unknown Pamirs; the Second Danish Pamir Expedition, 1899–99* (London: William Heinemann, 1904). 'Then all evidence of Zoroastrian communities disappears from Central Asia, except in the Pamirs and Badakhshān where in the 7th/13th century some people still claimed to follow the teachings of Zoroaster.' D.A. Scott,

faith of the Badakhshānīs, including whether it was Zoroastrianism or Buddhism, as well as the possible survival of pre-Islamic rituals. There is no doubt that Buddhism also existed in some parts of Badakhshān, in particular along the routes of the Silk Road, one such being the Wakhān corridor.[66] Similarly Zoroastrianism was a dominant religion and tradition for thousands of years, such that many of its traditions survived including specific features of the Nawruz (Persian New Year) celebrations and of Pamiri houses, graveyards, burial rites and customs, as well as Avestan toponims.[67] Most importantly the recent discovery of the ancient city of Karān, including the Fire Temple there, has provided more evidence to support the theory that the Darvās district of Badakhshān of Afghanistan, which lies on the border with Tajikistan, and which was the southern periphery of ancient Bactria, was most probably the birthplace of Zoroaster.[68] Similarly, many Fire Temples have been discovered in Badakhshān of Tajikistan, Afghanistan, the Northern Areas of Pakistan and, most recently, in the Chinese part of Badakhshān.[69]

'Zoroastrian Traces along the Upper Amu Darya (Oxus)', *The Journal of the Royal Asiatic Society of Great Britain and Ireland*, 2 (1984), pp. 217–228; 'Expatriate Sogdians at Dunhuang in China are known to have maintained Zoroastrian ceremonies until at least the beginning of the 10th century', Frantz Grenet and Zhang Guangda, 'The Last Refuge of the Sogdian Religion: Dunhuang in the Ninth and Tenth Centuries', *Bulletin of the Asia Institute*, 10 (1996 [1998]), pp. 175–1986; Frantz Grenet, 'Zoroastrianism in Central Asia', in Michael Stausberg et al., ed., *The Wiley Blackwell Companion to Zoroastranism* (Chichester, 2015), pp. 129–147. Also, Wu Xin, 'Zoroastrians of Central Asia: evidence from the Archeology of Art', *FEZANA Journal* (Summer 2014), pp. 22–30.

[66] Hyechʻo noted on their religion that 'The king, the chiefs, and the common people all serve Buddha and do not belong to any other religions.' Further he provided a brief description of the religion of Shughnān to the north explicitly saying that Buddhism was not observed there. Hyechʻo, *The Hye Chʻo Diary: Memoir of the Pilgrimage to the Five Regions of India*, ed. and tr. Han-Sung Yang and Yün-Hua Jan (Berkeley, CA: Asian Humanities Press, 1984), p. 52. See, Beben, *The Legendary Biographies*, p. 51.

[67] Yusufsho Yaqubov, *Davlati Kaëniën* [The Kayyanian State] (Dushanbe, 2012); Abusaid Shokhumorov, *Pamir – Strana Ariev* [Pamir: Land of the Aryan people] (Dushanbe, 1997).

[68] Yusufsho Yaqubov and Dagikhudo Dagiev, 'A Badakhshāni origin for Zoroaster', in Dagikhudo Dagiev and Carole Faucher, ed., *Identity, History and Trans-Nationality in Central Asia*, pp. 79–90.

[69] Zoroastrian Cemetery found in Xinjiang, Tashkurgan Tajik Autonomous County, Jirzankal, 2013. Available online at http://www.kaogu.cn/en/News/New_discoveries/2013/1026/43277.html [Last accessed, 18 October 2020]. For more details see, Shokhumorov, *Pamir – Strana Ariev*, pp. 71–74.

Meanwhile, a review of the Soviet literature in Ismaili studies appears rather confusing, as on the one hand there were scholars who somehow undermined Ismaili teachings and doctrines, and on the other hand, there were a number of other scholars who were open-minded in their attempt to understand the nature of Ismailism. Clear examples of this would be quotations from two Tajik scholars, which reflect their scholarship. A quotation from Lutfullo Buzurg-zoda (1909–1943) is a good example to illustrate the case in point:

> The situation in Egypt in that period [i.e. under the reign of the Fatimids] is characterised, to a great extent, by a highly centralised state machinery and a higher degree of *adāb* in the state administration. Manufacture and commerce flourished there and more religious tolerance was observed for perfectly explicable mundane reasons, namely religious tolerance was conducive to commercial and diplomatic relations with non-Muslim states.[70]

Buzurg-zoda also presented a progressive view of the conversion to Ismailism of Nāṣir-i Khusraw which he considered had two purposes: on the one hand it led to the formation of a great *dāʿī* of the Ismaili faith, but on the other it was part of his mission to fight against the oppression of his people in Khurāsān at the hand of foreign rulers.[71]

Equally, another Tajik scholar, Kamol Ayīnī (1928–2010), discussed the tragedy and crisis faced by Nāṣir in his life and saw his acceptance of Ismailism as the only possible way to fight feudalism and the ideology of 'orthodox' Islam.[72] For these reasons, the way Nāṣir-i Khusraw courageously confronted the trials of his life was an important factor in his popularity with his contemporaries and in particular with the later generations who admired and respected his bravery, his compassion and his love for Khurāsān that included, of course, its people and his mother tongue:

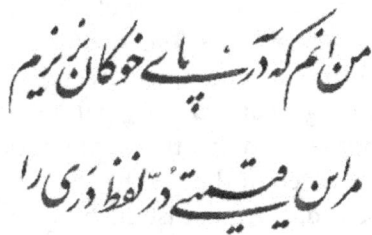

---

[70] Lutfullo Buzurg-zoda, *Iskatel' pravdy i spravedlivosti Nosir Khisroy* [Nāṣir-i Khusraw, Seeker of Truth and Justice] (Stalinabad, 1953), p. 9.

[71] Ibid., p. 10.

[72] Kamol Aĭynī, ed. and intr., *Nosiri Khusrav. Gulchine az devoni ashor* [Nāṣir-i Khusraw. Selected Poems from *Dīvān*] (Stalinabad, 1957).

I am he who does not throw before swine
These precious pearls of the Persian language [73]

(Nāṣir-i Khusraw, *Dīvān*, 64:32)

In the Soviet era some of these scholars had to make a choice between either conforming to Communist ideology, or attempting to follow purely academic lines of examination, which involved compromise and manoeuvring between state ideology and academic objectivity. Apart from the Marxist element in Soviet works, other factors should also be considered while reviewing the literature on the Ismailis by Russian and Soviet scholars. Some scholars, perhaps understandably since the written source material was limited, were influenced by the medieval Sunni sources, as has been discussed. Still others, evidently driven by a belief in Communist ideology, carried out their studies in the service of the Communist Party with the expectation of achieving promotion for their ideologically-sound writings.

Manuscripts Discovered in Badakhshān

An important work written in Badakhshān is *Silk-i gawhar-rīz*, which was found in the GBAO during the 1959–1963 field expedition organised by the Academy of Sciences of the USSR and the Institute of Oriental Studies of the Academy of Sciences of the Republic of Tajikistan. The work was significant for identifying the genealogy of the Ismaili imams and the religious hierarchy of the *pīr*s of Badakhshān. In contrast to previous texts found in Badakhshān, it is not about theology or philosophy, but is mainly concerned with history and, therefore, represents a source of reference for the study of the history and the genealogy of the *pīr*s as well as the Ismaili imams. Initially, it was assumed to be only about Nāṣir-i Khusraw's journey to Badakhshān. Some local people even believed that it was an eastward continuation of his *Safar-nāma* and therefore referred to it as *Safar-nāma-yi mashriq*, assuming that the original text had disappeared. However, textual study has verified that these assumptions were wrong.[74]

Silk-i gawhar-rīz was written in the first half of the 13th/19th century in Badakhshān in present-day Afghanistan, by a local author named

---

[73] Nāṣir-i Khusraw. *Dīvān*, ed. M. Mīnuvī, and M. Muḥaqqiq (Tehran, 1388 Sh./2009), p. 143.

[74] Ėl'chibekov, *Ierarkhiia Dukhovenstva*, p. 7.

Gawhar-rīz, son of Khwāja 'Abd al-Nabī, son of Ṣāliḥ-i Yamgī. He considered himself to be a descendant of Sayyid Khwāja Suhrāb Valī Badakhshānī (d. after 856/1452), who was erroneously assumed to be a companion of Nāṣir-i Khusraw. The book has been portrayed as an intellectual and social history of the Ismailis, and similar to many other works about religion, analyses the concepts of ancient religious beliefs, nature, society and the perception of the Badakhshānī Ismailis regarding their own belief system. As mentioned earlier, there is no specific work that deals with the Ismaili hierarchy although the *Silk-i gawhar-rīz* is a very significant source in this context due to the details it provides on this subject. Even though a few anonymous Ismaili sources such as: *Bāb dar bāyn-i dānistān-i 'ālam-i dīn*, *Risāla dar bāb-i haft ḥudūd al-dīn* and *Dawāzdah faṣl* provide some information about the Ismaili hierarchy, none of them is as detailed as *Silk-i gawhar-rīz*. However *Silk-i gawhar-rīz*, like some of the other manuscripts discovered, contains misreadings and misunderstandings of historical events particularly regarding Ismaili history, as the 'author does not provide sources for his information' and 'invokes Nāṣir-i Khusraw throughout the text, [but] narratives about him are scarce'.[75]

There are three copies of the *Silk-i gawhar-rīz*; one is listed in the Alphabetical Catalogue of the Manuscripts collected by Andreĭ Bertel's and Muhammadvafo Bakaev.[76] It is preserved as MS number 195 in the collection of the Institute of Oriental Studies, Academy of Sciences of the Republic of Tajikistan. The second manuscript was found by a learned man in Khārūgh, the administrative centre of the GBAO, in 1970. Since the first manuscript was found in the Rūshān district, it was listed under the letter 'R', and the second manuscript from the Shughnān district is listed under the letter 'S'. Following the study of both manuscripts, it appears that manuscript 'S' is the more complete and accurate one.[77] A third copy is an uncatalogued manuscript held in Semënov archive in the Institute of History, Archaeology and Ethnography of the Academy of Sciences of Tajikistan.[78]

---

[75] Gulamadov, *The Hagiography of Nāṣir-i Khusraw*, p. 242; Iloliev, *The Ismā'īlī-Sufi Sage of Pamir*, p. 33.

[76] A.E. Bertel's and M. Bakaev, *Alfavitnyĭ katalog rukopiseĭ* [Alphabetical Catalogue of Manuscripts], pp. 85–86.

[77] Ėl'chibekov, *Ierarkhiia Dukhovenstva*, p. 60.

[78] Ibid.; Beben, *The Legendary Biographies*, p. 346.

Sīlk-i gawhar-rīz was written in 1224 *hijrī* (1828–1829) in the Jurm district of Badakhshān and as verses in the book reveal, the author was sixty when he wrote it:

My precious life has reached sixty
The load of guilt has broken my back

Although the author gives his name as Gawhar-rīz, this seems to be his nickname. He was the son of Khwāja 'Abd al-Nabī b. Khwāja Ṣāliḥ-i Yamgī, and was born around 1181–82/1768–69 (there is no reference to his place of birth).

The 'S' copy of the manuscript, consisting of 113 folios, was copied in a very beautiful *nasta'līq* style by the renowned Ismaili *pīr* Sayyid Shāhzāda Muḥammad b. Sayyid Farrukh Shāh in 1337/1918 (in the village of Sarā-yi Bahār, Pārshinev district) at the request of an influential local figure of the time, Sayyid Mursal (first half of the 20th century), as indicated in the colophon. The 'R' copy, found and collected by the Bertel's and Bakoev expedition in the district of Rūshān in 1381/1961,[79] is a complete text copied in *nasta'līq mutawassiṭ*. It contains many grammatical mistakes, which are quite commonly found in texts copied by the local people.[80] The work is only known of in Badakhshān, and Wladimir Ivanow noted that he 'failed to find the manuscript even though he made a great effort to do so'.[81]

The book consists of two parts: poetry and prose. It begins with the conventional practice of talking about the creation of the world and a discussion of Ismaili philosophy of the medieval era. It further argues that the concepts in Ismaili philosophy, which was based a combination of Neoplatonic teaching and interpretation of Qur'anic verses, originated among Ismaili thinkers in Egypt in the 4th–5th/10th–11th centuries and

---

[79] A.E. Bertel's and M. Bakaev, *Alfavitnyĭ rukopiseĭ*, pp. 238–239.

[80] Author's interview with Qudratbek Ėl'chibekov, Senior Research Associate at the Oriental Institute of Manuscript Studies Academy of Sciences of the Republic of Tajikistan (Dushanbe, 2015).

[81] A.E. Bertel's and M. Bakaev, *Alfavitnyĭ rukopiseĭ*, p. 88.

later spread over the present territories of Iran and Central Asia. However, as already stated here, the latest studies have established that Ismaili teachings were infused with Neoplatonic philosophy in Khurāsān by Persian Ismaili thinkers.[82]

The author of *Silk-i gawhar-rīz* continues with this Ismaili philosophical understanding regarding the creation of the universe, beginning with the ʿaql-i kull (the Universal Intellect), *nafs-i kull* (the Universal Soul) and *chahār ʿanāṣir* (the four elements), in line with Nāṣir-i Khusraw's religio-philosophical understanding of the world.[83] The historical part of the book is important for scholars studying the Ismailis of Badakhshān, as it attempts to outline a historical narrative about the spread of Ismailism at the time of Nāṣir, as well as providing accounts of the activities of *dāʿī*s and other religious authorities who followed Nāṣir's tradition. However, as already

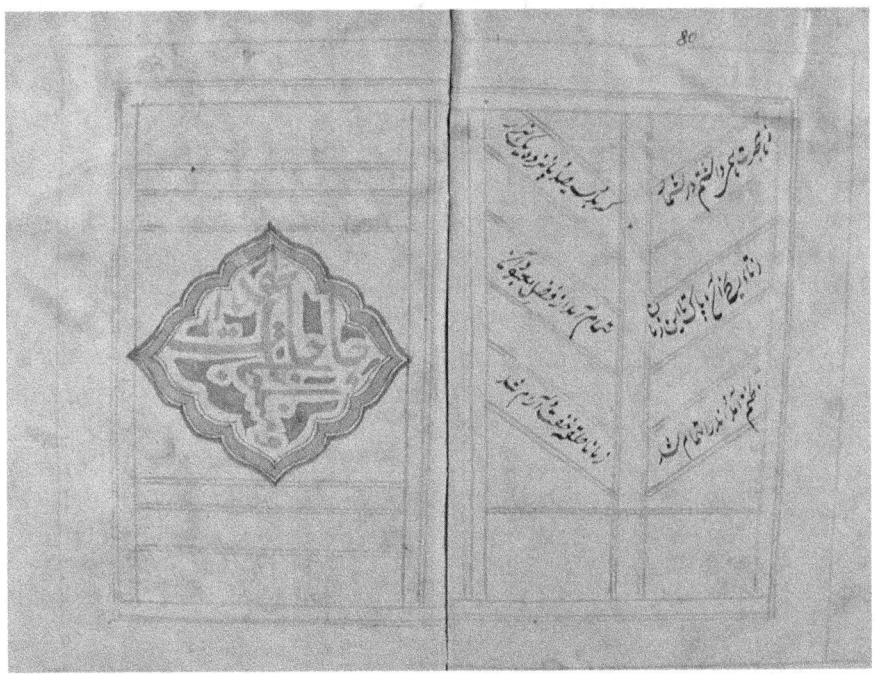

Ḥājat va Munājāt-i Mubārak-i Wakhānī

---

[82] For further information in this regard see, pp. 9–10, 12.

[83] Kudratbek Ėl'chibekov, 'Istoricheskie istochniki v Badakhshane' [Historical Sources in Badakhshān], *IAN (TSSR)*, 1 (1975), pp. 27–31.

mentioned, an examination of the text has demonstrated that *Silk-i gawhar-rīz* cannot be a reliable source as a narrative of the history of the Ismailis of Central Asia. In the historical part, the author mentions Nāṣir-i Khusraw meeting the Imam of the time, al-Mustanṣir bi'llāh, and receiving the title of *ḥujja* of Khurāsān, which is not found in any Fatimid historical sources.[84] However, E. Bertel's assumed that these details are not given in Nāṣir's *Safar-nāma* because the original copy of the *Safar-nāma* was probably lost.[85]

The book provides information about religious leaders in Badakhshān such as Sayyid Suhrāb Valī and Bābā ʿUmar-i Yamgī who were regarded as disciples of Nāṣir-i Khusraw, although Suhrāb Valī lived in the 9th/15th century and 'has nothing to do with Nāṣir-i Khusraw and does not even belong to his school, but coincides with the Alamūt tradition'.[86] But it also presents a detailed account of the Ismaili hierarchy and the ranks of *imām, ḥujja, dāʿī, maʾdhūn-i akbar, maʾdhūn-i aṣghar, muʿallim, mustajīb*. A significant part is devoted to the Nizārī imams, the activities of the *dāʿī*s and the rulers of Badakhshān from Nāṣir-i Khusraw's time until that of the author. Although earlier works have been written about the history of Badakhshān, none of them provides such a broad, comprehensive study of the Ismailis and of the activities of the *daʿwa* in Badakhshān.

As mentioned earlier, the basis for understanding the culture and tradition of the indigenous people of the mountain region of Badakhshān was established through the study of Ismailism by Russian scholars. I.I. Zarubin (1887–1964), was one of the first to visit Shughnān in 1916 and collected eleven manuscripts amongst which were: *Umm al-kitāb, Wajh-i dīn, Haft bāb, Sih faṣl-i ʿAṭṭār, Dīvān-i Shams-i Tabrīzī, Markaz al-adwār-i Fāyḍ-i Dakkanī, Zilzila-nāma, Ḥikāyat-i qahqaha, Saʿādat-nāma* and *Mirʾat al-Muḥaqqiqīn*.[87] These, together with some other materials with

---

[84] 'It is interesting to note that Khurāsān, of which Nāṣir-i Khusraw claimed to be the *ḥujja* in the second half of the 5th/11th century, does not appear as a *jazīra* in al-Nuʿmān's list'. Daftary, *The Ismāʿīlīs* (2nd ed., Cambridge, 2007), p. 218.

[85] E. Bertel's assumed that the present text of the *Safar-nāma* is incomplete and that the original version has not come down to us. 'The present copy of the *Safar-nāma* is incomplete and has been much distorted, as one can see in several places the narrative is in the third person.' Bertel's, preface to his translation of *Nasir-i Khusraw: Safar-nāma* (Moscow–Leningrad, 1933).

[86] Wladimir Ivanow, *A Guide to Ismaili Literature* (London, 1933), p. 93. See, Iloliev, *The Ismāʿīlī-Sufi Sage of Pamir*, p. 34.

[87] Wladimir Ivanow, 'Ismailitskie rukopisi Aziatskogo Muzeīa', Sobranie I. Zarubina, 1916 g.' [Ismaili Manuscripts of the Asiatic Museum. I. Zarubin's Collection, 1916], *Izvestiīa Rossiĭskoĭ Akademii Nauk*, 6 série, 11 (1917), pp. 359–386.

Ivan Ivanovich Zarubin (1887–1964)

Sufi and Ismaili contents acquired from the local people, were eventually moved to the Asiatic Museum in St Petersburg where they are still preserved at the Institute of Oriental Manuscripts.

However, these pioneering Russian scholars were only able to collect manuscripts that were known amongst the larger portion of the community and hence generally accessible.

A few years later Semënov also collected eight more manuscripts, which are also held by the Asiatic Museum. Yet many more manuscripts and related literature on poetry, philosophy, history and religious matters were still held and preserved by local people, particularly in remote rural areas. Many of these manuscripts only became known and available to scholars during the Soviet period as a result of the several field trips to those regions undertaken by members of the Academy of Sciences of Tajikistan. In 1967, Andreï Bertel's and Muhammadvafo Bakaev compiled a list of the manuscripts found in the region of Gorno-Badakhshān. Their work is regarded as one of the most important manuscript studies for this region. During the five years of fieldwork (1959–1963) it undertook, the academic expedition to the GBAO mentioned earlier examined 117 manuscripts. Palaeographic descriptions were prepared, and the manuscripts were photographed and then returned to their owners. The present catalogue has been compiled from photostat copies from the photographs and the diaries that were the result of the expedition. This material is now kept at the Department of Oriental Studies in Dushanbe. The collection described in the present catalogue consists of 186 works. At least 30 manuscripts have been ascertained to be completely new findings.

The manuscripts found as a result of these field trips have contributed towards a better understanding of the spread of Ismailism in the region from the 4th/10th century up to the present time. One of the oldest manuscripts is a copy of the *Rasā'il Ikhwān al-Ṣafā'* and the most recent is a collection of poetry by poets such as Nazmī, Maḥmūd, Ghiyāthī, Fārighī, Mīrzā 'Ibādī Shidzī, Shāh Fitūr and many other Badakhshānī poets of the 12th/18th and 13th/19th centuries, a collection which clearly reflects the life and religious activities of the Ismaili community at that particular period of time. One popular book was the *Ẓafar-nāma*, whose original text, according to Ḥājī Khalīfa, was translated by Ibn Sīnā (370–428/980–1037) for Nūḥ b. Manṣūr Sāmānī (r. 366–387/977–997). Other works discovered include the *Pand-nāma* of Shaykh Farīd al-Dīn 'Aṭṭār (Persian poet, Sufi theoretician of mysticism, and hagiographer,

Kulliyat-i Mubārak-i Wakhānī

540–618/1145–1221) and the *Ṣad naṣīḥat* of Luqmān al-Ḥakīm.[88] In the Academy of Sciences of the Republic of Tajikistan there is a special section for the Ismaili manuscript collections which were discovered during the five years of fieldwork in Badakhshān, including the *Zubdat al-ḥaqā'iq* and *Kashf al-ḥaqā'iq* of ʿAzīz al-Dīn Nasafī (a famous Persian Sufi scholar and author of the 7th/13th century), *Uṣūl al-ādāb* and *Āfāq-nāma* (attributed to Nāṣir-i Khusraw), and the anonymous work, *Umm al-kitāb*. It was thought that *Umm al-kitāb* was written by Nāṣir-i Khusraw, or the Persian polymath and Ismaili scholar, Naṣīr al-Dīn Ṭūsī (597–672/1201–1274). However, the original of the *Umm al-kitāb* is thought to have been produced in Arabic in the early Shiʿi *ghulāt* groups of southern Iraq in the second half of the 2nd/8th century, and then translated in the early decades of the 6th/12th century into Persian and expanded by the Persian Nizārī Ismailis.[89]

Several copies of the manuscript were discovered by Russian Orientalists among the collections of the Nizārī Ismailis of Badakhshān. Even though the text does not contain any known Ismailis doctrines, still the Central Asian Ismailis regard it as one of their most sacred and secret works. Ivanow was one of the first Orientalists to introduce the *Umm al-kitāb* to the scholarly world and in 1936 published a critical edition of it.[90]

Along with these materials discovered as a result of the fieldwork, there are also collections of folklore literature produced by local poets and writers, such as *Qiṣṣa-yi Chihil-tanān*, *Jang-nāma-yi Amīr-i Sīstān*, *Dāstān-i dukhtar-i Shaykh Manṣūr-i Ḥallāj* and other works. Moreover, amongst the materials collected there is also a pseudo-biography of Nāṣir-i Khusraw, *Dar nadāmat-i rūz-i qiyāmat*, and Ḥasan-i Ṣabbāḥ's *Haft Bāb* or *Qiṣṣa-yi Sargudhasht-i Bābā Sayyidnā*, still both very popular with the people of Badakhshān.

The majority of these collections consists of works by local poets, which bring to the fore the popularity of, and admiration for, poetry and the Persian poetic tradition, among the Badakhshānī Ismailis. The main

---

[88] Sometimes considered to be the Aesop of Arabic literature, wise sayings and epithets have been attributed to this pre-Islamic poet who is mentioned in Q. 31:23: 'We bestowed wisdom on Luqmān'.

[89] Daftary, *The Ismāʿīlīs* (2nd ed., Cambridge, 2007), pp. 93–95.

[90] For a comprehensive discussion of this work, see, Farhad Daftary, 'Omm al-ketāb', *EIR*. Available online at: http://www.iranicaonline.org/articles/omm-al-ketab [Last accessed, 15 June 2020].

sources of poetic inspiration were the beauty of nature, love of God and his creation, the relationship between the Prophet and the *ahl al-bayt* (the Prophet's immediate family), philosophy and the ethical aspects of human life. Also, the influence of the great and respected poet, Nāṣir-i Khusraw, is supreme among the poets and poetic traditions of Badakhshān, with most local poets having followed his style when composing their works. However, the literature of the local poets of Badakhshān has not been properly studied as yet. Well-known local poets include Mubārak-i Wakhānī (d. 1903), Shāh Fitūr, Mullā Timī, Shamsherbek, to mention but a few. Besides being a respected poet, Mubārak-i Wakhānī also produced a scholarly work on philosophy and astrology.[91] The emergence of these manuscripts highlights the fact that the people living in the high mountains of the Pamirs were well aware of Persian classical literature, such as the works of Aḥmad-i Jāmī (d. 536/1141), Shaykh ʿAṭṭār (d. 618/1220), Jalāl al-Dīn Rūmī (d. 672/1273), Saʿdī Shīrāzī (d. 691/1291), Maḥmūd Shabistarī (d. after 740/1339), Bābā Farghānī (d. 749/1348), Ḥāfiẓ Shīrāzī (d. 792–1390).

The second part of these literary finds consists of a collection of historical sources written in Badakhshān. One of the first historical works identified as *Tārīkh-i Badakhshān* (The History of Badakhshān) was written by local author, Muḥammad Ḥusayn, in the first half of the 12th/18th century. However, it seems that this work has not survived. The second local history which includes a detailed historical work concerning the political and social history of Badakhshān by Mīrzā Sang Muḥammad Badakhshī (12th–13th/18th–19th centuries) and a history by Faḍl ʿAlī Bek Surkhafsar (13th–14th/19th–20th centuries) is also entitled *Tārīkh-i Badakhshān*.[92] *Tārīkh-i Badakhshān* consists of these two parts; the first part is the history of Badakhshān compiled by Mīrzā Sang Muḥammad Badakhshī in 1223/1808, and the second part belongs to Faḍl ʿAlī Bek Surkhafsar completed in 1325/1907, which also includes three appendices, and covers the events of 1905 [1657–58] in the territories of the present-day Tajikistan and northern Afghanistan. It reflects the bloody inter-tribal clashes in Rāgh, Shughnān, Khatlān, Chitrāl and Fayḍābād provinces of Afghanistan. Individual chapters are devoted to the history of the dynasties of the *amīr*s and *khān*s of Badakhshān from the Tajiks, Uzbeks,

---

[91] For more details see, Iloliev, *The Ismāʿīlī-Sufi Sage of Pamir*.
[92] Mirzo Sangmuhammadi Badakhshī and Mirzo Fazlalibeki Surkhafsar, *Tārīkh-i Badakhshon* [The History of Badakhshān] (Dushanbe, 2007).

Qaṭaghans, Qārluqs and Qalmūqs, the intervention of Tsarist Russia and the British empire in the region, and their division of Badakhshān. The book provides a genealogy of a range of the *shāh*s and *mīr*s of Shughnān, including a biography of Sayyid Shāh Khāmūsh and a genealogy of Sayyid ʿAlī Shāh Valī, the father-in-law of Shāh Khāmūsh.

Another source also entitled *Tārīkh-i Badakhshān* was written by Qurbān Muḥammadzāda Ākhūnd Sulaymān and Shāh Fitūr Muḥammad Shāhzāda.[93] The work was edited and published by a Tajik historian from Badakhshān, Bahodur Iskandarov, in 1973. This work is designated by the same title as the two previous ones, however it mainly describes and narrates the local oral tradition of Shughnān, and how it has been preserved and passed from generation to generation, and would probably have been more appropriately called a history of Shughnān rather than of Badakhshān. However, it does refer to events in the history of Badakhshān as well. It also recounts the arrival of the three brothers from Mashhad, Shāh Malang, Shāh Khāmūsh and Shāh Burhān. The work is divided into four parts: 1) the reign of a local ruler ʿAbd al-Raḥīm Khān the son of Qubād Khān (ca. 1207–1230/1792–1814); 2) a history of the local kings of Shughnān; 3) *Tārīkh-i Afghānistān*, which deals with the occupation of Badakhshān by the Afghans; and 4) the time of Tsar Nicholas II (r. 1894–1917) and the arrival of Russian soldiers in Badakhshān up to the October Revolution in 1917.

The *Qayd-hā-yi tārīkhī* was written by Qurbān Shāh Zuhūr Bekzāda and describes historical events in Badakhshān from 1274/1858 to 1920 and the hardships of life under the rule of the Afghan *amīr* ʿAbd al-Raḥīm Khān (r. 1845–1867), and his sons Muḥabbat Khān (r. 1867–1868) and Yūsuf ʿAlī Khān (1869–1874), the rulers of Shughnān and Rūshān. This work and Sayyid Ḥaydar Shāh Mubārak Shāhzāda's *Tārīkh-i Mulk-i Shughnān* contain some detailed discussions on the history of Shughnān and its relations with neighbouring areas such as Rūshān, Wakhān and Darvāz.[94] *Tārīkh-i Mulk-i Shughnān* was written at the request of the Russian scholar Aleksandr Semënov in 1912, who translated it into Russian four years later. The work begins with the story of Chinese rule in Shughān, but does not provide dates. It also says that the local people

---

[93] In the local pronunciation, known as Kurbon Mukhamadzoda (Okhun-Sulaïmon) and Mukhabbat Shokhzoda (Seid-Fitur-Sho), *Istoriiā Badakhshana* [The History of Badakhshān] (Moscow, 1973).

[94] Muborakshohzoda, *Tārīkh-i Mulk-i Shughnān*.

belonged to different religious confessions including Ismailism, Twelver Shi'ism and idol-worship, and that half of the population were Sunnis. The text also mentions the arrival from Khurāsān of Shāh Khāmūsh and the story of how he overthrew the oppressive fire-worshipping king and establish his own rule. A short manuscript, *Mathnawī-yi Tārīkhī*, which is dedicated to eight local rulers of Shughnān, is another historical source. The *Mathnawī-yi Tārīkhī* also known as the *Tārīkh-i Shāhān-i Shughnān*, is a history of the rulers of Shughnān written in verse which gives a brief survey of the reigns of eight rulers of Shughnān. The author was a local Ismaili *pīr* of Shughnān, Sayyid Farrukh Shāh (d. 1307/1889), the son of Shāh Partāwī.[95]

These discoveries suggest a rich tradition of literature and literacy amongst the inhabitants of Badakhshān. Learned people and poets held a position of respect in the community as well as being highly regarded by the rulers of their time for their knowledge and contributions to learning and scholarship. The appetite for knowledge and learning in the tradition of the Badakhshān Ismaili community can be attributed directly to the teachings of their *pīr*, Nāṣir-i Khusraw, who in his *Wajh-i dīn* lays particular importance on the role of the intellect and learning: '...in reality, the Intellect is Paradise'.[96] Therefore, the attainment of knowledge was regarded as the highest purpose of a human-being in the material world, being the only means of salvation for the soul.

Even though an analysis of the poetry and religious literature of the Ismaili community shows that they were generally isolated from the outside world in the remote high Pamir mountains, it also proves that they were well aware of the Persian literary tradition and its main themes such as love, beauty, ethics, religion and philosophy. They were also able to maintain their religious traditions and beliefs, passing them down through the generations over centuries despite living in a hostile environment, surrounded by a Sunni majority, and governed by autocratic rulers.

---

[95] In the 18th and 19th centuries, local scholars produced a number of historical works. For more details see, Kudratbek Èl'chibekov, 'Novye materialy po istorii Shugnana' [New Materials on the History of Shughnān], *IAN (TSSR)*, 2 (1973), pp. 3–11. Nourmamadchoev, *The Ismā'īlīs of Badakhshān*, pp. 2–3.

[96] Nosiri Khusravi Qubodiënī [Nāṣir-i Khusraw-i Qubādiyānī], *Wajhi din* [Wajh-i dīn], ed. Aliqul Devonaqulov and Nurmuhammad Amirshohiī (Dushanbe, 2002), p. 56.

In the *Tārīkh-i Badakhshān* of Sulaymān Qurbān Muḥammadzāda and Sayyid Shāh Fitūr Muḥabbat Shāhzāda, mentioned above, there is no mention of Nāṣir-i Khusraw's *daʿwa* or his teachings but the authors talk extensively about the Ismaili teachings given by four *darvīsh*es known as Sayyid Shāh Malang, Mīr Sayyid Ḥasan Shāh Khāmūsh, Shāh Kāshān and Shāh Burhān Valī. Nonetheless, the focus is on the socio-political life of Badakhshān, the ruling elite and their genealogies, rather than on religion. By contrast, the author of *Silk-i gawhar-rīz*, as is apparent from the text, was a follower of the Nizārī Ismaili *ṭarīqa* who constantly demonstrates his love and passion for Nāṣir-i Khusraw and his followers. Consequently, Gawhar-rīz is mainly concerned with Ismaili religious beliefs and practices, Nāṣir-i Khusraw, the religious hierarchy, and the influential *pīr*s and *dāʿī*s who played an important role in the spread of Ismaili teachings in the region.

Despite the essential shortcomings of Soviet studies, as a result of the all-pervasive influence of Marxism and the Communist Party's authoritarian rule, Soviet scholars in fact produced many positive insights in the field of Ismaili studies. They examined almost every aspect of the life of the Ismaili community using disciplines from anthropology to archaeology, ethnography, history, philosophy, ritual practice and most importantly the collection and preservation of Ismaili manuscripts. Most of the photostat reproductions of these manuscripts are held at the Rudaki Institute of Oriental Studies and Written Heritage of the Republic of Tajikistan and the Russian Federation and are now available to scholars and students. However, the sudden collapse of the Soviet Union in 1991 and the emergence of the national republics as independent states meant that various projects which were designed to locate manuscripts for future studies were left in tatters. However, since independence developments for the Ismaili community and scholars in Tajikistan have included the establishment of the Ismaili institutions and the AKDN there. Once these institutions were established in Tajikistan, they began collaborating with the Academy of Sciences of Tajikistan and other academic institutions in order to advance the study and preservation of manuscripts. Several projects, which had come to a halt as a result of financial and other difficulties in the newly independent countries, have been restarted.

Review of the Literature on the Ismailis in Post-Soviet Studies

In Soviet and post-Soviet Tajikistan, the Ismailis of Badakhshān, who are like the Yaghnābīs,[97] also referred to as Pamiris in official Tajik government and academic contexts, are regarded as the ancestors of the present Tajiks. Alongside the Bactrians, Sogdians, Saka and other sedentary peoples of Central Asia – the Pamiris and the Yaghnābīs have contributed to the core elements that formed and developed into contemporary Tajik ethnicity.[98] Since the Tajik government recognises the Pamiri peoples and the Yagnābis as a central part of the Tajik nation, accordingly, their languages are also an integral part of the Tajik common cultural heritage. In other words, they are as much a part of the common national cultural heritage as the official state language, which is Tajik-Farsi. This means that the state should pay the same attention and give as much funding to the development of these languages as it does to the official state language. The Tajik people including Pamiris and other Eastern Iranians by their origin, culture and tradition are part of a common historical heritage,

---

[97] 'Currently, one of the most ancient and smallest groups of people lives in the territory of modern Tajikistan, which it can be also said with confidence is one of the rarest nationalities in the world. From time immemorial, the Yagnābis have lived in the high, mountainous and impassable Yagnāb Gorge. Their ancestors are the Sogdians, thus the peoples who have been famous for their high culture since the existence of the Sogdian and Bactrian kingdoms. The inhabitants of Yagnāb, overcoming all the political and historical obstacles that fell to their lot, have managed to preserve and bring to our times their most precious wealth – the Sogdian language, better known today as "Yagnāb" or "new Sogdian". And here it is important to say that it was precisely due to their geographical location that the Yagnābis managed to preserve their language. The Yagnāb gorge is located between the Zarafshān mountain range in the north, and in the south, the Hiṣṣār mountain range. This territory is subordinate to the Ainy district of the Sughd region. The main occupation of the inhabitants of the gorge is agriculture and animal husbandry.' S. Mirzozoda, 'Yagnabskiĭ yazyk-bogatstvo tadzhikskogo naroda, kotoroe neobkhodimo peredat' sledíushchim pokoleniîam' [The Yaghnāb language is the wealth of the Tajik people, which must be passed on to the future generations]. Available online at: http://sugdnews.com/2017/10/30/mirzozoda-yagnobskij-yazyk-bogatstvo-tadzhikskogo-naroda-kotoroe-neobkhodimo-peredat-sleduyushchim-pokoleniyam-3/ [Last accessed, 29 October 2020].

[98] Dagikhudo Dagiev, 'Pamiri Ethnic Identity and Its Evolution in post-Soviet Tajikistan', in Dagiev and Faucher, ed., *Identity, History and Trans-Nationality in Central Asia*, pp. 23–44, 37.

which requires special attention in terms of its preservation and study. These languages are no longer purely oral. With these languages, people compose poems, write songs and correspond on social networks.[99] Thus, their development is still on going and is to be considered as an irreversible process; yet, the development and preservation have been done mainly by the people themselves, rather than by state institutions.

The disintegration of the Soviet Union and Tajikistan's 1991 declaration of independence opened up an opportunity for the Ismaili community in Badakhshān and Tajikistan to establish links once again with their imam and with the Imamate institutions worldwide from which they had been completely cut off during the Soviet period. Indeed, this was a significant and historical event for the Ismaili community in Tajikistan as well as for the Imamate institutions around the world. The Imamate institutions under the umbrella of the Aga Khan Development Network (AKDN) began providing assistance for every aspect of the community's life as well as humanitarian aid and support for local institutions in various fields including education. In this instance it was achieved by granting scholarships for students and scholars to carry on with their studies at Russian and Western universities, and providing funding for academic institutions in Tajikistan and other Central Asian states. One such important project was the collaboration with and the continuation of the Soviet scholarly tradition in Ismaili studies.

Since the disintegration of the Soviet Union, local, Russian and Western scholars have continued to work on Ismaili studies, including on the Ismailis of Central Asia. This also includes the publication and translation of many academic works into Russian, Persian and Tajik[100] by the Institute of Ismaili Studies (IIS), in London. The study and understanding of Ismaili beliefs and doctrines are undergoing a dramatic transformation due to increased access to the academic and non-academic literature produced in Western countries. Prior to independence only a very limited number of people had any access to the considerable body of Ismaili literature that has been published by Western scholars over the last several decades. However, thanks to the IIS, much of this material has

---

[99] Ibid.

[100] From the 1930s the Persian language in Soviet Central Asia became known as Tajik. The Arab/Persian script was abandoned and the Latin script adopted in 1929, and in 1940 it was changed again to the Cyrillic script, which is still in use in modern Tajikistan.

been translated into various local languages, including Tajik, enabling access to many people in the community as well as others interested in Ismaili studies. The seminal works by Farhad Daftary, such as *The Ismāʿīlīs: Their History and Doctrines*, *The Assassin Legends* and *A Short History of the Ismailis*,[101] have been instrumental for both academic and non-academic audiences in the post-Soviet era in understanding Ismaili history and doctrines.[102] Farhad Daftary's works on the study of the history of the Ismailis and their doctrines are clear and comprehensible, but they are mainly focused on the areas that have been either the bases of the Ismaili imams or the focus of *daʿwa* activity, such as North Africa, Egypt, Iran and lately India. Generally speaking, Central Asia was viewed as peripheral in this regard and received less scholarly attention in the West.

Nevertheless, in post-Soviet Central Asia, in a fashion similar to that initiated by Russian scholars in the Tsarist era and continued by Soviet scholars under the guidance of the famous Soviet Orientalists, Andreĭ Bertel's and Mamadvafo Baqoev, a group of orientalist scholars and other academics travelled to the Western Pamirs to identify and digitise

---

[101] Farhad Daftary, *The Ismāʿīlīs: their History and Doctrines* (1st ed., Cambridge, 1990; 2nd ed., 2007); *The Assassin Legends: Myths of the Ismaʿilis* (London, 1994); *A Short History of the Ismailis* (Edinburgh, 1998).

[102] See the list of IIS translations and publications in Russian, Tajik, Chinese and Uyghur:

1. Daftary, Farhad. *A Short History of the Ismailis*, tr. A. Alimardonov (in Tajik).
2. – ed., *Intellectual Traditions in Islam*, tr. M. Dinorshoev (in Tajik).
3. – *A Short History of the Ismailis*, tr. Leila Dodykhudoeva and Lola Dodkhudoeva (in Russian).
4. – *Ismailis in Medieval Muslim Societies*, tr. L. Dodykhudoeva (in Russian).
5. – *The Assassin Legends*, tr. L. Dodykhudoeva (in Russian).
6. – *The Assassin Legends*, tr. A. Mamadnazarov (in Tajik).
7. – *The Ismailis: Their History and Doctrines*, tr. L. Dodykhudoeva (in Russian).
8. – *The Ismailis: Their History and Doctrines*, 2nd ed., tr. A. Mamadnazarov (in Tajik).
9. – *A Short History of the Ismailis*, tr. A. Saidula (in Chinese).
10. – *A Short History of the Ismailis*, tr. A. Saidula (in Uyghur).
11. – ed., *A Modern History of the Ismailis. Continuity and Change in a Muslim Community*, tr. L. Dodykhudoeva (in Russian).
12. – *Historical Dictionary of the Ismailis*, tr. L. Dodykhudoeva (in Russian).
13. – *A History of Shiʿi Islam*, tr. L. Dodykhudoeva (in Russian).
14. Hunsberger, Alice. *The Ruby of Badakhshan*, tr. N. Zurobekov (in Tajik).
15. – *The Ruby of Badakhshan*, tr. L. Dodykhudoeva (in Russian).
16. Lalani, Arzina. *Early Shiʿi Thought*, tr. N. Terletskiy (in Russian).
17. Shah-Kazemi, Reza. *Justice and Remembrance: Introducing the Spirituality of Imam ʿAlī*, tr. N. Terletskiy (in Russian).

manuscripts. The IIS launched this project in 1995 in order to identify, preserve and digitise the manuscripts and literary heritage of the Ismailis of Badakhshān in conjunction with the then Ismaili Tariqa and Religious Education Committee (ITREC) in Khārūgh, Tajikistan. In 2013, the Institute of Ismaili Studies established the Ismaili Special Collections Unit (ISCU) that now directs and manages the work of the manuscript project in Khārūgh, Tajikistan (previously managed under different entities in the IIS).

Outline of the Activities and Projects Conducted by the Manuscript Office

Since 1995, the manuscript project in Khārūgh has conducted many field trips in Badakhshān of Tajikistan. As a result, a great deal of material has been collected and periodic reports have been submitted to the IIS. A selected number of reports produced by the team in the Khārūgh Manuscript Office and the ISCU have been used in writing this brief section.[103]

The work of the Khārūgh Manuscript Office can be divided into the following broad categories:

(i) Identifying manuscripts and other literary sources

(ii) Preparing working handlists/catalogues

(iii) Digitising identified manuscripts and other literary sources

(iv) Analysing the content of identified manuscripts

Identifying and digitising manuscripts and other literary sources in Badakhshān of Tajikistan is still a work in progress. Hence, the Manuscript Project in Khārūgh produces working lists and reports which are used by

---

[103] The following reports have been used in writing this section: N. Nourmamdchoev, *Analytical Mapping of Persian Manuscripts from Badakhshan of Tajikistan: Revised version* (November 2019); N. Nourmamdchoev, *Analytical Mapping of Persian Manuscripts from Badakhshan of Afghanistan: Revised version* (November 2019); S. Sherzodshoev, 'Discovery of Documents in Badakhshan of Tajikistan' (Unpublished Report for the IIS, 2016); N. Nourmamadchoev, *Review of the Hand-List of Manuscripts from Badakhshan of Tajikistan* (20 January 2016); S. Sherzodshoev, 'Report from the Khorog Office: Discovery of Historical Documents' (Unpublished Report for the IIS, 2015); S. Mamadsherzodshoev, 'Excerpt from a report by ISCU Khārūgh Unit' (Unpublished Report for the IIS, 2014).

scholars at the ISCU, IIS, for preparing catalogues of manuscripts found in the broader Badakhshān region. The work the Khārūgh Manuscript Office undertook can be divided into two phases: phase one covered the period from 1995 to 2007 when the project was focused on identifying and digitising manuscripts, archival material and other sources relating to the heritage of the mountain regions of the GBAO of Tajikistan only. The originals are still held in private collections. Phase two covered the period from 2007 to 2016 when the project extended its field trips to include Badakhshān of Afghanistan as well. Unfortunately, the fieldwork in Badakhshān of Afghanistan did not last long due to the political instability, becoming infrequent from the end of 2010 and eventually stopping in 2016. Therefore, the southern parts of Badakhshān of Afghanistan where a small pocket of Ismailis resides remain uncovered by the project.

Even though the fieldwork in Badakhshān of Tajikistan and Afghanistan proved to be difficult because of the harsh climate and the natural environment as well as political instability in these regions, they resulted in the collection of a great deal of material. This was used in the creation of working handlists of various treatises in prose and poetry preserved in the manuscripts that had been discovered, the manuscripts being then digitised.

A working hand-list of manuscripts from Badakhshān of Tajikistan written in the Persian script by Shozodamamad Sherzodshoev and Mamadhusayn Alimadadshoev. This hand-list describes a total of 310 manuscripts which are either single-volume works or collections of treatises, known as a *majmūʿa*s. These 310 manuscripts contain more than 570 titles of various lengths and genres. Most of the texts are either copied from older manuscripts or from printed/lithographed copies which were not readily available in Badakhshān. A prominent place is given to a small number of manuscripts which are considered unique and were copied between 1049/1648 and 1101/1690.[104]

The Ismailis of Badakhshān preserved various copies of collections of poetry, *Dīvān*s, by famous Sufi poets such as Shams al-Dīn Muḥammad Ḥāfiẓ (d. 791/1389) [MS BT 301 and MS BT 308], and Jalāl-al-Dīn Muḥammad Rūmī (d. 672/1273) [MS BT 3; MS BT 13; MS BT 70; MS BT 96, MS BT 97; MS BT 120; MS BT292]. Apart from these *Dīvān*s there is a prevalence of Sufi works generally, such as those of the famous

---

[104] N. Nourmamdchoev, *Analytical Mapping of Persian Manuscripts from Badakhshan of Tajikistan: Revised version* (November, 2019), p. 9.

5th/11th-century author Abū Ismāʿīl ʿAbd Allāh Anṣārī (d. 481/1081) [MS BT 309 and MS BT 144]. Apart from this, the collection includes works by local Ismaili authors such as Naẓmī-i Shughnānī (12th/18th century) [MS BT 274], Sayyid Jaʿfar b. Sayyid Tīmūr b. Sayyid Shāh Muẓaffar (13th/19th century [MS BT 161 and MS BT 162]), and Mubārak-i Wakhānī [MS BT 145, MS BT 149, MS BT 151, and MS BT 154].[105]

Another important discovery made during the fieldwork in Badakhshān of Tajikistan was a short Ismaili *risāla* known as *Haft bāb-i Bābā Sayyidnā*. This brief work, which has been ascribed to Ḥasan-i Ṣabbāḥ, was found among the treatises in MS BT 9, MS 157 and MS BT 171 and then used as the basis of the critical edition and English translation with a proper ascription to Ḥasan-i Maḥmūd-i Kātib. The new critical edition was prepared for publication by S.J. Badakhchani in 2017.[106]

Another working hand-list of manuscripts from Badakhshān of Afghanistan was prepared on the basis of digital copies of manuscripts identified in Badakhshān of Afghanistan since 2007. It too was written in Persian by Shohzodamamad Sherzodshoev, and then later translated into English by Mamadhusayn Alimadadshoev. The hand-list presents descriptions and codicological information on 168 manuscripts containing more than 287 titles of various lengths and genres.[107] A prominent place in this collection is also given to two manuscripts from the 10th/16th and 12th/18th centuries. These are MS BA 5 *Maẓhar al-ajāʾib* by Farīd al-Dīn ʿAṭṭār-i Tūnī (fl. 9th/15th century) dated 10 Muḥarram 918/7 April 1512 and MS BA 46 *Majmūʿa* dated Muḥarram 1127/January–February 1715.

As part of these research projects, the ISCU at the IIS utilises codicological and palaeographic information from various hand-lists to prepare systematic catalogues of manuscripts identified in Badakhshān of Tajikistan and Afghanistan. This work is is anticipated to result in the publication of catalogues in the coming years.

As part of the Manuscript Analysis Project, the ISCU commissions scholars to produce research using manuscripts in its holdings including the

---

[105] Ibid., p. 8.

[106] For more information, see Badakhchani, *Spiritual Resurrection in Shiʿi Islam*, pp. 37–42.

[107] N. Nourmamdchoev, *Analytical Mapping of Persian Manuscripts from Badakhshan of Afghanistan: Revised version* (November 2019), pp. 2, 5–6.

digital copies referred to above. Scholars such as Shozodamamad Sherzodshoev, Jalal Badakhchani, Shafique Virani, Umed Sherzodshoev, Orkhan Mir-Kasimov, Karim Javan, Otambek Mastibekov, Nourmamadcho Nourmamadchoev, Daniel Beben, Shaftolu Gulamadov and many others, work on manuscripts from these collections.

Several articles featuring a discussion of some of the manuscripts digitised by the project in Khārūgh will form part of the conference proceedings to be published by the IIS under the title *Texts, Scribes and Transmission: Manuscript Cultures of the Ismaili Communities and Beyond*. These articles were originally presented at a symposium organised by the Ismaili Special Collections Unit in 2017.[108]

Post-Soviet Scholarship on the Ismailis

In the last two decades, many volumes of academic writing on Islam have been produced by scholars in Russia. These include *Khrestomatiĩa po Islamu* (Readings on Islam) edited by the Russian Orientalist, Stanislav M. Prozorov.[109] The work does not deal directly with the Ismailis or Ismaili studies. Prozorov himself argues that the aim of the book is to help the Russian-speaking audience, for the first time in the post-Soviet period, gain an impartial and accurate view of the religion of Islam as an elaborate and flexible ideological system. This was seen as a new area of Islamic Studies in Russian scholarship. The editor introduces three dimensions of Islamic history and discusses the problem of correlation between the fundamental principles of doctrinal Islam and their regional interpretations in multifarious social, cultural and ethnic contexts.

In the post-Soviet era, a wealth of new studies has been produced on the history, religion, culture and tradition of the Ismailis of Central Asia. Among Tajik scholars, mention can be made of the work of Khaëlbek Dodikhudoev, Abusaid Shokhumorov, N. Davlatbekov, Kudratbek Ėl'chibekov, Elbon Hojibekov, Sunatullo Jonboboev, Tohir Qalandarov, Hokim Qalandarov, Davlat Niyozbekov, Abdulmamad Iloliev, Muzaffar

---

[108] I would like to thank Dr(s) Wafi Momen and Nourmamadcho Nourmamadchoev of the Ismaili Special Collections Unit at the IIS for their support and their help in providing updates on the manuscript project in Khārūgh, Tajikistan.

[109] S.M. Prozorov, ed., *Khrestomatiĩa po Islamu* [Readings on Islam] (Moscow, 1994).

Zoolshoev, Nourmamadcho Nourmamadchoev, Otambek Mastibekov, Shaftolu Gulamadov, as well as those of a small number of Western scholars with Alice Hunsberger, Daniel Beben and Jo-Ann Gross undoubtedly being among the most significant.[110]

Scholars and research on the Ismailis in the post-Soviet era can be divided into three categories: (i) scholars influenced by Soviet or Marxist historical materialism despite the collapse of the Communist regime; (ii) scholars who have embarked on Ismaili studies since the disintegration of the Soviet Union, who have not been greatly affected by Soviet scholarship, and who can also access the relevant literature in Western languages; and (iii) scholars approaching Ismaili studies from Western perspectives including Western scholars and indigenous Tajik scholars who have received a Western education.

One of the publications that appeared in 1996 was *Anglo-Russkoie Sopernichestvo v TSentral'noĭ Azii i Ismailizm* (Anglo-Russian Rivalry in Central Asia and Ismailism) by Leonid N. Khariukov, a military serviceman who served in Badakhshān during the Soviet era. He had access to archival material including some private sources and his work conforms to Soviet ideology even though it was published several years after the collapse of the Soviet Union. He expresses a biased attitude towards Ismaili history and particularly towards what he sees as Aga Khan III's pro-British stance in the international arena. Although Khariukov's book falls far short of being an academic work, it is however valuable in terms of utilising unpublished material.

As already mentioned, the foremost scholar in the study of Ismaili philosophy during the Soviet and post-Soviet eras, is the Tajik academician Khaëlbek Dodikhudoev whose scholarship was introduced and examined in the previous section.[111] It is imperative for us to examine and assess his stance on Ismaili studies in the post-Soviet era given that his case reveals how in the Soviet era, the official ideology constrained him and his colleagues in their approach to the Ismailis and their faith.

In his recent work *Filosofskiĭ Ismailism* (2014), Dodikhudoev admits that in the totalitarian atmosphere engendered by the prevailing Communist ideology Ismaili studies was not a safe option for any Soviet scholar.[112]

---

[110] More details on their works are provided in Chapter 3.

[111] See, *Review of the Literature on the Ismailis in Soviet Scholarship*, pp. 71–90.

[112] Khaëlbek Dodikhudoev, *Filosofskiĭ ismailizm* [Philosophical Ismailism] (Dushanbe, 2014), pp. 6–7.

For this reason, many aspects of Ismaili history remained unexplored, even though considerable work on the study of Ismaili history, religious belief, doctrine and philosophy had been undertaken by scholars in other parts of the world. Nevertheless, according to Dodikhudoev, as regards the medieval era, the Ismailis were viewed by the Soviet authorities as a branch of Shiʻi Islam with a rational philosophy and shared with the other branches a long history of tragic events going back to the middle of the 2nd/8th century.[113] According to Dodikhudoev, the Ismaili legacy in the history of Islamic thought and Iranian philosophy and culture is unique due to the contributions made by Ismaili thinkers from the 3rd/9th to the early 14th/20th century. He argues that this contribution is primarily based on the following: 1) the Ismailis were amongst the first in Islamic history to compose works on philosophy and science in the Persian language, replacing Arabic usually used for these subjects (*Umm al-kitāb*, al-Sijistānī, Nāṣir-i Khusraw); 2) the Ismailis added the comparative study of religion and the philosophy of religion to the scholarship of their time (Abū Ḥātim al-Rāzī); 3) in their writings they formed a synthesis of Islamic prophetic wisdom and ancient philosophy (al-Nasafī, al-Rāzī, al-Sijistānī, al-Kirmānī, al-Shīrāzī, Nāṣir-i Khusraw and many others); 4) in scientific and religious thought, the Ismailis developed rationalism and raised up the role of reason (Abū Mūsā Jābir b. Ḥayyān, Ibn al-Haytham and other Ismaili philosophers, including the authors of the *Rasāʾil Ikhwān al-Ṣafāʾ*); 5) they were the first to carry out experiments in chemistry and optics (Jābir b. Ḥayyān, Ibn al-Haytham); 6) they created the first encyclopaedia in the form of the *Rasāʾil Ikhwān al-Ṣafāʾ*; 7) they established the world's first university, al-Azhar, in Cairo; 8) they developed the concept of sacred history in Islam; 9) they were the first group in Iran to create a national liberation movement to counter the domination of the Turkic tribes (the Nizārī Ismaili movement in Iran, from the 5th/11th to the 7th/13th century); 10) they established the first people's state in the history of Islam (Ḥasan-i Ṣabbāḥ).[114] However, he concludes, not all of these elements and contributions in terms of science and civilisation have been fully investigated and studied.

Abusaid Shokhumorov's final work *Razdelenie Badakhshana i sud'by Ismailizma* discusses the major events of the late 19th and early 20th centuries in Badakhshān and their impact on the Ismailis of the region.

---

[113] Ibid., p. 13.
[114] Ibid.

The author examines the main reasons for the ultimate subjugation and division of Badakhshān between the colonial powers. He also assesses and examines the major role played during the partitioning of Badakhshān by the religious and political figures of the time. The work presents a new approach to the study of historical events in the region, with the author questioning some of the assumptions of previous scholars.[115] Even though Shokhumorov attempted to introduce a new approach to the study of the Central Asian Ismailis, which should have been different from the Soviet one, still the work suffers from certain shortcomings as occasionally the claims regarding certain historical events are not supported by evidence.

Kudratbek Ėl'chibekov's work takes into account the theory of the hierarchy of the clergy discussed earlier, making use of a large number of the Ismaili sources discovered in Badakhshān during the expeditions carried out between 1957 and 1963. However, Ėl'chibekov's study is still in line with the Soviet approach to the study of religion in which the development of the Ismaili movement was interpreted as an instance of 'class struggle' taking place in medieval Muslim society.

Elbon Hojibekov's work presents an analysis of the little-known activities of the Ismaili *pīrs* in the political life of the of the Pamir region, particularly in the Shughnān district, between the end of the 13th/19th and the first half of the 20th century. Even though Hojibekov's work suffers from misreading and misquotation of the primary and secondary sources, the work is important because it includes a trove of recorded material and interviews that he conducted.

The Russian scholar, Andreï Vadimovich Smirnov (b. 1958), who studied Ismaili philosophy, wrote in his introduction to the Russian translation of al-Kirmānī's work *Rāḥat al-ʿaql*:

> Among the many discoveries of our century, we can rightly count the world's discovery of Ismaili philosophy. For centuries surrounded by an aura of mystery, generating fanciful and not always friendly legends, this most mysterious of the Shiʿi Islamic sects has only in recent decades allowed the publication of the key works of its theoretical thought.[116]

---

[115] Shokhumorov, *Razdelenie Badakhshana*. The unexpected death of Abusaid Shokhumorov in 1999 delayed the publication of this monograph for almost nine years but with the support of his friends and family members it was published in 2008.

[116] Ḥamīd al-Dīn al-Kirmānī, *Uspokoenie razuma* [*Rāḥat al-ʿaql*]. Vvedenie, perevod s arabskogo i kommentarii A.V. Smirnova [Intr., and tr., from Arabic with a commentary by A.V. Smirnov]. (Moscow, 1995), p. 5.

Another academic, Muso Dinorshoev, in the introduction to an edition of *Zād al-musāfirīn*,[117] identified reasons for the persecution of the Ismailis in the medieval period under various Muslim empires. He writes:

> [T]his phenomenon was due to several reasons. First, with their new call announcing happiness, justice and equality the Ismailis attracted the attention of various sectors of society. Secondly, of all the religious movements, sects and schools, only the Ismailis called for resistance to the Saljūq invaders. This patriotic call of the Ismailis was perceived positively by noble people and was headed by a true patriot such as Nāṣir-i Khusraw. On this basis, we can surely say that the persecution and oppression of Nāṣir by the Saljūqs had confessional and political reasons.[118]

Since the disintegration of the Soviet Union, several books have been published on the Ismaili community, which have more or less demonstrated impartiality and which have given credit to the Ismaili community and their imam for their work in the development of health services, educational programmes and economic growth all over the world. Sergeï Plekhanov's *Raskrytaīa Ladon': Aga-Khan i Ego Mīuridy*[119] presents in a broad historical context the significance of Aga Khan IV and his community in the world today. Plekhanov used various sources, domestic and foreign, to examine and provide a realistic picture of Ismaili movement as a unique cultural phenomenon. Plekhanov also says that his personal acquaintance with the life of the Ismaili communities and the work of AKDN institutions in different countries has enabled him not only to experience the diverse nature of AKDN programmes in the fields of economy, culture, education and health, but also to understand the Ismailis through the prism of human history.

Plekhanov further argues that the medieval Ismailis were the target of attacks by both Muslim and Christian orthodoxy, who presented them as assassins in the service of a secret organisation. He notes that it is only in recent decades that the perception has changed and people have started to understand that the bizarre legends circulating about the Ismailis were spawned to create an ideology of intolerance. Plekhanov's book serves as a

---

[117] Muso Dinorshoev, *Nasir-i Khusraw i ego 'Zad al-musafirin'* (Pripasy putnikov) [Nāṣir-i Khusraw and his *Zād al-Musāfirīn*], tr. from Tajik (Dushanbe, 2005).
[118] Ibid., p. 12.
[119] Sergeï Plekhanov, *Raskrytaīa ladon': Aga Khan i ego Mīuridy* [An Open Hand: the Aga-Khan and His *Murīds*] (Moscow, 2008).

source of inter-civilisational, inter-religious dialogue. It allows the Russian reader, as well as readers from the former Soviet territories, to have a better understanding of the Ismaili community and the role of its spiritual leader Aga Khan IV, one of the most prominent religious leaders in the world today.

Hokim Qalandarov's book entitled *Rūdakī va Ismoiliia*,[120] is a product of post-Soviet scholarship on the Ismailis. It considers one of the most debated topics amongst scholars of Persian literature about the life and work of the great poet Rūdakī, who is regarded as a master of Persian/Tajik poetry. The author was able to consult all the sources available in order to shed light on Rūdakī's affiliation with the Ismailis and the contribution he made to Persian poetry and his glorification of the Sāmānid state. He has also tried to highlight the differences between the Ismailis and the Qarmaṭīs who, due to hostile historical sources, were for a long time depicted as a single group.[121] However, the author not only differentiates the Ismailis from the Qarmaṭīs in this study, but dismisses the notion that Rūdakī had any association with the Qarmaṭīs. Furthermore, in the course of the analysis and the study of the topic, Qalandarov was able to respond to some of the anti-Ismaili publications of recent years.

A scholar such as Otambek Mastibekov represents another interesting case in Ismaili studies which is a combination of both Soviet and Western educational backgrounds. In his work under the title *Leadership and Authority in Central Asia: the Ismaili Community in Tajikistan* (2014) he provides a detailed study on religious leadership and authority in the context of the Ismailis of Tajikistan over the last a hundred years or so. The work is rich in terms of sources in both Tajik and Russian, revealing the role of the *pīrs* and *khalīfas* in the pre-Soviet and early-Soviet periods with a particular reference to Stalin's anti-religious policy as a result of which most religious authorities, and in particular *pīrs*, were eliminated. He further argues that with the elimination of the *pīrs* as key religious figures since the 1930s, the *khalīfas* became important in the preservation of Ismaili religious knowledge not only by passing it on to the next generation, but also by concealing religious manuscripts. However, he does not elaborate on the roles of the *khalīfas* during the establishment of Imamate institutions in post-Soviet Tajikistan.

---

[120] Qalandarov, *Rudakī va Ismoiliia*.
[121] For further on this point, see Daftary, *The Ismāʿīlīs*, especially 'The Ismāʿīlī-Qarmaṭī Schism of 286/899', pp. 116–126.

A study of the Darvāz district of the Gorno-Badakhshān region, where a small Ismaili community lives surrounded by a Sunni majority, was published by another Russian scholar, Nadezhda Emel'ianova. In the conclusion to her work she argues that a certain custom and tradition of the Darvāz Ismailis differs from those of the Ismailis in Shughnān and Rūshān.[122] Their focus on education, which comes out of their attitude to knowledge and the activities of the AKDN institutions in the region, is obvious and she further states, 'the Ismailis are trying to improve the life of their community through economic measures and by raising their educational level'.[123]

In addition to these individual studies, a series of conferences was organised with the support of the Institute of Ismaili Studies, London, and the Academy of Sciences of the Republic of Tajikistan. These conferences have enabled scholars and students to further their knowledge and understanding of the Ismailis and their beliefs by exploring the material collected in the course of a hundred years or so by Russian and Soviet Orientalists in Central Asia and Russia. Two large conferences were organised and sponsored by the Institute of Ismaili Studies in Khārūgh and Dushanbe (2003). Many scholars and academics were brought together at the conference to commemorate Nāṣir-i Khusraw's millennium, which ultimately resulted in the publication of a collection of articles under the title *Nāṣir-i Khusraw: Yesterday, Today, Tomorrow*[124] in English, Russian and Tajik. Even though many of Nāṣir's works were published in Tajik and Russian during the Soviet era, recent years have seen a positive surge in the publication of his works. In recent decades, with the support of the IIS in joint projects with many academics and academic institutions in Tajikistan, almost the entire corpus of Nāṣir's works and those of many other Ismaili thinkers have been translated and published, which has opened up new opportunities for research and further advances in Ismaili studies.

More recently, a conference was organised by the Institute of Ismaili Studies and the Russian Academy of Science's Institute of Oriental

---

[122] Nadezhda Emel'ianova, *Darvaz: religioznaia i kul'turnaia zhizn' Tadzhiksko-Afganskogo prigranich'ia* (po materialam polevykh issledovanii 2003–2006 gg.) [Darvāz – Religious and Cultural Life of the Tajik-Afghan Borders (based on field research between 2003 and 2006)] (Moscow, 2007), p. 107.

[123] Ibid.

[124] Sarfaroz Niyozov and Ramazon Nazariev, ed., *Nasir Khusraw: Yesterday, Today, Tomorrow* (Khujand, 2005).

Manuscripts in St Petersburg in celebration of the 125th anniversary of the birth of the prominent Russian Iranist, Wladimir Ivanow. Many scholars from the former Soviet countries as well as the Western world participated, including Farhad Daftary who had recently edited and annotated the English translation of Ivanow's memoirs.[125]

Another factor in the changing landscape of Ismaili studies is the influence of globalisation. Globalisation and modern technology have opened up a new dimension in Ismaili studies worldwide, as most of the works on the Ismailis have now become accessible to scholars regardless of their geographical location, political and religious views, or even language.

Therefore, since the disintegration of the Soviet Union, Ismaili studies has dramatically changed and there have been many positive developments. Prior to 1917, studies were conducted in the region mostly by Russian military officers and a few scholars, who in the main were on intelligence missions, but although their work is less significant academically, it contains important material that can be regarded as primary source material.

Ismaili studies in the Soviet era resulted in the discovery of a remarkable body of Ismaili manuscripts during fieldwork in the GBAO and a range of academic publications related to Ismaili studies, in fields such as history, religion, philosophy, and ethnography. However, as argued earlier, most of the time this academic study was undermined by the imprint of Communist ideology which had profound impact on much of the literature produced. Nevertheless, the achievements of the scholarship during this period outweigh the shortcomings resulting from any ideological constraints. Since then, with the disintegration of the Soviet Union, the Ismaili community as well as scholars in the field have been provided with fresh opportunities to further their knowledge and understanding of Ismaili history and traditions in Central Asia.

---

[125] Stanislav M. Prozorov and Hakim Elnazarov, ed., *Russian Scholars on Ismailism* (St Petersburg, 2014).

Bibliography of Works by Imperial Russian, Soviet and Post-Soviet Scholars[1]

This section is a detailed bibliography of books, articles, published and unpublished material, including also documents and recorded material. It is an attempt to bring together the vast range of material on the history, thought and practices of the Ismailis of Central Asia, most of which has been hitherto unknown to Western scholarship. It is hoped that this effort will contribute to further development of Ismaili studies and encourage scholars to engage even further in the study of the history and heritage of the Ismailis of Central Asia.

A

1   Abaeva, Tamara Grigor'evna (1927–). *Ocherki po istorii Badakhshana* [Essays on the History of Badakhshān], Akademiiā nauk UzSSR. Tashkent: Institut vostokovedeniiā, 1961. pp. 15. (in Russian).

2   —— *Ocherki istorii Badakhshana* [Essays on the History of Badakhshān]. Tashkent: Nauka, 1964. pp. 163. (in Russian).

The information provided in this study is based on archival material collected by Orientalists and the extensive literature which they systematised regarding aspects of the history of Badakhshān. The volume also presents data of a socio-economic nature as well as on the external relations of Badakhshān during the second half of the 19th century. It contains information about the religious beliefs of the mountain Tajiks, and also provides information on Shi'i, Ismaili and officially accepted Sunni practices.

3   —— *Pamiro-Gindukushskiĭ region Afganistana v kontse XIX – nachale XX veka* [The Pamir-Hindukush Region of Afghanistan at the end of the 19th – Beginning of the 20th Century]. Tashkent: Fan, 1987. pp. 118. (in Russian).

A study of the history of religious and ethnic minorities of the Pamir-Hindu Kush region in Afghanistan. The work traces the dynamics of relations

---

[1] 'Post Soviet' includes Western as well as Russian and Tajik academic writing.

between the *amīrs* of Kabul and the small ethnic groups and tribes of Badakhshān in the last quarter of the 19th century during the formation of the Afghan state. The book also touches upon the role of Aga Khan III and his *murīds* in Badakhshān province in the era of Anglo-Russian rivalry.

4 —— 'Ismaility Pripamir'ia i sektantskoe dvizhenie pandzhabaev v pamirskom ismailizme (20–30–i gody XX veka)' [The Pamir Region Ismailis and the Sectarian Movement of the Pamir Panjebhai (1920s–1930s)], Unpublished Report. Institute of Oriental Manuscripts of the Academy of Sciences of the Republic of Uzbekistan, 12 February 1997, pp. 13. (in Russian).

The paper focuses on the importance of the Persian (Tajik) language and its impact on the production of Ismaili literature, particularly in Nāṣir-i Khusraw's works. It highlights the unifying character of this language despite the diversity of the spoken dialects in each district of Badakhshān. The author emphasises the role of the *ishāns* or *pīrs* as the most distinctive members of the Pamir Ismaili community and she includes in her analysis a study of the Panjebhai movement in the Pamir area.

5 Abbas, Najam and Sultonbek Aksakolov. 'Taking Stock: Conventional and non-conventional Sources on the Ismailis of Central Asia', Unpublished Report for the IIS, 2008, pp. 1–73.

The work aims to serve as a historical record and guide to bibliographic efforts on Central Asian sources, and is intended to be a primary resource on the Ismailis of Central Asia.

6 Abibov, Amirbek (1916–1998). *Az tārīkh-i adabiëti tojik dar Badakhshon* [On the History of Tajik Literature in Badakhshān]. Dushanbe: Donish, 1971. pp. 195. (in Tajik).

A history of written literature in Badakhshān, dating back to the time when modern Persian/Tajik emerged in the major cities. The further development and promotion of written literature in Badakhshān is very much associated with the arrival of Nāṣir-i Khusraw (ca. 1060), who played a key role in the teaching and spread of the Ismaili *daʿwa*. The impact of his personality, religious teachings and philosophical ideas has been detectable in the written literature of Badakhshān ever since.

7 —— 'Chashmai Nosir: rivoiathoi khalqī dar borai Nosiri Khusrav' [Nāṣir's Spring: Folk Traditions about Nāṣir-i Khusraw], *IH*, 9 (1990), pp. 9–11. (in Tajik).

Popular folktales about Nāṣir-i Khusraw and his personality found among the Ismaili population of Badakhshān.

8 Adalis, Adelina Efimovna (1902–1969). 'Nosir Khisrou: O razume i prosveshchenii' [Nāṣir-i Khusraw: On Reason and Enlightenment], tr. of the

Qaṣīda into Russian, in I.S. Braginskiĭ, ed., *Antologiia tadzhikskoĭ poezii* [Anthology of Tajik Poetry]. Moscow: Goslitizdat, 1951, pp. 261-263. (in Russian).

This paper discusses the philosophical ideas of Nāṣir-i Khusraw, which differed from Sunni Islam. It also provides a Russian translation of his poem.

9   Agaev, I.A. and K.D. Dodikhudoev. 'Kontseptsiia religii v rannem ismailizme' ('Dīn al-falasifa', 'Brat'ev chistoty i druzeĭ vernosti') ['The Concept of Religion in Early Ismailism' ('The Faith of Philosophers', 'The Ikhwān al-Ṣafā' and the Friends of Faithfulness')], *IAN* (TSSR), 2 (1989), pp. 47-52. (in Russian).

The Ikhwān al-Ṣafā' was a group of 4th/10th century encyclopaedists, whose works had a significant influence on the formation of the philosophy of the Ismaili movement.

10 Akimushkin, Oleg Fedorovich (1929–2010), V.V. Kushev and N.D. Miklukho-Maklaĭ. *Persidskie i tadzhikskie rukopisi Instituta Narodov Azii. AN USSR: kratkiĭ alfavitnyĭ katalog* [Persian and Tajik Manuscripts of the Institute of the Asian Peoples. AN USSR: short alphabetical catalogue], part I. Moscow: Nauka, 1964. pp. 633. (in Russian).

The collection of Persian and Tajik manuscripts of the Institute of the Asian peoples of the Academy of Sciences of the Russian Federation is one of the oldest collections of written records in Persian, and includes a very important collection of Ismaili manuscripts.

11 —— V.V. Kushev and M.A. Salakhetdinova. *Persidskie i tadzhikskie rukopisi Instituta Narodov Azii. AN USSR (kratkiĭ alfavitnyĭ katalog)* [Persian and Tajik Manuscripts of the Institute of the Asian Peoples. AN USSR: short alphabetical catalogue], part II. Moscow: Nauka, 1964. pp. 145. (in Russian).

12 —— 'Predislovie, publikatsiia teksta i primechaniia. Avtobiographicheskaia spravka Vladimira Alekseevicha Ivanova (1886–1970)' [Foreword, the Publication of the Text and Notes. Autobiographical Reference of Wladimir Alexeevich Ivanow (1886–1970)], *PV*, 10 (2002), pp. 446–458. (in Russian).

A 'Biographical note' on Wladimir Alekseevich Ivanow, the outstanding Orientalist and scholar of Iranian Studies, an internationally recognised expert in Ismaili studies, who laid the foundations for the modern study of Ismaili history and philosophy.

13 Akramov, Nariman Mansurovich (1932–1996). *Voprosy istorii, arkheologii i etnographii narodov Pamira i Pri-Pamir'ia v trudakh B.L. Grombchevskogo* [Problems in the History, Archaeology and Ethnography of the Pamir People and Pamir Region in the Works of B.L. Grombchevskiĭ]. Dushanbe: Irfon, 1974. pp. 132. (in Russian).

The little-studied region of Pamir and the adjacent areas are known for fabulous minerals, and have long attracted the attention of travellers and academics. Records show that in the Middle Ages the region was visited by Chinese, Arab and other travellers.

14 Aksakolov, Sultonbek. *Islam in Soviet Tajikistan: State Policy, Religious Figures and the Practice of Religion (1950–1985)*, PhD dissertation, SOAS, University of London, 2013. pp. 211.

This thesis explores the religious life of Muslim communities in Soviet Tajikistan from 1950 to 1985 with a particular focus on the districts of Shughnān, Rūshān, Wakhān and other parts of Badakhshān where the Ismaili community is based.

15 Alekseev, Anton Kirillovich. 'Rossiia na "kryshe mira": pamirskiĭ otriad v politicheskoĭ i kul'turnoĭ zhizni Badakhshana. K 115–letiiu pokhoda generala M.E. Ionova v Zapadnyĭ Pamir (1894 g.)' [Russia on the "Roof of the World": The Pamir Military Detachment in the Political and Cultural Life of Badakhshān. Towards the 115th Anniversary of the Campaign of General M.E. Ionov in the Western Pamirs (1894)], *Vestnik Sankt-Peterburgskogo Universiteta* [St Petersburg University Newsletter], vol. 13, *Istoriia i Istochnikovedenie* (2013), pp. 76–90. (in Russian).

16 Al-Ḥusaynī, Shihāb al-Dīn Shāh. *Kitāb-i Khiṭābāt-i ʿāliya* [The Book of Excellence], transliterated from Persian to Tajik by Qimatshoh Qadamshoev and Mirsaid Navrūzbekov. Dushanbe: 'Tabʿ va Nashr', 2017. pp. 78. With an English foreword by W. Ivanow. Ismaili Society Series A, 14. Bombay: Ismaili Society, 1963. pp. xv (English) + 82 (Persian).

The treatise on *Excellence* was written in Persian by Shihāb al-Dīn Shāh (1851–1884), brother of Aga Khan III, and consists of sixty-four solutions related to Muslim ethics and Ismaili spiritual matters.

17 Alidonshoev, Dilbarsho. 'On the Advice of Nasir Khusraw', in Sarfaroz Niyozov and Ramazon Nazariev, ed., *Nasir Khusraw: Yesterday, Today, Tomorrow*. (Proceedings of a conference held in Khārūgh, Tajikistan). Khujand: Noshir, 2005, pp. 197–201.

'On the Advice of Nāṣir-i Khusraw', analyses a chapter of the *Rawshanā'ī-nāma* in which virtues are seen as a basis for developing the human soul and achieving its perfection.

18 Alimardonov, Amriiazdon. 'Dakholati paĭravoni mazohib dar "Safarnoma"-i Nosiri Khusrav' [The Intervention of Belief in Nasir-i Khusraw's 'Safar-nāma'], *NP*, 4 (2003), pp. 111–124. (in Tajik).

Many stories and legends have been told with regard to Nāṣir-i Khusraw. However, most of these stories were fabricated in an attempt to portray a negative image of him. The author has challenged and unravelled some of these stories by demonstrating out-dated aspects of the chronology and geography of Nāṣir-i Khusraw's *Safar-nāma*.

19 —— 'Attempts to Change Perceptions and Misrepresentations of Nasir Khusraw's Personality and Legacy down the Centuries', in Sarfaroz Niyozov and Ramazon Nazariev, ed., *Nasir Khusraw: Yesterday, Today, Tomorrow*. (Proceedings of a conference held in Khārūgh, Tajikistan). Khujand: Noshir, 2005, pp. 307–314. (in Tajik).

This article points out the origin of, and reasons for, these changes and misinterpretations. Evidence is presented from many sources to indicate the fallacies and generalisations of those who have studied the *Safar-nāma* over the centuries.

20 —— and N. Amirshohī, ed. *Nosir-i Khusraw. Devoni ash'or: Rushnoinoma va Saodatnoma* [Nāṣir-i Khusraw. Dīvān of Poetry: the *Rawshanā'ī-nāma* and the *Saʿādat-nāma*], vol. 1. Dushanbe: Shujoiën, 2009. pp. 663. (in Tajik).

Nāṣir-i Khusraw's *Dīvān* consists of *qaṣīda*s on philosophical and theological issues, singing the praise of human intelligence and dignity, and a description of the beauty of nature as God's creation, *inter alia*. It also includes two poems – the *Rawshanā'ī-nāma* (The Book of Enlightenment) and the *Saʿādatnāma* (The Book of Happiness).

21 —— S. Shokhumorov and T. Murodova, ed. *Nosir-i Khusraw. Zod-ul-musofirin* [Nāṣir-i Khusraw. *Zād al-musāfirīn*]. Dushanbe, 2010. pp. 511. (in Tajik).

22 —— 'Uspokoenie razuma' (Otryvki) ['The Rāḥat al-ʿaql' (Selected Chapters)], *Ishrāk* [Illumination], *EIF*, 4 (2013), pp. 319–261.

An annotated translation by A. Smirnov of 'quarters' 1.6–7, 2.1 and 7, 3.1, 4.5 and 7, 5.2, 7.9–10 and 12–13 of al-Kirmānī's *Rāḥat al-ʿaql* ('Quietude of Intellect'), completely revised and with extended commentaries.

23 Almazova A.Z., ed. *Pamirskai͡a Ėkspedit͡sii͡a (stat'i i materialy polevykh issledovanii)* [Pamir Expedition (articles and field research data)]. Moscow: RAN Institut Vostokovedenii͡a, 2006. pp. 272. (in Russian).

A collection of articles, *The Pamir Expedition* introduces the reader to the history, life, traditions and culture of the people living in the mountain region called 'the Roof of the World', i.e. Tajik and Afghan Badakhshān. The publication has been prepared by a team of scholars from Russia, Tajikistan and Canada. A number of the articles are written on the basis of collected field data and others are the result of scholarly research in Moscow, London, Dushanbe and Khārūgh.

24 Amirifar, Maryam. 'The Influence of the Sayings and Poetry of Hazrat ʿAli on Nasir Khusraw's Poetry', in Sarfaroz Niyozov and Ramazon Nazariev, ed., *Nasir Khusraw: Yesterday, Today, Tomorrow*. (Proceedings of a conference held in Khārūgh, Tajikistan). Khujand: Noshir, 2005, pp. 510–513.

This paper focuses on the religious and spiritual dimensions of Nāṣir-i Khusraw's poetry, citing examples from his devotional poetry. The author suggests that Nāṣir-i Khusraw's poetry introduces the words of Ḥaḍrat ʿAlī as the starting point for Ismaili doctrine, and as such, everything becomes invaluable and sacred in the eyes of the poet.

25 Amonbekov, N. 'Aspekty ismailitskoĭ spet͡sifiki, kotorye nuzhno uchityvat' pri formirovanii nat͡sional'nogo gosudarstvo v Tadzhikistane' [A Consideration of Specific Aspects of Ismailism in the Establishment of the Nation-State of Tajikistan], in *Postroenie Doveriia͡ Mezhdu Islamistami i Secularistami* [Building Trust between Islamists and Secularists]. Dushanbe: Devashtich, 2004, pp. 229–240.

The author presents some important and specific aspects of Ismailism that should be taken into consideration by the architects of modern Tajikistan during the establishment of the Tajik nation-state.

26 Andreev, Mikhail S. and Aleksandr Aleksandrovich Polovt͡sov. 'Materialy po ėtnografii iranskikh plemën Sredneĭ Azii. Ishkashim i Wakhan' [Materials on the Ethnography of the Iranian Tribes of Central Asia. Ishkāshim and Wakhān], *Sbornik Muzeia͡ Antropologii i Ėtnografii*, 9 (1911), pp. 1–41. (in Russian).

An ethnographical study of Ishkāshim and Wakhān, which includes historical legends, remnants of the old social order, social practices, rituals and beliefs.

27 —— *Tadzhiki doliny Khuf* (Verkhov'ia͡ Amu Dar'i) [The Tajiks of the Khuf Valley (The Upper Reaches of the Amū Daryā)], vol. 1. Stalinabad: Izd-vo AN Tadzh., 1953. pp. 251. (in Russian).

28 —— *Tadzhiki doliny Khuf* (Verkhov'ia͡ Amu Dar'i) [The Tajiks of the Khuf Valley (The Upper Reaches of the Amū Daryā)], vol. 2. Stalinabad: Izd-vo AN Tadzh., 1958. pp. 524. (in Russian).

This is a study of the beliefs of the Pamir (Ismaili) people. It is a significant contribution in the field of classical Central Asian ethnography. *The Tajiks of the Khuf Valley* is an important source for the material and spiritual culture of the mountain peoples of the Pamir region. The last chapter of the first volume deals with the funeral and memorial ceremonies of the Khuf population, which is said to have many similarities with the rites of the Bartang Ismailis.

29 —— *Tadzhiki doliny Khuf* [The Tajiks of the Khuf Valley], ed. Ė. Kochumkulovoĭ. Dushanbe: 'Dzhem Keĭ Dzhi', 2020. pp. 794. (in Russian).

30 Andreyev, Sergeĭ. 'Ismaili Sects – Central Asia', *EMA*, vol. 3, pp. 183–184.

The article is about the Ismaili areas in Central Asia, their ethnolinguistic composition, religious history, beliefs and practices, and community organisation.

31 —— 'Ismailis of Central Asia', Unpublished Report for the IIS, 1998. pp. 195.

A report on the Ismail communities in Tajikistan, Afghanistan and the Northern Area of Pakistan. It details the ethno-linguistic and religious composition of Badakhshān (Afghanistan and Tajikistan), the Ismaili population of Badakhshān and their neighbours including their socio-economic and religious history.

32 Anvarzod, Mahram, ed. *Pīr Sabz ʿAlī*. Dushanbe: Paëmi Oshno, 2003. pp. 60. (in Tajik).

The work presents a series of interesting stories about the life and journeys to Central Asia of Pīr Sabz ʿAlī.

33 Arabzoda, Nozir. 'Mafhumi zamon dar falsafai Nosiri Khusrav' [The Concept of the Time in Nāṣir-i Khusraw's Philosophy], *AAF* (RSST), 1 (1985), pp. 34–40 (in Tajik).

This article deals with the ontological status of the category of time in the Nāṣir-i Khusraw's philosophical system. The philosopher traces the connection and continuity of the teachings and writings of previous Ismaili thinkers, looking at Peripatetic as well as Platonic perspectives on 'time'.

34 —— 'Ratsionalizmi shoirona' [Poetic Rationalism], *MS*, 10 (1986), pp. 35–37 (in Tajik).

This article focuses on disproving the accusations against Nāṣir-i Khusraw of being a dualist, since he never emphasised the independent existence of nature nor sought to separate religion from knowledge.

35 —— 'Muḥīṭī maʿrifat' [The Circle of Enlightenment], *SS*, 12 (1986), pp. 114–120 (in Tajik).

This analysis is focused on the two ways human beings acquire knowledge: by sensation and intellection. Through observation, sensation allows human beings to attain a knowledge of particulars, whilst through the *ʿaql* understanding of the invisible side of substances and accidents is reached.

36 —— 'Tavsifi kategoriia makon dar falsafai Nosiri Khusrav' [The Description of the Category of Space in Nāṣir-i Khusraw's Philosophy], *AAF* (RSST), *Seriiai falsafa, iqtisodiët va huquqshinosī*, 1 (1988), pp. 15–18 (in Tajik).

Nāṣir-i Khusraw shared the Peripatetic concept of space, recognising the eternity of the world and its attributes, thus also embracing Ibn Sīnā's philosophical stances.

37 —— 'Andarzi Hakimi Qubodiēnī' [The Teaching of the Ḥakim of Qubādiyān], *SS*, 12 (1989), pp. 124–130 (in Tajik).

In the moral teachings of Nāṣir-i Khusraw the existence of good and evil is traditionally linked to the realm of the soul (*nafs*). If evil and indecency are the products of ignorance, good is the fruit of moral intentions, which are triggered by knowledge.

38 —— 'Zarurati ma'rifati olam az nazari Nosiri Khusrav' [The Necessity of the Gnosis of the World According to Nāṣir-i Khusraw], *AAF* (RSST), *Seriiai falsafa, iqtisodiët va huquqshinosī*, 4 (1989), pp. 3–8 (in Tajik).

Throughout his writings, Nāṣir-i Khusraw justifies the need for knowledge *en large* in order to recognise the world. The process of learning involves understanding both the intrinsic quality and the quantitative characteristics of the material world. As a follower of Ismaili theology, Nāṣir-i Khusraw simultaneously held both theological and teleological positions, suggesting that any person is authorised by God to comprehend the world we live in.

39 —— 'Harakat az didi Nosiri Khusrav' [Motion from Nāṣir-i Khusraw's Point of View], *IH*, 12 (1989), pp. 31–33 (in Tajik).

In order to explain the various degree of motion (*haraka*) occurring in existence, Nāṣir-i Khusraw follows philosophers such as Aristotle and Ibn Sīnā and speaks of generation (*kawn*) and corruption (*fasād*), improving imperfection (*nuqṣ*), and changes and transformations in terms of motion taking place in prime matter (*hayūla*).

40 —— 'Andeshai ofarinish dar falsafai Nosiri Khusrav' [The Idea of the Creation in Nasir-i Khusraw's Philosophy], *Farhang*, 7 (1991), pp. 57–61 (in Tajik).

In Nāṣir-i Khusraw's worldview, knowledge, mysticism, philosophy and religion are intertwined; the essence of his teaching is that if any of these components separates from the others, its functionality will lose specificity and effectiveness.

41 —— 'Javhariiati jism, modda va surat az nazari Nosiri Khusrav' [The Essence of Body, Matter and Form from Nāṣir-i Khusraw's Point of View], *IH*, 2 (1991), pp. 9–11 (in Tajik).

Nāṣir-i Khusraw's ideas on matter (*hayūla*), form (*ṣūra*) and body (*jism*) followed those of the philosophers, in that 'form (*ṣūra*) is above essence (*jawhar*) and prime matter (*hayūla*), since action actualises from form (*ṣūra*) and not from prime matter (*hayūla*)'.

42 —— 'Sushchnost' dushi. Traktovka psikhofizicheskoĭ problemy v filosofii Nosiri Khusrava' [The Quintessence of Soul. The Explanation of Psychophysical Problems in Nāṣir-i Khusraw's Philosophy], *AAF* (RSST), *Seriiai falsafa, iqtisodiët va huquqshinosī*, 1 (1991), pp. 29–39. (in Russian).

For Nāṣir-i Khusraw the ratio between soul and body is effectively explained in his philosophical works. He denounces some of the inconsistencies held by the philosophers regarding the concepts of soul and body.

43 —— 'Ėjodiëti Nosiri Khusrav' (Osori adabī, falsafī, dīnī) [Nāṣir-i Khusraw's Works (Literature, Philosophy and Religion], *Ma'rifat*, 2 (1992), pp. 13–17. (in Tajik).

A brief overview and reflection of Nāṣir-i Khusraw's religio-philosophical works.

44 —— 'Shakkokii Nosiri Khusrav' [The Concept of Doubt in Nāṣir-i Khusraw's Thought], *Adab*, 5 (1992), pp. 53–59. (in Tajik).

This paper discusses Nāṣir-i Khusraw's independent thought and the courage of his philosophical-poetical expression. The author also considers Nāṣir's alleged threat to the religious establishment, for which he was condemned as a *kāfir* (unbeliever) by the Sunni *'ulamā'*.

45 —— 'Nosiri Khusrav dar borai nubuvvat va imomat' [Nāṣir-i Khusraw on Prophethood and Imamate], *IH*, 7–8 (1993), pp. 29–31 (in Tajik).

The Ismaili philosopher believed that the hierohistory of mankind develops in seven cycles or eras (sing. *dawr*) each one inaugurated by a speaking-prophet or enunciator (*nāṭiq*) of a revealed message. In the first six eras of human history the enunciator-prophets were Adam, Noah, Abraham, Moses, Jesus and Muhammad. Each *nāṭiq* was succeeded by a legatee or executor (*waṣī*). The legatees in the first six eras were Sīth (Seth), Shem, Ishmael, Aaron, Shamʿūn and ʿAlī.

46 —— 'Ta'vili Qur'on dar ilohiëti Nosiri Khusrav' [Qur'anic Esoteric Interpretation in Nāṣir-i Khusraw's Theology], *Farhang*, 1 (1993), pp. 29–31 (in Tajik).

According to Nāṣir-i Khusraw, *ta'wīl* is the knowledge possessed by the Universal Soul whose aim is to elevate the individual soul, thus enabling its return to the Origin.

47 —— *Nosir Khusrav* [Nāṣir-i Khusraw]. Dushanbe: Maʿorif, 1994. pp. 176. (in Tajik).

In his introduction, Arabzoda argues that his endeavours have produced one of the most complete works on Nāṣir-i Khusraw's philosophy. The author claims to have consolidated all previous studies on Nāṣir-i Khusraw in the former Soviet Union. The book is divided into five main topics: (i) the search for truth and justice, (ii) theology, (iii) the puzzle of being, (iv) the cognition of being, and (v) ethical teaching.

48 —— 'Odobi sukhan guftan dar taʿlimoti akhloqii Nosiri Khusrav' [The Ethics of Speech in Nāṣir-i Khusraw's Ethical Teachings], *Adab*, 7 (1996), pp. 33–37. (in Tajik).

In his poetic and religious works, Nāṣir-i Khusraw teaches the reader to communicate through a moral, philosophical, aesthetic and literary language. Speech is deemed the most fundamental aspect of the human essence.

49 —— *Ismailitskaīa filosofiīa Nosira Khusrava* [The Ismaili Philosophy of Nāṣir-i Khusraw]. Dushanbe, 1997. pp. 307. (in Russian).

50 —— *Ismailitskaia filosofiia Nosira Khusrava* [The Ismaili Philosophy of Nāṣir-i Khusraw], Dissertatsii na soiskanie uchënoĭ stepeni doktora filosofskikh nauk [PhD Candidate for the Degree of Doctor of Philosophy]. Dushanbe: Akademi Nauk, 1997–1998. pp. 293. (in Russian).

Nāṣir-i Khusraw is portrayed as a thinker whose legacy has had a major impact on the history of philosophy and the development of Tajik literature. One of the first philosophers to write in Farsi, he managed to syncretise his Weltanschauung, theology and religion with scientific knowledge, his faith with reason. His doctrine is a valid synthesis of religious and philosophical outlooks. Nāṣir-i Khusraw is, undoubtedly, the founder of the religious and philosophical genre of the *qaṣīda*.

51 —— 'Fazilati nekī va nakūkorī dar ta'limoti akhloqii Nosiri Khusrav' [The Virture of Kindness and Compassion in Nāṣir-i Khusraw's Ethical Teachings], *IH*, 1 (1999), pp. 4–6 (in Tajik).

As a medieval Muslim philosopher and an Ismaili *dāʿī*, ethical issues were at the heart of Nāṣir-i Khusraw's teachings. He argued that virtuous behaviour was meant to guide others; his ethics called for a two-fold use of the intellect: to learn and to teach.

52 —— *Mir ideĭ i razmyshleniĭ Nosira Khusrava* [Nāṣir-i Khusraw's World of Ideas and Thought]. Dushanbe: Nodir, 2003. pp. 264. (in Russian).

Nāṣir-i Khusraw is a thinker whose work has left its mark on the history of philosophy, Ismaili theology, and on the history of the literary process. He was one of the first Persian thinkers who managed to combine organically a philosophical worldview with theology, religion with scientific knowledge, and faith with reason.

53 —— 'Intellectual Trends in Nasir Khusraw's Philosophy', in Sarfaroz Niyozov and Ramazon Nazariev, ed., *Nasir Khusraw: Yesterday, Today, Tomorrow*. (Proceedings of a conference held in Khārūgh, Tajikistan). Khujand: Noshir, 2005, pp. 126–130.

In this paper it is suggested that in Nāṣir-i Khusraw's philosophy, intellect and reasoning, knowledge and learning, are objects for special analysis in epistemological, ethical and religious terms. Knowledge and learning, philosophy and theology are all so intertwined in his worldview that they make up the fundamental elements of his philosophy, and if we were to try to separate them from each other, it would very probably lose its central meaning.

Arabzoda, Nozirjon, see Arabzoda, Nozir.

54 Arapov, Aleksandr. 'Kontseptsiia Mirovogo Razuma i Mirovoĭ Dushi v russkoĭ religioznoĭ filosofii i ismailizme' [The Concepts of the Universal Intellect and Universal Soul in Russian Religious Philosophy and Ismailism], in Stanislav M. Prozorov and Hakim Elnazarov, ed., *Russian Scholars on*

Ismailism. (Proceedings of a conference held in St Petersburg in 2011). St Petersburg: Nestor-Istoriiā, 2014, pp. 92–100. (in Russian and English).

The Platonic concepts of the Universal Intellect and Universal Soul are common to both Ismaili philosophy and the Russian religious philosophy of the Silver Age (the period between 1880 and 1920, which is characterised by the emergence of various intellectual movements in Russia), whilst being alien to classical Christian philosophy.

Russian philosophers who belonged to the Russian Orthodox Church were exposed to these ideas and developed a cosmological framework which was much closer to the Ismaili teaching than to Christian theology. The paper explores this subject in detail.

55 Ashurov, Gafor Ashurovich. 'Nosiri Khisrav i ego filosofskiĭ traktat Zod al-musofirin' [Nāṣir-i Khusraw and his Philosophical Treatise *Zād al-musāfirīn*], in *Tezisy nauchnoĭ konferentsii molodykh uchënykh, posvi͡ashchennoĭ 30-letii͡u Tadzhikskoĭ SSR* [Abstracts of the Academic Conference of Young Scholars, Dedicated to the 30th Anniversary of the Tajik SSR]. Stalinabad, 1959, pp. 82–83. (in Russian).

56 —— 'Filosofskiĭ traktat Nosiri Khisrava Zod al-musofirin' [Nāṣir-i Khusraw's Philosophical Treatise *Zād al-musāfirīn*], *AAF* (RSST), 2 (1960), pp. 53–60. (in Russian).

The most significant philosophical work by Nāṣir-i Khusraw is his *Zād al-musāfirīn*. Nāṣir himself pointed this out, presenting it as his major opus. In one place Nāṣir-i Khusraw expresses his attitude to this work in the following form:

Zād al-musāfirīn – one of my creations,

If read over Plato's grave,

Plato's dust will give me praise.

57 —— 'Ob otnoshenii Nosiri Khisrava k Abu Bakru ar-Razi' [The Relationship of Nāṣir-i Khusraw and Abū Bakr al-Rāzī], *AAF* (RSST), 2 (1963), pp. 41–49. (in Russian).

58 —— 'Reshenie osnovnogo voprosa filosofii Nosiri Khisravom (na osnove analiza filosofskogo traktata Zad al-musafirin)' [The Solving of the Main Question in Philosophy by Nāṣir-i Khusraw (on the basis of an analysis of the philosophical treatise *Zād al-musāfirīn*)], *AAF* (RSST), 2 (1963), pp. 80–92. (in Russian).

According to Ashurov, Nāṣir-i Khusraw's philosophical views appear to be those of an objective idealist. However, despite his general attitude in conveying concepts as an idealist, on some occasions, Nāṣir-i Khusraw seems to propound outlooks of a somewhat more pragmatic character. Thus, according to his theory of knowledge, practice neither acts as a criterion for attaining knowledge nor as the grounds for knowledge, but finds its validity as an application of knowledge, ultimately confirming the truth of the divine revelation.

59 —— 'Nasir Khosrov' [Nāṣir-i Khusraw], *FE*, vol. 3, pp. 555–556. (in Russian).

A brief biography of Nāṣir-i Khusraw and his main works.

60 —— 'Nasirėddin Tusi' [Naṣīr al-Dīn Ṭūsī], *FE*, vol. 3, p. 556. (in Russian).

A brief biography of Naṣīr al-Dīn Ṭūsī and his works.

61 —— *Filosofskie vzgliady Nosiri Khisrava. (Na osnove analiza traktata Zad al-musafirin)* [Nāṣir-i Khusraw's Philosophical Views (based on an analysis of *Zād al-musāfirīn*)], Dissertat͡sii na soiskanie uchënoĭ stepeni kandidata filosofskikh nauk [PhD Candidate for the Degree of Doctor of Philosophy]. Dushanbe: Akademi Nauk, 1964. pp. 208. (in Russian).

62 —— *Filosofskie vzgliady Nosiri Khisrava. (Na osnove analiza traktata "Zad al-musafirin")* [Nāṣir-i Khusraw's Philosophical Views (based on an analysis of *Zād al-musāfirīn*)]. Dushanbe: Donish, 1965. pp. 113. (in Russian).

63 —— 'Aqidahoi filosofii Nosiri Khisrav' [Nāṣir-i Khusraw's Philosophical Ideas (based on an analysis of *Zād al-musāfirīn*)], ANT (SSR), *OF* (1965), pp. 11. (in Tajik).

Ashurov argues that *Zād al-musāfirīn* must be regarded as one of Nāṣir-i Khusraw's most important works of philosophy. According to the scholar, this pivotal work, which is analysed from a Marxist point of view, presents the fundamental questions of philosophy in an idealistic manner not unlike that of major medieval thinkers.

64 Asoev, A. *Ahamii͡ati ateistii tanqidi ismoilii͡a* [The Importance of the Atheist Critiques of Ismailism]. Dushanbe, 1978. (in Tajik).

65 A'wani, Gholam-Reza. 'Abu Khatim Razi i ego A'lām an-nubuvva' [Abū Ḥātim al-Rāzī and His *A'lām al-nubuwwa*], *EIF*, 4 (2013), pp. 135–139. (in Russian).

This is an abridged version of the author's introduction to al-Rāzī's *A'lām al-nubūwwa*, a critical edition of which he published together with S. al-Sawī in 1977, and of which a revised second edition was produced in 2002. A'awani praises the *A'lām al-nubuwwa* as a monumental contribution to the Islamic thought of the late 3rd/9th–early 4th/10th century. He also discusses its influence on later Ismaili thinkers, in particular Nāṣir-i Khusraw and Ḥamīd al-Dīn Kirmānī.

66 Aynī, Kamol, ed. and tr. *Nosiri Khusravi Qabodiënī. 'Gulchine az devoni ash'or* [Nāṣir-i Khusraw of Qubādiyān. *Selected Poems from the Dīvān*]. Stalinabad, 1957, pp. 35. (in Tajik).

In his introduction to this edition of selected poems from Nāṣir-i Khusraw's *Dīvān*, Kamol Aynī provides a historical background and argues that Nāṣir-i Khusraw was one of the most spirited thinkers of his time who was not cowed by the rulers of the age and advocated and spread his ideas and religious beliefs with courage.

B

67 Babaeva, Navrasta S. *Drevnie verovaniiā gornykh tadzhikov I͡Uzhnogo Tadzhikistana v pokhoronno-pominal'noĭ obri͡adnosti (konet͡s XIX – nachalo XX vv.)* [The Ancient Beliefs of the Mountain Tajiks of Southern Tajikistan in Funeral and Memorial Rites (late 19th – early 20th century)]. Dushanbe: Donish, 1993. pp. 156. (in Russian).

This is the first general ethnographic study of the traditions, particularly the funeral rites, common among the mountain Tajiks of southern Tajikistan.

68 Badakhshi, Mirzo Sangmuhammad, and Mirzo Fazlalibek Surkhafsar. *Tārīkh-i Badakhshon* [The History of Badakhshān]. Dushanbe: Donish, 2007. pp. 274. (in Tajik).

Tārīkh-i Badakhshon is a valuable historical work which covers 250 years of the history of the Tajik people in Badakhshān from around 1657 to 1907.

The work is of great value particularly in terms of the accuracy of its sources relative to the Badakhshān area and its cities. It details Badakhshān's relations with the neighbouring regions such as Khatlān, Darvāz, Chitrāl, Kāshghar, Qaṭaghan and Yarqand. The socio-political and the economic structure of the region as well as the religio-ethnic identity of the people are also discussed.

The book is divided into three parts: (i) the genealogy and hierarchy of certain personalities amongst the Shughnān *mīrs*, (ii) the biography of Sayyid Shāh Khāmūsh, and (iii) the genealogy of Sayyid ʿAlī Shāh Valī, the father-in-law of Shāh Khāmūsh.

69 Badakhshi, Saidjalol. *Bahr ul-Akhbor: silsilai hikoi͡atho doir ba haëti Nosiri Khusrav va saëhati u dar Badakhshonzamin* [The Ocean of Tales: A sequence of Legends about the Life and the Travels of Nāṣir-i Khusraw in Badakhshān]. Khārūgh: 'Pomir', 1992. pp. 70. (in Tajik).

A collection of legends and stories about Nāṣir-i Khusraw and his travels in Badakhshān.

70 Bahromova, Nasiba Arturovna. 'Ėtnokonfessional'nai͡a kul'tura pamirskikh tadzhikov: sovremennoe sostoi͡anie' [Ethnic-Confessional Culture of the Pamiri Tajiks: the Current Situation]. Bachelor thesis, Tomsk University, 2017. pp. 69. (in Russian).

Despite the long Ismaili history in the Pamirs, many traditional customs and beliefs relating to the life of the Pamiri peoples can still be observed. However, the pre-Islamic traditions have been adapted and addressed in accordance with Ismaili canons and practices.

71 Baĭburdi, Chingiz Gulam-Ali (1925–2012). 'Srednevekovyĭ persidskiĭ poèt Nizārī v Zakavkaz'e' [The Medieval Persian Poet Nizārī in the Trans-Caucasus], *IFZ*, 4 (1959), pp. 233–243. (in Russian).

Descriptions of the journey recounted in Nizārī's poetic work, *Safar-nāma*. The work reports the poet's conversation with local scholars on religious themes in the form of short stories.

72 —— *Zhizn' i tvorchestvo Nizārī – persidskogo poèta XIII-XIV vekov* [The Life and Works of Nizārī, a Persian Poet of the 13th–14th Centuries], Dissertat︠s︡ii na soiskanie uchënoĭ stepeni kandidata filologicheskikh nauk [PhD Candidate for the Degree of Doctor of Philosophy]. Leningrad, 1963. pp. 245. (in Russian).

73 —— *Zhizn' i tvorchestvo Nizārī – persidskogo poèta XIII–XIV vekov* [The Life and Works of Nīzārī, a Persian Poet of the 13th–14th Centuries]. Moscow: Nauka, 1966. pp. 272. (in Russian).

Persian (tr.), *Zindagī va āthār-i Nīzārī* [The Life and Works of Nīzarī], tr. Mahnaz Ṣadrī. Tehran: Intishārāt-i 'Ilmī, 1370 Sh./1991. pp. 290. (in Persian).

This work by Baĭburdi is a study of the life and work of the once very famous Persian Ismaili poet, Nizārī Quhistānī, who lived during the Mongol invasion of Iran and Central Asia between the 7th/13th and 8th/14th centuries.

74 —— 'Rukopisi proizvedeniĭ Nizārī' [The manuscript of Nizārī's Works], *KSINA*, 65 (1964), pp. 13–24. (in Russian).

This is a study of the works of Nizārī Quhistānī, a well-known Persian-Ismaili poet who lived in the 7th/13th and 8th/14th centuries. The study of the literary heritage of Nizārī which was initiated by Bertel's has since progressed further and several poems and two *Dīvān*s by Nizārī have been discovered.

75 —— 'Nasirèddin Tusi' [Naṣīr al-Dīn Ṭūsī], *KLE*, vol. 5, pp. 125–126. (in Russian).

A brief entry on Naṣīr al-Dīn Ṭūsī.

76 —— 'Nizari, Sadaddin ibn Shamsaddin Nizariĭe Kuhistani' [Nizārī, Saʿd al-Dīn b. Shams al-Dīn Nizārī Quhistānī], *KLE*, vol. 6, pp. 270–271. (in Russian).

A brief entry on Nizārī Quhistānī.

77 —— 'O perepiske Malik-shakha s Khasanom ibn Sabbakhom' [The Correspondence between Malik-Shāh and Ḥasan b. Ṣabbāḥ]. *Kratkoe izlozhenie dokladov nauchnoĭ konferent︠s︡ii, posvi︠a︡shchënnoĭ 60-leti︠u︡ professora A.N. Boldyreva* [Summary of Scholarly Conference Reports, Dedicated to the 60th Anniversary of Professor A.N. Boldyrev]. Moscow (1969), pp. 9–12. (in Russian).

In this article, the author analyses and edits four letters, which it is sometimes thought, the Saljūq sultan of Iran in the late 5th/11th century, Malik-Shāh and his famous vizier Niẓām al-Mulk exchanged with the dāʿī of the Iranian Ismailis and founder of the Ismaili state in Alamūt, Ḥasan-i Ṣabbāḥ.

78 —— 'Ob ideologicheskoĭ obshchnosti nekotorykh doktrin ismailizma i babizma' [Some Commonalities of the Ideological Doctrines of Ismailism and Bābism], in *FISZAA, Tezisy dokladov nauchnoĭ konferentsii, posvi͡ashchënnoĭ 120–letii͡u osnovanii͡a Vostfaka LGU.* Leningrad, 1974, pp. 58–61. (in Russian).

According to recent scholarship, the religio-philosophical ideas of Bābism can be directly attributed to the founder of the movement, Sayyid ʿAlī Muḥammad Shīrāzī. Despite the accuracy of this position, a number of scholars believe that Bābism's main ideas were actually derived from Ismaili teachings.

79 Baĭkov, A.A. 'Pechat' fatimidskogo khalifa Zakhira' [The Seal of the Fatimid Caliph Ẓāhir], *ZKV*, 5 (1930), pp. 201–219. (in Russian).

A collection of carved stones found in the State Hermitage. Cut out on flat stones with polished surfaces, the inscriptions, mostly executed in Kufic script, include the following:

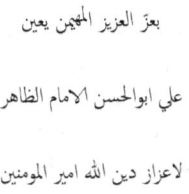

80 Baiza, Yahya. 'The Concept of *'Ilm* in the Writings of Nasir Khusraw', in Sarfaroz Niyozov and Ramazon Nazariev, ed., *Nasir Khusraw: Yesterday, Today, Tomorrow.* (Proceedings of a conference held in Khārūgh, Tajikistan). Khujand: Noshir, 2005, pp. 270–279.

This article explores some of Nāṣir-i Khusraw's major discussions on concepts such as *tawḥīd, taʾwīl* and *ʿilm.* The author regards Nāṣir-i Khusraw's notion of knowledge as an educational approach based on a systematic understanding of the purpose of creation and life in the material/physical world. Similarly, Nāṣir regards *taʾwīl* as the best method for enquiring into the religious truths.

81 —— 'Religion, Language or Ethnicity? Hybridised Identity among the Ismaili Youth of Afghanistan in Germany', in F. Ahmad and M. Seddon, ed., *Muslim Youth: Challenges, Opportunities and Expectations.* UK: Continuum International Publication Group, 2012, pp. 78–98.

This study explores the role of religion, language and ethnicity in the formation of identity among the Shiʿi Ismaili youth of Afghanistani origin who are primarily concentrated in four major regions of Essen

(Nordrhein-Westfalen), Frankfurt (Hessen), Munich (Bavaria) and Hamburg (or Freie und Hansestadt Hamburg).

82 —— 'The Hazaras of Afghanistan and their Shi'a Orientation: An Analytical Historical Survey', *Journal of Shi'a Islamic Studies*, 7, 2 (2014), pp. 151–171.

This paper begins with a critique of the existing hypotheses and interpretations, and continues with an analysis of the early Ghūrids and the Ismaili *da'wa* and their influence on the Hazara's adoption of Shi'i Islam.

83 —— 'Ismailis in Afghanistan and their Security Concerns: A Brief Synopsis', in ACCORD (Austrian Centre for Country of Origin and Asylum Research and Documentation), *Anfragebeantwortung zu Afghanistan: Sicherheitslage für Ismailiten in der Provinz Baghlan; Berichte über gezielte Angriffe durch die Taliban oder Hezb-e Islami* [Briefing on the Security Situation of Ismailis in Baghlan Province of Afghanistan; Reports of Targeted Attacks by the Taliban or Hezb-e Islami]. Vienna: ACCORD, European Country of Origin Information Network, 2015. Available online at: https://www.ecoi.net/en/document/1058514.html [Last accessed, 9 December 2018].

84 —— 'The Shi'a Isma'ili *Da'wat* in Khurasan: From its Early Beginning to the Ghaznawid Era', *Journal of Shi'a Islamic Studies*, 8, 1 (2015), pp. 37–59.

This article focuses on the rise and development of Shi'i Ismaili history in Khurāsān, from its earliest beginnings to the end of the Ghaznawid era. It demonstrates that the success of the Ismaili *da'wa* in Khurāsān was due to the high value that the Ismaili imams placed on Khurāsān as a territory ripe for their *da'wa* mission.

85 —— 'A Dream-Work: An Analysis of Nāṣer Ḳosrow's Dream and Intellectual Transformation', *International Journal of Iranian Heritage*, 1, 1 (2016), pp. 1–20.

The work analysis the contexts and the concepts of the dream which is described in Nāṣir-i Khusraw's *Safar-nāma*, and how this dream turned into a dream-work that transformed his life and enabled him to leave behind a rich intellectual legacy.

86 —— 'Authority and Rituals in the Shi'a Ismaili Tradition: An Interpretative Analysis', in A. Poya and F. Suleiman, ed., *Unity and Diversity in Contemporary Muslim Thought*. Cambridge: Cambridge Scholars Publishing, 2017, pp. 150–173.

This paper provides a brief introduction to the Nizārī Ismailis followed by an analysis of the Weberian notion of authority. There follows an analytical discussion of authority from the Shi'a, and specifically the Ismaili, perspective. It continues with a discussion on change and continuity in religious rituals, and concludes with an interpretative analysis of two concrete cases of *shahāda* (testimony) and *zakāt* (alms-giving) in the Ismaili context.

87 —— 'Authority, Identity, and Pluralism in the Modern Ismāʿīlī Religious Education Programme: A Critical Reflection', in *2017 Proceedings of the Third Annual International Conference on Shiʿi Studies*. London: ICAS Press, 2018, pp. 183–211.

This chapter presents an exploratory analysis of how the modern Ismaili religious education programme approaches the concepts of authority, identity and pluralism, and how it negotiates them with other parallel values in both Muslim-majority and minority contexts.

88 —— 'Ismāʿīliyya', *Dānishnāma-i Hazāra* (The Encyclopaedia of the Hazāra). Tehran: Hazāra Encyclopaedia Foundation, 1397 Sh./2018, pp. 471–486.

89 Bakaev, Mamadvafo. 'V poiskakh vostochnykh rukopiseĭ' [In Search of Oriental Manuscripts], *NAA*, 3 (1962), pp. 236–238. (in Russian).

At the end of August 1961, an expedition headed by Bakaev went to Badakhshān. This turned out to be very productive, with several valuable manuscripts on the history of the region being retrieved. Among the important findings was a second copy of Khwāja ʿAbd al-Nabī b. Khwāja Ṣāliḥī Yamgī's *Sīlk-i gawhar-rīz*.

90 —— 'Novye nakhodki na Pamire' [New Discoveries in the Pamirs], *NAA*, 4 (1963), pp. 236–237. (in Russian).

Towards the end of 1962, the Institute of Oriental Studies and Manuscript Heritage of the Academy of Sciences of Tajikistan organised an expedition to the GBAO region in search of manuscripts.

91 —— 'Pi͡ata͡ia pamirskai͡a ėkspedit͡sii͡a po sboru vostochnykh rukopiseĭ' [The Fifth Pamir Expedition in Search of Oriental Manuscripts], *NAA*, 3 (1964), p. 212. (in Russian).

In August 1963, the Institute of Oriental Studies and Manuscript Heritage of the Academy of Sciences of Tajikistan organised a fifth Tajik expedition to the GBAO in search of rare and valuable oriental manuscripts.

92 —— 'Fond vostochnykh rukopiseĭ AN Tadzhikskoĭ SSR i ego izuchenie' [Repository of the Oriental Manuscripts of the Academy of Sciences of the Tajik Soviet Socialist Republic], *NAA*, 6 (1965), p. 223. (in Russian).

93 —— O.F. Akimushkin et al. 'Persidskie i tadzhikskie rukopisi Instituta narodov Azii AN SSSR (Kratkiĭ alfavitnyĭ katalog)' [Persian and Tajik manuscripts of the Institute of the Peoples of Asia of the Academy of Sciences of the USSR], *NAA*, 1 (1966), p. 199. (in Russian).

94 Bamyani, Muhammad Ibrahim. 'Nasir Khusraw: Miraculous Life', in Sarfaroz Niyozov and Ramazon Nazariev, ed., *Nasir Khusraw: Yesterday, Today, Tomorrow*. (Proceedings of a conference held in Khārūgh, Tajikistan). Khujand: Noshir, 2005. pp. 632–640.

The work is the result of the author's field trips to the Badakhshān province of Afghanistan in the 1990s. He collected over 30 stories about Nāṣir-i

Khusraw. Some of these can also be found in the written historical literary sources, but the ones identified by the author are different versions of the same tales and therefore are of special importance for scholarly research on Nāṣir-i Khusraw's tradition.

95 Bandalieva, Shodigul. 'Intellect and Knowledge as the Source of the Philosophy of Hakim Nasir Khusraw', in Sarfaroz Niyozov and Ramazon Nazariev, ed., *Nasir Khusraw: Yesterday, Today, Tomorrow*. (Proceedings of a conference held in Khārūgh, Tajikistan). Khujand: Noshir, 2005, pp. 37–44.

Human understanding of the spiritual realities such as the Intellect and the Soul is said to be possible through the material world that, via sense perception, allows the human mind to grasp the spiritual realm.

96 —— 'Sootnoshenie Razuma i Very v uchenii Nasir Khusrava' [The Balance of Reason and Faith in the Teachings of Nāṣir-i Khusraw], *IANRT*, 4 (2015), pp. 51–58.

This is an article that deals with the correlation between the soul and the intellect according to Nāṣir-i Khusraw's view as reflected in his religious and philosophical works.

97 —— *Nravstvennaia filosofiia Nasira Khusrava* [Nasir-i Khusraw's Moral Philosophy], Institute Filosofy, Politologii i Prava im A. Bakhovaddinova Akademii Nauk Respubliki Tadzhikistan [A. Bakhovaddinova Institute of Philosophy, Political Science and Rights of the Academy of Science of the Republic of Tajikistan]. Dissertatsiia na soiskanie uchenoĭ stepeni doktora filosofii PhD [PhD Candidate for the Degree of Doctor of Philosophy]. Dushanbe: Akademi Nauk, 2018. pp. 200.

The origin of the ethical philosophy of Nāṣir-i Khusraw is analysed on the basis of his major philosophical works, in particular, his *Zād al-musāfirīn*, *Khwān al-ikhwān*, *Gushāyish va Rahāyish* and *Jāmiʿ al-ḥikmatayn*, as well as his *Dīvān*. In both his poetic and religious works, Nāṣir-i Khusraw teaches the reader to communicate through a moral, philosophical, aesthetic and literary language. Speech is deemed the most fundamental aspect of the human essence.

98 Bartol'd, V.V. *K istorii krestʾi͡anskikh dvizheniĭ v Persii* [On the History of Peasant Movements in Persia]. *Sochineniia*, vol. VII. Moscow: Nauka, 1971, pp. 438–449. (in Russian).

99 —— 'K istorii krestʾi͡anskikh dvizheniĭ v Persii' [On the History of Peasant Movements in Persia], *Iz dalekogo i blizkogo proshlogo. Sbornik ėti͡udov iz vseobshcheĭ istorii v chestʾ 50-letii͡a nauchnoĭ zhizni N.I. Kareeva* [On a Distant and Near Past. A Collection of Sketches from Universal History in Honour of the 50th Anniversary of the Scholarly Activity of N.I. Kareev]. Moscow: Myslʾ, 1923, pp. 54–62. (in Russian).

The author has tried to draw a connection between the Ismaili movement and the peasant masses revolting against the mainly land-owning local aristocracy in the medieval era.

100 Battis, Matthias. *Aleksandr A. Semenov (1873–1958): Colonial Power, Orientalism and Soviet Nation-building*, PhD dissertation, University of Oxford, 2016. pp. 269.

An examination of Semënov's career, scholarship and personal networks on the basis of his personal archive in Tajikistan's Academy of Sciences, which has not been researched in a systematic way since the 1970s. This thesis also includes a section on 'Semënov and the Ismailis in Tashkent 1912–1916'.

101 Beben, Daniel. *The Legendary Biographies of Nāṣir-i Khusraw: Memory and Textualization in Early Modern Persian Ismāʿīlism*, PhD dissertation, Indiana University, 2015. pp. 444.

This is an examination of the legendary biographical traditions concerning the 5th/11th-century Ismaili philosopher and missionary Nāṣir-i Khusraw and their significance for the history of the Badakhshān region of Central Asia.

102 —— 'Islamisation on the Iranian Periphery: Nasir-i Khusraw and Ismailism in Badakhshan', in A.C.S. Peacock, ed., *Islamisation: Comparative Perspective from History*. Edinburgh: Edinburgh University Press, 2017, pp. 317–335.

This study examines the spread of Islam in Asia through a case study of the Shiʿi Ismaili community of the highland Badakhshān region of Central Asia, a historical province encompassing the mountainous districts of present-day north-eastern Afghanistan and eastern Tajikistan, along with bordering areas of northern Pakistan and north-west China.

103 —— 'Religious Identity in the Pamirs: The Institutionalisation of the Ismāʿīlī *Daʿwa* in Shughnān', in Dagikhudo Dagiev and Carole Faucher, ed., *Identity, History and Trans-Nationality in Central Asia: The Mountain Communities of Pamir*. London: Routledge, 2018, pp. 123–142.

This paper explores the Shughnān region in Ismaili history and examines the process by which the Ismaili *daʿwa* (summons), with its roots in Iran and the Near East, came to be embedded in the social and political structure of Shughnān, resulting in the close affiliation of Ismaili and Pamiri identity that is present in the region today. In particular, the paper examines a critical and yet uncharted development that occurred between the 11th/17th and 13th/19th centuries, in which a resurgence of the Ismaili *daʿwa* in the broader Badakhshān region coincided with a new process of state formation in Shughnān.

104 —— 'The Ismaili of Central Asia', *Oxford Research Encyclopedia of Asian History*, Online Publication Date: Apr 2018. Available online

at: http://oxfordre.com/asianhistory/view/10.1093/acrefore/9780190277727.001.0001/acrefore-9780190277727-e-316 [Last accessed, 11 June 2019].

The work is a historical survey of the Ismailis in Central Asia from the arrival of the Ismaili daʿwa in Central Asia in the early 4th/10th century up to the present time.

105 —— 'The *Kalām-i Pīr* and Its Place in the Central Asian Ismaʿili Tradition', *Journal of Islamic Studies* (2018), pp. 1–34.

This paper is a study of the *Kalām-i pīr*, a text on religious doctrine preserved among the Shiʿi Ismaili community of the Badakhshān region of Central Asia, attributed to the 5th/11th-century Ismaili author, Nāṣir-i Khusraw.

106 —— 'Aḥmad Yasavī and the Ismāʿīlīs of Badakhshān: Towards a New Social History of Sufi–Shīʿī Relations in Central Asia', *Journal of the Economic and Social History of the Orient* (2020), pp. 643–681.

The paper examines how a text attributed to the renowned Central Asian Sufi figure Aḥmad Yasavī came to be found within a manuscript produced within the Ismaili Shiʿi community of the Shughnān district of the Badakhshān region of Central Asia.

107 —— 'The *Ṣaḥīfat al-nāẓirīn*: Reflections on Authorship and Confessional Identity in a Fifteenth-Century Central Asian Text', in Wafi Momin, ed., *Texts, Scribes and Transmission: Manuscript Cultures of the Ismaili Communities and Beyond*. London, (forthcoming).

This paper contends that Ghiyāth al-Dīn ʿAlī b. Amīrān Sayyid al-Ḥusaynī al-Iṣfahānī (fl. 9th/15th century) should most probably be identified as the original author of the *Ṣaḥīfat al-nāẓirīn*. Further, the author examines some of the possibilities that may explain the apparent shift in the text's attribution to Sayyid Suhrāb, which in turn may shed some additional light on the biography of this important yet enigmatic figure in the Ismaili history of Central Asia.

108 —— 'Reimagining *Taqiyya*: The "Narrative of the Four Pillars" and Strategies of Secrecy among the Ismāʿīlīs of Central Asia ', *History of Religions*, 59 (2019), pp. 81–107.

The article examines the issue through a case study of the Ismaili community of the mountainous Badakhshān region of Central Asia. It reassesses the place of *taqiyya* in the relationship between Ismailism and Sufism, which has frequently been cited as constituting a form of disguise for Ismailis engaged in the practice of precautionary dissimulation.

109 Behronov, Jumʾa S. 'Koran i Nasiri Khusrav' [The Qurʾan and Nāṣir-i Khusraw], *IANRT*, 2 (2010), pp. 98–102. (in Russian).

Nāṣir-i Khusraw's relationship to the Qurʾan. As a devoted Muslim, Nāṣir quoted the Qurʾan widely in his works. All his written works are in the spirit of, and refer to, Qurʾanic verses and prophetic *ḥadīth*s.

110 —— 'Ispol'zovanie aīatov Korana v kasydakh Nosira Khusrava' [The Use of Qur'anic verses in the *Qaṣīdas* of Nāṣir-i Khusraw], Izvestiīa Akademii nauk Respubliki Tadzhikistan, *Nauchnyĭ zhurnal* [Proceedings of the Academy of Sciences of the Republic of Tajikistan, Scientific Journal], 2 (2010), pp. 131–135. (in Tajik).

111 —— 'Rol' ta'vil v poėzii Nasiri Khusrava' [The Role of *Ta'wīl* in Nāṣir-i Khusraw's Poetry], *IANRT*, 3–4 (2010), pp. 98–110. (in Russian).

The important role of *ta'wīl* in poetry from Nāṣir-i Khusraw's standpoint.

112 —— 'Ėticheskie myshleniīa v poėzii Nosira Khusrava' [Ethical Thinking in the Poetry of Nāṣir-i Khusraw], *VTNU SFN*, 8 (2011), pp. 33–37. (in Russian).

This article is devoted to the ethical problems in Nāṣir-i Khusraw's poems. The poet touches upon many cosmic issues whilst simultaneously examining human ethics. He emphasises the point that ethics and enlightenment are the source of the religion of Islam. The author, very precisely, formulates his position on the role of poetry in addressing social problems.

113 —— 'Ssylki na Sury Korana v poėzii Nosira Khusrava' [References to *Sūras* of the Qur'an in Nāṣir-i Khusraw's Poetry], *VTNU SFN*, 8 (2014), pp. 220–224. (in Russian); also in: *VTNU SFN*, 4–5 (2014), pp. 91–95.

The article provides a short background on the usage of Qur'anic references in the works of Nāṣir-i Khusraw. As well as a semantic analysis of the poetic texts, the author studies some Qur'anic verses.

114 —— 'Nosiri Khusrav dar tazkiraho' [Nāṣir-i Khusraw in Anthologies], *VTNU SFN*, 8 (2014), pp. 98–102. (in Tajik). In *VTNU SFN*, 4 (2014), pp. 220–224.

The article analyses a number of sources, particularly anthologies where the authors have focused on Nāṣir-i Khusraw. Behronov investigates and questions some of the information provided in these anthologies and offers an objective evaluation of comments on the poetry of Nāṣir-i Khusraw. He achieves this by showing the significance of Nāṣir-i Khusraw's works in the context of the Persian poetic tradition.

115 —— 'She'ru shoiri dar nazari mazhabii Nosiri Khusrav' [Poem and Poetry in Nāṣir-i Khusraw's Religious View], *VKU*, Seriīa 10 (2014), pp. 84–88. (in Tajik).

The task and duty of poetry, according to Nāṣir-i Khusraw, is to promote religious moral values. In his view, religion must be based on reason and it must improve human behaviour.

116 —— *Koranicheskie motivy v poėzii Nosira Khusrava* [Qur'anic motives in the poetry of Nāṣir-i Khusraw], Dissertatsiīa na soiskanie uchënoĭ stepeni kandidata filologicheskikh nauk [PhD Candidate for the Degree of Doctor of Philosophy]. Dushanbe: Akademi Nauk, 2015. pp. 176. (in Russian).

The main purpose of this dissertation is to identify Qur'anic verses in the Persian-Tajik poetry of the 5th/11th century with a particular focus on Nāṣir-i Khusraw as an outstanding representative of this literary genre. The thesis analyses the process of how Qur'anic motifs imbued Nāṣir-i Khusraw's poetry.

117 Bekov, Komildzhon. 'Ikhvan-us-safa' [Ikhwān al-ṣafā'], in *Istoriia tadzhikskoĭ filosofii (s drevneĭshikh vremën do XV v.)* [The History of Tajik Philosophy (from Ancient times to the 15th century)], ed. A. Mukhammadkhodzhaev and K. Olimov. Dushanbe: Donish, 2011, vol. 2, pp. 288–311. (in Russian).

Some modern scholars are inclined to regard the *Ikhwān al-Ṣafā'* as followers of the Ismaili faith whilst a number of them have also argued that the epistles of the *Ikhwān al-Ṣafā'* were produced by the early Ismaili imams. One common aspect between the 'Brethren of Purity' and the Ismailis is that the two ideological schools pursued their ultimate spiritual goal in secret. Despite the similarities, the author holds that the *Ikhwān al-ṣafā'* and the Ismailis differ from each other in several aspects of their philosophical interpretations and understanding of the world.

118 Bekzoda, Komil. 'Nosiri Khusrav va muammoi falsafai milli' [Nāṣir-i Khusraw and the Puzzle of National Philosophy], *NP*, 4 (2003), pp. 131–136. (in Tajik).

119 —— 'Nasir Khusraw and the Puzzle of National Philosophy', in Sarfaroz Niyozov and Ramazon Nazariev, ed., *Nasir Khusraw: Yesterday, Today, Tomorrow*. (Proceedings of a conference held in Khārūgh, Tajikistan). Khujand: Noshir, 2005. pp. 44–49.

Notwithstanding the fact that Nāṣir-i Khusraw faced persecution, his love and affection for his native Khurāsān, where he lived as an *āzādmard*, never diminished. In his works, he considered the intellect, wisdom and reasoning as genuine tools for reaching the real meaning of humanity. His rationalist approach is still today deemed the hallmark of his intellectual contribution.

120 —— ed. *Nosir-i Khusraw. Khon-ul-ikhvon* [Nāṣir-i Khusraw. Khwān al-ikhwān]. Dushanbe: ER-graff, 2012. pp. 331. (in Tajik).

Khwān al-Ikhwān occupies a special place among Nāṣir's works as it explicitly invokes his philosophical teachings but demonstrates implicitly the influence of other esoteric philosophical systems.

121 Beliaev, E.A. (1895–1964). 'Ismaility' [The Ismailis] in his *Musul'manskoe sektantsvo (istoricheskie ocherki)* [Muslim Sectarianism (historical essays)]. Moscow, 1957, pp. 47–54. (in Russian).

The author examines different religious *ṭarīqa*s in Islam, including that of the Ismailis. Its origins are traced back to the time of Ismāʿīl (d. 136/754), son of the Imam Jaʿfar al-Ṣādiq. The article also discusses the emergence of the Qarmaṭī movement and its relationship to the early Ismailis.

122 Berezin, Il'iā Nikolaevich (1818–1896). 'Vostochnye reformatory-assasiny' [The Oriental Reformers – The Assassins], *Sovremennik* (St Petersburg), 10 (1857), pp. 93–122. (in Russian).

One of the first works on Ismaili studies by a Russian scholar, this article focuses mainly on the reformers who acted under the leadership of Ḥasan-i Ṣabbāḥ at Alamūt and the resistance mounted by the Ismaili *dāʿī*s and *fidāʾī*s during this period to their opponents.

123 Bertel's, Andreĭ Evgen'evich (1926–1995). *Nasir-i Khosrov i ego vremiā* [Nāṣir-i Khusraw and his Time], Dissertatsii na soiskanie uchënoĭ stepeni kandidata filologicheskikh nauk [PhD Candidate for the Degree of Doctor of Philosophy] (Moscow, 1952). pp. 260. (in Russian).

124 —— 'Rudaki i karmaty' [Rūdakī and the Qarmaṭīs], in *Rudaki i ego ėpokha* [Rūdakī and his Epoch] (Stalinabad, 1958), pp. 63–78. (in Russian).

Following the deposition of Amīr Naṣr I (301–331/914–943) as ruler of the Sāmānid state, the author argues, the Ismailis could have become the subject of detractors who condemned them as 'Qarmaṭīs' and were therefore liable to be persecuted.

125 —— *Nasir-i Khosrov i ismailizm* [Nāṣir-i Khusraw and Ismailism]. AN USSR, IV. Moscow: Izdatel'stvo Vostochnoĭ Literatury, 1959. pp. 289. (in Russian). Persian tr., *Nāṣir-i Khusraw va Ismāʿīliyān*, tr., Yaḥyā Āriyanpūr. Tehran, 1346 Sh./1967. pp. 323.

In *Nāṣir-i Khusraw and Ismailism*, the author addresses the development of the Ismaili community during the time of Nāṣir-i Khusraw against the backdrop of contemporary society. He explores the role of Nāṣir in this, presenting an analysis of his philosophical treatises and poetic verses.

126 —— 'Nakhodki novykh rukopiseĭ v Tadzhikistane' [New Manuscript Discoveries in Tajikistan], *PV*, 6 (1959), pp. 222–223. (in Russian).

In August 1959, the Institute of Oriental Studies and Manuscript Heritage of the Academy of Sciences organised an expedition to the GBAO region where several valuable and rare oriental manuscripts were discovered. Amongst these, a biography of Ḥasan-i Ṣabbāḥ, *Uṣūl al-ādāb*, *Rūḥnāma* and a few small manuscripts such as the *Kitāb al-majmūʿ az haft gūnāh*, *Dar bayān-i haft jasad-i jismānī* attributed to Nāṣir-i Khusraw. Other works include *Ṭulūʿ-i Shams* by Khākī Khurāsānī, a copy of the *Rasāʾil Ikhwān al-Ṣafāʾ*, and *Rawḍa-yi taslīm* by Naṣīr al-Dīn Ṭūsī.

127 —— 'Otchet o rabote pamirskoĭ ėkspeditsii otdela vostokovedeniiā i pis'mennogo nasledii͡a Akademii Nauk Tadzhikskoĭ SSR (avgust 1995)' [Report on the Work of the Pamir Expedition of the Department of Oriental Studies and Written Heritage of the Academy of Science of the Republic of Tajikistan (August 1959)], *IAN* (TSSR), 2 (1959), pp. 11–16. (in Russian).

This collection of manuscripts, published in 1959, is of great academic importance. It enhances our understanding of the cultural life of the people in the Pamirs before the October 1917 Revolution.

128 —— 'Nakhodki rukopiseĭ na Pamire' [Discoveries of Manuscripts in the Pamirs], *NAA*, 2 (1961), pp. 234–236. (in Russian).

A detailed list of the manuscripts discovered during the author's fieldwork in the Pamir region.

129 —— 'Ismailitskai͡a literature' [Ismaili Literature], *KLE*, vol. 3, pp. 203–204. (in Russian).

Brief information on Ismaili literature and the leading Ismaili intellectuals.

130 —— and Mamadvafo Bakaev. *Alfavitnyĭ katalog rukopiseĭ obnaruzhennykh v Gorno-Badakhshanskoĭ avtonomnoĭ oblasti ėkspedit͡sieĭ 1959–1963 gg.* [Alphabetic Catalogue of Manuscripts Found by the 1959–1963 Expedition to the GBAO], ed. Bobojon G. Ghafurov and A.M. Mirzoev. Moscow, 1967, pp. 120. (in Russian).

Persian tr., *Fihrist-i nuskhahā-yi khaṭṭī-yi mawjūd dar wilāyat-i Badakhshān-i Tājikistān*, tr. Qudrat-Beg Īlchī and Sayyid Anwar Shāh Khomarov. Qumm, 1376 Sh./1997. pp. 140.

During five years of fieldwork in the GBAO (1959–1963), the expedition examined 117 manuscripts. Palaeographic descriptions were prepared, the manuscripts were photographed and then the originals were returned to their owners who regard them as family heritage. The catalogue was compiled on the basis of photocopies and diaries written in the course of the expedition. This material is now kept at the Department of Oriental Studies in Dushanbe.

The collection described in the catalogue consists of 186 works. At least 30 manuscripts were shown to be absolutely new discoveries.

131 —— 'Nosir Khosrov' [Nāṣir-i Khusraw], *KLE*, vol. 5, p. 125. (in Russian).

Brief information on Nāṣir-i Khusraw's life and works.

132 —— *Vvedenie v izuchenie tekstov traktatov "Āfāqnāma". Pi͡at' filosofskikh traktatov na temu "Afaq va anfus"* (O sootnoshenii mezhdu chelovekom i vselennoĭ)' [Introduction to the Study of the Text of the Treatises. Five Philosophical Treatises on *Āfāq va Anfus* (On the Relationship Between Man and the Universe)]. Moscow, 1970. pp. 511. (in Russian).

Bertel's argues that the book *Five Philosophical Treatises on Āfāq va Anfus* is of exceptional importance for the study of Ismaili philosophical and theological concepts. The volume critically analyses some of the pivotal philosophical and theological ideas of the Ismailis of Badakhshān. Although Bertel's manages to explain objectively many questions of Ismaili philosophy and theology, in contrast to previous authors he does not address each of these problems individually.

133 —— 'Arzish-i mīrāth-i adabī-yi Nāṣir-i Khusraw' [The Value of Nāṣir-i Khusraw's Works], *Sophia Perennis*, 1 (1975), pp. 31–42. (in Persian).

This monograph is the most comprehensive work on the life and work of Nāṣir-i Khusraw in terms of history and philology. Bertel's, who was a prominent Russian academic, challenges the one-sidedness of a number of his colleagues and their failure to evaluate Nāṣir-i Khusraw's literary heritage in its entireity.

134 —— 'Naẓariyāt-i barkhī az ʿurafā va Shīʿayān-i Ithnāʿasharī rājiʿ bi arzish-i mīrāth-i adabī-yi Nāṣir-i Khusraw', in *Yādnāma-yi Nāṣir-i Khusraw*, ed. Dānishgāh-i Firdawsī, Dānishkada-yi Adabiyyāt va ʿUlūm-i Insānī (Faculty of Letters and Humanities of the University of Mashhad), Mashhad: Dānishgāh-i Firdawsī, 1355 Sh./1976, pp. 96–121. (in Persian).

135 —— 'Nasir Khosrov' [Nāṣir-i Khusraw], *BSE*, vol. 17, p. 880. (in Russian); also as 'Naser-e Khosrow' [Nāṣir-i Khusraw], in *GSE*, New York: Macmillan; London: Collier Macmillan, 1978, vol. 17, p. 349.

A brief biography and bibliographical list of Nāṣir-i Khusraw's works.

136 —— 'Poėticheskiĭ kommentariĭ shakha Niʾmatullakha Vali na filosofskuiu kasydu Nasir-i Khusrau' [A Poetic Commentary by Shāh Niʿmat Allāh Walī on a Philosophical *Qaṣīda* by Nāṣir-i Khusraw], in *Sad odnogo t͡svetka* [The garden of one flower]. Moscow: Nauka, 1991, pp. 7–30. (in Russian).

Bertel's talks about his peregrinations in the villages in Badakhshān in the summer of 1960, during which he acquired a small collection of poems, edited by the copyist Sayyid Muḥammad Shāh Zāda between 1906 and 1922. This was then the object of study by the Russian Orientalist, A.A. Semënov, who analysed Shāh Zāda's deep knowledge of philosophy and his love for poetry.

In the collection, Bertel's admits to having been struck by one particular '*Qaṣīda* that was attributed to Sayyid Nāṣir-i Khusraw and for each of the *bayt*s (couplets) Shāh Niʿmat Allāh Walī provided a commentary'. Bertel's questions the authenticity of this work, and asks, among other things, why a Sufi master would have produced a commentary on an Ismaili poem 300 years after its author's death.

137 Bertel's (Berthels), Evgeniĭ Ėduardovich (1890–1957). 'Nasir-i Khusrau i ego vzgli͡ad na poėzii͡u' [Nāṣir-i Khusraw and his View of Poetry], *IANRT*, 4 (1953), pp. 139–153; also in *Izbrannye Trudy*. Moscow: Nauka, 1988, pp. 139–153. (in Russian).

According to Bertel's, the Sufi concept of ecstasy does not find any place in Nāṣir-i Khusraw's poetry.

138 —— 'Ismaility' [Ismailis], *BSE*, vol. 19. 2nd ed., Moscow: BSE, 1953. (in Russian).

139 —— 'Nasir Khisrav' [Nāṣir-i Khusraw], *BSE*, vol. 29. 2nd ed., Moscow: BSE, 1954. (in Russian).

140 Bliss, Frank. *Social and Economic Change in the Pamirs (Gorno-Badakhshan, Tajikistan)*, tr. from German by Nicola Pacult and Sonia Guss with the support of Tim Sharp. Abingdon: Routledge, 2005, pp. 400.

This book deals with the history, anthropology and recent social and economic developments of the Pamiri people in Gorno-Badakhshān. Following the collapse of the Soviet Union, such high mountain areas were more or less forgotten and people would have suffered severely from the region's isolation had an AKF project in 1993 not afforded broader support.

141 Bobo, Faizulloev. 'The Characters of Muhammad Mustafa and 'Ali Murtaza in Nasir Khusraw's Poems', in Sarfaroz Niyozov and Ramazon Nazariev, ed., *Nasir Khusraw: Yesterday, Today, Tomorrow* (Proceedings of a conference held in Khārūgh, Tajikistan). Khujand: Noshir, 2005, pp. 142–150.

The article attempts to describe the personality of both the Prophet of Islam and the fourth caliph, 'Alī, giving prominence to their distinctive relationship. In addition to Nāṣir-i Khusraw's poems, the author employs many other sources to analyse what is for many Muslims an ethical issue.

142 Bobrinskoĭ, Alekseĭ Aleksandrovich (1852–1927). 'Sekta ismail'ia̍ v russkikh i bukharskikh predelakh Sredneĭ Azii' [The Ismaili Denomination in Russian and Bukharan Central Asia], *EO*, 2 (1902), pp. 1–20; also published separately, Moscow, 1902. pp. 18. (in Russian). Also in Stanishevskiĭ, A.V. *Ismailizm na Pamire* (1902–1931) [Ismailism in the Pamirs (1902–1931)]. Sbornik documentov [Collection of Documents], compiled by A.V. Stanishevskiĭ. Academiia̍ Nauk USSR, Glavnoe Arkhivnoe Upravlenie pri-Sovete Ministrov Uzbekskoĭ SSR: Institut Vostokovedeniia̍ [The Main Archive Directorate of the Council of Ministers of the Uzbek SSR: Institute of Oriental Studies], pp. 87–108. (in Russian).

In 1901, Bobrinskoĭ visited the region of Badakhshān where he met the local Ismailis, their *pīr*s, and representatives of Sunni and Shi'i Muslims. Following such encounters, he became convinced that the English sources he analysed were correct with regard to the information they provided on the Ismaili inhabitants of the Wakhān, Ishkāshim, Ghārān, Shughnān and Rūshān districts.

143 —— *Gort͡sy verkhov'ev pi͡andzha* (wakhant͡sy i ishkashimt͡sy) [The Mountain People of the Upper Panj (the Wakhīs and Ishkāshimīs)]. Moscow: n.p., 1908. pp. 158. (in Russian).

The book begins with a general description of the headwaters of the Panj River (Amū Daryā) located between the southwestern slopes of the northern spurs of the Pamir and Hindu Kush ranges. The subsequent chapters are observations on the mountain tribes of Wakhān and Ishkāshim and the legends surrounding these mountain tribes, which resulted in a general characterisation of the population of the region in the late 19th–early 20th centuries. The seventh chapter provides brief historical information on Wakhān. Further, the author provides an ethnographic description of the inhabitants of the upper reaches of the Panj River, and discusses the handicraft industry and commerce of the local tribes, their ritual practices and customs. In the final chapters of Bobrinskoĭ describes the ruins of local castles, shrines and caves.

144 Bogoutdinov, Alautdin Mukhmudovich (1911–1970). 'Nasir Khisrau' [Nāṣir-i Khusraw], in *Obshchestvenno-filosofskai͡a mysl' tadzhikskogo naroda v period XI-XV vekov. Izbrannye proizvedenii͡a.* Dushanbe: Donish, 1980, pp. 277–285. (in Russian).

Bogoutdinov examines Nāṣir-i Khusraw's philosophical and religious perception, with a reference to Marxist ideology. Nāṣir is depicted as a representative of the progressive ideology of the peasants, focusing on protecting and defending the interests of the working people.

145 —— 'Nasir Khisrau' [Nāṣir-i Khusraw], in *Ocherki po istorii tadzhikskoĭ philosofii* [Essays on the History of Tajik Philosophy]. 3rd ed., Dushanbe: Donish, 2011, pp. 148–159. (in Russian).

Adopting the outlook of Marxist materialist philosophy, the author interprets Nāṣir-i Khusraw as an irreconcilable fighter against the ruling elite who protected the interests of the working class. Nāṣir-i Khusraw was a mirror of his time: the anger of the working masses against their cruel feudal exploitation, the fight against official religion, disputes between the different groups in Islam, and the struggle of science against religious ignorance, are all themes reflected in his writings.

146 Boldyrev, Aleksandr N. (1909–1993). 'Byl li Rudaki ismailitom?' [Was Rūdakī an Ismaili?], *Archiv Orientalni*, 30 (1962), pp. 541–542. (in Russian).

Even though scholars such as A. Krymskiĭ and S. Nafīsī undoubtedly regarded Rūdakī as a Qarmaṭī-Ismaili, according to more cautious perspectives, such as that of A. Mirzoev and A. Bertel's, Rūdakī's relationship with the Ismailis consisted of a series of episodic conjunctures; therefore, Rūdakī can be neither considered an active figure of the Ismaili movement nor an Ismaili poet.

147 —— 'Tragedii͡a pravdoiskatelia͡' [The Tragedy of the Truth Seeker], *ZV*, 10 (1966), pp. 158–168. (in Russian).

148 —— 'Tragedii͡a pravdoiskatelia͡' [The Tragedy of the Truth Seeker], in *Iz istorii persidskoĭ i tadzhikskoĭ literatury* [On the History of Persian and Tajik Literature]. Moscow: Nauka, 1972, pp. 303–326. (in Russian).

Nāṣir-i Khusraw believed in the power of human cognition. On the basis of two causes that trigger the existence of all creatures, both spiritual and physical, he divided the objects of knowledge into speculative and sensual.

149 Bol'shakov, Oleg G. 'Al-Fatimiíun', in *IES* [The Fatimids], *A Concise Dictionary*. Moscow, 1991, pp. 253–354. (in Russian).

The Fatimid dynasty of the Shi'i Ismaili caliphs traces its origins from Fāṭima bint Muḥammad, through Ismā'īl b. Ja'far. However, according to the author, the true genealogy of the imams during the occultation remains obscure; he believes that even Ismaili sources suggested different times and names, whilst the Sunnis, in most cases, deny the 'Alid origins of the Fatimids.

150 Boyko, Vladimir. 'On the Margins of the Amanullah Era in Afghanistan: The Shughnan Rebellion of 1925', *International Journal of Central Asian Studies*, 7 (2002), pp. 67–78.

In the summer of 1925 the civil unrest which took place in the Ismaili districts of Shughnān and Rūshān, a mountainous area lying across the Afghan-Soviet border, became one of the events that eventually led to the overthrow of Afghan reformist ruler, King Amanullah in 1929.

151 Browne, Edward G. 'Nasir-i-Khusraw, Poet, Traveller, and Propagandist', *The Journal of the Royal Asiatic Society of Great Britain and Ireland* (Apr., 1905), pp. 313–352.

The article discusses the biography of Nāṣir-i Khusraw and disputes amongst scholars with regard to his personality and place of birth. Browne refers to Professor Rieu, who argued that there were two Nāṣir-i Khusraws, having the same name and the same *kunya* or cognomen.

152 Bubnova, M.A. *Proíavleniía drevnikh kul'tov v religioznoĭ praktike ismailitov Gorno-Badakhshanskoĭ Avtonomnoĭ Oblasti (po arkheologicheskim istochnikam)* [Manifestations of Ancient Cults in Religious Practices of the Ismailis of GBAO (according to archaeological sources)], *Materialy XXXIII sredneaziatsko-kavkazskikh chteniĭ 2008–2009 gg, EIAK* (2009), pp. 358–364. (in Russian).

According to this research, pre-Islamic faiths and beliefs are deeply rooted in the views and religious practices of the Ismailis of the western Pamir, and they appeared long before the acceptance of the Ismaili faith in Badakhshān.

153 Buniíatov, D. Ziía-Ogly. *Vosstaniía karmatov (IX-X v.v.)* [The Revolt of the Qarmaṭis (9th–10th century)]. Baku: 'Ėlm', 1988. pp. 124. (in Russian).

The research is devoted to the Qarmaṭīs, one of the most radical religious communities of their time, who led an armed struggle against Sunni Islam and the Abbasid caliphate for many years. Their ideological programmes propounded equality for all members of the community, whilst their slogans called for the coming of the True Imam.

154 Bushkov, Valentin and Tokhir Kalandarov. 'Ismaility Tadzhikistana: Traditsii i Sovremennost' [The Ismailis of Tajikistan: Tradition and Modernity], *Central Asia and the Caucasus*, 6 (2002), pp. 130–135. Available online at: http://www.ca-c.org/journal/2002/journal_rus/cac-06/15.busrus.shtml [Last accessed, 9 Nov. 2014]. (in Russian and English).

This article discusses issues of the lives, as well as the religious beliefs, of the poorly studied peoples of the western Pamir, who inhabit the Gorno-Badakhshān Autonomous Region of Tajikistan.

155 Buzurg-Zoda, Lutfullo, and B. Niëzmuhammadov. 'Nosiri Khisrav' [Nāṣir-i Khusraw], *Kommunist Tadzhikistana* [Communist of Tajikistan], 13 (1940). (in Russian).

In this article, the authors praise Nāṣir-i Khusraw for his 'sincere and fervent' criticism of the ruling class and the clergy on account of their 'wrongdoings' and for his 'selfless' and 'brave' struggle against 'the corruption of those in power'.

156 Buzurg-Zoda, Lutfullo. *Iskatel' pravdy i spravedlivosti Nosir Khisrou* [Nāṣir-i Khusraw, Seeker of Truth and Justice]. Stalinabad: Izbrannoe, 1949, pp. 232. (in Russian).

157 —— *Iskatel' pravdy i spravedlivosti Nosir Khisroy* [Nāṣir-i Khusraw, Seeker of Truth and Justice], in Valii Samad and Dovari Samad, ed., *Durakhshi īak akhtari sūzon* [A Flash of Sparkling Light]. Dushanbe: Matbuot, 2001, pp. 87–94.

Devotion to his beliefs was, according to Buzurg-Zoda, the misfortune of Nāṣir-i Khusraw life's journey. He argues that, without realising it, Nāṣir-i Khusraw was engaged in a humanistic struggle for justice and truth. However, his works, which the author claims are deeply permeated with Marxist teachings, were also at odds with his Ismaili religiosity.

C

158 Charoghabdolov, Alisho. 'Movement and Time from Nasir Khusraw's Perspectives and their Relation to the Perspectives of Contemporary Thinkers', in Sarfaroz Niyozov and Ramazon Nazariev, ed., *Nasir Khusraw: Yesterday, Today, Tomorrow* (Proceedings of a conference held in Khārūgh, Tajikistan). Khujand: Noshir, 2005, pp. 221–227.

This is a comparative analysis of a medieval philosophical problem, the question of time and movement. It offers comparisons with the views of the 20th-century scientist Albert Einstein. The author also discusses the theological aspect of the issue as expressed in Nāṣir-i Khusraw's works.

159 Chorshanbe, Goibnazarov. *Qaṣīda-khonī: A Musical Expression of Identities in Badakhshan, Tajikistan Tradition, Continuity, and Change*, PhD dissertation, Humboldt-Universität zu Berlin, 2018. pp. 273.

This dissertation explores *qaṣīda-khonī*, a musical performance tradition practiced among the Pamiri Ismaili Muslim community living in the mountainous Gorno–Badakhshān province of Tajikistan. This study analyses the importance of *qaṣīda-khonī* for the Pamiri Ismaili Muslims of Badakhshān in terms of how it participates in the construction of a distinct geo-cultural identity, and how it is embedded in broader social and cultural contexts and histories. This dissertation therefore studies *qaṣīda-khonī* as a distinct musical, cultural practice of Central Asia that has been shaped by history, language, geography and religion, and shows how its performance helps in fulfilling various socially cohesive functions.

160 Corbin, Henry. 'Nāṣir-i Khusrau and Iranian Ismāʿīlism', in R.N. Frye, ed., *The Cambridge History of Iran*, vol. 4, 'The Period from the Arab Invasion to the Saljuqs'. Cambridge: Cambridge University Press, 1975, pp. 520–542.

In order to appreciate the importance of Nāṣir-i Khusraw in the history of Iranian thought, it is necessary to place him in the Ismaili setting as a whole, for he was one of its most outstanding personalities. This chapter investigates the survival of the Ismailis under the cloak of Sufism; it is perhaps under such a guise that the true grandeur of Ismaili Islam and the inspiration of its distant origins is found rather than in the Fatimid court in Egypt.

D

161 Daftary, Farhad. *Ismoiliën: tarʾīkh va aqoid* [The Ismāʿīlīs: Their History and Doctrines], Tajik tr. by Abdusalom Mamadnazarov. Moscow: Ladomir, 1999. pp. 816.

162 —— *Sunnathoi aqlonī dar Islom* [Intellectual Traditions in Islam], Tajik tr., Muso Dinorshoev. Dushanbe: Nodir, 2002. pp. 327.

This work explores the role of the intellect in the legal, theological, philosophical and mystical traditions of Islam. It also addresses the impact of the intellect in the contemporary Muslim world and the challenges of modernity. Contributors include leading scholars such as Mohammad Arkoun, Norman Calder, John Cooper, Muhsin Mahdi, Abdulaziz Sachedina and Annemarie Schimmel.

163 —— *Kratkaia istoriia ismailizma: Traditsii musulʾmanskoĭ obshchiny* [A Short History of the Ismailis: Traditions of a Muslim Community], with a foreword by Oleg F. Akimushkin and a new preface by the author, tr. into Russian by Leila R. Dodykhudoeva and Lola N. Dodkhudoeva. Moscow: Ladomir, 2003. pp. 274; repr. 2004.

The translation of F. Daftary's work offers Russian readers access to Ismaili history as one of the main branches of Shiʿi Islam. The study of the history of the Ismaili state and its religio-philosophical doctrines are described as having been hitherto essentially dependent on material in heresiographical writings including the works of Sunni Muslim polemicists and European chroniclers of the Crusades, which led to misunderstanding and misrepresentation.

164 —— *Mukhtasare dar tārīkh-i Ismoilia: sunnathoi yak jamoati Musulmon* [A Short History of the Ismailis: Traditions of a Muslim Community], tr. into Tajik by Amriiazdon Alimardonov. Dushanbe: Nodir, 2003. pp. 368.

165 —— *Traditsii ismailizma v srednie veka* [Ismailis in Medieval Muslim Societies], tr. into Russian Zulaĭkho Odzhieva, ed. Leila R. Dodykhudoeva. Moscow: Ladomir, 2006. pp. 319. Includes a foreword by F. Daftary, pp. 1–19, and a 'Bibliography of the Publications of F. Daftary', pp. 270–279. (in Russian).

The author focuses on the formation of the Fatimid caliphate and the Nizārī state of Alamūt, especially the development of the Ismaili philosophical tradition, and the birth and progress of Ismaili literature through some of the most prominent representatives such as Nāṣir-i Khusraw, Nizārī Quhistānī, al-Nasafī, Ḥamīd al-Dīn al-Kirmānī, al-Sijistānī and Naṣīr al-Dīn al-Ṭūsī.

166 —— Dodykhudoeva, Leila R. and Roshchin, M.IU. 'Ismaility. Ismailitskaia Literatura' [Ismailis. Ismaili Literature], *Bol'shaia Rossiĭskaia Ėntsiklopediia*, vol. 12. Moscow, 2008, pp. 243–244. (in Russian).

167 —— *Legendy ob assasinakh. Mify ob ismailitakh* [The Assassin Legends: Myths of the Ismaʿilis], tr. into Russian, Leila R. Dodykhudoeva and ed. Oleg F. Akimushkin. Moscow: Ladomir, 2009. pp. 210. (in Russian).

In the 6th/12th century, the mythical tale of the Assassins and the legend of the Old Man of the Mountain excited the European imagination. These fables appeared when the Crusaders first encountered the Syrian Nizārī Ismailis, reportedly ready to go to their deaths on the orders of their leader.

The apogee of such myth-making was reached in the narrative by Marco Polo, which told how the Old Man of the Mountain lured his followers into a secret 'garden of Eden' by intoxicating them with *hashish*. As a result, the word 'assassin' from the Arabic term *ḥashshāshūn* (lit.: one who uses hashish), became in European languages a synonym for 'murderer'.

168 —— *Ismaility. Ikh istoriia i doktriny* [The Ismāʿīlīs: Their History and Doctrines], 2nd ed., tr. into Russian Leila R. Dodykhudoeva, ed. Lola N. Dodkhudoeva. Moscow: Natalis, 2011. pp. 264.

The authoritative research by Farhad Daftary is dedicated to the complex history of the Ismailis, the second largest Shiʿi Muslim community, now scattered through more than twenty countries across the world. The work describes all the major stages of Ismaili history, presents new material and investigates the historical context. It covers a period of over twelve centuries, from the formation of the Ismaili movement, through the founding of the Fatimid empire in Egypt, the Nizārī Ismaili state in Iran and Syria, and the post-Alamūt period, up to the present time which sees the Ismailis as a confessional minority in the Muslim world.

169 —— *Afsonahoi Avrupoi dar borai Ismoiliyon* [The Assassin Legends: Myths of the Ismaʻilis], with a new introduction by Karomatullo Olimov and Sunatullo Jonboboev, tr. into Tajik by Abdusalom Mamadnazarov. Dushanbe: ER-graf, 2011. pp. 259. (in Tajik).

170 —— *Ismoiliën: tar'īkh va aqoidi onho* [The Ismāʻīlīs: Their History and Doctrines], 2nd ed., tr. into Tajik, Abdusalom Mamadnazarov (Cyrillic transcription). Dushanbe: Er-graf, 2012. pp. 782. (in Tajik).

171 —— *Noveĭshaia istoriia ismailitov* [A Modern History of the Ismailis: Continuity and Change in a Muslim Community], tr. into Russian, Leila R. Dodykhudoeva, ed. Lola N. Dodkhudoeva. Moscow: Natalis, 2013. pp. xxiii and 616. (in Russian).

The Russian translation of *A Modern History of the Ismailis: Continuity: and Change in a Muslim Community* has a special place among the numerous publications on the contemporary history of Islam. For the first time the Ismailis' unique experiences, through the use of academic and archive material, are made available to the Russian-speaking audience, particularly as regards the identity and beliefs of this community in the rapidly changing world of the last two centuries.

172 —— 'Wladimir Ivanow and Modern Ismaili Studies', in Stanislav M. Prozorov and Hakim Elnazarov, ed., *Russian Scholars on Ismailism* (Proceedings of a conference held in St Petersburg, Russia in 2011). St Petersburg: Nestor-Istoriia, 2014, pp. 24–37. (in Russian and English).

Until the middle of the 20th century, the Ismailis were studied and evaluated almost exclusively on the basis of evidence produced, or often fabricated, by their detractors. Wladimir Ivanow played a key role in the initiation of modern Ismaili studies. This book presents the historical development of Ismaili studies and Ivanow's major contributions to the field of Islamic studies.

173 —— *Ismaility. Istoricheskiĭ slovar'* [Historical Dictionary of the Ismailis], tr. into Russian, Leila R. Dodykhudoeva, ed. Lola N. Dodkhudoeva. Moscow: Natalis, 2015. p. 335. (in Russian).

This dictionary covers all the main phases of Ismaili history, as well as the central doctrine of the community and provides systematic information on the main aspects of the life of the Ismaili community, including institutions, traditions and key figures.

174 —— *Piatʹdesi͡at Let na Vostoke: vospominanii͡a V.A. Ivanov; vstupitelʹnye statʹi, kommentarii i prilozhenii͡a* [Fifty Years in the East. The Memoirs of Wladimir Ivanow, ed. with annotations by Farhad Daftary], tr. into Russian A.Kh. I͡Ulgusheva, ed. V.I. Martyni͡uk. Moskva: Nauka, 2019. pp. 222. (in Russian).

The book is the second Russian edition of the memoirs of W.A. Ivanow, the outstanding Iranianist and founder of modern scholarship on Ismailis studies. It also includes a bibliography of his works and a detailed introduction by F. Daftary.

Daftary, Farkhad see Daftary, Farhad.

175 Dagiev, Dagikhudo. 'Falsafai akhloqii Nosiri Khusrav' [The Ethical Philosophy of Nāṣir-i Khusraw], Department of Humanities (Classical Tajik-Persian Literature and Languages), Unpublished thesis, Khārūgh State University, Tajikistan, 1999. pp. 89. (in Tajik).

The origin of the ethical philosophy of Nāṣir-i Khusraw is analysed on the basis of his major philosophical works, in particular, his *Dīvān, Zād al-musāfirīn, Rawshanāʾī-nāma* and *Saʿādat-nāma*.

176 —— and Carole Faucher, ed., *Identity, History and Trans-Nationality in Central Asia: The Mountain Communities of Pamir*. London: Routledge, 2018. pp. 299.

This book represents the first collection of scholarly articles in English entirely focused on the Ismaili population of the Pamir mountains. The book explores the identity, history and religious/philosophical stances of the Tajik Ismailis of the Pamir mountains, who are a small group of Iranic peoples inhabiting the mountainous region of the Pamir-Hindu Kush, a historical region of Badakhshān.

177 —— 'Pamiri Ethnic Identity and its Evolution in post-Soviet Tajikistan', in Dagikhudo Dagiev and Carole Faucher, ed., *Identity, History and Trans-Nationality in Central Asia: The Mountain Communities of Pamir*. London: Routledge, 2018, pp. 23–44.

The chapter examines and discusses the work of several academics and ethnographers with regard to the origin, development and evolution of Tajik Pamiri identity in Soviet and post-Soviet Tajikistan.

178 —— 'The Ismāʿīlī Hierarchy – Ḥudūd al-Dīn – in the Context of Central Asia', *JSIS*, 10, 3 (2019), pp. 343–370.

The work examines the scholarly findings of Wladimir Ivanow, Henry Corbin, Andreĭ Bertelʹs and Farhad Daftary; and with the help of important Ismaili manuscripts discovered in the Badakhshān region of Tajikistan during the Soviet era, also investigates how, particularly in Central Asia, the *ḥudūd al-dīn* were structured and how their role and function served the Ismaili community which lived in the midst of a Sunni majority.

179 Dastambuev, Nazarkhudo. *Sot͡sial'nye doktriny sovremennogo ismailizma* [Social Doctrines of Modern Ismailism], Dissertat͡siia na soiskanie uchenoĭ stepeni doktora filosofii PhD [PhD Candidate for the Degree of Doctor of Philosophy]. Dushanbe: Akademi Nauk, 2018. pp. 149. (in Russian).

180 —— *Sot͡sial'nia͡ filosofiia͡ sovremennogo ismailizma: problemy i resheniia͡* [The Social Philosophy of Modern Ismailism: Problems and Solutions]. Dushanbe: Dushanbe-Print, 2020. pp. 152. (in Russian).

The purpose of this book is to study the holistic reconstruction of Ismaili social doctrines and determine the extent of their importance for modern social philosophy, education and culture for the Ismaili community and the Islamic world.

181 Davlatbekov, N.D. *Osveshchenie religii i verovaniĭ naseleniia͡ verkhov'ev reki Pi͡andzha v trudakh russkikh issledovateleĭ* [The Religion and Beliefs of the Population in the Upper Reaches of the Panj River in the Works of the Russian Researchers], Dissertat͡sii na soiskanie uchënoĭ stepeni kandidata istoricheskikh nauk [PhD Candidate for the Degree of Doctor of Philosophy]. Dushanbe: Akademi Nauk, 1986. pp. 218. (in Russian).

The author's research is devoted to a historiographical analysis of pre-revolutionary Russian scholarship, discussing issues surrounding the remnants of pre-Islamic belief in the Pamir region, and Ismaili rites, rituals and customs.

182 —— *Doislamskie verovaniia͡ naseleniia͡ Zapadnogo Pamira* (po materialam russkikh isledovateleĭ) [Pre-Islamic Beliefs of the People of the Western Pamirs (in material by Russian researchers)]. Dushanbe: Orieno, 1995. pp. 80. (in Russian).

Davlatbekov's studies are devoted to the historiographic analysis of the writings of Russian and pre-revolutionary researchers. He examines the problems of the remnants of pre-Islamic beliefs in the Pamirs, and ceremonies, rituals and customs associated with the Ismailis in the works of Russian researchers.

183 —— *Osveshchenie ismailizma na Pamire v trudakh russkikh dorevoliu͡ut͡sionnykh issledovateleĭ* [Ismailism in the Works of Pre-Revolutionary Russian Researchers]. Dushanbe, 1995. pp. 57. (in Russian).

This detailed study of Ismailism by Russian Orientalists is in line with historical Marxism. The author considers the emergence of the Ismailis as the result of a socio-political movement against the unjust feudal rule of the Arab conquerers. It includes stories and legends about Nāṣir-i Khusraw and ʿAlī b. Abī Ṭālib and captures theological and philosophical debates concerning the imam's role as understood by the Ismailis of Badakhshān.

184 Davlatnazarov, Khushnazar. *Shughnoni Boston dar osori khattī va shifoī* [Ancient Shughnān in Oral and Written Sources]. Dushanbe: *AIT*, 1998. pp. 156. (in Tajik).

This research is devoted to the study of the region of Shughnān and its history from ancient times when Aryan tribes inhabited the region. It also investigates the ethnography, language and religious beliefs of it inhabitants.

185 Davydov, I. 'Zemnoĭ raĭ Aga-Khana' [The Worldly Paradise of the Aga Khan], *NR*, 12 (1966), pp. 48–49. (in Russian).

This article is devoted to Shāh Karīm al-Ḥusaynī, Aga Khan IV, who succeeded his grandfather to become the 49th Ismaili Imam. A very rare study from the Soviet era about the current Ismaili leader's life and activities.

186 Devonaqulov, Aliqul. 'Nosiri Khusrav (vasii͡atnoma)' [Nāṣir-i Khusraw (testament)], *Farhang*, 11 (1991), pp. 40–45. (in Tajik).

The author recounts a story consisting of two sections: the first part, beginning with the words, *bismi'llāh al-raḥmān al-raḥīm*, details Nāṣir-i Khusraw's intention to perform the pilgrimage and his preparations for it. The second part analyses the will that Nāṣir-i Khusraw wrote for his brother.

187 Dinani, Gholamhosseyn Ibrahimi. 'Tri filosofskie problemy: ot Nasir ad-Dina Tusi do Mully Sadry' [Three Philosophical Problems: From Naṣīr al-Dīn Ṭūsī to Mullā Ṣadrā], *EIF*, 4 (2013), pp. 379–393. (in Russian).

The article deals with three philosophical questions posed by Naṣīr al-Dīn Ṭūsī to his older contemporary Shams al-Dīn Khusrawshāhī (d. 652/1254), a scholar, philosopher and physician (who, to the best of our knowledge, never provided answers to them).

188 Dinorshoev, Muso. *Filosofii͡a Nasriddina Tusi* [Naṣīr al-Dīn Ṭūsī's Philosophy]. Dushanbe: Donish, 1968. pp. 157. (in Russian).

While analysing the philosophy of Naṣīr al-Dīn Ṭūsī, this study pays special attention to his teachings on the classification of sciences, matter and form, and the categories of being and essence.

189 —— 'Gnoseologii͡a Ghazali i ego mirovozzrencheskai͡a sushchnost' [Ghazālī's Epistemology and the Essence of His Worldview], *IAN (TSSR)*, 4 (1976), pp. 59–68. (in Russian).

Two opposite approaches relative to the classification of sciences – the religious/idealistic (Ghazālī) and materialistic (Peripatetic) – are analysed in this study. In particular, Ghazālī's worldview is at variance with the outlook of the self-proclaimed Peripatetic philosophers such as Ibn Sīnā and Naṣīr al-Dīn Ṭūsī.

190 —— ed. *Nosir-i Khusrav. Izbrannoe* [A Selection from Nāṣir-i Khusraw's Works]. Dushanbe, 2003. pp. 349. (in Russian).

This selection from Nāṣir-i Khusraw's works includes *Zād al-musāfirīn* and his *Safar-nāma* and reveals the essence of his philosophical views, and also, in particular, his talent in composing poems. It looks at how the philosophical and political views of Nāṣir-i Khusraw and his religious convictions were formulated under the influence of his great Ismaili predecessors – in line with Aḥmad al-Nasafī, Abū Ḥātim al-Rāzī, Abū Yaʿqūb al-Sijistānī and Ḥamīd al-Dīn al-Kirmānī in the 4th/10th century during the Ismaili mission in the Iranian lands.

191 —— 'Nasir Khusrav's Heritage', in Sarfaroz Niyozov and Ramazon Nazariev, ed., *Nasir Khusraw: Yesterday, Today, Tomorrow* (Proceedings of a conference held in Khārūgh, Tajikistan). Khujand: Noshir, 2005, pp. 111–125.

The author briefly spells out the content of the philosophical and theological heritage of Nāṣir-i Khusraw, including his philosophical-theological works, poetry and other prose genres such as the *tadhkira*.

192 —— *Nasir-i Khusraw i ego 'Zad al-musafirin'* (Pripasy putnikov) [*Nāṣir-i Khusraw's Zād al-musāfirīn*], intr., ed. and tr., from Persian into Russian. Dushanbe: Nodir, 2005. pp. 635.

Zād al-musāfirīn is considered the main religious and philosophical work of the 5th/11th-century philosopher, Nāṣir-i Khusraw. It analyses the most important religious and philosophical problems of the author's era such as the concepts of knowledge, material and spiritual existence, the nature and destiny of man and his place in the world and in society.

193 —— 'Traktat Nasir-i Khusrava *Zād al-musāfirīn*' [Nāṣir-i Khusraw's Treatise *Zād al-musāfirīn*], *EIF*, 4 (2013), pp. 326–332. (in Russian).

The article examines Nāṣir-i Khusraw's *Zād al-musāfirīn* (which was translated into Russian by the author, a well-known Tajik scholar). The author believes that Nāṣir's theory of knowledge must be treated as propaedeutic to his doctrines, and discusses its similarities and differences with Peripatetic Gnosticism.

194 Dobrovol'skiĭ, I. 'O monetakh ismailitov Alamuta' [On the Coins of the Ismailis of Alamūt], *SGE*, 45 (1980), pp. 66–68. (in Russian).

This is a study of one of the eight coins, recorded by G.C. Miles as minted in 542/1147, which is stored in the collection of the Hermitage, St Petersburg. It is a poorly preserved, heavily dented dinar, broken in two places. This coin was purchased in Tehran by J. Bartholomew for the Hermitage. It is a rare coin which was probably minted under Muḥammad b. Buzurg-Umīd, the second lord of Alamūt.

We are informed that the Hermitage has only one dinar of the same type belonging to Muḥammad b. Buzurg-Umīd which is well preserved, but minted in 556/1160. A similar coin, but dating to 536/1142, is held in the numismatic collection of the History Museum of Armenia, in Erevan.

A significant feature of this coin dating to the era of the Ismailis of Alamūt is the presence of the title 'Sulṭān', which has not previously been found on the coinage associated with Alamūt.

195 Dodikhudoev, Ëdgor. 'Taʼsiri oët va ahodis dar sheʻri Nizorii Quhistonī' [The Impact of *Āya*s and *Ḥadīth*s in Nizārī Quhistānī's Poetry], *Majalai ilmī bakhshi filologī*, 4, 1 (2012), pp. 180–186. (in Tajik).

This study highlights the Qurʼanic verses and *ḥadīth*s used in the works of the famous Ismaili poet of the 7th–8th/13th–14th centuries, Nizārī Quhistānī, and their Ismaili interpretation.

196 —— 'Taʻsiri andeshahoi mazhabi bar sheʻri Nizorii Quhistonī' [The Impact of Religious Thought on Nizārī Quhistānī's Poetry], *Majalai ilmī bakhshi filologī*, 4, 3 (2014), pp. 239–248. (in Tajik).

This article reviews the ideas of Nizārī Quhistānī who is presented as an important religious poet in the era of the Mongol invasions.

197 Dodikhudoev, Khaëlbek. 'Mirovozzrenie ismailitov' [The Ismaili Worldview], *Tezisy dokladov konferent͡sii molodykh uchënykh AN(T) SSR*. Dushanbe: Donish, 1966, p. 118. (in Russian).

In five points, the author, defines the worldview of the Ismailis by arguing that their philosophical concepts and ideological systems are based on Ancient Greek teachings, especially Pythagoreanism, Platonism and Peripatetism. The article also refers to the beliefs of the Ancient Persians, the Hindus, and other Eastern religions.

198 —— *Musulʼmanskie sekty* [Muslim Denominations]. Dushanbe: Irfon, 1967. pp. 16. (in Russian)

199 —— *Istoricheskie formy ateizma* [Historical Forms of Atheism]. Dushanbe: Irfon, 1967. pp. 16. (in Russian).

200 —— *Mazhabi ismoiliı͡a va mohiı͡ati ijtimoii on. Rohhoi bartaraf namudani boqimondai din* [The Ismaili Belief and its Social Aspects. Ways of Eliminating Traces of Religion]. Dushanbe: Donish, 1967. pp. 48. (in Tajik).

Based on Ismaili religious manuscripts and archival material, this work reflects a strictly Marxist approach to the study of religions, looking at Ismailism as an ideology for the ruling class. The work is part of the Marxist-atheist propaganda of the Soviet era which aimed at negating its religious aspect and depicting it as a class struggle for control over the means of production.

201 —— *Filosofiı͡a ismailizma (kharakteristika osnovnykh print͡sipov doktriny)* [Ismaili Philosophy (A Sketch of the Main Principle of the Doctrine)], Dissertat͡sii na soiskanie uchënoĭ stepeni kandidata filosofskikh nauk [PhD Candidate for the Degree of Doctor of Philosophy]. Dushanbe: Akademi Nauk, 1969. pp. 249 (in Russian).

An analysis of Ismaili philosophical doctrine shows that it played a major role in the development of freethinking and contained many ideas opposed to the teachings of Sunni Islam. This primarily refers to the Ismaili method of allegorical interpretation (*ta'wīl*) of the Qur'an.

202 —— *Osnovnye cherty filosofii ismailizma* [The Main Features of Ismaili Philosophy], *IAN (TSSR)*, 3 (1972), pp. 88–93. (in Russian).

Ismaili doctrine, in contrast to other faiths, is presented as a socio-political concept, refuting feudal forms of exploitation and their ideology.

203 —— *Ocherki filosofii ismailizma: obshchaia kharakteristika filosofskoĭ doktriny X–XIV* [Essays on Ismaili Philosophy: A Sketch of Doctrinal Philosophy X–XIV]. Dushanbe: Donish, 1976. pp. 142. (in Russian).

This book take a general look at the religio-philosophical doctrines of the medieval Ismailis. It displays a Marxist-Leninist approach to the study of religion and religious movements. It also tries to explain the success of the Ismaili *dāʿīs* and their *daʿwa* by arguing that the Ismaili movement was characteristically an anti-feudal one which gained momentum in the 4th/10th and 5th/11th centuries in the present territories of Iran, Central Asia and Syria.

204 —— 'Aliilohiën' ['Alī Allāhiyān], *EST*, vol. 1, p. 340. (in Tajik).

Encyclopaedia entry examining the origin and meaning of the term "Alī Allāhiyyān', or Ahl-i ḥaqq, as the members of this Shiʿi denomination prefer to call themselves.

205 —— 'Aqli kull' ['Aql-i kull], *EST*, vol. 1, p. 970. (in Tajik).

An encyclopaedia entry examining the origin and meaning of the notion of the ʿAql-i kull (universal intellect), as a philosophical and religious concept.

206 —— 'Duruziia' [Druzes], *EST*, vol. 2, p. 1038. (in Tajik).

Encyclopaedia entry examining the origin and meaning of the religious group called the Druze. A group of the Shiʿa, founded in the 5th/11th century in Egypt by al-Darazī, from which the Ismailis distanced themselves early on. Large Druze communities still exist in Syria, Lebanon and Israel.

207 —— 'Imom' [Imam], *EST*, vol. 3, p. 567. (in Tajik).

An encyclopaedia entry examining the origin and meaning of the term 'imām'. In Ismaili doctrine, the imam is regarded as the religious leader responsible for the esoteric hermeneutical interpretation of the Holy Scripture.

208 —— 'Ismoiliia' [Ismāʿīlīs], *EST*, vol. 3, pp. 78–80. (in Tajik).

An encyclopaedia entry examining the origin and development of Ismaili *daʿwa* as a branch of Shiʿi Islam. The formative period was grounded in a feudal-structured society whilst the spread of the *daʿwa* is associated with the socio-political contradictions and tensions characterising the Abbasid caliphate.

209 —— 'Nafsi kull', *EST*, vol. 1, p. 333. (in Tajik).

Encyclopaedia entry examining the origin and meaning of the notion 'Nafs-i kull' (universal soul), as a philosophical and religious concept.

210 —— *Filosofiia krest'ianskogo bunta* (o roli srednevekovogo ismailizma v razvitii svobodomysliia na musul'manskom Vostoke) [The Philosophy of the Peasant Revolt (the role of the medieval Ismailis in the development of thought in the Muslim East)]. Dushanbe: Irfon, 1987. pp. 432. (in Russian).

This work analyses Ismaili teachings, according to the Marxist-Leninist approach to the study of religion. The Ismaili movement and its relationship to Sunni Islam are interpreted as an ideological battle which mobilised the masses, the peasants and artisans, against the ruling class and feudalism. The historical experience of the Ismaili working masses is investigated and portrayed as a struggle against religious bigotry and the obscurantism of Sunni 'orthodoxy'.

211 —— *Ismoiliia va ozodandeshii Sharq* [Ismailism and Freedom of Thought in the East]. Dushanbe: Irfon, 1989. pp. 283. (in Tajik).

This work, focusing on the history of the Ismaili movement during the Middle Ages, is written from a Marxist perspective and analyses the works of both medieval philosophers and Soviet and Western scholars. It provides a distinctive understanding of the role of the Ismailis in the development of philosophical ideas and freethinking in the East in the 4th/10th–8th/14th centuries.

212 —— 'Razum ne mozhet predstavit' tvortsa (Koran s tochki zreniia Nosir-i Khusrava)' [Reason cannot Conceive the Creator (the Qur'an from Nāṣir-i Khusraw's viewpoint)], *Shelkovyĭ put'*, *Al'manakh* (1990), pp. 149–164. (in Russian).

At the core of Nāṣir-i Khusraw's negative theology is the thesis of the fundamental impossibility of any human being grasping the essence of God. The Creator is beyond comprehension; God defies any definition and cannot be categorised.

213 —— 'B. Ghafurov kak pioner issledovaniia ismailizma v Tadzhikistane', *Akademik Bobodzhon Ghafurov i izuchenie istorii i tsivilizatsii TSentral'noĭ Azii (tezisy dokladov)* ['Ghafurov as a Pioneer of Ismaili Studies in Tajikistan', in *Bobojon Ghafurov and the Study of the History and Civilisation of Central Asia (abstracts)*]. Dushanbe: Irfon, 1998, pp. 56–57. (in Russian).

214 —— 'Filosofskiĭ ismailizm' [Philosophical Ismailism], in A. Mukhammadkhodzhaev and K. Olimov, ed., *Istoriia tadzhikskoĭ filosofii (s drevneĭshikh vremen do XV v.)* [The History of Tajik Philosophy (from Ancient times to the 15th century], in three volumes, vol. 2. Dushanbe: 'Donish', 2011, pp. 196–287. (in Russian).

215 —— 'Eretik protiv filosofii eretika (k polemike Abu Khatima al-Razi i Abubakra ar-Razi)' [The Heretic against the Philosophy of the Heretic (in the Polemics of Abū Ḥātim al-Rāzī and Abū Bakr al-Rāzī], Stat'i͡a 1. *IAN (TSSR),* 3 (2012), pp. 21–26. (in Russian).

The article, which for the most part consists of translated or paraphrased passages from Abū Ḥātim al-Rāzī's (d. 934) *A'lām al-nubuwwa,* provides a detailed account of the Ismaili *dā'ī*'s polemic against his contemporary and compatriot, the famous physician and philosopher, Abū Bakr Muḥammad b. Zakariyyā al-Rāzī (d. between 925 and 935 CE).

216 —— 'Polemika Abu Khatima ar-Razi i Abu Bakra ar-Razi' [The Polemic between Abū Ḥātim al-Rāzī and Abū Bakr al-Rāzī], *EIF,* 4 (2013), pp. 140–161. (in Russian).

217 —— 'Suhrab Vali o pervonachalakh materii [Sayyid Khwāja Suhrāb Valī on the First Primary Matter]', *VKU, NZ,* serii͡a 2, 10 (2013), pp. 208–221. (in Russian).

Focusing on the study of the Universal Intellect and the Universal Soul, Sayyid Suhrāb Valī presented his views on matter and form and their relationship with the first being systematically. His understanding of the process of emanation differs from any known Ismaili philosophical concept of the 9th–10th/15th–16th centuries.

218 —— *Filosofskiĭ ismailizm* [Philosophical Ismailism]. Dushanbe: 'Ėr-graf', 2014. pp. 495. (in Russian).

Philosophical Ismailism investigates Ismaili philosophical trends, along with Eastern Peripateticism, *Kalām,* Sufism and Ishrāqism. It examines the philosophical aspects of key Ismaili notions such as *tawḥīd, ẓāhir, bāṭin, sharī'a, ḥaqīqa, tanzīl* and *ta'wīl,* probing into ontology, cosmogony, cosmology, epistemology, the classification of sciences, natural, social and political philosophy, ethics and anthropology.

219 —— 'Filosofskie debaty Abubakra Razi i Abuhatima Razi' [The Philosophical Debate between Abū Bakr al-Rāzī and Abū Ḥātim al-Rāzī], *Izvestii͡a instituta filosofii, politologii i prava,* ANRT, 3 (2016), pp. 17–29. (in Russia).

The author investigates the philosophical debates between Abū Bakr al-Rāzī and Abū Ḥātim al-Rāzī and their dispute on topics such as the nature of different groups in Islam and the coexistence of the world and God.

220 Dodikhudoeva, Lola. 'Svadebnye obri͡ady ismailitov Pamira' [Wedding Rites of the Pamiri Ismailis], *PIKFSA,* 1 (1973), pp. 31–39. (in Russian).

This article discusses the features of the wedding ritual of the Ismailis of Badakhshān based on oral traditions and historical sources. The work reveals the significant impact of pre-Islamic beliefs on the wedding ritual.

221 —— 'Nasir Khusraw: The Challenges of being One of the Chosen', in Sarfaroz Niyozov and Ramazon Nazariev, ed., *Nasir Khusraw: Yesterday, Today, Tomorrow*. (Proceedings of a conference held in Khārūgh, Tajikistan). Khujand: Noshir, 2005. pp. 289–299.

The scholar suggests that Nāṣir-i Khusraw approached the problems and tensions of his time by choosing a different interpretation of religion. The particular situation in Badakhshān forced Nāṣir-i Khusraw to play not simply the role of an Ismaili *dāʿī*, but also that of a *dāʿī* of Islam in general. In his role as a *ḥakīm*, Nāṣir emphasises the importance of the four tenets of Islam: *Qurʾān, sharīʿa, taʾwīl* and *tawḥīd*.

222 Dodykhudoeva, Leila R. and Reisner, Marina L. 'The Concept of the "Good Word" (Sukhan-i nik) in Nasir Khusraw's Didactic Qasidas', in Sarfaroz Niyozov and Ramazon Nazariev, ed., *Nasir Khusraw: Yesterday, Today, Tomorrow*. (Proceedings of a conference held in Khārūgh, Tajikistan). Khujand: Noshir, 2005, pp. 503–509.

Through an analysis of a number of verses from *qaṣīda*s in Nāṣir-i Khusraw's *Dīvān*, the authors highlight a significant point, that the *sukhan-i nīk* (i.e. the good word) is part and parcel of the 'Logos, or Divine Word'. The authors go as far as affirming that Nāṣir-i Khusraw's poetry is divinely inspired in both content and form. As such, his poetry requires an esoteric allegorical interpretation (*taʾwīl*).

223 —— and Reĭsner, Marina L. *Poėticheskiĭ iazyk kak sredstvo propovedi: kontseptsiia 'Blagogo Slova' v tvorchestve Nasira Khusrava* [Poetry as a Means of Preaching: the Concept of the 'Good Word', in Nāṣir-i Khusraw's Poetry]. Moscow: Natalis, 2007. pp. 383. (in Russian).

Dedicated to the poetic work of the outstanding Ismaili writer and religious leader, Nāṣir-i Khusraw, the book is designed to offer the modern reader a better understanding of Nāṣir's role in the history of classical Persian literature. It focuses particularly on delineating Nāṣir's function as a preacher and genuine innovator of poetic language. The biographical aspect of this research is supported by historical, theological and cultural material from Nāṣir-i Khusraw's own works.

Dzhonboboev, Sunatullo, see Jonboboev, Sunatullo.

E

224 Ėdelʾman, A.C. 'Shoir, mutafakkir, saëh va khodimi buzurgi jamʾiati Tojik dar asri XI Nosir Khisrav' [A Prominent Tajik Poet, Thinker, Traveller and Public Figure of the 11th Century, Nāṣir-i Khusraw], *MS* (Stalinabad), 12 (1952), pp. 32–44 (in Tajik).

In Persian/Tajik literature, Nāṣir-i Khusraw emerged as a dedicated fighter against encroaching social evil, and as a courageous thinker and a talented poet.

225 —— 'Nekotorye dannye o nauchnykh i filosofskikh vzgli͡adakh Nosiri Khisrau' [Some Facts on the Scientific and Philosophical Views of Nāṣir-i Khusraw], *IAN (TSSR)*, 4 (1953), pp. 155–159. (in Russian).

This study of the intellectual life of Nāṣir-i Khusraw clearly shows that he was an outstanding thinker and, in many ways, ahead of his time.

226 —— *Nosiri Khisrau i ego mirovozzrenie* [Nāṣir-i Khusraw and his Worldview], Dissertat͡sii na soiskanie uchënoĭ stepeni kandidata filosofskikh nauk [PhD Candidate for the Degree of Doctor of Philosophy]. Stalinabad, 1955. pp. 260. (in Russian).

The author analyses the socio-political, philosophical, ethnical and anti-clerical views of Nāṣir-i Khusraw. However, Ėdel'man has tried to identify some materialistic propensities in the idealistic philosophy and theology of Nāṣir-i Khusraw.

227 Ėl'chibekov, Kudratbek. 'Novye materialy po istorii Shugnana' [New Materials on the History of Shughnān], *IAN (TSSR)*, 2 (1973), pp. 3–11. (in Russian).

Shāh Fitūr Muḥabbat Shāh-Zāda, one of the authors of the *Tārīkh-i Badakhshān*, indicates that the book was completed on 6 Rajab 1365 (3 June 1946). The manuscript identifies some rulers of Shughnān, beginning with Shāh Khāmūsh, 459–531/1066–1137, and his son Shāh Khudādād, up to the last ruler of Shughnān, Yūsuf ʿAlī Khān. Between the first and the last ruler, the author also names, Davlat-shāh, Shāh-Vanjī, Shāh-Amirbek, Shāh-Vanjī II, Shāh-Qubād-khān and the father of Yūsuf ʿAlī-khān, ʿAbd al-Raḥmān Khān. Ėl'chibekov himself admits that he has been able to provide only the names of those rulers of Shughnān of whom he has heard.

228 —— 'Obshchie religiozno-filosofskie i fol'klorno-mifologicheskie obosnovanii͡a ierarkhii dukhovenstva v sufizme i ismailizme' [A Common Religio-Philosophical and Folklore-Mythological Faith Hierarchy in Sufism and Ismailism], *ROMSV* (1974), pp. 299–319. (in Russian).

As is apparent from the title of the article, the author has attempted to define the common features of Sufism and Ismailism, in particular with regard to the ideology and organisation of both currents of thought. He focuses on their historical and traditional sources, which should enable us to understand the intricacies of the religious ideologies found in a number of Eastern countries today. At the beginning of the article the author admits that his approach reflects a Marxist explanation of religion, which is also presented as the only scientific method.

229 —— 'Istoricheskie istochniki v Badakhshane' [Historical Sources in Badakhshān], *IAN (TSSR)*, 1 (1975), pp. 27–31. (in Russian).

The work deals with three historical sources written by local authors in Badakhshān including a copy of *Silk-i gawhar-rīz*, an important discovery which was hitherto unknown.

230 —— *Ierarkhii͡a dukhovenstva v ismailizme i eë politicheskai͡a rol'* [The Ismaili Hierarchy of the Clergy and its Political Role], Na osnove materialov sobrannykh ėkspeditsieĭ v Gornom Badakhshane Tadzhikistana v 1959–1970) [Based on Materials Collected by the Expedition to the Gorno-Badakhshān Region of Tajikistan in 1959–1970], Dissertatsii na soiskanie uchënoĭ stepeni kandidata istoricheskikh nauk [PhD Candidate for the Degree of Doctor of Philosophy] (Moscow, 1977). pp. 159. (in Russian).

The object of this thesis is to identify the causes which led to the formation of the religious and philosophical structure of the Ismaili hierarchy. The study of the Ismaili spiritual hierarchy is presented as being based on the Ismaili sources discovered in the territory of the GBAO.

231 —— 'Piry i ikh rol' v ismailizme' [*Pīrs* and their Role in Ismailism], *Trudy respublikanskoĭ konferentsii molodykh uchënykh Tadzhikskoĭ SSR, posvi͡ashchënnoĭ XXV sʻezdu KPSS* [Proceedings of the Republican Conference of Young Scholars of the Tajik SSR, Dedicated to the 25 Congress of the CPSU]. Dushanbe, 1977, pp. 73–74. (in Russian).

This work presents the role of the *pīr*, one of the most important in the religious hierarchy in Badakshān; it examines the *pīr*'s task of teaching Ismaili beliefs in the region and of maintaining the link between the Imam of the Time and his *murīds*.

232 —— 'Mansha'-i rivoët dar bora-i Nosir-i Khusrav' [The Sources of the Legends about Nāṣir-i Khusraw], *NP*, 4 (2003), pp. 157–164. (in Tajik).

This work investigates the sources of the legends about Nāṣir-i Khusraw.

233 —— 'The Sources of Stories about Nasir Khusraw', in Sarfaroz Niyozov and Ramazon Nazariev, ed., *Nasir Khusraw: Yesterday, Today, Tomorrow.* (Proceedings of a conference held in Khārūgh, Tajikistan). Khujand: Noshir, 2005, pp. 402–406.

This is an attempt to identify the origins of the myths portraying Nāṣir-i Khusraw as a sacred person, revered by both the Sunni and Shiʻi populations of Badakhshān, by studying oral and written accounts.

234 —— 'Religioznye verovanii͡a ismailitov Badakhshana. Islamskie tsennosti TSentral'noĭ Azii: tolerantnost' i gumanizm' [Religious Beliefs of the Ismailis of Badakhshān. Islamic Values in Central Asia: Tolerance and Humanism], *IFKA*, Tashkent (2008), pp. 200–203. (in Russian).

235 —— *Ierarkhiia dukhovenstva v ismailizme Badakhshana (na osnove rukopisi 'Silk-i gawhar-riz')* [The Religious Hierarchy among the Ismailis of Badakhshān (based on the manuscript *Silk-i gawhar-rīz*). Dushanbe: 'Iste'dod', 2016. pp. 216. (in Russian).

The objective of this work is to identify the causes of the formation and development of religious and philosophical studies on the Ismaili clerical hierarchal structure.

Ėl'chibekov, Qudratbek, See Ėl'chibekov, Kudratbek.

236 Elnazarov, Hakim. 'The Russian Pioneer of Modern Scholarship on the Ismailis of Central Asia', in Stanislav M. Prozorov and Hakim Elnazarov, ed., *Russian Scholars on Ismailism*. (Proceedings of a conference held in St Petersburg, Russia in 2011). St Petersburg: Nestor-Istoriia, 2014, pp. 101–122. (in Russian and English).

A general overview of the emergence of Ismaili and Pamiri studies in Russian scholarship.

237 —— 'The Luminous Lamp: The Practice of *Chirāgh-i Rawshan* among the Ismailis of Central Asia', in Farhad Daftary and Gurdofarid Miskinzoda, ed., *The Study of Shiʿi Islam: History, Theology and Law*. London: I.B. Tauris, 2014, pp. 529–541.

238 —— 'Chirāgh-i Rawshan', *EIS*, vol. 5, pp. 676–680. Available online at: http://referenceworks.brillonline.com/entries/encyclopaedia-islamica/chiragh-i-rawshan-COM_05000087 [Last accessed, 4 October 2017].

The *chirāgh-i rawshan* is one of the most important traditional practices of the Central Asian Ismailis. The practice assisted the community in the preservation of its religious identity as well as providing a medium for the Ismaili *pīr*s and *dāʿī*s to disseminate their teachings to various parts of Central Asia.

239 —— and Sultonbek Aksakolov. 'The Nizari Ismailis of Central Asia in Modern Times', in Farhad Daftary, ed., *A Modern History of the Ismailis: Continuity and Change in a Muslim Community*. London: I.B. Tauris, 2011, pp. 45–75.

240 —— and Sultonbek Aksakolov. 'Ismaility nizarity Tsentral'noĭ Azii v Novoe vremia' [The Nizārī Ismailis of Central Asia in Modern Times], in Farhad Daftary, ed., *Noveĭshaia istoriia ismailitov: Preemstvennost' i peremeny v musul'manskoĭ obshchine* [A Modern History of the Ismailis: Continuity and Change in a Muslim Community], Russian tr. R. Leila Dodykhudoeva, ed. Lola N. Dodkhudoeva. Moscow: Natalis, 2013, pp. 69–102. (in Russian).

The work presents the Ismailis of Central Asia as having a distinct set of religious, cultural and social practices, values, achievements and challenges.

241 ——, Ramazon Nazariev, Shukrat Karamkhudoev and Mirzo Mabatqadamov, ed. and tr. *Ravzai Taslim* [Paradise of Submission by Naṣīr al-Dīn Ṭūsī (597–672)]. Dushanbe: 'Ėr-graf', 2016. pp. 243. (in Tajik).

The significance of this treatise lies in its comprehensive treatment of medieval Ismaili thought, including theology, philosophy and esotericism, as well as being regarded as the major doctrinal work of the Nizārī Ismailis to survive the destruction of Alamūt by the Mongols.

Ėl'nazarov, Khakim, see Elnazarov, Hakim

242 Emadi, Hafizullah. 'Minority Group Politics: The Role of Ismailis in Afghanistan's Politics', *Central Asian Survey*, 12, 3 (1993), pp. 379–392.

The focus of this article is to study the emergence of the Ismaili *daʿwa* in Afghanistan, to examine the role of Ismaili missionaries in preaching Ismaili doctrines, and to explore factors that compelled the Ismailis to collaborate with the dominant powers in the post-Alamūt period.

243 —— 'The End of *Taqiyya*: Reaffirming the Religious Identity of Ismailis in Shughnan, Badakhshan and Political Ramifications for Afghanistan', *Middle Eastern Studies*, 34, 3 (1998), pp. 103–120.

The focus of this article is to examine how the Ismaili *daʿwa* unfolded and became consolidated in Badakhshān, to explore factors that led to politicisation of the Ismaili intelligentsia in Shughnān in the 1960s and 1970s, to study the basis of their support for the pro-Soviet government during the Soviet occupation of Afghanistan.

244 —— 'Politics of Transformation and Ismailis in Gorno-Badakhshan, Tajikistan', *Internationales Asienforum*, 29, 1–2 (1998), pp. 5–22.

The work is a short history of the Ismailis of the GBAO, a region in modern-day Tajikistan, from the spread of the Ismaili *daʿwa* in the area up to modern times, the declaration of independence of Tajikistan and the challenges that the Ismaili community of Badakhshān faces.

245 —— 'Praxis of *Taqiyya*: Perserverance of the Pashaye Ismāʿīlī Enclave, Nangarhar, Afghanistan', *Central Asian Survey*, 19, 2 (2000), pp. 253–264.

This article is about the history of the spread of Ismaili doctrine through the *dāʿī*s, the agents of the *daʿwa*, in Badakhshān of Afghanistan, and how the Ismailis have been able to maintain the principle of *taqiyya* in practising their beliefs, thereby preserving their religious literature and safeguarding their identity.

246 —— 'Struggle for Recognition: Hazara Ismaʿili Women and their Role in the Public Arena in Afghanistan', *Asian Journal of Women's Studies*, 8, 2 (2002), pp. 76–103.

247 —— 'Nahzat-e-Nawin: Modernisation of the Badakhshani Ismaʿili Community of Afghanistan', *Central Asian Survey*, 24, 2 (2005), pp. 165–189.

This study focuses on the politics of Islamic insurgency and its impact on the lives of the Ismailis of Badakhshān of Afghanistan in the 1980s and 1990s. It explores factors that led the AKDN to engage in the rehabilitation of Badakhshān, a district inhabited by Sunnis and Shiʿis with opposing political views. The article also examines efforts by the Ismaili leadership to modernise Ismaili communities by establishing new institutional structures and appointing a new generation of leaders to guide the Ismailis and facilitate their interaction with other communities.

248 Emeli͡anova, Nadezhda. 'Nasir Khusraw: The Light that Illuminates the History of the Peoples of Pamir', in Sarfaroz Niyozov and Ramazon Nazariev, ed., *Nasir Khusraw: Yesterday, Today, Tomorrow.* (Proceedings of a conference held in Khārūgh, Tajikistan). Khujand: Noshir, 2005, pp. 651–656.

The author briefly describes the impact which some of the major events in Nāṣir-i Khusraw's life have had in delineating diversity in the Pamir region. She concludes that the passage of time has not diminished the popularity and devotion of the Pamiri people to Nāṣir-i Khusraw.

249 —— 'Badakhshanskiĭ dnevnik' [Badakhshān Diary], in A.Z. Almazova, ed., *Pamirskai͡a Ėkspedit͡sii͡a (stat'i i materialy polevykh issledovaniĭ)* [The Pamir Expedition (articles and materials of field research)], Moscow: RAN Institut Vostokovedenii͡a, 2006, pp. 12–23. (in Russian).

In August–September 2002, the first scientific expedition in Badakhshān, Afghanistan by a group of Russian scholars from the Institute of Oriental Studies took place. The author, who participated in this event, shares her expertise, experiences and observations.

250 —— *Darvaz – religioznai͡a i kul'turnai͡a zhizn' Tadzhiksko-Afganskogo prigranich'i͡a (po materialam polevykh issledovaniĭ 2003–2006 gg.)* [Darvaz – Religious and Cultural Life of the Tajik-Afghan Border (on the basis of field research)]. Moscow, 2007. pp. 111. (in Russian).

The book is based on material gathered by the author during her field studies in 2003–2006. It discusses processes occurring in both Afghan and Tajik Badakhshān. It attempts to provide answers to questions such as: what opportunities exist for the development of a pluralistic society, and to what degree has traditional society been challenged by the processes which modernisation has brought to the mountain areas.

F

251 Farmand, Ḥusayn, ed. *Dānā-yi Yumgān: Majmūʿa-i maqālāt-i simūnār-i bayn al-milalī-yi Nāṣir-i Khusraw* [Sage of Yumgān: Proceedings of the International Seminar on Nāṣir-i Khusraw]. Kabul: Akādemī-yi ʿUlūm, Markaz-i Zabān va Adabiyāt, 1366 Sh./1987. (in Persian).

252 Frolova, E.A. 'Religioznaĭa filosofiĭa: filosofskoe uchenie v ismailizme' [Religious Philosophy: Philosophical Doctrine in Ismailism], in *Istoriĭa srednevekovoĭ arabo-islamskoĭ filosofii* [The History of Medieval Arabo-Islamic Philosophy]. Moscow: RAN, 1995, pp. 58–76. (in Russian).

Ismailism is regarded as one of the main branches of Shi'i Islam in which major philosophical concepts and religious precepts are based on rationalism and rational philosophy, including ontological and epistemological approaches.

253 —— 'Filosofskoe uchenie v ismailizme' [Philosophical Doctrine in Ismailism], in *Istoriĭa arabo-musul'manskoĭ filosofii. Srednie veka i sovremnnost'* [The History of Arabo-Muslim Philosophy. Medieval and Contemporary periods]. Moscow: RAN, 2006, pp. 42–56. (in Russian).

This study deals with the development of Ismailism as one of the branches of Shi'i Islam which emerged during the 2nd/8th century. It also discusses important concepts in Ismaili philosophy such as God, the Universal Intellect, the Universal Soul, the imam, and creation, the law of nature in accordance with the writings of Ismaili thinkers such as al-Nasafī, al-Sijistānī, al-Kirmānī, Nāṣir-i Khusraw and others.

G

254 Ghaforova, U. and N. Salimov, tr., *Nasiruddini Ṭūsī, Akhloqi Nosirī* [Naṣīr al-Dīn Ṭūsī's *Akhlāq-i Nāṣirī*] (The Institute of Ismaili Studies in collaboration with Khujand University). Dushanbe, 2009. pp. 386. (in Tajik).

Naṣīr al-Dīn Ṭūsī's *Akhlāq-i Nāṣirī* is devoted to philosophical ethics; the study is divided into three parts: ethics, economics and politics.

Gafurov, Bobodzhan G., see Ghafurov, Bobojon G.

255 Ghafurov, Bobojon G. *'Ob ismailizme'* [On Ismailism]. Stalinabad: Gosizdat Tadzhikistan, 1943. pp. 47. (in Russian).

The work is the result of a request by the Communist Party leadership to produce polemical propaganda. This booklet was aimed at presenting the Aga Khan as an anti-revolutionary bureaucrat who advised his *murīd*s and *pīr*s to spread detrimental rumours against the Communist government in the Soviet Union, urging his followers to resist its rule.

256 —— ed. *Religiĭa i obshchestvennaĭa mysl' stran Vostoka* [The Religion and Social Thought of the Eastern Countries]. Sb. Stateĭ: Moscow, 1971, pp. 265. (in Russian).

A collection of articles covering a wide range of issues providing a religious assessment of the ideological struggle occurring in India, Pakistan, Indonesia, Thailand, Afghanistan and Iran. The author examines the evolution of the role of religion in the various stages of the history of the East.

257 —— 'Interview; Russian Professor's View on Ismailism', *Ismaili Mirror Magazine* (December 1974), pp. 16–17.

To one of the most salient questions posed during the interview ('What is your impression of the Ismailis in general?'), Bobojon Ghafurov replies: 'The Ismailis are always peace-loving people. I have studied the history of the Ismaili imams, and feel that union of the universal mind and universal soul can be achieved through the leadership of the imam. The Ismailis are guided by their imam, and this is why they are a well-organised and well-disciplined community. Their attitude towards women is also progressive. Generally speaking, religious fanaticism is a hindrance to progress, and this is why Sufi thought (the Bāṭini philosophy) helps to develop freedom of thought.'

258 —— 'Nahzat-i ismoiliho' [The Ismaili Renaissance], in *Tojikon (tārīkh-i qadimtarin, qadim, asrhoi miëna va davrai nav)* [The Tajiks (Earliest, Ancient, Medieval and Modern histories)]. Dushanbe: Donish, 2008, pp. 400–402. (in Tajik).

Ismailism is labelled here as a revolutionary movement opposed to mainstream Islam, and led by medieval feudal lords, encouraging an uprising amongst ordinary people and followers of other movements such as *taṣawwuf* and other innovative currents of thought.

259 —— 'Nosiri Khisrav' [Nāṣir-i Khusraw], in *Tojikon (tārīkh-i qadimtarin, qadim, asrhoi miëna va davrai nav)* [The Tajiks (Earliest, Ancient, Medieval and Modern histories)]. Dushanbe: Donish, 2008, pp. 433–435. (in Tajik).

A brief biography of Nāṣir-i Khusraw focussing on his conversion.

260 Ghulomi, Ali Muhammad. 'Hakim Nasir Khusraw as a Bright Sun', in Sarfaroz Niyozov and Ramazon Nazariev, ed., *Nasir Khusraw: Yesterday, Today, Tomorrow.* (Proceedings of a conference held in Khārūgh, Tajikistan). Khujand: Noshir, 2005, pp. 524–535.

The paper explores the religious ideas and beliefs of Nāṣir-i Khusraw through his poetry while comparing his interpretations with those of other Ismaili philosophers and writers. One of the subjects analysed is the position and authority of the imam, the spiritual leader of the Ismailis. The author considers Nāṣir-i Khusraw's teachings on *nubuwwa* (prophecy) and *imāma* (the imamate) in the light of his poetry and tries to define their value and status in terms of artistic and creative expression.

261 Gornenskiĭ, Ioann. *Legendy Pamira i Gindukusha* [Legends of the Pamirs and Hindu Kush]. Moscow: Aleteĭi͡a, 2000. pp. 208. (in Russian).

For many years the author travelled in the Pamirs, collecting ancient legends, which still survive in remote corners of the high valleys. The Pamir range is an ancient crossroads of trade routes, a reserve of secrets, a repository of legends of various peoples and religions.

262 Gotfrid, L. and M. Gafiz. *Krasnyĭ flag na Kryshe mira. Pamirskie ocherki* [Red Flag on the Roof of the World. Essays on the Pamir], Chapter 11, 'Ismaility' [Ismailis]. Tashkent; Stalinabad: Tadzhikgiz, 1930, pp. 94–102. (in Russian).

Having arrived in the Pamir region in 1923, Pīr Sabz ʿAlī prepared and organised a number of *anjuman*s (societies/committees). The local *pīr*s, who were losing their influence as a consequence of the innovative teaching propounded by the Panjebhai movement, revolted against the latter's newly-proposed religious rites which had not yet received the Aga Khan's endorsement.

263 Grigorīan, Sergeĭ Nikolaevich. *Iz istorii filosofii Sredneĭ Azii i Irana VII-XII vekov* [On the History of Philosophy in Central Asia and Iran from the 7th to the 12th Centuries], Moscow: IAN USSR, 1960. pp. 330. (in Russian).

The outstanding thinkers of Central Asia and Iran are depicted as bearers of new ideas, and philosophical, scientific and doctrinal approaches to the study of religious teachings. They are credited with having mapping out new paths of research and having made a vast contribution to the world cultural heritage.

264 —— *Srednevekovaīa filosofiīa narodov Blizhnego i Srednego Vostoka* [Medieval Philosophy of the People of the Near and Middle East]. Moscow: Nauka, 1966. pp. 352. (in Russian).

This work is an excursus on the history of the philosophy of science relative to the philosophical heritage of the people of Central Asia, Iran and the Arab East. It presents a unified picture of their materialist and rationalist ideas set against the religion and ideology of the Middle East during the Middle Ages.

265 Grigor'ev, Sergeĭ Evgen'evich. 'Ismaility Afganistana: nekotorye zamechaniīa i nabliūdeniīa' [The Ismailis of Afghanistan: Some Notes and Observations], *Vestnik Vostochnogo Instituta*, vol. 2 (1996), pp. 88–106. (in Russian).

266 —— 'K voprosu o rodoslovnoĭ ismailitskikh pirov Afghanistana' [On the Lineage of the Ismaili *Pīr*s of Afghanistan], *Strany i narody Vostoka*, vol. 30 (1998), pp. 242–251. (in Russian).

As suggested by the title of the article, the author has attempted to define the features common to Sufism and Ismailism in terms of ideology and organisation. The primary intent is to identify their historical and traditional sources, which should enable us to understand the intricacies of the religious ideologies in a number of eastern countries today. At the beginning of the article, the author admits that his approach is in accordance with the Marxist explanation of religion that is to say historical materialism, which is presented as the only scientific method.

267 Gross, Jo-Ann. 'Introduction', *Journal of Persianate Studies*, 4 (2011), pp. 109–116.

The papers, according to the author, in this symposium address four main themes: (i) issues of religious and ethno-linguistic identity; (ii) the effects of institutional, structural and environmental change, particularly in Tajikistan and Kyrgyzstan where socio-economic dislocation and nation building followed the break-up of the Soviet Union; (iii) the ecological, spiritual and socio-cultural dimensions of geographical space and the natural landscape; and (iv) indigenous knowledge, legend and history.

268 —— 'Foundational Legends, Shrines, and Isma'ili Identity in Gorno-Badakhshan, Tajikistan', in Margaret Gormack, ed., *Muslims and Others in Sacred Space*. Oxford: Oxford University Press, 2013, pp. 164–192.

The aim of this study is to explore the geography of sacred knowledge in the Pamirs through its foundational traditions. It discusses their relationship with the sacred landscape of shrine networks in the regions of Shughnān, Rāshtqala, Ishkāshim, and Wakhān.

269 —— 'The Motif of the Cave and the Funerary Narratives of Nāṣir-i Khusrau', in Julia Rubanovich, ed., *Orality and Textuality in the Iranian World*. Leiden: Brill, 2015, pp. 130–165.

This study examines the motif of the cave as it relates specifically to the oral and written traditions regarding Nāṣir-i Khusraw's death and burial in Yumgān. The analysis is based on two primary sources: (i) oral traditions collected during field research in Tajik Badakhshān; (ii) the funerary narrative contained in a *Risāla* written in the voice of Nāṣir-i Khusraw and his brother, Abū Sa'īd.

270 —— 'Preliminary Notes on the *Naṣab-nāmah*s of Badakhshan', *Shii Studies Review*, 2 (2018), pp. 365–371.

The project draws attention to the history of the Ismaili tradition in the context of Islamic Central Asia and engages in a new field of inquiry concerning the local cultural practices of Islamic documentation in the Persianate world, specifically the documentation of genealogically-based sanctity and *sayyid* pedigree among familial communities of *shāh*s, *pīr*s and *khalīfa*s in Badakhshān.

271 Gulamadov, Shaftolu. *The Hagiography of Nāṣir-i Khusraw and the Ismā'īlīs of Badakhshān*, PhD dissertation, University of Toronto, 2018, pp. 471.

The thesis examines Badakhshānī Ismaili hagiographical texts written between, approximately, the late 10th/16th and the late 14th/20th century in their socio-political contexts. It analyses the narratives by drawing attention to how the authors expressed ideals, values, beliefs, practices and concerns through the medium of hagiography.

H

272 Hasan Mahmud Kotib. *Devoni Qoimiët* [*Dīvān-i Qā'imiyyāt*], ed. Jalal Badakhchani and Ato Mirkhoja. Dushanbe: Bukhoro, 2015. pp. 593. (in Tajik).

Ḥasan-i Maḥmūd-i Kātib's *Dīvān-i Qā'imiyyāt* is a collection of Ismaili religious poems of the 7th/13th century. This newly discovered work is significant for Persian culture and language in particular, and Ismaili studies in general, and is of remarkable value from historical, social, political and religious perspectives. Jalal Badakhchani, the editor of this volume adds important biographical information about the author of many of the poems. Ḥasan-i Maḥmūd-i Kātib was also known as Ḥasan-i Ṣalāḥ Munshī; he was a contemporary of four imams of the Alamūt period, from Ḥasan 'alā dhikrihi al-salām (d. 561/1166) to 'Alā' al-Dīn Muḥammad (d. 653/1255). He was probably born in north-west Iran, in the region of Qazwīn, and joined the Ismaili community at a young age. For a long period he worked as a scribe for the Ismaili rulers of Quhistān. He moved to Alamūt, the centre of the Nizārī Ismaili state in Iran, around 637/1240 and died there in 644/1247. It is argued that Ḥasan-i Maḥmūd-i Kātib's *Dīvān* has been deemed instrumental in the compilation of Naṣīr al-Dīn Ṭūsī's *Rawḍa-yi taslīm*.

273 Hojibekov, Elbon. 'Nazare ba tārīkh-i i͡ak pareshoni dar sunnati ismoiliëni Shughnonu Rushon, ë marosimi 'Charoghravshan'-i ajdodi va paĭdoishi 'panj tasbeh'-i panjobhai (panjaboi)' [A Glance at the History of Misapprehension in the Ismaili Traditions of Shughnān and Rūshān, or the 'Ceremony of the Ancestors' 'Chirāgh-i Rawshan' and the emergence of the 'Panj Tasbeḥ' of the Panjabhai (Panjebhai)], *Donishgohi Davlatii Khārūgh* (1999), pp. 1–5. (in Tajik).

The article investigates the Panjebhai movement and the role of Sayyid Munīr as the movement's missionary in Badakhshān in the early Soviet period.

274 —— 'Naqshi pironi mazhabī dar khudikhtiërī hamroh kardani Pomir ba Rossii͡a' [The Role of the Ismaili *pīrs* in the Voluntary Entry of the Pamirs into Russia]. *Paëmi Donishgohi Khārūgh*, 3 (1999), pp. 120–125. (in Tajik).

Historical evidence suggests that it was mainly due to Ismaili *pīrs* that the Pamir region entered voluntarily into a union with Tsarist Russia. They viewed this union as the only means of safeguarding the Ismaili community from Sunni and Afghan persecution.

275 —— *Ismailitskie dukhovnye nastavniki (piry) i ikh rol' v obshchestvenno-politicheskoĭ i kul'turnoĭ zhizni Shugnana: vtorai͡a polovina XIX veka – 30-e gody XX v.* [Ismaili Spiritual Mentors (*pīrs*) and their Role in the Socio-Political and Cultural Life of Shughnan: the second half of the 19th Century – 1930s], Dissertat͡sii͡a na soiskanie uchënoĭ stepeni kandidata filosofskikh

nauk [PhD Candidate for the Degree of Doctor of Philosophy]. AN Tajikistan: Dushanbe: Akademi Nauk, 2002. pp. 189. (in Russian).

276 —— 'Mahmadalishoh Saidiūsufalishoev – okhirin piri aholii Shughnon' [Mahmad ʿAlī Shāh Sayyid Yūsuf ʿAlī Shāh, the Last Pīr of Shughnān], *Paëmi Donishgohi Khārūgh*, 1, 2 (2002), pp. 146–151. (in Tajik).

Following the death of Sayyid Yūsuf ʿAlī Shāh, an Ismaili *pīr* from the Shughnān district, his followers decided to elect Maḥmad ʿAlī Shāh as their next *pīr*, and this appointment was later on approved by the *farmān* of the Imam of the time. He was later captured by the Soviet agents on the Afghan side of Shughnān and probably shot to death.

277 —— 'The Representations of Historical Time and Some Humanistic Ideas in Nasir Khusraw's Poetry', in Sarfaroz Niyozov and Ramazon Nazariev, ed., *Nasir Khusraw: Yesterday, Today, Tomorrow*. (Proceedings of a conference held in Khārūgh, Tajikistan). Khujand: Noshir, 2005, pp. 241–252.

Hojibekov engages in an analysis of Nāṣir-i Khusraw's ethical ideas, all of which clearly possess humanistic pathos. The author's analysis and conclusions indicate that, regardless of Nāṣir-i Khusraw's own suffering at the hands of the Saljūq rulers, he always propounded humanism, knowledge and reason.

278 —— 'On a Religious Tradition of the People of Badakhshan', in Sarfaroz Niyozov and Ramazon Nazariev, ed., *Nasir Khusraw: Yesterday, Today, Tomorrow*. (Proceedings of a conference held in Khārūgh, Tajikistan). Khujand: Noshir, 2005, pp. 605–610.

The author touches upon a popular tradition known as *Zinda daʿwa* in the Shughnān and Rūshān districts of Badakhshān and as *Daʿwat-i ṣafāʾ* in the Wakhān and Ghārān areas of the district of Ishkāshim. This tradition, which the author considers is part of the concept of *Daʿwat-i baqāʾ*, is no longer practised.

279 —— 'Repressii 30-kh godov XX veka i ismaility Badakhshana' [The Repression of the 1930s and the Ismailis of Badakhshān], in A.Z. Almazova, ed., *Pamirskaiā Ėkspedit͡siiā (statʾi i materialy polevykh issledovaniĭ)* [Pamir Expedition (articles and materials of field research)]. Moscow: RAN Institut Vostokovedeniiā, 2006, pp. 101–110. (in Russian).

The virtual 'elimination' of the Ismaili *pīrs* in Badakhshān in the 1930s is presented as having been facilitated by the local people themselves. Amongst the causes, the author identifies illiteracy, a lack of experience (especially among young people) and political short-sightedness as factors which led to mass repression.

280 —— 'Rudakī va davlati Somoniën' [Rūdakī and the Sāmānid State], in *Simpoziumi baĭnalmilalii ʿRudakī va farhangi jahonīʾ*, 6–7 senti͡abrī, 2008

[International Symposium 'Rūdakī and the World Culture' (6–7 September 2008)]. Dushanbe, pp. 179–180. (in Tajik).

This paper points out the similarity between the ideas and views of Rūdakī and the *Ikhwān al-Ṣafāʾ* due to their common historical, ideological and literary circumstances.

281 —— 'The History of the Ismaili *Pirs* of Shughnan in the Works of Russian, Soviet and Contemporary Scholars', in Stanislav M. Prozorov and Hakim Elnazarov, ed., *Russian Scholars on Ismailism*. (Proceedings of a conference held in St Petersburg, Russia in 2011). St Petersburg: Nestor-Istoriiā, 2014, pp. 218–228.

The author of the paper examines the major issues in the history of the Ismaili *pīrs* of the Shughnān district of the GBAO of Tajikistan as presented in the works of Russian and Soviet scholars.

282 —— *Ismailitskie dukhovnye nastavniki (piry), ikh rol' v obshchestvennoĭ zhizni Shugnana (vtoraiā polovina XIX – 30-e gody XX vv.)* [Ismaili Spiritual Mentors (*pīrs*) and their Role in the Social Life of Shughnān: the Second half of the 19th Century – 1930s]. Dushanbe: 'Bukhoro', 2015. pp. 282. (in Russian).

The monograph focuses on the Ismaili *pīrs* of Pārshnëv and mainly on Sayyid Farrukh Shāh and his son Sayyid Yūsuf ʿAlī Shāh, the religious leaders of Shughnān. It analyses the struggle during the second half of the 19th century against the Afghan and the Bukharan rulers, who regarded the Ismailis as heretics. These rulers abused and jailed thousands of Ismailis, and shipped others to Kabul and other central regions of Afghanistan as slaves.

Honsberger, Alis, see Hunsberger, Alice.

283 Hunsberger, Alice C. 'Nasir Khusraw: Fatimid Intellectual', in Farhad Daftary, ed., *Intellectual Traditions in Islam*. London: I.B. Tauris, 2001, pp. 112–129.

For Nāṣir-i Khusraw, reason is not opposed to faith, but it does represent an alternative way of life. Reason is integral in both leading a believer to proper faith and strengthening that conviction.

284 —— *Nasir Khusraw the Ruby of Badakhshan: A Portrait of the Persian Poet, Traveller and Philosopher*. London: I.B. Tauris, 2003. pp. xxiii + 292.

285 —— *Laʿli Badakhshan* [The Ruby of Badakhshān], tr. N. Zurobekov. Dushanbe: Nodir, 2003. pp. 328. (in Tajik).

286 —— *Nasir Khusrav – Rubin Badakhshana. Portret persidskogo poèta, puteshestvennika, filosofa* [Nasir Khusraw: the Ruby of Badakhshān: A Portrait of the Persian Poet, Traveller and Philosopher], tr. Leila R. Dodykhudoeva. Moscow: Ladomir, 2005. pp. 288. (in Russian).

The first large-scale study of the life and creative heritage of Nāṣir-i Khusraw, one of the greatest Persian poets; a writer and traveller, who was above all an Ismaili thinker and influential preacher. A unique synthesis of magnificent poetry and original theological constructions made the subject of this book one of the outstanding figures of medieval Islamic culture.

287 —— 'Cosmos into Verse: two Examples of Islamic Philosophical Poetry in Persia', in Omar Alí-de-Unzaga, ed., *Fortresses of the Intellect: Ismaili and other Islamic Studies in Honour of Farhad Daftary*. London: I.B. Tauris, 2011, pp. 343–367.

This paper examines the genre of philosophical poetry in the Persian language, specifically the composition of philosophical *qaṣīda*s by Nāṣir-i Khusraw who expressed highly sophisticated ideas in this genre of poetry.

288 —— *Pearls of Persia: The Philosophical Poetry of Nāṣir-i Khusraw*. London: I.B. Tauris, 2012. pp. 286.

This volume is based on a conference, 'The Philosophical Poetry of Nāṣir-i Khusraw', convened in 2005 by Alice Hunsberger in collaboration with Doris Behrens-Abouseif at the School of Oriental and African Studies (SOAS) in London, as part of the international commemorations of the 1000th anniversary of the birth of Nāṣir-i Khusraw. The chapters are arranged in three main sections: (i) Speech and Intellect; (ii) Philosophical Poetry: Enlightening the Soul; and (iii) Nāṣir-i Khusraw's Poetics; the volume consists of 13 chapters and an introduction.

289 Hunzai, Faquir Muhammad. 'The Necessity of the *Ta'wīl* of the Qur'an and the *sharīʿa* According to Nasir Khusraw', in Sarfaroz Niyozov and Ramazon Nazariev, ed., *Nasir Khusraw: Yesterday, Today, Tomorrow*. (Proceedings of a conference held in Khārūgh, Tajikistan). Khujand: Noshir, 2005, pp. 165–171.

Through *ta'wīl*, the seekers of the truth are taken beyond the apparent meaning of words, reaching their original and deepest sense. Thus, the method of *ta'wīl* is a means to a broader interpretation of apparent meanings. Moreover, *ta'wīl* is portrayed as a 'path' to rationalism and an instrument triggering pluralism through discussion.

290 Hunzai, Fida Ali Isar. 'Nasir Khusraw's Approach to Ethics', in Sarfaroz Niyozov and Ramazon Nazariev, ed., *Nasir Khusraw: Yesterday, Today, Tomorrow*. (Proceedings of a conference held in Khārūgh, Tajikistan). Khujand: Noshir, 2005, pp. 280–288.

The roots of ethics are to be found in the Qur'an and in the sayings and actions of the Prophet of Islam, whose personality embodies for Muslims the highest ethical standard. Nāṣir's position on ethics suggests that the straight path for any individual is a reflection of virtuous acts and behaviour.

291 Hunzai, Ghulam Abbas. 'The Concept of Pleasure Propounded by Nāṣir-i Khusraw'. MA dissertation, Institute of Islamic Studies, McGill University, Montreal, 1993. pp. 133.

This study investigates the views of Nāṣir-i Khusraw on a cardinal religio-philosophical concept, that is, pleasure, and places it in historical contexts by attempting to find out the origins of its philosophical explanation.

292 —— 'The Meaning of Pleasure in the Philosophy of Nasir Khusraw', in Sarfaroz Niyozov and Ramazon Nazariev, ed., *Nasir Khusraw: Yesterday, Today, Tomorrow*. (Proceedings of a conference held in Khārūgh, Tajikistan). Khujand: Noshir, 2005, pp. 59–67.

According to Nāṣir-i Khusraw, the concept of pleasure is not simply an ethical one, but a cosmic issue, which is active and functional on all existential levels. On the sub-human level (i.e. mineral, vegetable and animal), the principle of pleasure is a driving force, which enables man to preserve the well-being of all entities belonging to this dominium. However, from the human level up to the level of the Universal soul, this principle acquires an increasingly epistemological character as it is connected to the soul's activity of gaining knowledge.

293 —— 'Nasir-i Khusraw's Intellectual Contribution: the Meaning of Pleasure and Pain in His Philosophy', in Dagikhudo Dagiev and Carole Faucher, ed., *Identity, History and Trans-Nationality in Central Asia: The Mountain Communities of Pamir*. London: Routledge, 2018, pp. 106–122.

The chapter consists of two parts. The first part makes an attempt to present a synoptic vision of Nasir-i Khusraw's contribution as an Ismaili *dāʿī*, Persian poet, Muslim philosopher and founder of the faith tradition in Central Asia. In the second part, it endeavours to examine Nasir-i Khusraw's notion of pleasure (*lazzat*) as one of the central principles of his philosophical worldview.

294 Hunzā'ī, Naṣīr al-Dīn. *Charoghi ravshan va olami donishi Hakim Nosiri Khusrav* [Charāgh-i Rawshan and Ḥakīm Nāṣir-i Khusraw's World of Knowledge], tr. from English, Parwona Jamshed. Dushanbe, 1998. pp. 71. (in Tajik).

A translation from English into Tajik of *Charāgh-i Rawshan*, a work by ʿAllāma Naṣīr al-Dīn Hunzāʾī. He argues that the text of the *Charāgh-i Rawshan* requires a spiritual explanation (*taʾwīl*; esoteric hermeneutical interpretation) because of the meaning hidden in it. The *Charāgh-i Rawshan* ceremonies have been divided into 21 *ḥikma*s, each one having a specific spiritual meaning in the performance of the ceremony.

295 Hunzai, Shahnaz Salim. 'The Significance of the Tradition of Nasir Khusraw and the Reinvigoration of its Intellectual Aspect in Northern Pakistan', in Sarfaroz Niyozov and Ramazon Nazariev, ed., *Nasir Khusraw: Yesterday, Today, Tomorrow*. (Proceedings of a conference held in Khārūgh, Tajikistan). Khujand: Noshir, 2005, pp. 626–631.

The work discusses the important geo-political changes of the 20th century, such as the partition of the Indian sub-continent. As a result of colonial policy, the Ismaili *daʿwa* centred in Badakhshān gradually lost its active influence in Northern Pakistan. This, in turn, brought about the decline of the Persian language in the area.

I

296 Iloliev, Abdulmamad. 'Mubarak Wakhani's Intellectual Contributions to Nasir Khusraw's Tradition in Pamir', in Sarfaroz Niyozov and Ramazon Nazariev, ed., *Nasir Khusraw: Yesterday, Today, Tomorrow*. (Proceedings of a conference held in Khārūgh, Tajikistan). Khujand: Noshir, 2005, pp. 611–619.

Through an examination of the life and legacy of Mubārak-i Wakhānī, a Persian mystical poet, the author identifies connections between the Ismaili tradition introduced by Nāṣir-i Khusraw and the Sufi tradition. Mubārak-i Wakhānī was able to reconcile Sufi vocabulary, methods and symbolism with Ismaili esotericism in the context of the Pamir region.

297 —— *The Ismāʿīlī-Sufi Sage of Pamir: Mubarak-i Wakhani and the Esoteric Tradition of the Pamir Muslims*. Amherst, NY: Cambria Press, 2008. pp. 238.

This book is the first introductory study on the subject, and provides a systematic presentation of a seminal Islamic figure. In an endeavour to establish an accurate biography of Mubārak-i Wakhānī and to render his Ismaili-Sufi ideas as lucidly and coherently as possible, the author concentrates on assessing his life and thoughts in their historical and religious context. In addition he explores how far Mubārak's works represent the indigenous Pamiri perception of Ismaili thought and where he stands in relation to it in general.

298 —— 'Popular Culture and Religious Metaphor: Saints and Shrines in Wakhan Region of Tajikistan', *CAS*, 27, 1 (2008), pp. 59–73.

This is a study of Ismaili saints (*awliyāʾ*) and shrines (sing. *qadamgāh*) in the Wakhān region of Tajikistan along with their historical context. It draws a succinct historical and ethnographical picture of shrine culture in the region and determines its religious significance in the broad frame of the socio-cultural context of Wakhān.

299 —— 'Pirship in Badakhshan: The Role and Significance of the Institute of the Religious Masters (*Pirs*) in Nineteenth and Twentieth Century Wakhan and Shughnan', *JSIS*, 6, 2 (2013), pp. 155–175.

This is an examination of how the Ismailis, like many other Muslim communities, have developed their own distinctive ways of practising Islam and being Muslim. These are also deeply rooted in their indigenous histories and cultures, but theoretically framed in relation to the Shiʿi doctrine of the imamate.

300 —— 'King of Men: 'Ali Ibn Abi Talib in Pamiri Folktales', *JSIS*, 8, 3 (2015), pp. 307–323.

Examining the traditional Pamiri accounts associated with 'Alī b. Abī Ṭālib, the paper explores the hagiographic image of 'Alī.

301 —— 'The Concept of *Wilāya* in Mubārak-i Wakhānī's *Chihil Dunyā*: A Traditional Ismaili–Sufi Perspective on the Origins of Divine Guidance', in Orkhan Mir-Kasimov, ed., *Intellectual Interactions in the Islamic World: The Ismaili Thread*. London: I.B. Tauris, 2019, pp. 381–403.

This article aims to examine the concept of *wilāya* ('the exercise of authority'), which denotes devotion for and allegiance to the Shiʿi imams, in Wakhānī's *Risāla-yi Chihil Dunyā* ('The Epistle of the Forty Worlds') in relation to the special role and spiritual authority of 'Alī b. Abī Ṭālib (d. 40/661) in Shiʿi and Sufi thought. Discussing Wakhānī's perception of *wilāya* as the divinely given spiritual authority of 'Alī, Iloliev explores how Sufi ideas are used alongside, and in conjunction with, the Ismaili concept of *imāma*.

302 Ilolov, Mamadsho. 'The Themes of Intellect and Knowledge in Nasir Khusraw and their Balance in Contemporary Science', in Sarfaroz Niyozov and Ramazon Nazariev, ed., *Nasir Khusraw: Yesterday, Today, Tomorrow*. (Proceedings of a conference held in Khārūgh, Tajikistan). Khujand: Noshir, 2005, pp. 201–205.

The intellect is portrayed as God's creation according to Nāṣir-i Khusraw's views. The understanding of religion and its development is achieved not through blind imitation and dogmatic defensiveness, but through the laws of science, especially logic.

303 Inostrant͡sev, Konstantin Aleksandrovich (1876–1941). *Torzhestvennyĭ vyezd fatymidskikh khalifov* [The Ceremonial Procession of the Fatimid Caliphs]. St Peterburg, 1905. pp. 113. (in Russian).

304 —— *Torzhestvennyĭ vyezd fatymidskikh khalifov* [The Ceremonial Procession of the Fatimid Caliphs]. Izdatel'stvo: 'ЁЁ Media' (Kniga po trebovanii͡u [Print on Demand]), 2012. pp. 120. (in Russian).

This is a Russian annotated translation from Arabic describing the perception which the Egyptian chronicler al-Maqrīzī (1364–1442) had of the court ceremonials in the Fatimid state. The latter (297–567/909–1171) being described as a medieval Shiʿi (Ismaili) Arab state with its centre in Cairo (from 972), ruling over Egypt, North Africa, and parts of Syria.

305 Iqbol, Shaĭkh Muhammad and Khonum Z̤avohir Nur Ali. *Taʾrīkh-i ismoiliia*. Tahii͡ai matn, peshguftor va lughotu tavzehot az Saidanvar Shohkhumorov va Amrii͡azdon Alimardonov [Ismaili History. The Draft of the Text, Preface and Explanation of Vocabulary by Saidanvar Shokhumorov and Amriyazdon Alimardonov]. Dushanbe: n.p., 1997; 2nd ed., 2006. pp. 195. (in Tajik).

Ismaili History was written by Shaykh Muḥammad Iqbāl and Zawahir Noorally in Urdu. However, the Tajik text with minor editing is a translation from the Persian text published in Karachi in 1979.

The book consists of four parts and each part covers a particular period of Ismaili history. The first part is from the early period of Islam up to the Fatimids in Egypt. The second part relates to the history of the Fatimid caliphs. The third part focuses on the history of the imamate in Iran, and the fourth part begins with the history of the imamate in India.

306 Iṣfahānī, Ghiyāth al-Dīn. *Nujūm* [Astronomy], tr. and ed. Umed Shohzodamuhammad. Khārūgh: Nashriëti "Meros", 1995. pp. 95. (in Tajik).

Ghiyāth al-Dīn Iṣfahānī was one of the most celebrated Ismaili *dāʿī*s sent to Badakhshān during the time of the 32nd Nizārī Ismaili Imam, Mustanṣir bi'llāh II (d. 885/1480) in the 9th/15th century. The works of Ghiyāth al-Dīn Iṣfahānī became well known in Badakhshān. Among his interests was the elucidation of the development of astronomy in Badakhshān. Despite the fact that there were no *madrasa*s in Badakhshān at the time, astronomers taught their students in private schools, and observed the galaxy and the planets in order to determine auspicious and inauspicious times.

307 Iskandarov, B. *Sotsial'no-ėkonomicheskie i politicheskie aspecty istorii Pamirskikh knīazhestv (X v. - pervaīa polovina XIX v.)* [Socio-Economic and Political Aspects of the History of the Pamir Kingdoms (10th–first half of 11th centuries]. Dushanbe: 'Donish', 1983. pp. 159. (in Russian).

This work deals with the socio-political and economic aspects of the life of the people in the Pamir region over thousands of years.

308 Iskhog, Tavonofar Murod Ali. *Religiozno-filosofskie i sotsial'no-politicheskie vozzreniīa nizaritov Alamuta* [The Religio-Philosophical and Socio-Political Views of the Nizārīs of Alamūt], Dissertatsiīa na soiskanie uchënoĭ stepeni kandidata filosofskikh nauk [PhD Candidate for the Degree of Doctor of Philosophy]. Dushanbe: Akademi Nauk, 2015. pp. 162. (in Russian).

The work investigates the religio-philosophical and socio-political views of Nizārī Ismailis from a number of hitherto unexplored historical sources.

309 'Ismoiliīa va adabiëti ismoilī dar asrhoi XII–XIV' [Ismailism and Ismaili Literature in the 12th–14th Centuries], in Rasul Hodizoda, ed., *Adabiëti forsu-tojik dar asrhoi XII-XIV* [Persian-Tajik Literature in the 12th–14th Centuries], Part I. Dushanbe: Donish, 1976, pp. 181–214. (in Tajik).

This work was designed for graduate students of Tajik/Persian language and literature. It provides detailed studies of Ismaili history from the Marxist perspective which considered the work of the Ismaili *daʿwa* as a struggle for the control of political power among different factions of society.

Ivanov, Vladimir Alekseevich, see Ivanow, Wladimir.

310 Ivanow, Wladimir (1886–1970). 'Ismailitskie rukopisi Aziatskogo Muzeĩa. Sobranie I. Zarubina, 1916 g.' [Ismaili Manuscripts of the Asiatic Museum. The I. Zarubina Collection, 1916], *Izvestiĩa Rossiĭskoĭ Akademii Nauk* (Petrograd). *BAISR*, 6 serie, 11 (1917), pp. 359–386. (in Russian). English summary in E. Denison Ross, 'W. Ivanow, Ismaili MSS in the Asiatic Museum, Petrograd, 1917', *JRAS* (1919), pp. 429–435.

A list of the extremely valuable Ismaili manuscripts brought from Shughnān and Rūshān to the Asiatic Museum by I.I. Zarubin.

311 —— 'An Ismailitic Pedigree', *JASB*, NS, 18 (1922), pp. 403–406.

A review of a manuscript containing a rare Persian work detailing the theoretical system of Shiʿism. The manuscript is extensive and provides some information about Shiʿi tendencies and references to the extensively used principles of *taqiyya*.

312 —— *Ismailitica*, in *Memoirs of the Asiatic Society of Bengal*, 8 (1922), pp. 1–76.

A short text which, according to its author, contains an exposition of some secret Ismaili doctrines, as well as a few notes on the present state of the Ismailis in Persia.

313 —— 'Notes on the Ismailis in Persia', in his *Ismailitica*, in *Memoirs of the Asiatic Society of Bengal*, 8 (1922), pp. 50–76.

A study relative to the Ismailis in Persia: their lifestyle; geographical location in Iran; family structural organisation and family ties; beliefs and understanding of their imam.

314 —— 'Imam Ismail', *JASB*, NS, 19 (1923), pp. 305–310.

According to Ivanow, some interesting casual references to Imam Ismāʿīl are found in a little known and rare Shiʿi book, *Maʿrifat akhbār al-rijāl*, composed sometime in the 4th/10th century by Abū ʿUmar Muḥammad b. ʿUmar b. ʿAbd al-ʿAzīz al-Kishshī. Although such references do not add much to our current knowledge of Imam Ismāʿīl, they deserve attention for two main reasons: (i) such references are extremely rare in Islamic literature and, (ii) they come apparently from early and very reliable sources.

315 —— 'Alamut', *Geographical Journal*, 77 (1931), pp. 38–45.

The paper is based on Ivanow's personal observations of the fortress of Alamūt. It is shaped by both the literary sources and reports which he collected directly from members of the Ismaili community in Iran.

316 —— 'An Ismailitic Work by Nasiru'd-din Tusi', *JRAS* (1931), pp. 527–564.

The work is an important introduction to the life and the works of Naṣīr al-Dīn Ṭūsī. Of particular interest to the reader is the question of Ṭūsī's relationship with his Ismaili patrons. The work also analyses Ṭūsī's philosophical investigations and his views on Ismaili doctrine.

317 Ivanow, Wladimir. 'An Ismaili Interpretation of the Gulshani Raz', *JBBRAS*, NS, 8 (1932), pp. 69–78.

The treatise called *Gulshan-i Rāz* is probably one of the most popular sources on Sufism, largely imitated and commented upon, particularly by Persian poets. One of such commentary is a short work titled *Baʿḍī az Taʾwilāt-i Gulshan-i Rāz* which offers Ismaili explanations of selected passages from the original treatise.

318 —— 'Notes sur l'Ummu'l-kitab des Ismaëliens de l'Asie Centrale', *REI*, 6 (1932), pp. 419–481.

319 —— *A Guide to Ismaili Literature*. Royal Asiatic Society, Prize Publication Fund, XIII. London: Royal Asiatic Society, 1933. pp. xii and 138.

A Guide to Ismaili Literature is the first catalogue of Ismaili sources published in modern times. It demonstrates the richness and diversity of Ismaili literature and served as an invaluable tool, for several decades, for the advancement of Ismaili scholarship.

320 —— tr., into English from Persian with an Introduction, *Divan of Khaki Khorasani* [Khākī Khurāsānī]. Islamic Research Association (1). Bombay, 1933. pp. 128.

As Ivanow says in the introduction, the *Dīvān*, or collection of lyric poetry was the work of Imām-Qulī, who was the inhabitant of the village of Dizbād situated high up in the hills, half-way between Mashhad and Nīshāpūr. In his poetry, he used the *takhalluṣ*, or *nom-de-plume* of Khākī, and is known as Khākī Khurāsānī.

321 —— 'The Sect of Imam Shah in Gujrat', *JBBRAS*, NS, 12 (1936), pp. 19–70.

322 —— 'Some Muhammadan Shrines in Western India', *Ismaili*, Golden Jubilee Number, 5 (21 January, 1936), pp. 16–23.

323 —— 'A Forgotten Branch of the Ismailis', *JRAS* (1938), pp. 57–59.

In 1537, an extraordinary event took place in Aḥmadnagar, when the ruler Burhān Niẓām Shāh proclaimed Shiʿism the official religion of his kingdom. The paper is devoted to the central figure who inspired this policy: a rather enigmatic Persian emigrant, a learned theologian, philosopher, poet and politician, Shāh Ṭāhir, surnamed Dakkhanī Ḥusaynī.

324 —— 'Some Ismaili Strongholds in Persia', *IC*, 12 (1938), pp. 383–396.

The author's personal investigation and research into the medieval Ismaili fortresses of the Nizārī state, about which little was known. The author draws attention to the fact that, for his contemporaries there was no reliable information on the famous fortress of Alamūt linked to Ḥasan-i Ṣabbāḥ.

325 —— 'Tombs of Some Persian Ismaili Imams', *JBBRAS*, NS, 14 (1938), pp. 49–62.

The article investigates the nature of the tombs of the Ismaili imams during the period of concealment following the Mongol destruction of the Ismaili strongholds.

326 —— 'The Organisation of the Fatimid Propaganda', *JBBRAS*, NS, 15 (1939), pp. 1–35; reprinted in Bryan S. Turner, ed., *Orientalism: Early Sources*, vol. I: *Readings in Orientalism*. London: Routledge, 2000, pp. 531–571.

327 —— 'Ismailis and Qarmatians', *JBBRAS*, NS, 16 (1940), pp. 43–85.

Virtually all the early historians regarded the Ismailis and the Qarmaṭīs as members of the same religious group. This view that generally prevailed among the early Orientalists was that the term 'Qarmaṭīs' was actually the authentic name of the Fatimid caliphs.

328 —— 'Early Shiʿite Movements', *JBBRAS*, NS, 17 (1941), pp. 1–23.

According to Ivanow, historians too often regarded Shiʿi sectarian movements as purely religious developments resulting from the impact of pre-Islamic religious traditions on Islam. The need to counter-argue this conviction motivated him to produce this work.

329 —— *Ismaili Tradition Concerning the Rise of the Fatimids*. Islamic Research Association Series, 10. Bombay, etc.: Published for the Islamic Research Association by H. Milford, Oxford University Press, 1942. pp. xxii and 337 (English), 113 (Arabic).

The work is an attempt – apparently the first of its kind – to collect, analyse, and systematise as far as possible all the information contained in genuine Ismaili literature concerning the history of the Shiʿi moment which brought about the foundation of the Fatimid caliphate in North Africa in 297/909.

330 —— *The Alleged Founder of Ismailism*. Ismaili Society Series A, 1. Bombay: Published for the Ismaili Society by Thacker and Co., 1946. pp. xv and 197; 2nd revised edition as *Ibn al-Qaddāḥ (The Alleged Founder of Ismailism)*. Ismaili Society Series A, 9. Bombay: Ismaili Society, 1957. pp. 159.

The author challenges the centuries-old myth of ʿAbd Allāh b. Maymūn al-Qaddāḥ, the non-ʿAlid personality often regarded by anti-Ismaili polemicists of medieval times as the founder of the Ismaili movement and the progenitor of the Fatimid caliphs.

331 —— tr. into English from Persian, *True Meaning of Religion* [Risāla dar Ḥaqīqat-i Dīn]. Bombay, India: Published for the Ismaili Society by Thacker & Co., 1947. pp. xiv and 51.

A short treatise on the fundamental Ismaili principles. It represents a useful introduction to the study of the Ismaili doctrine in general and of its Nizārī facet in particular.

332 —— tr., into English from Persian, *On the Recognition of the Imam* [Faṣl dar Bayān-i Shinakht-i Imām]. Bombay, India: Published for the Ismaili Society by Thacker & Co., 1947. pp. x–xii, pp. 59.

According to Ivanow the pamphlet represents a remarkable discovery due to the outspoken treatment of specific esoteric subjects and to the abundance of references to authors and poets of Persian literature.

333 —— *Studies in Early Persian Ismailism*. Ismaili Society Series A, 3. Leiden: Published for the Ismaili Society by E.J. Brill, 1948. pp. 202; 2nd ed., Ismaili Society Series A, 8. Bombay: Ismaili Society, 1955. pp. 157.

The work is a combination of several articles written by Ivanow relative to early Ismaili history, particularly the early history of the Ismaili movement in Persia.

334 —— ed. *Collectanea*: vol. I. Ismaili Society Series A, 2. Leiden: Published for the Ismaili Society by E.J. Brill, 1948. pp. xii + 242.

The volume includes translations and collection of seminal Ismaili related literature.

335 —— *Nasir-i Khusraw and Ismailism*. Ismaili Society Series B, 5. Bombay: Ismaili Society, 1948. pp. 78. Persian tr., *Nāṣir-i Khusraw va Ismāʿīliyān*, tr., Yaʿqūb Āzhand, in B. Lewis et al., *Ismāʿīliyān dar tārīkh*, pp. 403–463.

The work was intended to elucidate Nāṣir-i Khusraw's relationship with Ismailism, a point which in his biography remained for a long time rather obscure.

336 —— 'Noms bibliques dans la mythologie Ismaélienne', *JA*, 237 (1949), pp. 249–255.

An analysis of the Biblical names occurring in Ismaili mythological tales.

337 —— *Brief Survey of the Evolution of Ismailism*. Ismaili Society Series B, 7. Leiden: Published for the Ismaili Society by E.J. Brill, 1952. pp. 92.

As the author argues, this work is an attempt to provide the gist of the revolution that Ismaili ideas, as a whole, underwent in the course of the twelve centuries of Ismaili history.

338 —— 'Abū ʿAlī Sīnā va Ismāʿīliyān-i makhfī', in *Jashn-nāma-yi Ibn Sīnā/Le livre du millénaire d'Avicenne*, vol. 2. Tehran: Anjuman-i Āthār-i Millī, 1334 Sh./1955, pp. 450–454.

The article investigates whether Ibn Sīnā adhered to the same religious belief, that of the Ismailis, as his father and brother.

339 —— 'Shums Tabrez of Multan', in S.M. Abdullah, ed., *Professor Muḥammad Shafīʿ Presentation Volume*. Lahore: Majlis-i Armughān-i ʿIlmī, 1955, pp. 109–118.

Ivanow propounded that there was a shrine in Multan in the name of Shams Tabrīzī, claimed as a co-religionist by the Ismailis. However, recent studies seem to have shown that the Shams buried in Multan may be identified with an Ismaili *pīr*, Shams al-Dīn.

340 —— 'Ismaili Mission in Indo-Pakistan', *Imamat*, 1, 2 (November, 1956), pp. 19–24.

341 —— *The Ismaili Society of Bombay: The Tenth Anniversary (16-2-1946/16-2-1956)*. Bombay: Ismaili Printing Press, 1956. pp. 13.

The aim of the Ismaili Society, founded in Bombay on 16 February 1946, was the promotion of the independent and critical study of all subject-matter relative to Ismaili literature, history and philosophy.

342 —— 'Ismailis in Russia', *Imamat*, 1, 2 (November, 1956), pp. 39–41; reprinted in *Read and Know*, 1, 12 (1967), pp. 11–15.

This article reports on Ismaili villages found in the valley of the River Panj (Amū Daryā) in Soviet Central Asia, present-day Tajikistan. The author argues that their Ismaili inhabitants were often wrongly called 'Pamir Ismailis', not because they inhabit the plateau of the 'Roof of the World', the Pamir, but because they reside on its borders, in the gorges which open into the Panj valley.

343 —— *Problems in Nasir-i Khusraw's Biography*. Ismaili Society Series B, 10. Bombay: Ismaili Society, 1956. pp. xiv + 88.

The author sought to clarify some of the problems related to Nāṣir-i Khusraw's biography and his connection with Ismailism.

344 —— 'Study Ismailism', *Imamat*, 1, 3 (October, 1957), pp. 15–18; reprinted as 'The Importance of Studying Ismailism', *Ilm*, 1, 3 (1975), pp. 8–9, 20, and as 'Why Should we Study Ismailism', *Ismaili Bulletin*, 4, 9 (May, 1978), pp. 13–15.

Ivanow believed that the Ismaili community attained prosperity because they were a well-organised body guided by their imams. This helped them to survive the catastrophes which overtook them in the course of history.

345 —— 'Sufism and Ismailism: *Chirāgh-nāmah*', *Majalla-yi Mardum-shināsī/ Revue Iranienne d'Anthropologie*, 3 (1338 Sh./1959), pp. 13–17 (English summary), 53–70 (Persian text).

According to Ivanow, Sufi philosophy is virtually the same doctrine as Ismaili esoterism, even though at the beginning Sufism was a purely Sunni development with, he argues, an undeniable Christian influence.

346 —— *Alamut and Lamasar: Two Mediaeval Ismaili Strongholds in Iran – An Archaeological Study*. Ismaili Society Series C, 2. Tehran: Ismaili Society, 1960. pp. xiv + 105. Persian tr. of chapter four as 'Nukātī tārīkhī dar bārah-yi Alamūt', tr. Masʿūd Rajab Niyā, in Riḍā Riḍāzāda Langarūdī, ed., *Yādigār-nāma: majmūʿa-yi taḥqīqī taqdīm shuda bi ustād Ibrāhīm Fakhrāʾī*. Tehran: Nashr-i Naw, 1363 Sh./1984, pp. 465–484.

As Ivanow himself says, the purpose of this publication is to provide students of Ismailism with reliable data on the drama of Alamūt. A proper understanding of the 170 years of the Alamūt era is fundamental for attaining a correct perception of the evolution which Ismaili religious and philosophical thought has undergone.

347 —— *Ismaili Literature: A Bibliographical Survey*. Ismaili Society Series A, 15. Tehran: Ismaili Society, 1963. pp. 245.

This book is a detailed inventory of the Ismaili literary heritage, including works which are still extant as well as lost works whose titles, however, may be traced in early literature.

348 —— 'My First Meeting with Ismailis of Persia', *Read and Know*, 1 (1966), pp. 11–14; reprinted in *Ilm*, 3, 3 (December, 1977), pp. 16–17.

The author narrates his initial meeting with Ismailis in Persia in February 1912. Although World War I loomed on the horizon, Persia was still living in an ancestral medieval fashion, with affairs largely carried on in a traditional way.

349 —— 'Hakim Nizari Kohistani', *African Ismailis*, 2, 7 (September, 1969), pp. 6–7.

A brief study by Ivanow regarding the views of various scholars on Nizārī Quhistānī's works and his religious affiliation.

350 —— 'Ismailism and Sufism', *Ismaili Bulletin*, 1, 12 (September, 1975), pp. 3–6.

351 —— ʿal-ʿIrq al-mansī fi'l-Ismāʿīliyya', abridged and translated by ʿĀrif Tāmir, *al-Bāḥith*, 7, 1 (1985), pp. 75–81.

352 —— 'Ismāʿīliyya', *EI2*, Supplement, pp. 98–102.

A brief entry on the Ismailis and their development, including a survey of how they have been variously named over the course of history.

353 —— 'Bohoras', 'Imām-Shāh', 'Ismāʿīlīya', 'Khodja', 'Ṭāhir', in *HI*.

354 —— 'Bohoras', pp. 64–65; 'Imām-Shāh', p. 167; 'Ismāʿīlīya', pp. 179–183; 'Khodja', pp. 256–257; 'Ṭāhir', p. 560; in *SEI*.

Brief entries on the subjects of the Bohoras, Imām-Shāh, Ismāʿīlīya, Khodja and Ṭāhir.

355 —— *Ocherki po istorii ismailizma: k 125-letiiu so dnia rozhdeniia Vladimira Alekseevicha Ivanova* [Essays on the History of Ismailism: Dedicated to the 125th Anniversary of Wladimir Alekseevich Ivanow]. St Petersburg: Zodchiĭ, 2011. pp. 199. (in Russian).

Wladimir Ivanow was at the forefront of modern Ismaili studies and made significant and original contributions to the academic account of the history of the Ismailis and their teaching. This publication represents the first Russian translation of Ivanow's works and serves to honour his academic achievements.

356 —— *Vospominaniĩa o Vostoke 1918–1968* [Memories of the East 1918–1968], preface and comments by B.V. Norika. St Peterburg, 2015. pp. 160. (in Russian).

The book is a publication of previously unreleased material from the private archives of Wladimir Ivanow. The documents are arranged in two parts: an autobiographical one and a section relative to the observations collected by Ivanow whilst living in the East, mostly in India and Iran.

J

357 Jamshedov, Parwona. 'The Debates (Deliberations) of Russian Scholars on Nasir Khusraw's Life and Personality', in Sarfaroz Niyozov and Ramazon Nazariev, ed., *Nasir Khusraw: Yesterday, Today, Tomorrow*. (Proceedings of a conference held in Khārūgh, Tajikistan). Khujand: Noshir, 2005. pp. 344–354.

The author examines the views of three Russian scholars (Bertel's, Semënov and Ivanow) on Nāṣir-i Khusraw's personality, poetic skills, and role in the development of Ismaili religious and philosophical thought as well as his position as a *ḥujja*. In particular, he regards Ivanow's view as subjective and biased and attempts to corroborate this point with references derived from Nāṣir-i Khusraw's works.

358 Jonboboev, Nazardod. 'Ba″ze aqidahoi ziddin dinii Nosir Khisrav' [Some of the Anti-Religious Ideas of Nāṣir-i Khusraw], *Badakhshoni Sovetī* [Soviet Badakhshān], 1960, p. 3. (in Tajik).

359 —— and Shohzodamamad Mamadsherzodshoev, ed. *Durdonahoi Badakhshon (asotirho va afsonaho)* [Pearls of Badakhshān (myths and legends)]. Khārūgh, 1992. pp. 54 (in Tajik).

This book explores the folklore of the Badakhshānī people including ancient legends and myths which are often linked to accounts of extraordinary phenomenological events and are often interwoven with religious beliefs.

360 —— ed. *Ismoiliën* [The Ismailis]. Khārūgh: Ittihodiĩai Istehsolii Matbaaho, 1992. pp. 40. (in Tajik).

This publication consists of a Tajik translation of Bobrinskoĭ's article, 'Sekta ismail'ĩa v russkikh i bukharskikh predelakh Sredneĭ Azii', with a foreword by the editors, as well as two other documents: i) 11 February 1904 – Report of the General Consul in Bombay, V.O. von Klemm, to the Foreign Ministry about his meeting with the Aga Khan; ii) Report of Ḥaydar Shāh Mubārak

Shāh Zāda and Shāhzāda Muḥammad regarding a dispute with Mullah Muḥammad-Ṣālīh of Peshawar.

361 Jonboboev, Sunatullo. 'Problema universaliĭ v filosofii Nosira Khisrava' [The Problem of Universals in Nāṣir-i Khusraw's Philosophy], *IAN (TSSR)*, 3–4 (1996), pp. 83–88. (in Russian).

362 —— 'Maqomi aql dar ash'ori shoironi faĭlasufi ahdi Somoniën' [The Category of Intellect in the Works of the Poet-Philosophers of the Sāmānid Era], in A. Muhammadkhojaev and M. Mahmadjonov, ed., *Falsafa dar ahdi Somoniën* [Philosophy during the Samanid Era]. Dushanbe: Donish, 1999, pp. 175–181. (in Tajik).

This article concerns the intellectual tradition of the poets of the Sāmānid and post-Sāmānid periods, such as Rūdakī, Firdawsī Ṭūsī, Abū Shakūrī Balkhī, Nāṣir-i Khusraw and Kasā'ī-yi Marvazī.

363 —— 'Nasir Khusraw on Human Condition', in Sarfaroz Niyozov and Ramazon Nazariev, ed., *Nasir Khusraw: Yesterday, Today, Tomorrow*. (Proceedings of a conference held in Khārūgh, Tajikistan). Khujand: Noshir, 2005, pp. 259–269.

Nāṣir-i Khusraw believed and propounded the notion that enmity and evil are not ingrained in human nature. He maintained that enmity is only a temporary condition for human beings, the result of an in-built ignorance which, however, can be removed by learning and by following the guidance of spiritual leaders.

364 —— 'Rudakī va Ikhvonussafo' [Rūdakī and the Ikhwān-al-ṣafā'], in Simpoziumi baĭnalmilalii 'Rudakī va farhangi jahonī', 6–7 sentiabria 2008 [International Symposium 'Rūdakī and World Culture', 6–7 September 2008], Dushanbe, pp. 180–183. (in Tajik).

The author observes the impact that the Ikhwān al-Ṣafā''s literature had on the religious and philosophical themes in Rūdakī's poetry.

365 —— 'Falsafai ta'rīkh, jam'iiat va davlat az nigohi ismoiliëni asrhoi miëna' [Philosophy of History, Society and State from the View Point of the Medieval Ismailis], *Falsafa va Huquq, Akhbori akademiiai ilmhoi Jumhurii Tojikiston*, 4 (2011), pp. 39–49. (in Tajik).

Ismaili thinkers understood the cycle of human history as being in strict connection with the motion and the events in the material universe.

366 —— 'Mas'alai rahbariiat va ė'tibori qudrat (imomat) dar falsafai ismoiliia: guzorishi mas'ala' [The Issue of Leadership and the Recognition of Authority in Ismaili Philosophy: Formulation of the Problem], *Falsafa va Huquq, Akhbori akademiiai ilmhoi Jumhurii Tojikiston*, 2 (2011), pp. 12–17. (in Tajik).

This article discusses the problem of leadership in the history of the Ismailis, developed in line with the Ismaili doctrine of the imamate, as one of the ultimate social, philological and religio-political issues in the history of Tajikistan and the Islamic world generally.

367 —— 'O spetsifike ismailitskoĭ kontseptsii filosofii istorii' [On the Particularities of the Concept of the Philosophy of History according to the Ismaili Tradition], *Izvestiia instituta filosofii, politologii i prava*, 1–2 (2013), pp. 35–44. (in Russian).

The concept of the philosophy of history occupies an important place in the Ismaili intellectual tradition. This article is based on a reading and analysis of works by Ismaili thinkers, whilst also providing a synthesis and assessment of Russian, Soviet and Western research on the Ismailis.

368 —— ed. *Nosir-i Khusraw. Safarnoma* [Nāṣir-i Khusraw. *Safar-nāma*], Dushanbe: Bukhoro, 2014. pp. 284. (in Tajik).

The *Safar-nāma* was, according to Nāṣir-i Khusraw, a biographical account of his adventurous life, although it does not encompass all his life. The travelogue, in fact, only recounts seven years of his journeys which began on 16 October 1045 and drew to a close on 23 October 1052, during which he visited the largest Islamic and non-Islamic civilisational centres and cities of his time.

369 —— 'Ismailitskaia ideia istorii v kontekste vseobshcheĭ filosofii istorii', in Stanislav M. Prozorov and Hakim Elnazarov, ed., *Russian Scholars on Ismailism*. (Proceedings of a conference held in St Petersburg, Russia in 2011). St Petersburg: Nestor-Istoriia, 2014, pp. 74–92. (in Russian and English).

This article is based on an analysis of the works of the Ismaili philosophers, as well as on the generalisations and evaluations made by Russian, Soviet and Western scholars of Ismaili studies. These generalisations served as the foundation for a comparison between the current conception of Ismaili history and other well-known, similar theories related to the philosophy of history.

K

Kalandarov, Hokim, see Qalandarov, Hokim.

370 Kalandarov, Tokhir. 'Religioznaia situatsiia na Pamire (k probleme religioznogo sinkretizma)' [The Religious situation in the Pamirs (on the problem of religious syncretism], *Vostok*, 6 (2000), pp. 37–49. (in Russian).

The religious situation in the Pamirs is characterised by a significant number of the population whose everyday beliefs and rituals go back to ancient times, often even to the most ancient, Indo-Iranian beliefs, although they have been reinterpreted and understood in an Ismaili context.

371 —— *Istoricheskie sud'by shugnantsev i ikh verovaniĭ* [The Historical Destiny of Shughnānīs and their Beliefs], Dissertatsiia na soiskanie uchënoĭ stepeni

kandidata istoricheskikh nauk [PhD Candidate for the Degree of Doctor of Philosophy]. Moscow, 2000. pp. 217. (in Russian).

372 —— *Shugnantsy (istoriko-ėtnograficheskoe issledovanie)* [Shughnānīs (historical-ethnographical studies)]. Moscow: IEA RAN, 2004. pp. 478. (in Russian).

This work is devoted to the study of the Shughnānī people and their beliefs, from the early stages of their history. The GBAO is identified with the remote valleys of the Panj river tributaries where the Pamiri people (such as the Yazghulāmīs, Rūshānīs, Bartangīs, Rashārwīs, Shughnānīs, Khūfīs, Bajūwīs, Ishkāshimīs, Wakhīs, etc.) reside. Due to their isolation from the lowland areas, these people have been able to preserve their languages as well as many ancient customs and traditions which have disappeared elsewhere in Central Asia.

373 —— 'Agiografiia "apostola pamirskikh ismailitov"' [Hagiography of the "Apostle of the Pamir Ismailis"], *Ėtnograficheskoe Obozrenie*, 2 (2004), pp. 58–49. (in Russian).

This article attempts to make a comparative analysis of the legends and traditions about Nāṣir-i Khusraw found among the people of Gorno-Badakhshān, on the one hand, and the reliably known facts of his biography, on the other.

374 —— 'Ismailism na Pamire: poisk novykh puteĭ i resheniĭ' [Ismailism in the Pamirs: Finding New Ways and Solutions], in *Rasy i narody: sovremennye ėtnicheskie i rasovye problem* [Races and People: Contemporary Ethnic and Racial Problems], *IEA RAN*, 2006, pp. 180–196. (in Russian).

This article focuses mainly on the transformations of the late 20th and early 21st centuries in the religious practices of the Pamiri Ismailis. It also analyses the role that Ismailism has played in the social and spiritual life of the inhabitants of GBAO.

375 —— 'Religiia v zhizni pamirtsev XX veka' [Religion in the Life of the Pamiris in the 20th Century], in A.Z. Almazova, ed., *Pamirskaia Ėkspeditsiia (stat'i i materialy polevykh issledovaniĭ)* [Pamir Expedition (articles and materials of field research)]. Moscow: RAN Institut Vostokovedeniia, 2006, pp. 24–50. (in Russian).

This article focuses primarily on the peoples of the Western Pamirs and their ethno-confessional relations throughout history. It assesses the role played by pre-Islamic beliefs and cultures in shaping the Ismaili doctrine in the region.

376 —— and V. Terekhov. *Puteshestvie v stranu rubinovykh gor* [Journey to the Ruby Mountains]. Moscow: Nauka, 2006. pp. 288. (in Russian).

'There are places on earth where man finds peace of mind and an exalted state of being. One of them is the High Pamir region.' The author investigates how in the sparsely inhabited valleys of the Panj River and its tributaries, there are people speaking eastern Iranian languages and adhering to Ismaili beliefs, until now a religion that only a few non-Ismailis have understood.

377 —— and Alauddin Shoinbekov. 'Some Historical Aspects of Funeral Rites among People of Western Pamir', *AME*, 3, 1 (2008), pp. 67–81.

378 —— and Alauddin Shoinbekov. 'Pokhoronno-pominal'naia obriadnost' u pamirskikh narodov: zabota o zhivykh ili osveshchenie puti umershego?' [Funeral and Commemoration Rites of the Pamir People: Concern for the Living or Illumination of the Path of the Deceased?], in *Vostokovedcheskie issledovaniia na postsovetskom prostranstve*, ed. E.I. Larina. *Sbornik nauchnykh statei pamiati professor Sergeia Petrovicha Poliakova* [Collection of Scholarly Articles in Memory of Professor Sergeĭ Petrovicha Poliakova]. Moscow, 2014, pp. 163–177. (in Russian).

A study of some aspects of the funeral rites taking place among the indigenous people of Badakhshān. Most of such ceremonies focus on ritual purifications aimed at enabling the departure of the deceased's soul into another world.

379 Kamolidin, Sayed Muhammad Boqer. 'The Spirit of Nasir Khusraw's Word', in Sarfaroz Niyozov and Ramazon Nazariev, ed., *Nasir Khusraw: Yesterday, Today, Tomorrow*. (Proceedings of a conference held in Khārūgh, Tajikistan). Khujand: Noshir, 2005, pp. 559–564.

The author touches upon some of the most fundamental themes of Nāṣir-i Khusraw's poetry, including truthfulness, knowledge of the self or self-awareness, freedom and free thinking, the renunciation of the material world, etc. These ideas are supported by the examples of Qurʾanic *āyāt* and prophetic *ḥadīth*s.

380 Karamkhudoev, Shukrat. 'The Contradictions between the Poem "Debate with God" and Other Works of Nasir Khusraw', in Sarfaroz Niyozov and Ramazon Nazariev, ed., *Nasir Khusraw: Yesterday, Today, Tomorrow*. (Proceedings of a conference held in Khārūgh, Tajikistan). Khujand: Noshir, 2005, pp. 150–157.

According to the author, 'Debate with God' is written in a poorer style than other poems by Nāṣir-i Khusraw. In addition, the subject matter is at odds with the main topics dealt with by Nāṣir-i Khusraw. Therefore, he argues, authorship of *Debate* cannot be attributed to Nāṣir-i Khusraw.

381 —— *Sopostavitel'nyĭ analiz religiozno-filosofskikh ideĭ Nosira Khusrava i Dzhalaleddina Rumi* [A Comparative Analysis of the Religious and Philosophical Ideas of Nāṣir-i Khusraw and Jalāl al-Dīn Rūmī], Dissertatsiia na soiskanie uchënoĭ stepeni kandidata filosofskikh nauk [PhD Candidate for the Degree of Doctor of Philosophy]. Dushanbe: Akademi Nauk, 2009. pp. 160. (in Russian).

A comparative analysis of Nāṣir-i Khusraw's and Jalāl al-Dīn Rūmī's religio-philosophical doctrines upholding the necessity of a balance between the spiritual and material world.

382 —— *Sopostavitel'nyĭ analiz religiozno-filosofskikh ideĭ Nosira Khusrava i Dzhalaleddina Rumi* [A Comparative Analysis of the Religious and Philosophical Ideas of Nāṣir-i Khusraw and Jalāl al-Dīn Rūmī]. Dushanbe, 2011. pp. 180. (in Russian).

383 —— 'Ėzotericheskaia kontseptsiia i problema eë interpritatsii v uchenii Nosira Khusrava' [Esoteric Concepts and Issues of their Interpretation in Nāṣir-i Khusraw's Doctrine], *VII*, 1 (2014), pp. 87–93. (in Russian).

This article deals with Nāṣir-i Khusraw's ideas on the hidden and manifest meanings in the Qur'an and the *sharīʿa*. According to Nāṣir-i Khusraw, each item or phenomenon in this world has an inner content, reflecting the purpose of the Creator.

384 —— 'Chelovek kak filosofskaia problema' [Man as a Philosophical Problem], *VPU*, 1 (2015), pp. 29–32. (in Russian).

Man, analysed from a philosophical perspective, bridges the differences between Eastern and Western philosophy.

385 —— 'Hikmati Rozi az nuqtai nazari Nosiri Khusrav' [Rāzī's Wisdom from Nāṣir-i Khusraw's Point of View], *VPU*, 1 (2015), pp. 8–11. (in Tajik).

The article investigates the dispute between Nāṣir-i Khusraw and Muḥammad b. Zakariyyā al-Rāzī on topics such as prime matter, space and time.

386 Karamshoev, Dodikhudo and I. Kharkavchuk. *Pogranichniki i zhiteli Pamira* [Border guards and the Inhabitants of Pamir]. Khārūgh: 'Pomir', 1995. pp. 148. (in Russian).

This book provides historical data, reports and records on military officers, border guards and other political agents who served in the Pamir region before the October Revolution of 1917. It opens with the first Russian expedition to the Pamir region, providing information on the lives of researchers such as Bronislav Grombchevskiĭ (1855–1926), a military officer, Dmitriĭ L'vovich Ivanov (1846–1924), a writer and traveller, Mikhail Efremovich Ionov (1846–1923) and Vasiliĭ Nikolaevich Zaĭtsev (1851–1933), both military officers, Andreĭ Snesarev (1865–1937), a military academic Orientalist, and Ivan Ivanovich Zarubin (1887–1964), one of the pioneers of Pamir studies, a folklorist, ethnographer and historian.

387 —— 'Peromuni duʻoho va rusumot-i mardumi Badakhshon' [About Duʻā and the Rituals of the Inhabitants of Badakhshān], *NP*, 4 (2003), pp. 139–159. (in Tajik).

Duʿās in the context of Badakhshān are similar to *duʿās* in other religious contexts. They are divided into two groups: one type is performed during funerals and the mourning period, and the second is performed at the harvest, at meals, social and convivial events, receptions, etc., *Duʿās* are recited mainly in Persian and partly in Arabic.

Kātib, Ḥasan-i Maḥmūd-i, see, Kotib, Hasan Mahmud.

388 Kazem, Saidfarrukhshokhzoda and Saidmursalzoda Shokhnom. *Vozzvanie k ismailitam i ko vsem musul'manam mira* [A Proclamation to Ismailis and all Muslims of the World]. Tashkent, 1944, pp. 1–7 (in Russian).

The Proclamation begins: 'In the name of God and of the Imam of the time Sulṭān Muḥammad Shāh and according to Nāṣir-i Khusraw's *Wajh-i dīn*', and contains a covering letter by the Muftiyat of the Muslims of Central Asia and Kazakhstan, Ishan Babakhan ibn Abdulmanzhidkhan. On 22 June 1944, the proclamation was sent to the people of the Pamirs in the name of Sayyed Kazem, Sayyed Farrukhshah-Zada and Shohnam Sayyed Mursal-Zada. Its core was actually an appeal to all Ismailis and to all Muslims to help the Red Army and Soviet State in their war against Fascism, as well as an exhortation to liberate all people from Nazi enslavement.

389 Khalīlī, Khalīl Allāh. *Yumgān* [Yumgān], ed. and introd. by ʿInāyat Allāh Shahrānī. Delhi, 1379 Sh./2000 [Kabul, 1959], pp. 46. (in Persian).

This treatise is the outcome of research on the tomb of Nāṣir-i Khusraw, the famous poet and Ismaili *dāʿī* of the 5th/11th century.

390 Khamenei, Sayyed Muhammad. 'Istoki Ismailizma' [The Beginnings of Ismailism], *EIF*, 4 (2013), pp. 25–31. (in Russian).

When dealing with Ismaili origins, Iranian and western scholars have identified the founder as Jaʿfar b. Ṣādiq's eldest son Ismāʿīl, whose descendants continued to expand and develop the military-political movement established by their ancestor. Given that most of the surviving Ismaili manuscripts pertain to the Fatimid or post-Fatimid era, the early period comprised between the imamate of Ismāʿīl b. Jaʿfar and ʿAbd Allāh al-Mahdī (here called ʿUbayd Allāh), the author argues remains, by and large, *terra incognita*.

391 Khan, Alisher Sher. 'Religious and Economic Development: Experience of Transformation among the Ismailis of Badakhshan, Tajikistan (field work)', Unpublished Report for the IIS, 2004. pp. 84.

On the basis of the ethnographical sources, this study has attempted to understand the hardship that Ismailis of Badakhshānī were faced with upon the collapse of the Soviet Union.

392 Khan, Mir Baiz. 'Living Traditions of Nasir-i Khusraw: A Study of Ismāʿīlī Practices in Afghan Badakhshan', Unpublished Report for the IIS, 2004. pp. 319.

This report explores the traditional (religious and cultural) practices of the Central Asian Ismailis.

393 —— 'Nasir Khusraw: A Man of Faith', in Sarfaroz Niyozov and Ramazon Nazariev, ed., *Nasir Khusraw: Yesterday, Today, Tomorrow*. (Proceedings of a conference held in Khārūgh, Tajikistan). Khujand: Noshir, 2005, pp. 619–625.

Nāṣir-i Khusraw's intellectual heritage reveals his search for the true knowledge of faith which led him to become a travelling philosopher and a poet of eminence. He considered faith to be a universal intellectual constant.

394 —— 'Znanie, traditsiia vospitanie: otnoshenie Nasira Khusrava k musul'manskomu ucheniiu' [Knowledge, Tradition and Education: the Approach of Nāṣir-i Khusraw to Muslim Teachings], in A.Z. Almazova, ed., *Pamirskaia Ėkspeditsiia (stat'i i materialy polevykh issledovaniĭ)* [The Pamir Expedition (articles and materials of field research)]. Moscow: RAN Institut Vostokovedeniia, 2006, pp. 131–141. (in Russian).

In this article, the author analyses Nāṣir-i Khusraw's views on knowledge, tradition and upbringing. His approach to these issues is important for our understanding of Islam and our contemporary world. Nāṣir-i Khusraw's choice of these three areas of interest was affected by the Fatimid *daʿwa*'s ideas on *taqwā* (humility, obedience), *siyāsa* (leadership, authority) and *ʿilm* (knowledge).

395 —— '*Chirāgh-i Rōshan*: Prophetic Light in the Ismāʿīlī Tradition', *Islamic Studies*, 52, 3–4 (2013), pp. 327–356.

The paper presents a core metaphor in the Ismaili religious ceremony called *Chirāgh Rawshan* (here *Chirāgh-i Rōshan*). This ceremony is a reference to the Prophetic tradition of divine guidance. For centuries, this ceremony has been critical for Ismaili Muslims in Afghanistan, Tajikistan, China and northern Pakistan including Chitrāl and Gilgit-Baltistan, in preserving and protecting their religious identity, and in expressing their devotion through the series of ritual acts which form this ceremony.

396 Khariukov, L.N. *Anglo-russkoe sopernichestvo v Tsentral'noĭ Azii i ismailizm* [Anglo-Russian Rivalry in Central Asia and Ismailism]. Moscow: Izdatel'stvo Moskovskogo Universiteta, 1995. pp. 237. (in Russian).

This work focuses mainly on the history of the Ismailis of Central Asia in the late 19th and early 20th centuries, with consideration given to Anglo-Russian rivalry in the region and its effect on the Ismailis living there.

Khodzhibekov, Ėl'bon, see Hojibekov, Elbon.

397 Khorāsānī, Fidāʾī. *Kitāb bi-Hidāyat al-muʾminīn al-ṭālibīn* ('Istoriia ismailizma') [Fidāʾī Khurāsānī, *Hidāyat al-muʾmīn al-ṭālibīn* ('Ismaili History')], tr. and intr. A.A. Semënov. Moscow: Izdatel'stvo vostochnoĭ literatury, 1959. pp. 254. (in Russian); repr. Tehran, 1362/1983.

This work by Fidā'ī Khurāsānī, which constitutes an extremely valuable source for the history of the Ismailis, has so far been known only in the form of a unique manuscript belonging to the Russian Orientalist, Semënov. The book includes annotations contained in a number of seminal works which are no longer extant.

398 Khudoërov, M.M. 'Ismailism in postsovetskom Pamire' [Ismailism in Post-Soviet Pamir], *IEA, RAN*, vol. 12. (2010), pp. 87–93. (in Russian).

This article examines the process of religious revival among the people of the Western Pamirs, in Rūshān, Shughnān, Bartang, Ishkāshim and Wakhān, who inhabit the GBAO of the Republic of Tajikistan. The article also investigates the changes that have been taking place in the Ismaili community since the late 1980s, as well as the role of the AKF in modern Pamiri society.

399 Khudonazarov, Davlat N. 'Graf A.A. Bobrinskoĭ – osnovopolozhnik izucheniiā dukhovnoĭ kul'tury tadzhikov Pamira' [Count A.A. Bobrinskoĭ – the Founder of the Study of the Spiritual Culture of the Pamiri Tajiks], *Religiovedenie*, vol. 3 (2008), pp. 175–187. (in Russian).

Bobrinskoĭ was one of the first Russian Orientalists to travel to Badakhshān with the aim of documenting the presence of the Ismaili community in Central Asia. There he met Ismaili religious leaders, such as *pīrs*. As a result of his travels and writings he was and still is regarded as an expert in Ismaili studies in Russian scholarly circles.

400 —— 'Count Alekseĭ Bobrinskoĭ – the Founder of Modern Ismaili Studies in Russian Scholarship', in Stanislav M. Prozorov and Hakim Elnazarov, ed., *Russian Scholars on Ismailism*. (Proceedings of a conference held in St Petersburg, Russia in 2011). St Petersburg: Nestor-Istoriiā, 2014, pp. 123–151. (in Russian and English).

The paper is devoted to an investigation of the beginning of Ismaili studies in Russian scholarship. The pioneer of Ismaili studies in the Russian domains was A.A. Boborinskoĭ, an ethnographer and specialist in cultural studies. Khudonazarov claims that Bobrinskoĭ's publication of 1902 was the first Russian, and in fact, the first European, study on Ismailism.

401 al-Kirmānī, Ḥamīd al-Dīn. *Uspokoenie razuma* [*Rāḥat al-ʿaql*]. Vvedenie, perevod s arabskogo i kommentarii A.V. Smirnova [Intr., and tr., from Arabic with a commentary by A.V. Smirnov]. Moscow: Ladomir, 1995, pp. 519. (in Russian).

An introduction and translation of al-Kirmānī's *Rāḥat al-ʿaql*, which was intended for a narrow circle of initiates, and which only became available to wider audiences at the beginning of the 20th century. One of the last works by the famous Persian thinker, 'Shaykh of the Ismaili philosophers', who has been credited with the systematisation of the Fatimid Ismaili philosophical system. As one of the most learned Ismaili *dāʿī*s, he opposed Druze teachings on the nature of the Ismaili Imam of the time, al-Ḥākim bi-Amr Allāh.

402 Klimovich, L. 'Ismailizm i ego reakt͡sionnai͡a rol'' [Ismailism and its Reactionary Role], *Antireligioznik*, 8 (1937), pp. 34–40. (in Russian).

'The Anti-religionist' (*Antireligioznik*), was a monthly journal of the League of Militant Atheists (Soi͡uz voinstvui͡ushchikh bezbozhnikov). In this article, Klimovich argues that Ismailism has a 'conspiratorial' nature and alerts the Soviets to what he asserted was the espionage of the Ismailis who were loyal to the imam. He calls the imam 'a loyal servant of British imperialism' and 'an enemy of the Soviet state.'

403 Klimovich, L. *Islam*. 2nd ed., Moscow: Izdatel'stvo 'Nauk', 1965. pp. 333. (in Russian).

Klimovich approached the study of religion from a Marxist standpoint, that of historical materialism, which was used by Communist and Marxist historiographers in the study of religion. In the author's view Ismailism in particular, and Shiʿi Islam in general, are the movements that served as a religious cover for the anti-feudal peasant movements directed against the prevailing feudal cliques.

404 Komilov, Rustam. 'Hikmati ismoilii͡a' [Ismaili Wisdom], in *Falsafai Tojik: az ahdi boston ta imruz* [Tajik Philosophy: from Ancient Times to the Present]. Dushanbe: Irfon, 2011, pp. 151–172. (in Tajik).

The religious understanding of Ismailism is presented through the thought of some of the most important Ismaili *dāʿī*s such as Abū Ḥātim al-Rāzī, al-Nasafī and Nāṣir-i Khusraw.

405 Korneeva, Tat'i͡ana Georgievna. 'Nasir Khusrav: Biografii͡a i tvorchestvo filosofa-ismailita' [Nāṣir-i Khusraw: Biography and Works of the Ismaili Philosopher], *Filosofii͡a i kul'tura*, 6 (2015), pp. 830–842. (in Russian).

The article is devoted to the life and works of the Persian Ismaili philosopher Nāṣir-i Khusraw who, according to the author, made a great contribution to the development of Persian literature and influenced the formation of its poetic language.

406 —— *Filosofskie vzgli͡ady Nasira Khusrav (na materiale traktata 'Raskrytie i osvobozhdenie')* [Philosophical Views of Nāṣir-i Khusraw (materials from the treatise 'Disclosure and release')], Dissertat͡sii͡a na soiskanie uchënoĭ stepeni kandidata filosofskikh nauk [PhD Candidate for the Degree of Doctor of Philosophy]. Moscow, 2016. pp. 233. (in Russian).

The study, based on an examination of the treatise, *Gushāyish va rahāyish* (translated into English as 'Knowledge and Liberation') demonstrates that the Ismaili philosopher did not just adhere to concepts developed by his predecessors, but actively reinterpreted and refined them, embedding them in his own philosophical system.

407 Krymskiĭ, A.E. 'Ismaility' [The Ismailis], *ESBE*, vol. 13. St Petersburg, 1894, pp. 394–395. (in Russian).

This article covers the split in Shi'i Islam in the second half of the 2nd/8th century which led to the rise of a new movement that became known by the name Ismaili. It further discusses the movement's development up to the Fatimid era in Egypt in the 4th–6th/10th–12th centuries.

408 —— 'Ismaility' [The Ismailis], *ES*, vol. 1. Moscow, 1953, p. 707. (in Russian).

Brief entry on the Ismailis and their religious leaders.

409 von Kügelgen, Anke. *A Society in Transition: Ismailis in the Tajik Pamirs*. Institut für Islamwissenschaft: Universität Bern, 2006. pp. 210.

The thesis presents anthropological studies on the Ismaili Tajiks of the Pamirs. The work provides a historical background to the history and the doctrines of the Ismailis and the introduction and diffusion of these beliefs in the region of present-day Badakhshān. The research is mainly based on interviews the author conducted in the Khārūgh, Shughnān and Ishkāshim districts on local Ismaili religious practices and education, particularly during the Soviet and post-Soviet period.

L

410 Lalani, Arzina R. *Ranniaia shi'itskaia mysl'* [Early Shi'i Thought], tr., N. Terletskiĭ. Moscow: Natalis, 2014. pp. 239. (in Russian).

This publication is the first systematic description of the life, work and teachings of Imam Muḥammad al-Bāqir. One of the most educated Muslims of his time, he played a significant role in the early Islamic history. Being both a spiritual leader and a versatile scholar, he was also an authority on the interpretation of the Qur'an, the traditions of his forebear, the Prophet Muhammad, and a variety of issues relating to Muslim rites, rituals and practices.

411 Landolt, Hermann. 'Early Evidence for the Reception of Nāṣir-i Khusraw's Poetry in Sufism: 'Ayn al-Quḍāt's Letter on the Ta'līmīs', in Omar Alí-de-Unzaga, ed., *Fortresses of the Intellect – Ismaili and other Islamic Studies in Honour of Farhad Daftary*. London: I.B. Tauris, 2011, pp. 369–386.

The article probes two somewhat different, earlier cases of possible 'cross-ties' between Ismailism and Sufism, both having to do with the 'multi-faceted personalities' of Nāṣir-i Khusraw. Landolt briefly discusses the general questions of Sufi influence on, and reception of, the great Ismaili poet.

412 Lashkarbekov, B., S. Yusufbekov and S. Khodjaniyazov. 'Ismailism and Central Asian Ismailis in Russian and Soviet Studies', Unpublished Report for the IIS, 2000. pp. 87.

A brief overview of Russian-Soviet studies on Ismailism including social, cultural, religious and other aspects of the Ismaili inhabitants of Soviet Central Asia.

413 Lashkariev, Amrisho Zokhirbekovich. *Pokhoronno-pominal'naia obri͡adnost' Bartangt͡sev* [Funeral and Memorial Rites of Bartangis], Dissertat͡siia na soiskanie uchënoĭ stepeni kandidata istoricheskikh nauk [PhD Candidate for the Degree of Doctor of Philosophy]. Moscow, 2007. pp. 195. (in Russian).

This thesis explores how the isolated life in the remote mountain region of the Pamirs has helped to preserve local culture in terms of their (eastern Iranian) languages and their particular faith, Ismailism.

414 —— 'Construction of Boundaries and Identity through Ritual Performance by a Small Ismaili Community of Gorno-Badakhshan', PhD dissertation, Eberhard Karls Universität Tübingen, 2014. pp. 276.

415 —— *The construction of Boundaries and Identity through Ritual Performance by a Small Ismaili Community of Gorno-Badakhshan*, Volume 24 of Beiträge zur Kulturkunde, Politischer Arbeitskreis Schulen, 2016. pp. 263.

The work examines the ritual performances of a small religious community in order to understand relationships in their villages and with the wider Darvāz district and Tajik society. The beliefs of the religious community differ from those of the Sunni majority of Darvaz, adhering to a different set of interpretations of Islam, that are the basis for drawing a boundary in terms of 'we' and 'they'. To a great extent this work uses approaches to performance to explore social interactions and relationships in the village communities. In this work, ritual is primarily used to understand how this religious community conceives of itself as a particular community in the region and how by means of performance the individuals in it relate themselves to other groups, to their nation-state and to the Ismaili 'global assemblage'.

416 Levin, Sergeĭ Fridrikhovich (1930–1984). 'Reformatorskoe dvizhenie v indiĭskoĭ torgovoĭ obshchine ismailitov-khodzha v 1829–1866 gg.' [The Reform Movement among the Ismaili-Khoja Indian Trading Community 1829–1866 years], *KSINA*, 51 (1962), pp. 89–121. (in Russian).

417 —— 'Organizat͡sii ismailitskoĭ burzhuazii v Pakistane' [The Organisation of the Ismaili Bourgeoisie in Pakistan], *KSINA*, 71 (1964), pp. 72–87. (in Russian).

This article argues that the Khoja Ismailis under the leadership of Aga Khan III played a major role in the reformation and re-organisation of Ismaili institutions not only in South Asia but also other countries where Ismaili communities reside.

418 —— *Torgovaia͡ kasta khodzha (iz istorii musul'manskoĭ burzhuazii Indii i Pakistana)* [The Khoja Trading Caste (towards a history of the Muslim bourgeoisie in India and Pakistan)], Dissertat͡sii na soiskanie uchënoĭ stepeni kandidata istoricheskikh nauk [PhD Candidate for the Degree of Doctor of Philosophy]. Moscow, 1964. pp. 361. (in Russian).

This thesis is an attempt to highlight the history of one of the different caste groups of the Muslim bourgeoisie of India and Pakistan, tracing the history of the Khoja Ismaili community.

419 —— 'Ob ėvoliu͡tsii musul'manskikh torgovykh kast v svia͡zi s razvitiem kapitalizma (na primere bokhra, memanov i khodzha)' [On the Evolution of Muslim Trading Castes in Connection with the Development of Capitalism (the case of Bohras, Memans and Khojas)], *Kasty v Indii* [Castes in India] (1965), pp. 233–261. (in Russian).

The development of capitalism in India has not led to the disappearance of the trading castes, present since the Middle Ages. In a number of works by Soviet and foreign researchers, attention has been drawn to the important role which continues to be played in shaping the commercial caste bourgeoisie of India and Pakistan by the Bohra, Meman and Khoja communities.

420 —— 'Finansovaia͡ imperiia͡ Aga-Khana IV' [The Financial Empire of Aga Khan IV], *NR*, 8 (1971), pp. 58–59. (in Russian).

The Aga Khan's modernisation of the Ismaili community's traditional organisation is aimed at involving the leadership and representatives of the bourgeois class of the Indian trading community, the Khojas, in it. Under the leadership of Aga Khan IV, the Khoja community has created an extensive network of Ismaili banks, financial corporations, insurance companies and cooperative societies in countries like India, Pakistan and Burma, and in East Africa.

421 —— 'Aga Khan III', *BSE*, vol. 1. Moscow: BSE, 1970, p. 503 (in Russian); also in *GSE*, vol. 1. New York: Macmillan; London: Collier Macmillan, 1973, pp. 128–129.

Brief information about the life and work of Aga Khan III (Sulṭān Muḥammad Shāh).

422 —— 'Ėtapy i osobennosti formirovaniia͡ musul'manksoĭ burzhuazii iz obshchiny ismailitov-khodzha' [Stages and Distinctive Features of the Transformation of the Ismaili-Khoja Community into a Muslim Bourgeoisie], *Islam i sotsial'nye struktury stran Blizhnego i Srednego Vostoka* (1990), pp. 39–50. (in Russian).

The article focuses on the position of the individual groups belonging to the Pakistani Ismaili bourgeoisie.

423 Levi-Sanchez, Suzanne. *The Afghan-Central Asia Borderland: The State and Local Leaders*. London: Routledge, 2016. pp. 196.

Based on extensive, long-term field work in the borderlands of Afghan and Tajik Badakhshān, this book explores the importance of local leaders and local identity groups for the stability of a state's borders, and ultimately for the stability of the state itself.

424 Lewisohn, Leonard. 'Hierocosmic Intellect and Universal Soul in a Qaṣīda by Nāṣir-i Khusraw', *Journal of Persian Studies*, 45 (2007), pp. 193–226.

This article attempts to decipher some of obscure religious, cosmological, theological, and psychological allusions found in Nāṣir-i Khusraw's metaphysical poetry. A single *qaṣīda* is translated, each line given exhaustive commentary and its key concepts – particularly Soul (*nafs, jān*), Intellect (*'aql*), Substance (*jawhar*), and Form (*ṣūrat*) – placed in their proper philosophical and literary context.

M

425 Maĭskiĭ, P.M. 'Sledy drevnikh verovaniĭ v pamirskom ismailizme' [Traces of Ancient Beliefs in Pamiri Ismailism], *SET*, 3 (1935), pp. 48–58. (in Russian).

From a Marxist perspective, in each stage of human social development the dominant ideology is that of the hegemonic class. Drawing on this attitude Ismailism is depicted as the ideology of a feudal aristocracy.

426 Makhmudov, N.S. *Kul'tura i byt naseleniĭa Pamira i Pripamir'ĭa v posledneĭ chetverti XIX – nachale XX vv. (po materialam russkikh vostokovedov)* [The Culture and Everyday Life of the Population of the Pamirs and Pamir region in the Last Quarter of the 19th and early 20th Centuries (according to materials of Russian Orientalists)], Dissertat͡sii na soiskanie uchënoĭ stepeni kandidata istoricheskikh nauk [PhD Candidate for the Degree of Doctor of Philosophy]. Khudjand, 1999. pp. 166. (in Russian).

427 —— *Kul'tura i byt naseleniĭa Pamira i Pripamir'ĭa v posledneĭ chetverti XIX – nachale XX vv. (po materialam russkikh vostokovedov)* [The Culture and Everyday Life of the Population of the Pamirs and Pamir region in the Last Quarter of the 19th and early 20th Centuries (according to materials by Russian Orientalists)]. Khudjand, 2010. pp. 166. (in Russian).

This work is an exploration of the views of pre-revolutionary Russian researchers on the physical, social and spiritual culture of the peoples of the Pamir region.

428 Makhmudov, Oybek. 'Rossiĭa i Ismaility: K istorii vzaimootnosheniĭ v Srendeĭ Azii' [Russia and the Ismailis: the History of their Relationship in Central Asia], *Istoriĭa: problemy ob"ektivnosti i nravstvennosti: Materialy*

nauchnoĭ konferentsii [History: Problems of Objectivity and Morality: Materials from the Academic Conference] (11 March, 2003). Tashkent, pp. 131–135. (in Russian).

The study introduces some features of the relationship between the local Ismaili population of the Pamirs and the Russian military deployment. It also presents features of the positive influence the Russian military had on the life of the local Pamiris under Ė.K. Kivekės, the long-serving head of the military unit.

429 —— 'Vliīanie doislamskikh kul'tov i filosofskikh system na ismailizm Pamiro-Gindukushskogo regiona' [The Impact of pre-Islamic Cults and Philosophical Systems on Ismailism in the Pamir-Hindu Kush Region], *Vostok-Zapad: Vzaimodeĭstviīa: Matrialy Nauchnoĭ Conferentsii* [East-West: Aspects of Interaction: Materials from the Academic Conference] (2006). Tashkent, pp. 125–129. (in Russian).

It is evident that various trends and philosophical beliefs have affected Ismailism in the Pamir-Hindu Kush region. This study questions whether these forms of belief have facilitated the existence of Ismailism in this part of the world and whether they differ from those in other regions.

430 —— 'Proniknovenie ismailizma na Pamir i kul'turnye posledstvie ego rasprostraneniīa' [Ismaili Penetration into the Pamir and the Cultural Consequences of its Spread], *Granitsy v Prostranstvie Proshlogo: Sotsial'nye, Kul'turnye, Ideĭnye Aspecty: Sb. St. uchastnikov Vseros. (s mezhdunarodnym uchastiem) nauch. konf. molodykh issledovateleĭ, posv. 35–letniū Tverskogo gosudarstvennogo universiteta Tver' 23–26 apriliā 2006 g.* [Borders in the Space of the Past: Social, Cultural and Ideological Aspects: A Collection of Articles by Participants in the All-Russian (with international participation) Academic Conference of Young Researchers, Dedicated to the 35th Anniversary of Tver University. Tver' 23–26 April 2006]. 2 vols, Tver': Nauchnaīa kniga, 2007, vol. 2, pp. 185–192. (in Russian).

The study is an examination of the process of the dissemination of Ismaili beliefs in the Pamir. Evidence is presented from various sources, including legends about the spread of the Ismaili *daʿwa* in the Pamir-Hindu Kush region.

431 —— 'Perezhitki drevnikh verovaniĭ v kalendare ismailitov Badakhshana' [Traces of Ancient Beliefs in the Calendar of the Ismailis of Badakhshān], *VII Kongress ėtnografov i antropologov Rossii: Doklady i Vystupleniīa 9–14 iūliā 2007 g. – Saransk, 2007* [7th Congress of Russian Ethnographers and Anthropologists: Reports and Speeches, Saransk 9–14 July 2007]. Saransk, 2007. pp. 260. (in Russian).

A brief study on some unique features in the traditional calendar of the Pamir Ismailis and their connection with pre-Islamic beliefs and ideas.

432 —— 'Trudy A.A. Semënov po issledovaniiu pamirskogo ismailizma (Kratkiĭ istoriograficheskiĭ Ocherk' [A.A. Semënov's Works on the Study of Pamiri Ismailism (A Brief Historiographical Essay)], *Izhtimoiĭ Fikr, Inson Huquqlari* [Social Opinion, Human Rights], 3 (2009), pp. 120-126. (in Russian).

This paper portrays Semënov as one of the first researchers of Pamiri Ismailism. It presents a brief analysis of his works and publications.

433 —— 'Trudy A.A. Bobrinskogo i A.A. Semënov po issledovaniiu pamirskogo ismailizma (kratkiĭ istoriograficheskiĭ ocherk)' [Bobrinskoĭ's and Semënov's Works on the Study of Pamiri Ismailism (A Brief Historiographical Essay)]. *Uzbekiston Tarikhning Dolzarb Muammolari: Uzbekiston Tarikhidan Ilmī Maqolalar Tūplami* [Actual Problems in the History of Uzbekistan: A Collection of Learned Articles on the History of Uzbekistan]. Tashkent, 2009, pp. 247-254. (in Russian).

The works of A.A. Bobrinskoĭ and A.A. Semënov examined in this study show them to be pioneers in the study of Pamiri Ismailism. A brief analysis of their publications and the issues related to their studies is presented here.

434 —— 'Ispol'zovanie naseleniia pamiro-gindukushskogo regiona Rossiĭkoĭ i Britanskoĭ razvedkami (vtoraia polovina XIX – nachalo XX vv)' [The Use of the Population of the Pamir-Hindu Kush Region by the Russian and British Intelligence Services (1850s – early 20th Century)], *Vestnik Natsional'nyĭ Universitet Uzbekistana*, Special Issue (2010), pp. 87-90. (in Russian).

This study is based on archival material and a number of research papers on the role played by the Ismaili religious leaders (*pīrs* and *khalīfa*s) during the era of Russian and British imperial rivalry in the region.

435 —— 'Izuchenie ismailizma v zapadnoĭ istoriografii (kratkiĭ obzor)' [Ismaili Studies in Western Historiography (Overview)], in *Uzbekiston Milliĭ Universiteti Arkheologiia Kafedrasining 70 Ĭilligiga Baghishlangan Ma"ruzalar Tūplamithe* [A Collection of Lectures devoted to the 70th Anniversary of the Archaeology Department of the National University of Uzbekistan]. Tashkent: Yangi Nashr, 2010, pp. 294-296. (in Russian).

The study investigates the main stages in the development of western historiography with regard to Ismaili history. The dynamics and processes of the changing and deepening knowledge about Ismaili history and teachings emerges through both researching original sources and the emergence of new avenues of enquiry.

436 —— 'Pandzhabkhaĭskoe dvizhenie na Pamire v 20-30s gg. XX v. (k voprosy o reformatsii v ismailizme)' [The Panjebhai Movement in the Pamirs in the 1920s and 1930s (On the Question of the Reformation of Ismailism)]. *Ėsh Sharqshunoslarning Akademic Ubaĭdulla Karimov Nomidagi IX Ilmiĭ-Amaliĭ Konferentsiiasi Tezislari* [The 9th Academic Conference of Eastern

Orientalists. Dedicated to Professor Ubaidulla Karimov]. Tashkent, 2011, pp. 111–112. (in Russian).

A paper on the under-studied Panjebhai movement which attempted to reform Pamiri Ismailism between the 1920s and 1930s but which, however, was ultimately abortive.

437 —— 'Nekotorye predstavleniia pamirskikh ismailitov o t͡siklicheskom ustroĭstve' [Some Views of the Pamiri Ismailis on the Cyclical Structure of the Universal Hierarchy], *Vestnik Nat͡sional'nyĭ Universitet Uzbekistana*, Special Issue, 2011, pp. 40–44. (in Russian).

Based on collected documents held in the Central State Archive of the Republic of Uzbekistan, this study includes the report of Ḥaydar Shāh Mubārak Shāh Zāda and Shāhzādamuḥammad regarding a dispute with Mullah Muḥammad-Ṣāliḥ of Peshawar. The study provides a summary of the speakers' arguments and comments, particularly on the Pamiri Ismailis and their perception of the cyclical and hierarchical structure of the universe.

438 —— *Ismailizm v T͡Sentral'noĭ Azii: sushchnost', osobennosti razvitiia i formy sushchestvovaniia (seredina XIX – nachalo XX veka)* [Ismailism in Central Asia: its Essence, the Distinctive Features of its Development and Form of Existence (mid-19th – early 20th centuries)], Dissertat͡sii na soiskanie uchënoĭ stepeni kandidata istoricheskikh nauk [PhD Candidate for the Degree of Doctor of Philosophy]. Tashkent, 2011. pp. 120. (in Russian).

This thesis studies aspects of and developments in Ismailism in Central Asia, especially in the Pamir region from the middle of the 19th to the early 20th centuries. It relies mainly on information provided by Russian academics.

439 —— 'Vzgli͡ad Russkikh voennykh na naselenie Pamira i Pripamir'i͡a (po materialam 'Sbornika Geograficheskikh, Topograficheskikh i Statisticheskikh Materialov po Azii')' [The Russian Military's View of the Population of the Pamir (based on materials from the 'Collection of geographical, topographic and statistical materials on Asia')], *Vestnik Nat͡sional'nyĭ Universitet Uzbekistana* [Bulletin of the National University of Uzbekistan], 4 (2012), pp. 74–79. (in Russian).

This research is an analysis of the contents of a number of publications on the Pamir collated in the 'Collection of geographical, topographical and statistical materials on Asia', including the opinion of the Russian military on the Pamir region and its population in the late 19th and early 20th century.

440 —— 'Vostochnyĭ chelovek kak nositel' "Orientalizma" (Pamir i Pripamir'e v trudakh B.L. Tageeva)' [Eastern Man as the Bearer of "Orientalism" (Pamir and the Pamir Area in the Works of B.L. Tageev], *Izhtimoĭ Fikr. Inson Huquqlari* [Social Thoughts. Human Rights], 4 (2012), pp. 85–91. (in Russian).

The works of B.L. Tageev, a military man and journalist, on the Pamir region are reviewed and analysed in this paper. He visited and observed the local inhabitants of the Pamirs and the region itself.

441 —— 'Izuchenie istorii ismailizma v Russkoĭ, Sovetskoĭ i post-Sovetskoĭ istoriografii: metody, podkhody, reprezentatsii i Innovatsii' [The Study of the History of Ismailism in Russian, Soviet and post-Soviet Historiography: Methods, Approaches, Representations and Innovations], *Ŭzbekiston Tarikhi Fanidagi Innovatsiĭa* [Innovation in the History of Uzbekistan], 2012, pp. 109–127. (in Russian).

A brief analysis of the features and approaches in the study, observation and representation of Ismaili doctrines in Imperian Russian, Soviet and post-Soviet historiography.

442 —— 'Nekotorye istochniki po istorii i ucheniiu isma'ilizma (kratkiĭ obzor)' [Some Sources on the History and Teaching of Ismailism (a brief overview)]. *Ŭzbekistondagi Amonaiĭ Izhtimoiĭ-madaniĭ Zharaënlarni Ėritishda Izhtimoiĭ Tarikhning Ŭrni. Respublika Ilmiĭghamaliĭ Anzhuman Materiallari* [The Role of Social History in the Coverage of Social-Cultural Processes in Uzbekistan. Materials of the National Academic Conference]. Tashkent, 2015, pp. 53–61. (in Russian).

This article is a brief description of the main sources on Ismaili history in Russian and Soviet studies, covering their characteristics and features.

443 Malysheva D.B. 'Ismaility' [Ismailis], *Voprosy Istorii*, 2 (1977), pp. 138–149. (in Russian).

The Ismaili *dāʿī*s actively promoted Ismaili ideology, philosophy, culture, and socio-political teachings, over the centuries to many people, from North Africa to the Indian subcontinent.

444 Mamadjonova, Muhiba. 'Symbolism in the Thought of Nasir Khusraw and Jalal al-Din Rumi', in Sarfaroz Niyozov and Ramazon Nazariev, ed., *Nasir Khusraw: Yesterday, Today, Tomorrow*. (Proceedings of a conference held in Khārūgh, Tajikistan). Khujand: Noshir, 2005, pp. 181–187.

In this article, the author argues that the Sufi convention of expression through symbols does not correspond to the notion of *ta'wīl*, which is widely used by Ismailis as the hermeneutical interpretation of the Qur'an. In the formative period of Sufism, Qur'anic sayings were interpreted in such a way that their meaning could be understood only in a state of ecstasy.

445 Mamadnazarov, Khudonazar. 'Shakhsi Boĭtarini Dunë' [The Richest Man of the World], in Khudonazar Mamadnazarov, *Dūstiro justujū dorem mo* [We are looking for Friendship]. Dushanbe: Irfon, 1975, pp. 59–76. (in Tajik).

A rare article written about Aga Khan IV during the Soviet era, by a Tajik Ismaili government official. The article is written from the Marxist perspective which views the Aga Khan as an imperialist bureaucrat on good terms with American and British imperialists.

446 Mamadsherzodshoev, Shozodamamad. 'The Contribution of Russian Scholars to the Collection and Study of the Written Heritage of the People of Mountainous Badakhshan', in Stanislav M. Prozorov and Hakim Elnazarov, ed., *Russian Scholars on Ismailism*. (Proceedings of a conference held in St Petersburg, Russia in 2011). St Petersburg: Nestor-Istoriiā, 2014, pp. 152–159. (in Russian and English).

The work describes the main stages in the study of the written heritage of Badakhshānī manuscripts and the role played by Russian scholars in the collection and examination of this heritage.

447 Maniëzov, A. and K. Sharipov. *Hakimi sukhanvar (bakhshida ba hazorai zodruzi Nosiri Khusraw)* [Eloquent Sage (on the millennium of Nāṣir-i Khusraw)]. Dushanbe, 2003. pp. 234. (in Tajik).

Besides being an Ismaili *dāʿī* who is regarded as a *pīr* and a *ḥujja* in Badakhshān, Nāṣir-i Khusraw also made a great contribution to the world of Persian literature throughout his writings by calling people to humanism, patriotism, the acquisition of knowledge, justice, friendship and brotherhood.

448 Mastibekov, Otambek. 'The Concept of Knowledge in Nasir Khusraw and Nasir al-Din Tusi's Thought', in Sarfaroz Niyozov and Ramazon Nazariev, ed., *Nasir Khusraw: Yesterday, Today, Tomorrow*. (Proceedings of a conference held in Khārūgh, Tajikistan). Khujand: Noshir, 2005, pp. 67–74.

In this paper it is argued that, according to Ṭūsī, we have to know Him (the Universal teacher) in order to acquire knowledge, while in Nāṣir-i Khusraw's thought we have to acquire knowledge in order to reach or know Him.

449 —— *The Leadership and Authority of Ismailis: A Case Study of the Badakhshani Ismaili Community in Tajikistan*, PhD dissertation, SOAS, University of London, 2011. pp. 202.

450 —— *Leadership and Authority in Central Asia: An Ismaili Community in Tajikistan*. London: Routledge, 2014. pp. 185.

The book identifies traditional forms of religious authority in the network of religious functionaries amongst the Central Asian Ismailis. The development of a religious structural authority is viewed as a necessity for the survival and evolution of the religious and political authorities of the Badakhshānī Ismailis in times of radical and political upheaval.

451 Matīnī, Jalāl. 'Nāṣir-i Khusraw va Madīḥa-sarāyī' [Nāṣir-i Khusraw and Eulogism], in *Yādnāma-yi Nāṣir-i Khusraw*, ed. Dānishgāh-i Firdawsī,

Dānishkada-yi Adabiyyāt va ʿUlūm-i Insānī (Faculty of Letters and Humanities of the University of Mashhad), Mashhad: Dānishgāh-i Firdawsī, 1355 Sh./1976, pp. 421–494. (in Persian).

The article argues that through his religious poetry Nāṣir-i Khusraw propagated the Ismaili daʿwa as a righteous religious faith.

452 Meskoob, Shahrokh. 'Manshaʾ va maʿnā-ī ʿAql dar andīshah Nāṣir-i Khusraw' [The Origin and Meaning of ʿAql (reason) in the Thought of Nāṣir Khusraw], *Iran Nameh: A Persian Journal of Iranian Studies*, 7, 2 (1989), pp. 240–253. (in Persian).

The concept of reason was fundamental to the creation of Nāṣir-i Khusraw's worldview, as well as his religious beliefs.

453 Middleton, Robert. *Legends of the Pamirs*. Khārūgh: University of Central Asia. 2013. pp. 67.

This is a study of the shrines found in the mountainous region of Badakhshān and the traditions attached to them.

454 Mirabulqosimī, Saĭid Muhammadtaqī. *Bozmondai merosi ismoiliĭa dar Ėron* [The Remnants of the Ismaili Heritage in Iran]. Dushanbe: Instituti Sharqshinosi va Merosi Khatti, 2006. pp. 167. (in Tajik).

The theme of the book is the socio-religious life of the Ismaili community in modern Iran, and the challenges and issues that it is faced with.

455 Mirboboev, Aziz. 'Taʾvili raqam va harf dar "Wajh-i dīn"' [The *Taʾwīl* of Number and Letter (*Ḥarf*) in "Wajh-i dīn"], *NP*, 4 (2003), pp. 119–130. (in Tajik).

The Ismailis place great religious significance in the concepts of the manifest (*ẓāhir*) and the hidden (*bāṭin*). In order to understand the concealed meaning of the *sharīʿa*, namely, the real meaning of the Revelation, it is necessary to decode the figures, characters, numbers and numerical values of the letters of the alphabet, to reveal the true significance of the Qurʾanic *āyāt*, Prophetic *ḥadīth*s and the *aḥkām* of the *sharīʿa*.

456 Mirhasan, Gulhasan. 'On Certain Relationships between Intellect and Soul in *Zad al-musafirin*', in Sarfaroz Niyozov and Ramazon Nazariev, ed., *Nasir Khusraw: Yesterday, Today, Tomorrow*. (Proceedings of a conference held in Khārūgh, Tajikistan). Khujand: Noshir, 2005, pp. 49–53.

The source of Nāṣir-i Khusraw's intellectual and ethical philosophy lies not in the blind imitation and repetition of ancestral practice and traditions, but in the individual intellect and knowledge, in personal effort (individual intellect), as well as in knowledge and social practice (active complete intellect).

457 —— *Filosofskiĭ analiz mirovozzreniĭa Muboraka Vakhani* [A Philosophical Analysis of Mubārak-i Wakhānī's Worldview], Dissertatsiĭa na soiskanie

uchënoĭ stepeni kandidata filosofskikh nauk [PhD Candidate for the Degree of Doctor of Philosophy]. Dushanbe: Akademi Nauk, 2015. pp. 158. (in Russian).

This is an analysis of the philosophical outlook of the Tajik Ismaili poet and thinker of the late 19th and early 20th centuries, Mubārak-i Wakhānī, who had a great influence on the lives of the Wakhānī Tajiks living in the mountainous regions of the Pamir and Hindu Kush ranges.

458 Mirshahi, Ghulam-Reza and Ahmad Yahyoyi Ilahi. 'Rationality as an Introduction to Religious Pluralism', in Sarfaroz Niyozov and Ramazon Nazariev, ed., *Nasir Khusraw: Yesterday, Today, Tomorrow*. (Proceedings of a conference held in Khārūgh, Tajikistan). Khujand: Noshir, 2005, pp. 171–180.

Inspired by Nāṣir-i Khusraw's writings, the author suggests that a diversity of views, or pluralism, is to be regarded as basis for establishing a civil society in contemporary terms.

459 —— and Ahmad Yahyoyi Ilahi. 'The Relationship between the lives and ideas of Nasir Khusraw and Mawlawna', in Sarfaroz Niyozov and Ramazon Nazariev, ed., *Nasir Khusraw: Yesterday, Today, Tomorrow*. (Proceedings of a conference held in Khārūgh, Tajikistan). Khujand: Noshir, 2005, pp. 383–394.

The article compares the lives, thought and teachings of Nāṣir-i Khusraw and Jalāl al-Dīn Rūmī through their poetry.

460 Mirshakar, Mirsaid (1912–1993). *Isëni khirad* [The Rebellion of Reason], Dushanbe: Irfon, 1982. pp. 80 (in Tajik).

An allegorical poem, in which the poet tells the story of Nāṣir-i Khusraw through the spring (*chashma*) that he was said to have generated. The spring is the symbol of the *khirad* (intellect), one of the powerful tools in the hands of humankind. He emphisises the importance of reason, knowledge and wisdom of human beings.

461 Mirzohasan, La'ljuba and Alidod Charoghabdol, ed. *Tazkirai Adiboni Badakhshon* [Biographies of the Badakhshānī Poets]. Dushanbe: Adib, 2005. pp. 544. (in Tajik).

The book is a study of the biographies and the poetry of Badakhshānī poets writing between the 17th and 20th centuries CE. There is very little evidence regarding the written literature of Badakhshān before the time of Nāṣir-i Khusraw; as a result Nāṣir-i Khusraw's poetry has had a great impact on the poetic, philosophical and religious literature of Badakhshān.

462 Mirzozoda, Kholiqzoda. 'Ismoiliĭa, qarmatiĭa, botiniĭa' [The Ismailis, Qarmaṭīs and Bāṭinīs], in his *Ta'rīkh-i adabiëti tojik (az davrai qadim to asri XIII)* [The History of Tajik Literature (from Ancient times to the 13th century)]. Dushanbe: Maorif, 1989, pp. 126–176. (in Russian).

Ismailism has been labelled a democratic tendency in the Shi'i tradition, and this led to its rise as a powerful literary movement and tradition. Ismailism is presented as having been led in Iran and Central Asia by eminent *dā'īs* who were able to convert the intelligentsia, artists and free thinkers, such as Rūdakī, Abu'l-Faḍl Bal'amī, Firdawsī, Nāṣir-i Khusraw and many others.

463 Monogarova, Lidiĩa F. *Preobrazovaniĩa v bytu i kul'ture pripamirskikh narodnosteĭ* [Changes in the Everyday Life and Culture of the Pamiri Peoples]. Moscow: Nauka, 1972. pp. 172. (In Russian).

This work examines processes taking place among the Pamiri nationalities mainly based on ethnographic material collected by the author as a result of the expedition which took place in 1964–1967. The work also shows the influence of radical changes in the socio-economic conditions of the Pamiri Ismailis that took place during the Soviet era.

464 —— 'Perezhitki ĩazychestva v musul'manskoĭ obrĩadnosti ismailitov Zapadnogo Pamira' [Pagan Elements in the Muslim Rites of the Ismailis of the Western Pamirs], in D.V. Frolov, ed., *Islam i problemy mezhtŝivilizatŝionnogo vzaimodeĭstviĩa* [Islam and the Problems of Inter-Civilisational Interaction]. Moscow: Institut Islamskoĭ TSivilizatsii, 1992, pp. 124–127. (in Russian).

Monogarova investigated remnants of pre-Islamic custom and ritual theraputic acts in the daily life of the Shughnānīs as well as other peoples of the Pamir region.

465 Mozheĭko, Igor'. 'Khozĩain zamka Alamut i ego nasledniki' [The Lord of the Castle of Alamūt and His Successors], *NR*, 7 (1987), pp. 59–64. (In Russian).

The article discusses the fearlessness of the Ismailis in the Alamūt fortresses under the leadership of Ḥasan-i Ṣabbāḥ whom the author regards as a 'selfless fighter for the people's happiness'.

466 Muborakshozoda, Haidarshoh. *Tārīkh-i mulk-i Shughnān* [The History of the land of Shughnān], ed. N. Jonboboev and A. Mirkhoja. Pomir: Khārūgh, 1992, pp. 35. (in Tajik).

It is thought that *Tārīkh-i mulk-i Shughnān* was the work of Sayyid Ḥaydar Shāh Mubārak Shāh Zāda. It provides detailed discussions on the history of Shughnān and its relations with neighbouring areas such as Rūshān, Wakhān and Darvāz on both the Afghan and Tajikistan sides of the Amū Daryā.

467 Muhabbati, Mehdi. 'The Impact of Nasir Khusraw on the Formation of Iranian Islamic Rationalism', in Sarfaroz Niyozov and Ramazon Nazariev, ed., *Nasir Khusraw: Yesterday, Today, Tomorrow*. (Proceedings of a conference held in Khārūgh, Tajikistan). Khujand: Noshir, 2005, pp. 102–110.

Nāṣir-i Khusraw tried to understand and develop rationalism in Perso-Islamic culture in four ways: (i) by moving away from the superficial religio-legal terms towards the true inner meaning of the teachings; (ii) by a rationalisation of culture and religion strongly expressing a practical dimension; (iii) by thinking of a prosperous exemplary society and the depiction of the city of his dreams in the form of the Fatimid state as it existed then; and (iv) by presenting a prosperous and exemplary society not as an imaginary utopia, but as a glimpse of the realities in which he had lived and worked.

468 Muhammadkhojaev, Ahmadjon. 'Ta'wil from the Perspectives of Nasir Khusraw and Sufism', in Sarfaroz Niyozov and Ramazon Nazariev, ed., *Nasir Khusraw: Yesterday, Today, Tomorrow.* (Proceedings of a conference held in Khārūgh, Tajikistan). Khujand: Noshir, 2005, pp. 158–164.

The scholar compares the Sufi interpretation of the Qur'anic *sūra* 12 (*sūrat Yūsuf*), and its Ismaili interpretations, showing both similarities and differences between the philosophies of these two groups and the way they engaged in *ta'wīl*.

469 —— 'Ta'vil az nigohi Nosir-i Khusrav va tasavvuf' [*Ta'wīl* from the View of Nāṣir-i Khusraw and *Taṣawwuf*], *Andeshaho peromuni irfon va falsafa*, (2012), pp. 93–103. (in Tajik).

For both the Ismailis and the Sufis the interpretation of the Qur'anic commands was not only intended to unveil the meaning of the *sharīʿa*, but also was a way to turn from a merely exoteric (*ẓāhir-parast*) understanding of the truth and to attain a more authentic meaning, thus enabling freedom of expression for the leading thinkers.

470 —— ed. *Nosir-i Khusraw. Kushoish va rahoish* [Nāṣir-i Khusraw. Gushāyish va Rahāyish]. Dushanbe: ER-graff, 2013. pp. 123. (in Tajik).

Gushāyish va Rahāyish contains responses to a series of 30 questions on theological and philosophical subjects, with special reference to the human soul, its relation to the world of nature and its quest for salvation.

471 Muḥaqqiq, Mahdī. 'Chihra-yi dīnī va madhhabī Nāṣir-i Khusraw dar *Dīvān*' [Faith and the Religious Figure of Nāṣir-i Khusraw in his *Dīvān*], in *Yādnāma-yi Nāṣir-i Khusraw*, ed. Dānishgāh-i Firdawsī, Dānishkada-yi Adabiyyāt va ʿUlūm-i Insānī (Faculty of Letters and Humanities of the University of Mashhad), Mashhad: Dānishgāh-i Firdawsī, 1355 Sh./1976, pp. 492–519.

Nāṣir-i Khusraw shunned the material world and the luxurious life of his age which he compared to darkness. It was in the spiritual world that he found knowledge, awareness and a faith that could lead to enlightenment and fulfilment.

472 —— 'New Comments on Nasir Khusraw's Divan', in Sarfaroz Niyozov and Ramazon Nazariev, ed., *Nasir Khusraw: Yesterday, Today, Tomorrow.*

(Proceedings of a conference held in Khārūgh, Tajikistan). Khujand: Noshir, 2005, pp. 367–382.

The *Dīvān* of Nāṣir-i Khusraw is full of symbolic expressions which derive from various sources and are not easy to comprehend. For this reason, Mahdī Muḥaqqiq, a well-known commentator on Nāṣir-i Khusraw, offers a brief and comprehensive interpretation of Nāṣir's poems.

473 Mujtahidi, Karim. 'Filosofskiĭ analiz *Kashf al-makhdzhub* Abu ĪAʻkuba Sidzhistani' [A Philosophical Analysis of Sijistānī's *Kashf al-Maḥjūb*], *EIF*, 4 (2013), pp. 199–203. (in Russian).

The article begins with a brief account of the Ismaili role in Iranian history. In particular, the author argues that the heroic defence of Alamūt changed the course of the history of Iran. The original Arabic version of *Kashf al-maḥjūb*, as far as we know, has not survived. The sole manuscript of the Persian translation (or, perhaps, paraphrase) of the book was discovered in the private library of Sayyid Naṣrullāh Taqawī. The translation, which was most probably made about a century after al-Sijistānī's death, was first described by Paul Kraus, later translated into French and published by Henry Corbin.

474 Mukhammadzoda, Kurbon (Okhon Sulaĭmon) and Shakhfutur (Seid-Fitur-Sho) Mukhabbatshozoda. *Istoriia Badakhshana* [The History of Badakhshān], tr. and ed. A.A. Egani and B.I. Iskandarova, AN (TSSR), In-t istorii im. Akhmada Donisha [Ahmad Donish History Institute]. Moscow: Nauk, 1973. pp. 250. (in Tajik).

The book is dedicated to the socio-political life and history of Badakhshān, and is divided into four parts. The first part begins with the reign of a local ruler ʻAbd al-Raḥmān Khān, the son of Qubād Khān (ca. 1792–1814); the second part relates to the history of the local kings of Shughnān; the third part which is titled *Tārīkh-i Afghānistān*, refers to the time of the occupation of Badakhshān by the Afghans; and the final part of the book focuses on a period from the reign of the Russian emperor Nicholas II and the arrival of Russian soldiers in Badakhshān to the victory of the October Revolution of 1917 in Russia.

475 Mukhiddinov, Ikrom M. 'Religioznye verovaniia, sviazannye s zhilishchem u pamirskikh tadzhikov', *Vsesoiuznaia sessiia, posviashchënnaia itogam polevykh ètnograficheskikh i antropologicheskikh issledovaniĭ 1976–1977 g.* ['Religious Beliefs Related to Homes among the Pamiri Tajiks', in *All-Union Session on the Results of the Field Ethnographic and Anthropological Research 1976–1977*]. Erevan, 1978, pp. 166–168. (in Russian).

476 —— 'Obychai i obriady, pamirskikh tadzhikov, sviazannye s zhilishchem: Konets XIX-nachalo XX v. (materialy k istoriko-ètnograficheskomu atlasu narodov Sredneĭ Azii i Kasakhstana)' [Rites and Customs of the Pamiri Tajiks Dealing with Housing: End of 19th – Beginning of 20th Century

(materials for a historical and ethnographic atlas of the peoples of Central Asia and Kazakhstan)], *SET*, 2 (1982), pp. 76–83. (in Russian).

—— 'Obychai i obri͡ady, svi͡azannye so stroitel'stvom zhilishcha u pripamirskikh narodnosteĭ v XIX-nachale XX v.' [Rites and Customs of the Pamiri Ethnic Groups dealing with the Building of Dwellings at the End of 19th – Beginning of 20th Century], *Ėtnografii͡a Tadzhikistana*, 4 (1985), pp. 24–29. (in Russian).

Pamiri customs and rituals are discussed in the work, as well as the leading role of the Ismaili *pīr*s and in particular *khalīfa*s in the daily practices of the community.

477 —— 'Osobennosti traditsionnogo zemledel'cheskogo khozi͡aĭstva pripamirskikh narodnosteĭ v XIX – nachale XX vv.' [Features of the Traditional Agricultural Economy of the Pamiri People in the 19th – early 20th Century]. Dushanbe: Donish, 1984. pp. 193. (in Russian).

Ancient folk representations associated with the cult of the ancestors were redefined under the influence of Ismaili theology; this shift can be witnessed in architectural elements such as basic load-bearing roof structures, including poles and support columns which now came to symbolise the God-creator and the holy Prophets.

478 —— *Relikty doislamskikh obychaev i obri͡adov u zemledel'tsev Zapadnogo Pamira (XIX-nach. XX v.)* [Relics of Pre-Islamic Customs and Rituals among the Agriculturists of the Western Pamir (19th-early 20th Century)]. Dushanbe: Donish, 1989. pp. 100. (in Russian).

A study of the cycle of agricultural labour among the Pamiri people, citing analogies of certain customs and beliefs linked to the production of a good harvest.

479 —— 'Proi͡avlenie astral'nykh predstavleniĭ v bytu ismailitov Zapadnogo Pamira' [Astral Beliefs as Mirrored in the Everyday Life of the Ismailis of the Western Pamir], S.Kh. Ki͡amilev and I.M. Smili͡anskai͡a eds., *Islam i problmy mezhtsivilizatsionnogo obshchenii͡a*, [Islam and the Problems of Inter-Civilisational Interaction]. Moscow: Institut Islamskoĭ TSivilizatsii, 1994, pp. 130–134. (in Russian).

It is argued here that, in an effort to ensure a good harvest and to increase the number of livestock, the Pamiri people combined traditional farming skills that took into account the characteristics of the natural environment along with rites associated with animistic beliefs, including those connected to astral cults.

480 Murodova, Tozhiniso O. 'Gumanizmi Nosiri Khisrav' [The Humanism of Nāṣir-i Khusraw], *MS*, 12 (1980), pp. 47–49. (in Tajik).

481 —— 'Rumuzi olam dar falsafai Nosiri Khisrav' [The Riddle of the World in Nāṣir-i Khusraw's Philosophy], *IAN (TSSR)*, 2 (1981), pp. 69–73. (in Tajik).

According to the author, Nāṣir-i Khusraw accepted the theory of the origination of the universe whilst simultaneously maintaining that the processes of generation and corruption are embedded in nature.

482 —— 'O nekotorykh aspektakh teorii ėmanat͡sii Avit͡senny i Nosiri Khisrava' [On Some Aspects of Avicenna's and Nāṣir-i Khusraw's Theories of Emanation], *IAN (TSSR),* 1 (1982), pp. 61–64. (in Russian).

483 —— 'O nekotorykh aspektakh naturfilosofii Nosir-i Khisrava' (na osnove 'Dzhome'-ul-khikmataĭn)' [On Some Aspects of Nāṣir-i Khusraw's Natural Philosophy (on the basis of *Jāmiʿ al-ḥikmatayn*)], *IAN (TSSR),* 2 (1984), pp. 28–33. (in Russian).

The discussion is based on Nāṣir-i Khusraw's philosophical treatise *Jāmiʿ al-ḥikmatayn*, which analyses the discourses of the universal cycle, the ratio of the moon and the sun, stars and other heavenly objects in connection to the Earth.

484 —— 'Nosiri Khisrav' [Nāṣir-i Khusraw], *EST*, vol. 5, pp. 691–698. (in Tajik).

A biography of Nāṣir-i Khusraw including an analysis of his main religio-philosophical works from a Marxist perspective.

485 —— *Dzhame'-ul-khikmataĭn' Nosir-i Khisrava kak filosofskiĭ trud* [Nāṣir-i Khusraw's *Jāmiʿ al-ḥikmatayn* as a Philosophical Work], Dissertat͡sii na soiskanie uchënoĭ stepeni kandidata filosofskikh nauk [PhD Candidate for the Degree of Doctor of Philosophy]. Alma-Ata, 1985. pp. 169. (in Russian).

The discussion is based on one of the essential works by Nāṣir-i Khusraw, the *Jāmiʿ al-ḥikmatayn*, which deals with a large range of ontological issues such as substantial and accidental origination, motion, space and time.

486 —— 'Kategorii dvizhenii͡a, prostranstva i vremeni v filosofii Nosiri Khisrava' [Categories of Movement, Space and Time in Nāṣir-i Khusraw's Philosophy], *IAN (TSSR),* 4 (1986), pp. 14–19. (in Russian).

The work deals with issues of movement, space and time according to Nāṣir-i Khusraw's understanding together with the ratio of form and substance.

487 —— 'K kharakteristike chuvstvennogo i rat͡sional'nogo poznanii͡a v filosofskoĭ kont͡sept͡sii Nosiri Khisrava' [The Characteristic Features of Sensory and Rational Knowledge in Nāṣir-i Khusraw's Conception of Philosophy], *IAN (TSSR),* 1 (1988), pp. 3–8. (in Russian).

Nāṣir-i Khusraw, unlike many thinkers of his time, did not disseminate ideas on the 'supernatural' origin of human knowledge and instead made attempts to explain the human mechanisms of reflection and reproduction.

488 —— 'O nekotorykh aspektakh problemy substant͡sii s tochki zrenii͡a Avit͡senny i Nosiri Khisrava' [Some Aspects of the Theory of Emanation

from the Standpoint of Avicenna and Nāṣir-i Khusraw], in G.A. Ashurov and M.S. Sultanov, ed., *Torzhestvo razuma* [The Triumph of Reason]. Dushanbe: Donish, 1988, pp. 133–135. (in Russian).

The author draws parallels between the theoretical thinking of Avicenna and that of Nāṣir-i Khusraw on pivotal philosophical topics such as accident and substance, form and matter, essence and existence.

489 —— 'Osnovnye polozheniiā filosofii Nosiri Khisrava' [The Main Hypothesis of Nāṣir-i Khusraw's Philosophy], *IAN* (TSSR), 4 (1989), pp. 9–14. (in Russian).

This article investigates Nāṣir-i Khusraw's main philosophical points, based on his major philosophical works such as the *Zād al-musāfirīn*, *Jāmiʿ al-ḥikmatayn*, and *Gushāyish va Rahāyish*. The issues of existence, the universe, the relationship between the soul and the body, the categories of motion, time and space, as well as the theory of natural philosophy are all discussed and analysed.

490 —— 'Problema bytiiā v uchenii Abu IAkuba Sidzhistoni' [The Problem of Being in the Teachings of Abū Yaʿqūb al-Sijistānī], *IAN* (TSSR), 2 (1990), pp. 38–42. (in Russian).

A comparative analysis of al-Sijistānī's and Nāṣir-i Khusraw's discourses on issues such as God's relationship to nature and mankind, His role as the Creator in respect to His creation. Murodova argues that even though both philosophers could be, from a Marxist perspective, identified as being objective idealists, their approach to certain philosophical matters differs substantially.

491 —— *Filosofiiā Nosir-i Khisrava* [Nāṣir-i Khusraw's Philosophy]. Dushanbe: Donish, 1994. pp. 88. (in Russian).

The work analyses metaphysical categories such as 'accidental' and 'substantial', space, time and matter, and the concepts of God and Nature, as expounded by Nāṣir-i Khusraw in his treatise, *Jāmiʿ al-ḥikmatayn*.

492 —— 'Abu Yakub Sidzhistani' [Abū Yaʿqūb al-Sijistānī], *Istoriiā tadzhikskoĭ filosofii (s drevneĭshikh vremen do XV v.* [The History of Tajik Philosophy (From Ancient Times to the 15th Century], vol. 2, ed. A. Mukhammadkhodzhaev and K. Olimo. Dushanbe: Donish, 2011, pp. 328–343. (in Russian).

The work analyses al-Sijistānī's Ismaili philosophy on subjects such as being, the relationship of the Creator and creation, matter and form, soul and body, and the categories of movement, space and time.

493 —— 'Nasir Khusrav' [Nāṣir-i Khusraw], in *Istoriiā tadzhikskoĭ filosofii (s drevneĭshikh vremen do XV v.*) [The History of Tajik Philosophy (from Ancient times to the 15th century], vol. 2, ed. A. Mukhammadkhodzhaev and K. Olimov. Dushanbe: Donish, 2011, pp. 344–372. (in Russian).

In Nāṣir-i Khusraw's ethical philosophy, man occupies an important place. The human being, in his opinion, has a speaking soul, which ensures his superiority over other earthly creatures.

N

494 Nafisi, Orash. *Istoriia̐ raspostraneniia̐ ismailizma v Khorasane i Moverannakhre* [The History of the Spread of Ismailism in Khurāsān and Māwarā' al-nahr], Dissertat͡siia̐ na soiskanie uchënoĭ stepeni kandidata filosofskikh nauk [PhD Candidate for the Degree of Doctor of Philosophy]. Dushanbe: Akademi Nauk, 2016. pp. 160. (in Russian).

The study is a comparative analysis of the Ismailis of Central Asia, in particular Tajikistan and Afghanistan and their dynamics. The study provides: i) a critical analysis of the history of the introduction and spread of Ismailism in the region; ii) an assessment of the influence and position of the Ismaili imams in strengthening the Ismaili community in Central Asia; iii) an investigation of the change in the position of Ismailism in the post-Soviet period.

495 Najib, Azizullah. 'The Intellect from Nasir Khusraw's Viewpoint', in Sarfaroz Niyozov and Ramazon Nazariev, ed., *Nasir Khusraw: Yesterday, Today, Tomorrow*. (Proceedings of a conference held in Khārūgh, Tajikistan). Khujand: Noshir, 2005, pp. 84–101.

This paper argues that Nāṣir-i Khusraw divides the Intellect into the universal or complete (*kullī*) and the individual (*juz'ī*). Nāṣir-i Khusraw regarded the universal or first intellect as the prime origin of creation, which emerged by God's command without reference to reason, space or time, simply by instantaneous *ibdāʿ* (creation *ex nihilo*). The individual intellect is a tool for perfecting the soul, which in turn is developed via learning and the gaining of knowledge.

496 Nanji, Azim. 'Nāṣir-i Khusraw', *EI2*, vol. 7, pp. 1006–1007.

A brief biographical entry on Nāṣir-i Khusraw.

Nāṣir Khusrau, see, Nasir-i Khusraw.

497 Nâsir-i-Khusrau [Nāṣir-i Khusraw], *Diary of a Journey through Syria and Palestine*, tr. Guy Le Strange. London: Palestine Pilgrims' Text Society, 1893. pp. 72.

Guy Le Strange translated from the Persian and annoted the first partial English language edition of the *Safar-nāma*.

498 —— *Safar-namė: kniga puteshestviia̐*, E.Ė. Bertel's per. i vstuplenie [*Safar-nāma*. Travelogue, E.Ė. Bertel's tr., and intr.], under the general editorship of V.A. Gordlevskiĭ and Academician I.I͡U. Krachkovskiĭ. Moscow-Leningrad: Akademiia̐, 1933. pp. 207.

The first Russian translation and edition of Nāṣir-i Khusraw's *Safar-nāma*.

499 —— *Safarnoma* [Safar-nameh]. Dushanbe: Irfon, 1970. pp. 118. (in Tajik).

500 —— *Forty Poems from the Divan.* tr. and introd., Peter Lamborn Wilson and Gholam Reza Aavani, ed. Seyyed Hossein Nasr. Tehran: Imperial Iranian Academy of Philosophy, 1977. pp. 144.

A selection of forty poems by Nāṣir-i Khusraw.

501 —— *Kulliët* [Complete Works]. Khārūgh: Pomir, 1992. pp. 34. (in Tajik).

502 —— *Ravshanoinoma* [Rawshanā'ī-nāma]. Khārūgh: Pomir, 1992. pp. 34. (in Tajik).

503 —— *Knowledge and Liberation: A Treatise on Philosophical Theology*, a new edition and translation of *Gushāyish va Rahāyish*, ed and tr. by Faquir M. Hunzai, with an introduction and commentary by Parviz Morewedge. London: I.B. Tauris, 1998. pp. 237.

Gushāyish va Rahāyish is the first major treatise by Nāṣir-i Khusraw to be translated into English. Consisting of a series of thirty questions and answers, it addresses some of the central philosophical and theological issues of his time from an Ismaili perspective, ranging from the creation of the world and the nature of the soul to questions of free will and responsibility.

504 —— *Vajhi din* [Wajh-i dīn], ed. Aliqul Devlonaqulov and Nurmuhammad Amirshohī. Dushanbe: Amr-i Ilm, 2002. (in Tajik).

505 —— 'Raushanai-nama' ('Kniga prosvetleniia') [*Rawshanā'ī-nāma* ('The Book of Enlightenment')], Introduction; Chapter on edification; Verses 1–162, *EIF*, vol. 4, pp. 333–344.

An annotated translation by N.I. Prigarina and M.A. Shakarbekova of both the introduction and the first chapter of Nāṣir-i Khusraw's *Rawshanā'ī-nāma*.

506 Nasr, S.H. 'Nasir i Khusraw', *ER*, vol. 10, pp. 312–313.

Brief information about Nāṣir-i Khusraw's life, thought and work, and influence on Islamic philosophy.

507 Nazaramonov, Shaboz Parvonaevich. *Problema cheloveka v filosofii Nasira Khusrava* [The Problem of Man in Nāṣir-i Khusraw's Philosophy], Dissertatsiia na soiskanie uchënoĭ stepeni kandidata filosofskikh nauk [PhD Candidate for the Degree of Doctor of Philosophy]. Dushanbe: Akademi Nauk, 2014. pp. 151. (in Russian).

The theme of the thesis is about the understanding the anthropology of Nāṣir-i Khusraw's concept of the historical and socio-cultural conditions that have influenced the formation of rational philosophy, including an analysis of human nature, the mind and the soul, and their relationship.

508 Nazariev, Ramazon. 'Nasir Khusraw's Views on Din and Dunya', in Sarfaroz Niyozov and Ramazon Nazariev, ed., *Nasir Khusraw: Yesterday, Today, Tomorrow*. (Proceedings of a conference held in Khārūgh, Tajikistan). Khujand: Noshir, 2005, pp. 53–58.

While human beings are generally subordinate to God, they are also relatively free in their actions. Nāṣir-i Khusraw describes this intermediate situation as 'neither compelled to do something, nor free in the full sense'.

509 —— *Allegoricheskai͡a interpretat͡sii͡a filosofsko-teologicheskikh problem v ismailizme* [The Allegorical Interpretation of Philosophical and Theological Problems in Ismailism], Dissertat͡sii na soiskanie uchënoĭ stepeni kandidata filosofskikh nauk [PhD Candidate for the Degree of Doctor of Philosophy]. Dushanbe: Akademi Nauk, 2000. pp. 156. (in Russian).

This study covers the basic philosophical, theological, epistemological and social issues – such as the nature of God, the transcendent world and its elements, the Qur'an, the nature and role of the prophets and imams as spiritual and charismatic leaders of society – from the point of view of different Ismaili thinkers. Particular attention is paid to the conceptual and systematic analysis of the above issues from the Ismaili doctrinal perspective.

510 —— *Sot͡sial'nai͡a filosofii͡a 'Ikhvan as-safa" - i Nasira Khusrava: sravnitel'nyĭ analiz* [The Social Philosophy of the 'Ikhwān al-Ṣafā'' and Nāṣir-i Khusraw: A Comparative Analysis], Dissertat͡sii na soiskanie uchënoĭ stepeni doktora filosofskikh nauk [PhD Candidate for the Degree of Doctor of Philosophy]. Dushanbe: Akademi Nauk, 2011, p. 293. (in Russian).

A comparative study of the social philosophy of the Ikhwān al-Ṣafā' and that of Nāṣir-i Khusraw.

511 —— 'The Contribution of Russian Scholars to the Study of Ismaili Philosophy and Theology, and Prospects for its Development', in Stanislav M. Prozorov and Hakim Elnazarov, ed., *Russian Scholars on Ismailism*. (Proceedings of a conference held in St Petersburg, Russia in 2011). St Petersburg: Nestor-Istorii͡a, 2014, pp. 64–73. (in Russian and English).

Many eminent scholars have studied Ismaili philosophical doctrines. Amongst these, a special role is given to Russian Orientalists. The study highlights the following periods: (i) pre-Soviet scholars: A.A. Bobrinskoĭ, A.A. Semënov, V.V. Bartol'd, V.A. Ivanov; (ii) Soviet scholars: A.E. Bertel's, A.K. Zakuev; and (iii) post-Soviet scholars: E.A. Frolova, A.V. Smirnov and A.A. Ignatenko.

512 —— and Shahboz Nazaramonov. *Farhangi zaboni Nosiri Khusraw* [A Guide to Nāṣir-i Khusraw's Philosophical and Literary Heritage]. Dushanbe: Andaleb, 2015. pp. 416. (in Tajik).

The work studies terms, concepts and phrases in the philosophical and poetic corpus of the *ḥakīm*, philosopher, traveller and the renowned poet of the 5th/11th century, Nāṣir-i Khusraw.

513 Nazriev, Jurabek and Amrii͡azdon Alimardonov. 'Nasir Khusraw – A Thinker and Poet of Truth, Wisdom and Humanity', in Sarfaroz Niyozov and Ramazon Nazariev, ed., *Nasir Khusraw: Yesterday, Today, Tomorrow.* (Proceedings of a conference held in Khārūgh, Tajikistan). Khujand: Noshir, 2005, pp. 435–441.

The authors illustrate the important role which, according to Nāṣir-i Khusraw, human beings play in society, highlighting the value of knowledge and wisdom, the significance of language, advice and good counsel.

514 Ne'matov, Numon. 'Harakati qarmatii͡a va mohii͡ati ijtimoii on' [The Qarmaṭī Movement and its Social Meaning], in *Davlati Somoniën: tojikon dar asrhoi IX–X* [The Sāmānid State: Tajiks in the 9th–10th Centuries]. 2nd ed., Dushanbe: Irfon, 1989, pp. 139–141. (in Tajik).

According to the author, the Qarmaṭī movement shows some common traits with Ismaili thought and Shiʿi thought in general. From the outset, the Qarmaṭīs were very critical of the feudal social structure and, as a result, gained support amongst the ordinary people. Ideologically, the Qarmaṭī movement used rationalism and philosophy on the one hand, whilst appealing to reactionary Sufism (*taṣawwuf-i irtijāʿī*) on the other.

515 Nicholson, R.A. 'Nāṣir Ibn Khusrau', *ERE*, vol. 9, pp. 186–187.

A brief biography of Nāṣir-i Khusraw.

516 Niëzbekov, Davlat. 'Filosofskai͡a teologii͡a Abu Khatima ar-Razi' [The Philosophical Theology of Abū Ḥātim al-Rāzī], *IANRT*, 4 (2008), pp. 1–12. (in Russian).

Abū Ḥātim al-Rāzī was a follower of the doctrine of the imamate, as well as an adherent of *taʿlīmiyya* teaching, believing that the source of true knowledge comes through the imam. In his book, *Kitāb aʿlām al-nubuwwa*, he set out to prove the necessity of the imam as the foremost means of attaining true knowledge of God.

517 —— 'Abu Khatim Razi' [Abū Ḥātim al-Rāzī], in *Istorii͡a tadzhikskoĭ filosofii (s drevneĭshikh vremen do XV v.)* [The History of Tajik Philosophy (from Ancient times to the 15th century], vol. 2, ed. A. Mukhammadkhodzhaev and K. Olimov. Dushanbe: Donish, 2011, pp. 328–343. (in Russian).

Abū Ḥātim al-Rāzī was regarded as the second thinker, after Nasafī, to make a significant contribution to the development of theology and philosophy in the Ismaili movement, as well as to the systematisation of theological terms in the Arabic language.

518 —— 'Abu Khatim Razi i ego vklad v stanovlenie filosofskogo ismailizma' [Abū Ḥātim al-Rāzī and His Contribution in the Development of Philisophical Ismailism], *VU (RTSU)*, 1 (2014), pp. 203–210. (in Russian).

This work focuses on Abū Ḥātim al-Rāzī's intellectual activities and the contradictions in his understanding and interpretation of the Qur'an.

519 —— 'Filosofskoe tvorchestvo Abu Khatima Razi' [The Philosophical Creativity of Abū Ḥātim al-Rāzī], *Seriia̐: Gumanitarnykh nauk*, 139 (2014), pp. 131–135. (in Russian).

Abū Ḥātim al-Rāzī not only played a huge role in the development of Ismaili philosophical ideas, but along with other followers of the Ismaili doctrine, he also contributed significantly to the development of a Shiʿi school of jurisprudence (*fiqh*) in Islam.

520 —— *Filosofskie vzgliady Abu Khatima ar-Razi* [Abū Ḥātim al-Rāzī's Philosophical Understanding], Dissertatsii na soiskanie uchënoĭ stepeni kandidata filosofskikh nauk [PhD Candidate for the Degree of Doctor of Philosophy]. Dushanbe: Akademi Nauk, 2014. pp. 150. (in Russian).

The study focuses on a synthesis of Islam and ancient philosophy in the works of Abū Ḥātim al-Rāzī, which played an important role for the further development of Islamic culture and civilisation.

521 —— 'Abu Khatim ar-Razi i antichnaia̐ mysl" [Abū Ḥātim al-Rāzī and Antique Thought], *Filosofiia̐*, TSentr Nauchnogo Sotrudnichestva 'Interaktiv pliu̐s'. Cheboksary, 2016, pp. 198–203. (in Russian).

This work is devoted to the origins of philosophical views in the history of philosophy of the East, particularly the works of Abū Ḥātim al-Rāzī, a philosopher and a preacher from the ranks of the Ismaili *ḥujjas*.

522 —— 'Ėticheskoe Uchenie Abu Khatima Razi' [The Ethical Teachings of Abū Ḥātim al-Rāzī], *Nauchnye Issledovaniia̐: ot teorii k praktike*, Sbornik materialov IX Mezhdunarodnoĭ nauchno-prakticheskoĭ konferentsii [Academic Research: From Theory to Practice, Collected Materials of the 9th International Academic Conference on Scholarly Practice]. Cheboksary, 2016, pp. 262–266. (in Russian).

This article sheds some light on Abū Ḥātim al-Rāzī's ethical philosophy, an area of study which has been so far overlooked.

523 —— *Filosofiia̐ Abu Khatima ar-Razi i ranniĭ ismailizm* [The Philosophy of Abū Ḥātim al-Rāzī and Early Ismailism]. Dushanbe, 2017. pp. 202. (in Russian).

The book covers little-studied questions on the ontology, epistemology and anthropology of Abū Ḥātim al-Rāzī as well as the formation of early Ismaili philosophical thought.

524 Nikitina, Vera Borisovna (1922–1993). *Nekotorye osobennosti liriki Nasir-i Khosrova* [Some Features of Nāṣir-i Khusraw's Texts], Dissertatsii na soiskanie uchënoĭ stepeni kandidata filologicheskikh nauk [PhD Candidate for the Degree of Doctor of Philosophy], Moskovskiĭ gosudarstvennyĭ universitet im. M.V. Lomonosova [Lomonosov University]. Moscow, 1955. pp. 260. (in Russian).

The author discusses the traditional poetic works of Nāṣir-i Khusraw. In her thesis she devotes a chapter to the use of poetic devices in his *Qaṣīdas*.

525 —— 'Nekotorye osobennosti v kasyde Nasir-i Khosrova' [Some Features of the Landscape in Nāṣir-i Khusraw's *Qaṣīdas*], *Filologicheskie nauki*, 3 (1961), pp. 172–180. (in Russian).

526 Nikol'skiĭ, B.K. *Religioznye verovaniia narodov SSSR* [The Religious Beliefs of the Peoples of the USSR], vol. 1, 'Ismailizm [Ismailism]'. Moscow-Leningrad: Moskovskiĭ rabochiĭ, 1931, pp. 364–375. (in Russian).

The study analyses the doctrines of the Central Asian Ismailis, their views about God, the Prophets and the imams, including the Ismaili hierarchy and the role of the *pīr*s, religious rituals and ceremonies.

527 Niyozov, Sarfaroz. 'Shi'a Ismaili Tradition in Central Asia: – Evolution, Continuities and Changes', *Central Asia and the Caucasus*, 24 (2003), pp. 39–46. Available online at: http://www.ca-c.org/journal/eng-06-2003/05.niyprimen.shtml [Last accessed, 7 May 2019].

The Tajik Ismaili community constitutes one of the largest and historically oldest concentrations of Ismailis in the world.

528 —— and Ramazon Nazariev, ed. *Nasir Khusraw: Yesterday, Today, Tomorrow*. (Proceedings of a conference held in Khārūgh, Tajikistan). Khujand: Noshir, 2005. pp. 682.

The collection of articles is from the conference celebrating the millennium of Nāṣir-i Khusraw, held in Tajikistan in September 2003. It captures the intellectual quality and diversity reflected in the presentations and discussions held in Khārūgh and Dushanbe, Tajikistan.

529 —— 'A Comparative Analysis of W. Ivanow's and A. Bertel's' Works on Nasir-i Khusraw and Ismailism: Toward Rethinking Central Asian Ismaili Studies', in Stanislav M. Prozorov and Hakim Elnazarov, ed., *Russian Scholars on Ismailism*. (Proceedings of a conference held in St Petersburg, Russia in 2011). St Petersburg: Nestor-Istoriia, 2014, pp. 160–208.

Despite post-Soviet advances in the study of Central Asian Ismailism, Wladimir Ivanow and Andreĭ Bertel's have remained foundational in this field. However, due to the opposing ideological camps in which these two scholars found themselves, their impact has been limited to their own spheres of influence. The paper advocates a re-examination of the ideological positioning of both authors, arguing that each played a critical role in the establishment of this subject within the context and constraints of their times.

530 Norboev, M. 'Sootnoshenie fiziki i metafiziki Aristoteliā i ego znachenie dliā razvitiiā filosofii Nasira Khusrava' [The Correlation of the Physics and Metaphysics of Aristotle and its Role in the Development of Nāṣir-i Khusraw's Philosophy], *VTNU SFN*, 3 (2015), pp. 127–133. (in Russian).

The main problems of physical and metaphysical significance in the teachings of Aristotle and Nāṣir-i Khusraw are expounded in comparative focus. Special attention is paid to an analysis of the correlations of the spiritual and material, cosmic and terrestrial, natural, corporal and spiritual.

531 Norik, Boris. 'W. Ivanow's Collection in the Archives of the Institute of Oriental Manuscripts of the Russian Academy of Sciences: A Short Survey', in Stanislav M. Prozorov and Hakim Elnazarov, ed., *Russian Scholars on Ismailism*. (Proceedings of a conference held in St Petersburg, Russia in 2011). St Petersburg: Nestor-Istoriiâ, 2014, pp. 38–44. (in Russian and English).

The paper is a survey of the Ivanow Collection in the Asiatic Museum (currently known as the Institute of Oriental Manuscripts) and its value for Orientalists.

532 Nourmamadchoev, Nourmamadcho. *The Ismāʿīlīs of Badakhshan: History, Politics and Religion from 1500–1750*, PhD dissertation, SOAS, University London, 2014. pp. 288.

This thesis analyses the political, religious, and cultural life of Badakhshān, set in the wider historical context of Central Asia and the Persianate world, from 905/1500 to 1163/1750. Its main focus is the scattered Ismaili communities of Badakhshān and the Pamir principalities. It also addresses the impact of politics on religion and religious communities, particularly the Shiʿi and Ismaili minority groups in Badakhshān.

533 —— 'Ismaili-Sufi and Ismaili-Twelver Relations in Badakhshān in the Post-Alamūt Period: The *Chirāgh-nāma*', in Orkhan Mir-Kasimov, ed., *Intellectual Interactions in the Islamic World: The Ismaili Thread*. London: I.B. Tauris, 2019, pp. 355–380.

This chapter focuses on Ismaili-Sufi and Ismaili-Twelver relations in Badakhshān. In modern studies, Badakhshān is referred to as 'a sort of cultural palimpsest, a recipient of a complex series of influences' such as the relations between the Sufis, Ismailis and Twelver Shiʿis. In this context, this chapter gives an overview of Ismaili-Sufi relations and also tries to explore the influence of Twelver Shiʿism on the *Chirāgh-nāma* and on other texts produced in Badakhshān.

534 —— 'Paying Homage to the *Ahl al-Bayt*: Shāh Ḍiyāʾ-yi Shughnānī's *Salām-nāma* in Central Asian Manuscripts', in Wafi Momin, ed., *Scribes and Transmission: Manuscript Cultures of the Ismaili Communities and Beyond*. London (forthcoming).

Shāh Ḍiyāī-i Shughnānī is a hitherto unknown Ismaili poet from the region of Shughnān. He lived in the 10th–11th/16th–17th centuries, a time when most of Badakhshān was ruled by the last Tīmūrids, namely Sulaymān Mīrzā (d. 997/1589) and his son Ibrāhīm Mīrzā (d. 967/1560). In the religious context, he was a contemporary of the Qāsim-Shāhī Imams, Murād Mīrzā (d. 981/1574) and Dhu'l-Fiqār ʿAlī (d. 1043/1634). This study concentrates comparing two different texts on the poem of allegiance known as *Salām-nāma*.

O

535 Odilbekov, R. 'Materialy k istorii Shugnana (konets XVIII–XIX vv.)' [Materials on the History of Shughnān (end of XVIII–XIX Century)], *IAN (TSSR)*, 1 (1974), pp. 3–17. (in Russian).

This study analyses new materials and historical documents on the socio-economic and political life of the Pamir region and in particular the district of Shughnān, before the October 1917 Revolution.

536 Odinaev, N.S. 'Az ta'rīkh-i omūzish va pazhūhishi ahvol va osori Nasiruddini Tusī' [The History of Research and Exploration into the Life and the Works of Khwāja Naṣīr al-Dīn Ṭūsī], *AAF* (RSST), SFH, 4 (2011), pp. 50–55. (in Tajik).

This article scrutinises of the life and works of the prominent 7th/13th-century thinker Khwāja Naṣīr al-Dīn Ṭūsī.

537 Olimov, K., K. Askardaev and A. Sharipov, ed. *Nosir Khusrav. Jomeʾ-ul-hikmataïn* [Nāṣir-i Khusraw. *Jāmiʿ al-ḥikmatayn*]. Dushanbe: ER-graff, 2011. pp. 310. (in Tajik).

Jāmiʿ al-ḥikmatayn was written at the request of the *amīr* of Badakhshān, Abu'l-Maʿālī ʿAlī b. Assad; it aims at providing answers to a *qaṣīda* by Abu'l-Haytham Aḥmad b. al-Ḥasan al-Jurjānī containing 91 questions on philosophy, logic, physics, syntax and the religious sciences.

538 Orënfar, Shamsulhaq. *Simoi Hazrati ʿAlī dar Farhangi Mardumi Forszabon* [The Reputation of Ḥaḍrat-i ʿAlī in Persian Culture]. Dushanbe, 2001. pp. 75. (in Tajik).

A series of legends about ʿAlī in the folklore of Persian-speaking countries such as Afghanistan, Iran and Tajikistan.

539 Ormsby, Eric, ed. and tr. *Between Reason and Revelation: Twin Wisdoms Reconciled: An annotated English translation of Nāṣir-i Khusraw's* Kitāb-i Jāmiʿ al-ḥikmatayn. London: I.B. Tauris, 2012. pp. 292.

This is the first English translation of the last known philosophical work of the great fifth/eleventh-century Ismaili thinker, poet and Fatimid emissary, Nāṣir-i Khusraw. Appointed by the Fatimid Imam-caliph al-Mustanṣir in Cairo to serve first as a *dāʿī*, and then as the *ḥujjat*, for the entire region of Khurāsān, he maintained his allegiance both to his mission and to his imam for the rest of his life, even when driven into exile.

540 Oshurbekov, Sharaf. *Places, Memories and Religious Identity: Muslim Places of Worship in Badakhshan Region of Tajikistan*. PhD dissertation, York University. Toronto, 2014. pp. 173.

This dissertation examines the ways in which the Ismailis of the Badakhshān region of Tajikistan understand, and relate to, their sacred sites. It explores the sacred sites of Badakhshān in the framework of anthropological literature on space and place.

P

541 Peerwani, Parvin E. 'Pir Nasir Khusraw's Concept of Intellect and Theory of Intellectual Education', *Ilm*, 12, 1 (July, 1989), published by ITREB, UK. Also, available online at: https://simerg.com/literary-readings/pir-nasir-khusraws-concept-of-intellect-and-theory-of-intellectual-education-2/ [Last accessed, 18 May 2019].

The relationship between intellect (*'aql*) and faith has always been of fundamental importance to Muslims and has been widely discussed amongst Muslim philosophers and intellectuals.

542 —— 'Hakim Nasir's Theory of Education (*ta'līm*) for the Development of Human Intellect', *Ilm*, 12, 1 (July, 1989), published by ITREB, UK. Also, available online at: https://simerg.com/literary-readings/pir-nasir-khusraws-theory-of-intellectual-education-2/ [Last accessed, 18 May 2019].

From the study of Nāṣir-i Khusraw's work it can be deduced that *ta'līm* (instruction or education) encompassed the study of *'ilm* and the practice (*'amal*) of various disciplines including the Qur'an and its *ta'wīl* or deeper meaning, the *ḥadīth* or the traditions of the Prophet, and the teachings of the legitimate imams from the Prophet's progeny.

543 Petrushevskiĭ, Il'iā P. 'Ismaility', 'Karamaty', ['Ismailis', 'Qarmaṭīs'], *BSE*. Moscow: BSE, 1972. (in Russian).; 'Ismailians', 'Karamathians', also in *GSE*. New York: Macmillan; London: Collier Macmillan, 1976–1977.

A brief overview of Ismaili history.

544 —— 'Ismaility' [The Ismailis], *BSE*, 3rd ed., pp. 1471–1472. (in Russian).

Brief information on Ismailism and its history.

545 Pidrom, Latif. 'The Neo-Aristotelian Thought of Nasir Khusraw', in Sarfaroz Niyozov and Ramazon Nazariev, ed., *Nasir Khusraw: Yesterday, Today, Tomorrow*. (Proceedings of a conference held in Khārūgh, Tajikistan). Khujand: Noshir, 2005, pp. 91–101.

The author asserts that the philosophy of the ancient Greeks, in particular that of Aristotle, had a major influence on Nāṣir-i Khusraw's thought. At the same time, in constrast to Ibn Sīnā and al-Farabī who were also influenced by Greek philosophy, Nāṣir-i Khusraw subjected Greek ideas and theories to much deeper scrutiny. Pidrom touches upon a number of themes in Nāṣir-i Khusraw's works, such as non-being, being and God.

546 Pigulevskai͡a, N.B., A.I͡U. Yakubovskiĭ., I.P. Petrushevskiĭ., L.B. Stroeva and A.M. Belenit͡skiĭ. 'Ismaility' [The Ismailis], in *Istorii͡a Irana s drevneĭshikh vremen do kont͡sa XVIII veka* [The History of Iran from Ancient times up to the End of the 18th Century]. Leningrad: Izdatel'stvo Leningradskogo Universiteta, 1958. pp. 118. (in Russian).

Following the split in Shiʿi Islam in the second half of the 2nd/8th century, a new religious movement emerged which later became known as Ismailism and in time further developed its doctrines.

547 —— A.I͡U. Yakubovskiĭ, I.P. Petrushevskiĭ, L.B. Stroeva and A.M. Belenit͡skiĭ. 'Ismaility v Irane' [The Ismailis in Iran], in *Istorii͡a Irana s drevneĭshikh vremen do kont͡sa XVIII veka* [The History of Iran from Ancient times to the end of the 18th Century]. Leningrad: Izdatel'stvo Leningradskogo Universiteta, 1958, pp. 151–152. (in Russian).

Following the decline of the Fatimid state in Egypt, Ḥasan-i Ṣabbāḥ became the leader of the Ismailis of Iran and Syria. Under his leadership they established a secret organisation at Alamūt whose members were bound to strict discipline under unconditional obligation to their leaders.

548 Plekhanov, Sergeĭ. *Raskrytai͡a ladon'*: *Aga Khan i ego Mi͡uridy* [An Open Hand: the Aga-Khan and His Murīds]. Moscow: Nat͡sional'noe obozrenie, 2008. pp. 206. (in Russian).

The book presents a broad historical context, without which it would not be easy to understand the significance of the Aga Khan and his followers in the world today.

549 Pomirzod, Khushnazar. 'Historical Events, Their Contemporary Significance and the Future of the Pir Shah Nasir Khusraw's Tradition', in Sarfaroz Niyozov and Ramazon Nazariev, ed., *Nasir Khusraw: Yesterday, Today, Tomorrow*. (Proceedings of a conference held in Khārūgh, Tajikistan). Khujand: Noshir, 2005, pp. 641–650.

The author discusses the rites and rituals of the people of Badakhshān, such as those of birth and death, the construction of houses and other more or less significant religious and non-religious ceremonies and holidays.

550 Prozorov, Stanislav Mikhaĭlovich. 'al-Ismāʿīlīi͡a', [Ismailism], *IES*, pp. 110–114. (in Russian).

Prozorov discusses the Ismailis as followers of one of the main branches of Shiʿi Islam, who played a significant role in the history of the Muslim East at different times and in different countries, who have also been known under different names such as al-Bāṭiniyya, al-Qarmaṭiyya, al-Taʿlīmiyya, al-Mulḥīda, etc. The work is divided into subsections: (i) the history of the Ismaili movement; (ii) propaganda organisation (hierarchy); (iii) teaching.

551 —— and Hakim Elnazarov, ed. *Russian Scholars on Ismailism*. (Proceedings of a conference held in St Petersburg, Russia in 2011). St Petersburg: Nestor-Istoriia̐, 2014. pp. 311. (in Russian and English).

In December 2011 the Institute of Ismaili Studies, London, and the Institute of Oriental Manuscripts, St Petersburg, held an international conference on the contribution of Russian scholars to Ismaili studies on the occasion of the 125th anniversary of the birth of the prominent Russian Iranist, W.A. Ivanow (1886–1970). The conference materials form the basis of this collection of articles.

552 Putiata̐, Dmitriĭ Vasil'evich. 'Ocherk ėkspeditsii v Pamir, Sarykol, Wakhan i Shugnan v 1883 g.' [Essays on an Expedition to the Pamir, Sarikūl, Wakhān and Shughnān in 1883], *Sbornik geograficheskikh, topograficheskikh i statisticheskikh*, 10 (1884). pp. 88. (in Russian).

Putiata̐'s work is one of the first ethnographic studies of the people of Shughnān, Wakhān and Sarikūl. The author also provided an account of their religious beliefs by arguing that these people are Muslim Shiʿi [Ismaili] followers.

Q

553 Qadamshoh, Qimatshohi. *Zaruriëti dinī-mazhabii ismoiliën* [The Religious Obligations of the Ismailis]. Dushanbe: Meʿroj-Graf, 2016. pp. 128. (in Tajik).

This book on Ismaili traditions and ceremonies was commissioned and approved by the Committee on Religious Affairs of the Government of Tajikistan. It provides a set of examples of *duʿā*(s), prayers, chants and verses of the Qur'an with translations.

554 Qalandarov, Hokim. 'Kist on "shoiri tirachasmi ravshanbin"?' ['Who is that Blind Sharp-Sighted Poet?'], *AS* (24 April 2008), pp. 1–2 (in Tajik).

A dispute between the author of the article and a contemporary scholar, Tojiddin Mardoni, who argued that when Nāṣir-i Khusraw asked the question, 'Who is a blind clairvoyant poet?' he was referring to the Arab poet al-Maʿarrī. Kalandarov disagrees with this identification and holds that the person referred to is actually Rūdakī.

555 —— 'Paĭvandi fikrii Imom Jaʿfari Sodiq va Imomi Aʿzam' [The Unity of the Views of Imam Jaʿfar al-Ṣādiq and Imam Abū Ḥanīfa], *IANRT*, 2 (2009), pp. 57–60. (in Tajik).

An important study on two key figures of the Islamic world: Imam Jaʿfar al-Ṣādiq, who the Ismailis regard as their fifth imam, and Abū Ḥanīfa one of the founders of the Sunni school. The study presents Abū Ḥanīfa as a pupil of Jaʿfar al-Ṣādiq, as a scholar who had a high regard for his master and was heavily influenced by his teachings.

556 —— 'Zikri qissai Azozil dar i͡ak ghazali Robiae Balkhī', in *Vzgli͡ad na zhizn' i tvorchestvo Robea Balkhi* [The Mention of Demon Legends in a *Ghazal* of Rābiʿa Balkhī, in *A View of the Life and Work of Rābiʿa Balkhī*], Collection of Essays. Dushanbe: Istiqbal, 2010, pp. 85–90. (in Tajik).

The famous Persian-Tajik poet Rābiʿa Balkhī lived in a time when Ismaili philosophy was dominant in the world of thought. The author has analysed one of Rābiʿa's *ghazal*s which narrates the story of ʿAzāzīl.

557 —— 'Rudakī va ismoilizm' [Rūdakī and Ismailism], *VTNU SFN*, 8 (2008), pp. 211–229. (in Tajik).

In this article, the author discusses Abū ʿAbd Allāh Rūdakī's view of the Ismailis using his poems and including other examples of Persian poetry in connection to this issue.

558 —— *Rudakī va ismoilii͡a* [Rūdakī and the Ismailis]. Dushanbe: Ėr-graf, 2012. pp. 235. (in Tajik).

Rūdakī's connection to the Ismailis is one of the most important aspects of the history of Tajik-Persian literature. The author of *Rūdakī and the Ismailis* claims that Rūdakī adhered to Ismaili ideas. The author also touches upon the important issue of the distinction between the Qarmaṭīs and the Ismailis.

559 —— 'Ėʿtiqod az nigohi Kisoī' [Faith in Terms of Kasāyī], *VTNU SFN*, 4, 6 (2012), pp. 207–212. (in Tajik).

The author emphasises the importance of Ismaili philosophical thought and its impact on the poetry of the 4th/10th century. He focuses on one of the most popular poets, Kasāyī Marvazī, analysing how faith and belief are reflected in his verse.

560 —— 'Muorizai Nosiri Khusrav va Kisoī' [The Verbal Dispute between Nāṣir-i Khusraw and Kasāyī], *Slovesnost' Nauchniyĭ zhurnal instituta i͡azyka, literatury, vostokovedenii͡a pis'mennnogo nasledii͡a*, 2 (2012), pp. 65–85. (in Tajik).

Nāṣir-i Khusraw often refers to the poet Kasāyī in his lyrics, a peculiarity which has attracted the attention of the experts. This issue is interpreted from different perspectives by Orientalists due to the fact that both scholars had the same religious affiliation. Despite noting Kasāyī's ideas, Nāṣir-i Khusraw did not welcome his arguments mainly deeming them anachronistic.

561 —— 'Zikri qissai *Oshūro* dar îak ghazali Kisoī' [Mention of the 'Āshūrā Tradition in Kasāyī's Ode], *IANRT*, 3–4. Dushanbe: Donish, 2013, pp. 36–50. (in Tajik).

This article focuses on one of the first religious elegies in the history of Persian-Tajik poetry. Kasāyī Marvazī was clearly an adept of the Prophet's Family, and this elegy dwells on the martyrdom of Imam Ḥusayn b. 'Alī b. Abī Ṭālib. The author, referring to historical sources, and using the comparative-historical method, undertakes a comprehensive examination of the elegy.

562 —— 'Maqomi Imom az nazari Sūzani Samarqandī' [The Imam and his Status from Sūzanī Samarqandī's Point of View], *VPU*, Seriîa pedagogicheskikh i filologicheskikh nauk, 2 (2013), pp. 315–321. (in Tajik).

An analysis of Sūzanī Samarqandī's *qaṣīda*s relative to Ismaili religious teachings and philosophical views.

563 —— 'Andeshahoi falsafii ismoiliën dar risolai "Haĭ ibni ĪAqzon")-i ibni Sino' [The Philosophical Views in the 'Ḥayy b. Yaqẓān' Treatise of Ibn Sīnā], *VPU*, Seriîa pedagogicheskikh i filologicheskikh nauk, 2 (2013), pp. 321–327. (in Tajik).

According to this article, Ibn Sīnā had close relations with the Ismailis, and besides being engaged in the study of secular sciences was also fascinated by Ismaili doctrines. Qalandarov believes that Ibn Sīnā wrote *Ḥayy ibn Yaqẓān*, intending to present it as an allegory on the Active Mind, yet, from a hidden and symbolic angle, one could identify in this story the doctrines and the core of the Ismaili faith.

564 —— 'Bahs peromuni tamoĭulhoi ě'tiqodii ibni Sino' [The Controversy around the Religious Tendencies of Ibn Sīnā], *VPU*, Seriîa obshchestvennykh, gumanitarnykh i filologicheskikh nauk, 4 (2013), pp. 18–27. (in Tajik).

This paper analyses the religious affiliation of Ibn Sīnā, which has often been a subject of debate in the works of Russian and European academics. During the Sāmānid era, the Ismaili movement was regarded as a progressive one that was spread by its preachers (sing. *dāʿī*).

565 —— 'Mafohim va mazomini mazhabī dar nazmi Nosiri Khusrav' [Religious Motives and the Content of Nāṣir-i Khusraw's Poetry], *VPU*, Seriîa obshchestvennykh, gumanitarnykh i filologicheskikh nauk, 6 (2013), pp. 16–25. (in Tajik).

This article presents an analysis of the impact of Nāṣir-i Khusraw's philosophical theology in outlining the main pillars of Islam.

566 —— 'Tafsiri ismoilii "Qasidai aĭniîa"-i ibni Sino' [The Ismaili Interpretation of Ibn Sīnā's 'al-Qaṣīda al-'Ayniyya'], *VTNU SFN*, 4, 3 (2013), pp. 214–219. (in Tajik).

The work examines Ibn Sīnā's *qaṣīda*, which has been translated repeatedly into Persian, through an Ismaili lens. From the perspective of Ismaili doctrine, it can be seen to recount the heavenly origin of the soul, believed to be in captivity and in pain in this earthly world.

567 —— 'Sūzanī va tamoĭuli aqidati ū' [Sūzanī and His Religious Affiliation], *VTNU SFN*, 4, 1 (2013), pp. 162–172. (in Tajik).

Although there have been certain assumptions with regard to Sūzanī Samarqandī's Ismaili religious adherence, this study sheds some new light on this issue, analysing Samarqandī's poetical works and concluding that he adopted the Ismaili faith during the second half of his life.

568 —— 'Joĭgohi adabiëti ismoilī dar ėjodiëti Ivanov V. A.' [The Place of Ismaili Literature in the Works of W.A. Ivanow], *VTNU SFN*, 4, 5 (2013), pp. 120–126. (in Tajik).

The article gives a brief overview on the works of the Russian Orientalist, Wladimir Ivanow, on Ismaili literature. The author points out the need to define the place of Ismaili literature in Persian-Tajik literary criticism.

569 —— 'Naqshi imom dar taʻlimoti ismoiliën va fahmishi Nosiri Khusrav' [The Role of the Imam in Ismaili Doctrine and Nāṣir-i Khusraw's Understanding of it], *VTNU SFN*, 4 (2013), pp. 148–150. (in Tajik).

Overall, this work sets out Nāṣir-i Khusraw's understanding of the role of the imam according to Ismaili doctrine. According to the author, Nāṣir-i Khusraw, as an Ismaili preacher, maintained that the imam is the treasure of God's wisdom and is, consequently, the only person who can interpret the Qurʾan and the *sharīʿa* transmitted by the Prophet.

570 —— 'Tafsiri ismoilī az 'Qasidai ruh'-i ibni Sino' [The Ismaili Interpretation of the '*Qaṣīda* Rūḥ' of Ibn Sīnā], *FS*, 4 (2013), pp. 159–169. (in Tajik).

Among the works by Ibn Sīnā, there is a *qaṣīda* which has been interpreted according to Ismaili wisdom, and which recounts the descent of the soul to the world of dust where it dwells in the human body, as well as its return to heaven (*aʻlām-i qudsī*). The *qaṣīda* is also known as *al-Qaṣīda al-ʻAyniyya* (the Poem on the Soul), *Qaṣīda ʻan al-Nafs*, *al-Qaṣīda al-Nafsiyya* and even as *Qaṣīda ʻan al-Rūḥ*.

571 —— 'Andar mansubiĭati ĭak qasida ba Hakim Kisoĭ' [Regarding One of the *Qaṣīda*s from the Pen of Ḥākim Kasāyī], *Slovesnost' Nauchniyĭ zhurnal instituta ĭazyka, literatury, vostokovedeniĭa pis'mennnogo nasledĭĭa* (2013), pp. 87–101. (in Tajik).

The author analyses the discussion which arguably took place between the Ismaili poets Kasāyī Marvazī and Nāṣir-i Khusraw. Some scholars have argued that Kasāyī, having composed the *qaṣīda* 'The soul and mind are fluid under the blue firmament', sent it to Nāṣir-i Khusraw, who wrote a *qaṣīda* in response, *Bālā ī haft charkh mudawwar du gawharand*. However, this work considers whether in fact *Bālā ī haft charkh mudawwar du gawharand* was composed by Kasāyī Marvazī.

572 —— 'Sababho va zaminahoi garoishi Nosiri Khusrav ba tariqai ismoiliĭa' [Preconditional Reasons for Nāṣir-i Khusraw's Commitment to Ismailism], *VPU*, Seriĭa obshchestvennykh, gumanitarnykh i filologicheskikh nauk, 1 (2014), pp. 3–6. (in Tajik).

Relying on the studies of many Orientalist scholars, as well as his own research findings, Qalandarov investigates the reasons behind Nāṣir-i Khusraw's conversion.

573 —— 'Qasidai forsii Khoja Abulhaĭsam va sharhhoi on' [Abu'l-Ḥaytham's *Qaṣīda* and its Commentary], *VTNU SFN*, 4, 2 (2014), pp. 202–207. (in Tajik).

Abu'l-Ḥaytham's *qaṣīda*s occupied a prominent place in the Ismaili literature of his time. The themes of his *qaṣīda*s concern mainly religious and philosophical issues such as the universe and man, God and the Prophet's successors, the role and scope of spiritual guidance and the role of the Ismaili imam.

574 —— 'Andeshahoi ismoili dar nazmi shoironi ahdi Rudakī' [Ismaili Motifs in Rūdakī's Contemporary Poetry], *VTNU SFN*, 4, 3 (2014), pp. 156–164. (in Tajik).

Persian-Tajik Ismaili poetry heralds the spread of the Persian language; its spiritual and religious development is linked with the works of Rūdakī and his contemporary poets. This paper discusses, in particular, the spiritual and religious realm propounded in the poetry of Rūdakī and his contemporaries.

575 —— 'Struktura i soderzhanie kasydy Khadzhi Abul'khaĭsama i kommentarii k neĭ' [The Structure and the Content of Abu'l-Ḥaytham's *qaṣīda* and the Commentaries on it], *VTNU SFN*, 1 (2014), pp. 257–263. (in Russian).

This article deals with the structure and content of the *qaṣīda* by the Ismaili poet and philosopher Abu'l-Ḥaytham as perceived by two major representatives of Ismaili literature, Nāṣir-i Khusraw and Muḥammad b. Surkh al-Nīshāpurī.

576 —— 'Karmaty i ikh vliĭanie na politicheskuĭu zhizn' perioda pravleniĭa Samanidov i Gaznevidov' [The Qarmaṭīs and their Influence on Political Life during the eras of the Sāmānids and Ghaznawids], *Vestnik Tadzhikskogo natsional'nogo universiteta prava, biznes i politiki*, 2 (2014), pp. 138–148. (in Russian).

The main purpose of this paper is to identify the influence of the Qarmaṭī movement on cultural and social aspects of the Sāmānid and Ghaznawid states.

577 —— 'Bahs peromuni tamoĭuli aqidatii Firdawsī' [The Controversy over the Religious Affiliation of Firdawsī], *VPU, Seriia͡ obshchestvennykh, gumanitarnykh i filologicheskikh nauk*, 3 (2014), pp. 286–294. (in Tajik).

This is a comparative analysis of Ismaili philosophy and its impact on Abu'l-Qāsim Firdawsī's worldview. Qalandarov argues that the main reason Firdawsī's renowned *Shāhnāma* was not well received by Sulṭān Maḥmūd was because Firdawsī belonged to a branch of Islam which the Ghaznawid rulers opposed.

578 —— 'Mesto ismailitskoĭ poèzii v persidsko-tadzhikskoĭ literature' [The Status of Ismaili Poetry in Persian-Tajik Literature], *Izvestiia͡ Rosiĭskogo gosudarstvennogo pedagogicheskogo universiteta*, 169 (2014), pp. 54–59. (in Russian).

The classical period of Persian-Tajik literature is divided into four currents of thought: i) the philosophy of language ii) collective rationality (*mashshā'ūn*), iii) mysticism, and iv) Ismailism. This work focuses on whether Ismaili doctrine was established based on the philosophy of words or other general literary trends.

579 —— 'Qasidai Khoja Abulhaĭsam – avvalin qasidai mazhabi ba zaboni forsī' [Abu'l-Ḥaytham's *Qaṣīda* – the First Religious *Qaṣīda* in Persian], *VTTU*, 2 (2014), pp. 144–149. (in Tajik).

Abu'l-Ḥaytham Jurjānī's *qaṣīda* aims to probe his contemporary scholars and philosophers on issues such as knowledge of God, the Prophet, the imam and the *dāʿī*, the universe and the end of the world, from the standpoint of Ismaili doctrine.

580 —— 'Ismailitskaia͡ poèziia͡' [Ismaili Poetry], *Slovesnost' Nauchniyĭ zhurnal instituta ia͡zyka, literatury, vostokovedeniia͡ pis'mennnogo nasledii͡a*, 1 (2014), pp. 64–71. (in Russian).

Excluding Sufi literature, the role of religious poetry in literature in general, and in Tajik literature in particular, has not yet been systematically analysed.

—— 'Boztobi andeshahoi ismoilī dar ash'ori shoironi ahdi Rudakī' [The Reflection of Ismaili Thought in the Poetry of the Poets of Rūdakī's Epoch], in A. Sattorzoda, ed., *Ėdnomai Ustod Rudakī*. Dushanbe: Shahpar, 2014, pp. 386–406. (in Tajik).

This is a study on Ismaili philosophy and its impact on the works of a number of Persian-Tajik poets from the 3rd/9th and 4th/10th centuries.

581 Qoimdod, Qozidavlat. *Didor* [Visit]. Dushanbe: Sharqi Ozod, 1994. pp. 85. (in Tajik).

In 1993 Qozidavlat Qoimdod, Deputy to the Supreme Council of the newly independent Tajikistan and the representative of Tajik Ismaili community, visited the Aga Khan IV in Geneva, Switzerland, for the first time. He gives details about his meetings with the Aga Khan, and describes the Ismaili Imam's life and his worldwide projects carried out through the AKDN network.

582 Qurboniev, Aslisho. 'Project Identity: the Discursive Formation of Pamiri Identity in the Age of the Internet', in Dagikhudo Dagiev and Carole Faucher, ed., *Identity, History and Trans-Nationality in Central Asia: The Mountain Communities of Pamir*. London: Routledge, 2018, pp. 227–248.

This paper suggests that the historical memory of the Pamiri Tajiks, as well as the social and political conditions in Soviet Tajikistan, contributed to the construction of a defensive communal identity with clearly defined cultural, religious and linguistic boundaries.

Qalandarov, Tohir, see Kalandarov, Tokhir.

Qulmatov, Nozir. See Arabzoda, Nozir.

R

583 Rachin, E.I. 'Ismailizm' [Ismailism], *NFE*, pp. 164–166. (in Russian).

Ismailism is portrayed as a medieval school of Arab-Muslim philosophy, with an intrinsic scientific and encyclopaedic nature and not purely as a secretive community.

584 Rahmonov, A. 'Nosiri Khisrav' [Nāṣir-i Khusraw], *EAST*, vol. 2, pp. 478–481. (in Tajik).

An entry describing Nāṣir-i Khusraw's seven-year journey and conversion to Ismailism, his return to his homeland and struggle against the Turkic Sunni establishment, as well as his major philosophical and religio-intellectual works.

585 Rizvonshoeva, Gulniso. 'An Image of Nasir Khusraw', in Sarfaroz Niyozov and Ramazon Nazariev, ed., *Nasir Khusraw: Yesterday, Today, Tomorrow*. (Proceedings of a conference held in Khārūgh, Tajikistan). Khujand: Noshir, 2005, pp. 576–580.

The author suggests that throughout the centuries, many stories were told about Nāṣir-i Khusraw that were of a type of folkloric genre enriched by the imagination and creativity of skilful and talented storytellers, and these tales were passed from one generation to another.

586 Rodionov, Mikhail A. 'Ad-Duruziia' [The Druze], *IES*, p. 71. (in Russian).

A brief entry on the emergence and the establishment of the Druze as a religious community, who live in various regions of present Syria, Lebanon and Israel.

587 Romanov, A. 'Pamirskie startsy' [The Pamiri Elders], *NR*, 7 (1969), pp. 36–39. (in Russian).

A conversation between a Pamiri elder and a correspondent of *Nauka i religiĩa* (Science and Religion), a journal on moral principles.

588 Roshchin, M.I. 'Khalif al-Khakim i ustanovlenie teokratii v Fatimidskom Egipte' [The Caliph al-Ḥākim and the Establishment of Theocracy in Fatimid Egypt], *SNAA*, 5 (1978), pp. 132–140. (in Russian).

Events during the reign of the caliph al-Ḥākim were marked by sharp turns and sudden changes of view, reflecting the vicissitudes of the struggle of centrifugal tendencies among the Fatimid ruling oligarchies in Egypt.

589 —— 'U Pamirskikh Ismailitov' [Among the Pamiri Ismailis], in A.Z. Almazova, ed., *Pamirskaiā Ėkspeditsiiā (stat'i i materialy polevykh issledovaniĭ)* [Pamiri Expedition (articles and materials of field research)], Moscow: RAN Institut Vostokovedeniiā, 2006, pp. 51–56. (in Russian).

Brief information on the role of the Ismaili *pīr*s in the GBAO of Tajikistan prior to the establishment of the Imamate institutions.

590 —— 'Osobennosti sovremennogo ismailizma na Pamire' [Features of Modern Ismailism in the Pamir], *Materialy XXXIII Sredneaziatsko-Kavkazskikh Chteniĭ 2008–2009 gg.* [Materials of the XXXIII Central Asia-Caucasus Reading 2008–2009], *EIAK* (2009), pp. 368–370. (in Russian).

According to the author, the key feature of the Ismaili *ṭarīqa* is that Imam Aga Khan IV guides and protects his community during times of socio-political upheaval, as shown by the example of the Ismaili community in Badakhshān, Tajikistan, following the disintegration of the Soviet Union and the civil war in Tajikistan (1992–1997).

591 Rozenfel'd, A.Z. 'Materialy po ėtnografii i perezhitkam drevnikh verovaniĭ tadzhikoiāzychnogo naseleniiā Sovetskogo Badakhshana' [Materials on Ethnography and Traces of Ancient Beliefs amongst the Tajik-speaking Population of Soviet Badakhshān], *SET*, 3 (1970), pp. 114–119. (in Russian).

Ismailism had a visible impact on the way of life of the population of the Western Pamirs. However, there are traces of pre-Islamic beliefs, ideas and customs there, indicating the very ancient origins of the earliest religion in the region. These traces can be found, *inter alia*, in the wedding and funeral ceremonies, and the custom of honouring ancient shrines.

592 Rzakulizade, Solmaz D. 'Nekotorye aspekty zhizni i tvorchestva Nasir ad-Dina Tusi' [Some Aspects of the Life and the Works of Naṣīr al-Dīn Ṭūsī], *EIF*, vol. 4, pp. 394–414. (in Russian).

The author argues that Naṣīr al-Dīn Ṭūsī's interest in Ismaili philosophy and doctrine was due to the influence of his paternal uncle, who was a student of Shahrastānī. It was probably following his advice, that Ṭūsī went to Quhistān, where he was commissioned by the local Ismaili ruler to translate Miskawayh's

Tahdhīb al-akhlāq into Persian. At some point during his sojourn in Quhistān he formally converted to Ismailism and later moved to Alamūt, where he made use of the rich library of Ismaili works. It is thought that Ṭūsī wrote about a hundred works in different fields of learning.

S

593 Saidaliev, Khurshed. *Hazrati Imom Huseĭn (a) dar farhangi ommai Tojikiston* [Ḥaḍrat-i Imam Ḥusayn in Popular Tajik Culture]. Dushanbe, 2002. pp. 70. (in Tajik).

The place and the role of Imam Ḥusayn in Tajik folk culture.

594 Saidula, Amier. 'The Nizari Ismailis of China in Modern Times', in Farhad Daftary, ed., *A Modern History of the Ismailis: Continuity and Change in a Muslim Community*. London: I.B. Tauris, 2011, pp. 77–92.

595 —— 'Landscape of Spirituality: the Topography of Ismaili Sacred Sites in Xinjiang, China', *Journal of the Anthropological Society of Oxford*, 3 (2016), pp. 348–371.

The article documents some important sacred sites and their relevance today, an age of economic and social change. Since in Islam the term 'pilgrimage' is often associated with the *ḥajj*, in order to avoid confusion the term 'visit' (*ziyāra*) is used for the local pilgrimage-like tradition being discussed here. The study is based on data collected in the Tashkurgan Tajik Autonomous County in Xinjiang in the summer of 2011.

596 —— and Mahmud Abduwali. 'A Short Analysis of the Concept of Identity in Modern Times', *Xinjiang Ijtima'i Pan Munbiri* (Social Sciences), 3 (2012), pp. 55–61. (in Uyghur).

This article analyses the modern theory of identity through examples of identity consumption among the Uyghurs and Tajiks in Xinjiang and other ethnic groups in modern China.

597 —— 'Ismaility nizarity Kitaĭa v Novoe vremĭa' [The Nizārī Ismailis of China in Modern Times], in Farhad Daftary, ed., *Noveĭshaĭa istoriĭa ismailitov: Preemstvennost' i peremeny v musul'manskoĭ obshchine* [A Modern History of the Ismailis: Continuity and Change in a Muslim Community], tr. Leila R. Dodykhudoeva, ed. Lola N. Dodkhudoeva. Moscow: Natalis, 2013, pp. 69–102. (in Russian).

The Ismaili community in China is an ethnic, religious, linguistic and racial minority. They are an autonomous group, with a history connecting them to the ancient eastern Iranian inhabitants of the region, and an ethnolinguistic and cultural heritage connecting them to the present-day Pamiri Ismailis of Tajikistan.

598 —— *Last Refuge: National Law, Traditional Dispute Resolution and Tajik Survival in Xinjiang, China*, PhD dissertation, University of Edinburgh, 2014. pp. 275.

This thesis deals with the processes by which Tajiks in the far west of China attempt to manage disputes inside an authoritarian state. By looking at the micro-politics of disputing, it analyses the relationship between everyday social values and norms and formal state law. In particular, the thesis focuses on the ethics of Tajik society, and the ways in which the Tajiks try to organise their internal relationships, as well as their relationship with the state. More broadly, the thesis is therefore also concerned with the dynamics of legal and political change among minorities in marginal areas of China.

599 —— 'Chirogh Rawshan: Shi'i Ceremonial Practised by the Ismaili Communities of Xinjiang China', in Fahmida Suleiman, ed., *People of the Prophet's House: Artistic and Ritual Expressions of Shi'i Islam*. London: Azimuth Editions in association with The Institute of Ismaili Studies, 2015, pp. 232–242.

This essay focuses on the ritual of the *Chirāgh-i rawshan*, a unique religious ceremony of the Nizārī Ismaili community in Xinjiang, in order to consider the internal diversity and richness of Shi'i ceremonial traditions.

600 —— 'The Tajiks of China: Identity in the Age of Transition', in Dagikhudo Dagiev and Carole Faucher, ed., *Identity, History and Trans-Nationality in Central Asia: The Mountain Communities of Pamir*. London: Routledge, 2018, pp. 61–75.

This chapter examines how ethnicity is imagined, fashioned, consumed and re-iterated, on the peripheries of a nation-state while a marginal community is involuntarily exposed to changes generated from outside.

601 Saidzoda, Jamoliddin. 'National Thought and Spirit in Nasir Khusraw's Poetry', in Sarfaroz Niyozov and Ramazon Nazariev, ed., *Nasir Khusraw: Yesterday, Today, Tomorrow*. (Proceedings of a conference held in Khārūgh, Tajikistan). Khujand: Noshir, 2005, pp. 252–258.

Throughout his works Nāṣir-i Khusraw emphasised themes such as freedom, patriotism, justice, national consciousness, bravery and truthfulness, which have influenced successive generations until today.

602 —— *Nosiri Khusrav – shoire khiradsitoĭ va donishgaroĭ* [Nāṣir-i Khusraw – a Poet of Wisdom and Knowledge]. Dushanbe: Irfon, 2014. pp. 100. (in Tajik).

The intellectual works of Nāṣir-i Khusraw are all dedicated to the call for learning and the acquisition of knowledge and wisdom.

603 Saĭnakov, Saĭnak Parpishoevich. 'Naqshi A.A. Semënov dar mardumshinosii Badakhshon' [A.A. Semënov's Contribution to the Study of the Ethnography of the Badakhshānī People], in K. Pirumshoev and A. Khudoĭdodov, ed., *Sbornik*

dokladov mezhdunarodnoĭ konferentsii, posviashchënnoĭ 140–letiiu akademika V.V. Bartol'da [Collected Reports from the International Conference on the 140th Anniversary of the birth of V.V. Barthold]. Dushanbe: Akademi Nauk, 2010, pp. 184–191. (in Tajik).

Semënov commented on the beliefs of the people of the Pamirs, pointing out that the Ismaili faith is found in India, Badakhshān, Tibet and Kashghar. He also provided important data on Ismaili ceremonies and religio-philosophical views.

604 —— 'A.A. Bobrinskoĭ – issledovatel' istorii ismailizma na Pamire' [A.A. Bobrinskoĭ – a Researcher on the History of Ismailism in the Pamirs], in Kh. Pirumshoev and A. Khudoĭdodov, ed., *Sbornik dokladov mezhdunarodnoĭ konferentsii, posviashchënnoĭ 140–letiiu akademika V.V. Bartol'da* [Collection of Reports of the International Conference on the 140th Anniversary of V.V. Barthold]. Dushanbe: Akademi Nauk, 2010, pp. 169–183. (in Russian).

Bobrinskoĭ participated in organising and conducting a series of expeditions to Central Asia with the goal of establishing the geographical location of the Ismailis and collecting data about their lifestyle. The author also highlights some of the controversial conclusions made by Bobrinskoĭ in the process of his study of Ismailism.

605 —— *Vklad dorevoliutsionnykh russkikh issledovateleĭ v izuchenie ėtnografii gornogo Badakhshana (Pamira)* [The Contribution of Pre-Revolutionary Russian Scholars to the Study of the Ethnography of Gorno-Badakhshān], Dissertatsii na soiskanie uchënoĭ stepeni kandidata istoricheskikh nauk [PhD Candidate for the Degree of Doctor of Philosophy]. Dushanbe: Akademi Nauk, 2015. pp. 207. (in Russian).

This thesis is a historiographical analysis of the materials of pre-revolutionary Russian researchers and their discussions on issues such as remnants of pre-Islamic beliefs in the Pamirs, the use of light in the Ismaili funeral ceremony (the *Chirāgh-i Rawshan*), and customs associated with them.

606 Sayf Āzād, 'Abd al-Raḥmān. *Tārīkh-i khulafā-yi Fāṭimī* [The History of the Fatimid Caliphs]. Dushanbe: Donish, 1990. pp. 242. Persian tr. Tehran: Idāra-yi Majalla-yi Īrān-i Bāstān, 1341 Sh./1962. pp. 311.

The book is a study of the history of the Fatimid caliphs in Egypt (909–1172).

607 Schadl, Marcus. 'The Shrine of Nasir Khusraw: Imprisoned Deep in the Valley of Yumgan', *Muqarnas*, 26 (2009), pp. 63–93.

Under God's protection I am here in Yumgān.
Look closely, and consider me not a prisoner.
No one says that silver or diamonds or rubies

Are prisoners in the rocks or lowly.
Even though Yumgān itself is lowly and worthless,
Here I am greatly valued and honoured.

As the author says, this study has only been able to provide a cursory analysis of certain aspects of the structure of Nāṣir-i Khusraw's shrine. The saint culture of the Ismailis of Badakhshān still remains an under-studied field. The *suras* and invocations enscribed on the ceiling of the shrine likewise deserve the attention of an expert, as they promise to yield further insights into the intellectual rapprochement between Ismaili thought and Sufi mysticism.

608 Schimmel, Annemarie. *Make a Shield from Wisdom: Selected Verses from Nāṣir-i Khusraw's Divan.* London: I.B. Tauris, 1993; rpr. 2001. pp. 103.

This book provides an important survey of the major themes and techniques deployed by Nāṣir-i Khusraw in his poetry, including a significant number of new English translations of some of his verse. Nāṣir-i Khusraw's poetry, in spite of being written by one of the finest Ismaili intellectuals and most renowned poets in Persian literature, has not been much translated so this publication is important in presenting his poetry to an English-speaking audience.

609 Semënov, Aleksandr Aleksandrovich. 'Iz oblasti religioznykh verovaniĭ gornykh tadzhikov' [On the Religious Beliefs of the Mountain Tajiks], *EO*, 47, 4 (1900), pp. 81–88. (in Russian).

Semënov argues that even though Islam spread among the mountain Tajiks a thousand years ago, due to the isolation and remoteness of their abode these people have preserved remnants of pre-Islamic religious beliefs. The people of the highlands piously honour their old ancestral beliefs and customs, which have almost disappeared among lowland Tajiks.

610 —— 'Iz oblasti religioznykh verovaniĭ shugnanskikh ismailitov' [On the Religious Beliefs of the Ismailis of Shughnān], *MI*, 1 (1912), pp. 523–561. (in Russian).

This article discusses the concept of God in the understanding of the mountain Tajiks. Semënov argued that a thousand of years of Islam among the mountain Tajiks did not completely remove traces of their ancient beliefs.

611 —— 'Rasskaz shugnanskikh ismailitov o bukharskom sheikhe Bekha-ud-Dine' [The Tale of the Shughnānī Ismailis about the Bukharan Shaykh Bahā' al-Dīn], *Zapiski Vostochnogo otdeleniĭa Imperatorskogo Russkogo Arkheologicheskogo obshchestva*. St Petersburg: Tipografiĭa Imperatorskoĭ Akademii Nauk, 22 (1915), pp. 321–326. (in Russian).

In the vast pantheon of saints in Central Asia, a very important place is occupied by a prominent figure and patron of Bukhārā, Shaykh Bahā' al-Dīn (Khwāja Bahā' al-Dīn Naqshband Bukhārī). Among the local orthodox Sufis, he is considered the 'imam of the *ṭarīqa, pīr* of the *ḥaqīqa* and the model worthy of emulation in the knowledge of *sharīʿa*'.

612 —— 'Sheĭkh Dzhelal-ud-Din-Rumi po predstavleniiam shugnanskikh ismailitov' [The Shughnānī Ismailis' View of Shaykh Jalāl al-Dīn Rūmī], *Zapiski Vostochnogo otdeleniia Imperatorskogo Russkogo Arkheologicheskogo obshchestva*. St Petersburg: Tipografiia Imperatorskoĭ Akademii Nauk, 22 (1915), pp. 247–256. (in Russian).

The article begins with an introduction by Semënov, which is written on the basis of recorded conversations with a resident of the Shughnān district whose name, for some reason, is not given. The article covers the meetings and conversations between Jalāl al-Dīn Rūmī and Shams-i Tabrīzī.

—— tr., 'Istoriia Shugnana' [History of Shughnān], *Protokoly Turkestanskogo kruzhka liubiteleĭ arkheologii*, 21 (1916), p. 24. (in Russian).

'Istoriia Shugnana' is the Russian translation of the original Persian work. As Semënov says, 'The work was written in Persian at the end of 1912, at my personal request, by a fairly literate person from Shughnān, Sayyid Ḥaydar Shāh, son of Mubārak Shāh, from the village of Porsheniev. He was one of the natives who was willing to talk about his country and about the different features of his life.'

613 —— 'Opisanie ismailitskikh rukopiseĭ sobrannykh A.A. Semënovym' [A Description of Ismaili Manuscripts from the Collection of A.A. Semënov], *Izvestiia Imperatorskoĭ Academii Nauk*, 12 (1918), pp. 2171–2202. (in Russian).

Semënov discusses how he and another Russian scholar, Ivan I. Zarubin, raised the issue of the collecting and study of Ismaili manuscripts at an academic level in Russian circles. Semënov is regarded as one of the first scholars to initiate the use of Ismaili primary sources.

614 —— 'Nasyri Khosrov o mire dukhovnom i material'nom' [Nāṣir-i Khusraw on the Spiritual and Material Worlds], in *Sbornik Turkestanskogo vostochnogo instituta v chest' A.Ė. Shmidta* [Collected Essays of the Turkestan Oriental Institute in Honour of A.E. Schmidt]. Tashkent: Turkgosizdat, 1923, pp. 124–133. (in Russian).

The cause of the material world is the imperfection of the Universal Soul, by virtue of which it is considered as lower in degree and rank than the Universal Intellect. This world belongs to the Universal Soul, as it serves as the main source through which the Universal Soul corrects its imperfections.

615 —— 'K biografii Nasyr-i Khosrova' [Towards a Biography of Nāṣir-i Khusraw], *Biulleten' Sredneaziatskogo gosudarstvennogo universiteta* [*Bulletin de l'Université d'Asie Centrale*], 3 (1924), pp. 214–231. (in Russian).

616 —— 'Kritika i bibliografiia ', *IJHM*, 1 (1973), pp. 215–231. (in Russian).

Critical studies of Nāṣir-i Khusraw's biography and works.

617 —— 'Protivorechiia vo vzgliadakh na pereselenie dush u pamirskikh ismailitov i u Nasyr-i Khosrova' [Contradictions in the Views on Metempsychosis of the Pamiri Ismailis and in the Works of Nāṣir-i Khusraw]. *Biulleten Sredneaziatskogo gosudarstvennogo universiteta* [*Bulletin de l'Universite de Asie Centrale*], 9 (1925), pp. 103–117. (in Russian). A Turkish translation of this study was published in *The Proceedings of the Istanbul University*, 7 (1926).

A study on the concept of the highest degree of accomplishments of the human soul which can only be achieved with a knowledge of the meaning and value of this material world.

618 —— *K dogmatike pamirskogo ismailizma XI glava "Litsa very" Nasyr-i Khosrova* [On the Dogmatics of Pamiri Ismailism: The 11th Chapter of the *Wajh-i dīn* of Nāṣir-i Khusraw]. Tashkent, 1926. pp. xiv and 52. (in Russian).

This is a work on Ismaili theology and philosophy. It discusses creation, the *ʿaql-i kull* and the *nafs-i kull* along with the mediation of the hierarchy of the religious ranks including the *nāṭiq*, *asās*, the imam and the *ḥujja*. It also talks about the spiritual mission of the prophets and the imams and the latters' continuing presence as a proof of God on earth.

619 —— 'Vzgliad na Koran v vostochnom ismailizme' [The Qurʾan from the Viewpoint of Oriental Ismailism], *IJHM*, 1 (1926), pp. 59–72. (in Russian).

The author expresses his personal fascination with the Ismaili philosophical interpretation of the Qurʾan and in particular with Nāṣir-i Khusraw's interpretation of Qurʾanic verses and arguments in *Wajh-i dīn*, where his reading appears to Semënov so far advanced from the ossified forms of Islamic orthodoxy that it could be easily modified to meet the needs of the time and environment.

620 —— 'Pamir Ismaililer abidelerine ait' [Ismaili Monuments in the Pamir], Turkish tr. Abdülkadir, *DIFM*, 2 (1928), pp. 81–88.

621 —— *Ismailitskaia oda, posviashchennaia voploshcheniiam Aliia boga* [An Ismaili Ode Dedicated to ʿAlī]. Tashkent, 1927, pp. 1–24. (in Russian).

622 —— 'Ismailitskaia oda, posviashchennaia voploshcheniam Aliia-Boga' [An Ismaili Ode Dedicated to ʿAlī], *IJHM*, 2 (1928), pp. 1–24. (in Russian).

An Ismaili ode known as the *Qaṣīda-i-Dhurriya* by Raqqāmī Khurāsānī includes a list of imams given by an Iranian Ismaili of the 11th/17th century.

623 —— 'Ismailitskiĭ panegirik obozhestvlënnomu Aliiu Fedai Khorosanskogo' [An Ismaili Eulogy of Imam ʿAlī by Fidāʾī Khurāsānī], *IJHM*, 3 (1929), pp. 51–70. (in Russian).

The author of this eulogy was a modern scholar and Ismaili *dāʿī*, Muḥammad b. Zayn al-ʿĀbidīn Khurāsānī, whose nickname was Fidāʾī.

624 —— 'Shugnansko-ismailitskai͡a redakt͡sii͡a "Knigi sveta" (Roushanaėinama) Nasyr-i Khosrova' [The Shughnānī-Ismaili Edition of the 'Book of Light' (*Rawshanā'ī-nāma*) of Nāṣir-i Khusraw], *Zapiski kollegii vostokovedov pri Aziatskom muzee AN SSSR* [Notes of the College of Orientalists of the Asian Museum of the Academy of Sciences, USSR], 5 (1930), pp. 589–610. (in Russian).

This article is about one of Nāṣir-i Khusraw's well-known works. The *Rawshanā'ī-nāma* or 'Kniga prosveshchenii͡a' [Book of Light] is a poem in the *mathnawī* form. There are two manuscripts of it in the Bibliothèque nationale de France (one formerly in the possession of M. Schefer), and one in Leiden, one in Gotha, and one in the India Office. A line in this poem, giving the date of the composition, forms the basis of the most serious argument in favour of the view that there were two separate *Rawshanā'ī-nāma*s by Nāṣir-i Khusraw.

The discussion is followed by the text of the *Rawshanā'ī-nāma*, which was brought to Semënov from Shughnān by A.V. Stanishevskiĭ.

625 —— *Izbrannie sochinenii͡a* [Selected Essays]. Dushanbe: Ofset-Imperii͡a, 2013. pp. 408. (in Russian).

This collection is dedicated to the 140th anniversary of the birth of A.A. Semënov, the outstanding scholar, Academician of the Academy of Sciences of Tajikistan and the first director of the Institute of History, Archaeology and Ethnography.

The collection covers all the main areas of Semënov's activities – from research to administration and his contribution to the study of the cultural history of the Central Asian nations, among other subjects. The collection is designed for professionals and students in the field of Oriental Studies, as well as for those interested in the history, culture and religion of the peoples of Central Asia.

626 Semënova, Lidii͡a Andreevna. *Iz istorii fatimidskogo Egipta. Ocherki i materialy* [On the History of Fatimid Egypt. Essays and Sources]. Moscow: Nauka, 1974. pp. 264. (in Russian).

The book is a study of Egyptian history. The author has consolidated her arguments through use of the Arabic primary sources that refer to the history of Egypt from the second half of the 4th/10th century to the first half of the 6th/12th century, a period when the Ismaili imams ruled over a great empire. The work also pays particular attention to the popular uprising of Abū Rakwa.

627 —— *Egipet pri Fatimidakh* [Egypt under the Fatimids], Dissertat͡sii na soiskanie uchënoĭ stepeni doktora istoricheskikh nauk [PhD Candidate for the Degree of Doctor of Philosophy]. Moscow, 1980. pp. 348. (in Russian).

In general, in the decade prior to 1980 Western scholars of Ismaili studies highlighted new facts gleaned from Ismaili literature, greatly expanding our understanding of the Fatimid Ismailis, and so taking account what is described as their social utopia, the author asserts that Egypt under the Fatimid rule was neither an oriental despotism in its classical interpretation, nor a feudal state.

628 —— 'Fatimidskiĭ ismailizm v sovremennom zapadnom islamovedenii' [Fatimid Ismailism in Modern Western Islamic Studies], in I.M. Smiliânskaiâ and S.Kh. Kiâmilev, ed., *Islam v Istorii Narodov Vostoka* [Islam in the History of the People of the East]. Moscow: Nauka, 1981, pp. 25–39. (in Russian).

This chapter tackles the problems related to the study of Ismaili thought of the Fatimid era and issues concerning the study of Islam in contemporary western scholarship.

629 —— 'Fatimidy' [The Fatimids], *BSE*, vol. 27, p. 218 (in Russian); also in *KLE*, vol. 27, pp. 112–113. (in Russian).

A brief historical account of the Arab-Muslim dynasty whose rulers, as it is put, claimed to be descended from Fāṭima, the daughter of the Prophet Muhammad.

630 Sergeev, L. 'Imperiiâ Aga-Khana IV' [The Empire of Aga-Khan IV], *AAS*, 9 (1965), pp. 22–23, 37. (in Russian).

The article includes photographs of Aga Khan IV and the US president John F. Kennedy (16 March 1961) and provides a brief historical overview of the Ismailis. However, the article is written in a Marxist spirit where the author accuses the Aga Khan of adhering to western imperialism.

631 Shahbozov, Mergand. 'Badakhshan's Affection for Nasir Khusraw', in Sarfaroz Niyozov and Ramazon Nazariev, ed., *Nasir Khusraw: Yesterday, Today, Tomorrow*. (Proceedings of a conference held in Khārūgh, Tajikistan). Khujand: Noshir, 2005, pp. 602–605.

The work succinctly notes some of the factors that contributed to the Badakhshānī people's affectionate and devoted attitude to Nāṣir-i Khusraw. In his exposition, the author refers to certain historical events and points out that Nāṣir-i Khusraw not only spread the Ismaili faith in Badakhshān but also, through his religious preaching, knowledge and wisdom, and notes that his legacy is kept alive by the people of the region.

632 Shakarmamadov, N. and N. Jonboboev. *Laʿl-i Kuhsor* [The Ruby of the Mountains]. Khārūgh: Maʿrifat, 2002. pp. 67. (in Tajik).

This work consists of a collection of oral and written accounts and stories about Nāṣir-i Khusraw, who has been depicted as a saint and the father of a religious tradition, as well as preaching the faith as a *dāʿī*.

633 —— *Folklori Pomir* [The Folklore of Pamir], vol. 2. Dushanbe: Imperialgrupp, 2005. pp. 432. (in Tajik).

Myths, legends and stories are rooted in the religion, tradition, customs and beliefs of the people of Badakhshān. The legends and stories clearly show that, during a thousand years of history, the residents of the GBAO have maintained social and cultural ties with other countries and peoples.

634 —— 'Popular Conceptions of Hakim Nasir Khusraw', in Sarfaroz Niyozov and Ramazon Nazariev, ed., *Nasir Khusraw: Yesterday, Today, Tomorrow*. (Proceedings of a conference held in Khārūgh, Tajikistan). Khujand: Noshir, 2005, pp. 592–598.

The author emphasises the fact that the number of tales developed about Nāṣir-i Khusraw is unprecedented in the history of Persian and Tajik literature, culture and tradition, and even if one comes across this sort of legacy for other poets or philosophers, it does not hold the same kind of meaning as the stories about Nāṣir-i Khusraw do.

635 —— *Ostonho – osori ta'rīkh va farhangi mardum (tadqiqi ziëratgohhoi Kuhistoni Badakhshon)* [Shrines – Historical Remains and the Tradition of the People (An Analysis of Shrines in Mountainous Badakhshān)]. Khārūgh: Logos, 2010. pp. 244. (in Tajik).

Materials and oral data collected on the religions, traditions, rituals, ceremonies and holy places in the mountainous areas of Badakhshān have demonstrated the impact of ancient beliefs on the religion of the inhabitants of Badakhshān, which to a certain degree differ from village to village, district to district, and valley to valley as regards their performance.

636 Shakarmamadov, Orif. 'Stories and Tales about Nasir Khusraw in Written Texts', in Sarfaroz Niyozov and Ramazon Nazariev, ed., *Nasir Khusraw: Yesterday, Today, Tomorrow*. (Proceedings of a conference held in Khārūgh, Tajikistan). Khujand: Noshir, 2005, pp. 599–602.

The study begins by referring to Abū Yaḥyā Zakariyyā b. Muḥammad al-Qazwīnī's *Āthār al-bilād wa-akhbār al-ʿibād* (Gazetteer of World Geography), and cites many examples of stories and tales devoted to Nāṣir-i Khusraw, which in the course of the centuries acquired mythical and imaginary elements.

637 Sharipov, Khudoī. 'Sukhanguĭ bedormaghz' [An Alert Spokesman], *Ma'rifat*, 2 (Jan–Feb, 2005), pp. 33–40. (in Tajik).

The author attempts to define the meaning of words in Nāṣir-i Khusraw's discourses, with reference to Nāṣir's hermeneutical understanding of Qur'anic verses.

638 —— *Rozi jahon* [The Secret of the World]. Dushanbe: Nodir, 2011. pp. 352. Reprinted in 2016. (in Tajik).

According to Nāṣir-i Khusraw, true beauty in human beings is a form of religious subordination through which mankind is able to overcome everyday challenges and reach spiritual and intellectual maturity.

639 Shoinbekov, Alovuddin A. *Traditsionnaia̐ pogrebal'no-pominal'naia̐ obria̐dnost' ismailitov Zapadnogo Pamira: konets XIX – nachalo XXI vv.* [Traditional Burial and Memorial Rites of the Ismailis of Western Pamir (end of 19th – beginning of 21st century]. Dissertatsii̐a na soiskanie uchënoĭ stepeni kandidata istoricheskikh nauk [PhD Candidate for the Degree of Doctor of Philosophy]. St Petersburg, 2007. pp. 176. (in Russian).

This study examines the complex issues related to the idea of death, with associated images and symbols which are embodied in the customs, rituals and ceremonies of the people of the Pamirs.

640 —— 'Predsmertnai̐a molitva ismailitov Zapadnogo Pamira' [The Deathbed Prayer of the Western Pamir Ismailis], *EB, Muzeia̐ antropologii i ėtnografii im. Petra Velikogo (Kunstkamera) RAN*, pp. 22–27. (in Russian). Available online at: http://www.kunstkamera.ru/lib/rubrikator/03/03_05/978-5-88431-150-3 [Last accessed, 17 April 2018].

An accepted tradition among the Ismaili population of the Western Pamir says that when death is approaching, the *khalīfa* must read a prayer to the dying person to facilitate his/her soul's salvation.

641 Shokhumorov, Abusaid. 'T̐Sennoe issledovanie po istorii Pamira' [Valuable Research on the History of the Pamir], *IAN* (TSSR), 2 (1984), pp. 102–103. (in Russian).

The article is a review of B.I. Iskandarov's book *Sot̐sial'no-ėconomicheskie i politicheskie aspekty istorii pamirskikh knia̐zhestv (X v.-pervaia̐ polovina XIX v.)* [Socio-Economic and Political Aspects of the History of the Pamir Principalities (10th century – the first half of the 19th century]. (Dushanbe: Donish, 1983) which is a socio-political and socio-economic history of the Pamir region covering a thousand years.

642 —— 'Otrit̐satel'nai̐a teologii̐a kak predposylka filosofskikh i politicheskikh vzglia̐dov Nosir-i Khusrava' [Negative Theology as an Argument in Nāṣir-i Khusraw's Philosophical and Political Views], in *Tezisy IV regional'nykh filosofskikh chteniĭ molodykh uchënykh respublik Sredneĭ Azii i Kazakhstana* [Abstracts of the 4th Regional Philosophical Papers of Young Scholars of the Republics of Central Asia and Kazakhstan]. Dushanbe, 1988, pp. 89–91. (in Russian).

The author proposes a hypothesis, which is that the idea of negative theology was formed by Nāṣir-i Khusraw and other Ismaili thinkers more under the influence of ancient Iranian Zoroastrian traditions than of other philosophical and religious currents.

643 —— 'Ṭarz-i daʿwat-i Fāṭimī va pīshwāyān-i barjasta-yi madhhab-i Ismāʿīliyya' [The Methods of the Fatimid *Daʿwa* and Famous Ismaili Leaders], in the collection *Dānāy-e Īūmgān*. Kabul, 1988, pp. 142–156. (in Persian).

The *dāʿī*s were selected from the intelligentsia and received instruction from the Fatimid caliphs for their mission, and then were sent to different cities, countries and areas termed *jazīra*s. Thus Nāṣir-i Khusraw was commissioned to spread the *daʿwa* in the region of Khurāsān. The article analyses the challenges and the success of Nāṣir-i Khusraw's mission.

644 —— *Kontseptsiia poznaniia Nosir-i Khusrava* [Nāṣir-i Khusraw's Concept of Knowledge], Dissertatsii na soiskanie uchënoĭ stepeni kandidata filosofskikh nauk [PhD Candidate for the Degree of Doctor of Philosophy]. Dushanbe: Akademi Nauk, 1990. pp. 155. (in Russian).

The philosophical core of Nāṣir-i Khusraw's speculative system lies in its theory of knowledge. Knowledge does not confine itself to the understanding of the Creator, as representatives of schools of thought in ancient and medieval Eastern philosophy had previously propounded. According to Nāṣir-i Khusraw, the comprehension of human essence and its role in the world order is attainable exclusively through an understanding of nature.

645 —— *Nosir Khusrav 'Strela vremeni'* [Nāṣir-i Khusraw, the 'Arrow of Time']. Dushanbe: Adib, 1991. pp. 47. (in Russian).

In Persian-Tajik literature, Nāṣir-i Khusraw's role is considered significant as he is regarded as the unique proponent of the genre of philosophical *qaṣīda*. According to his stance, knowledge is the only salvation for any man's soul.

646 —— 'Ravshanzamiri sarsupurda, qissae az ruzgori Said Muniri Suchonī dar darbori Oghokhoni III' [Enlightened and Devoted. The Biography of Sayyid Munīr of Suchān at the Court of Aga Khan III], *Farhangi Badakhshon*, 9 (1992), pp. 1–3. (in Tajik).

A story about Sayyid Munīr Badakhshānī, a renowned public and religious figure in Badakhshān during the first decades of the 20th century.

647 —— *Pamir - strana Ariev* [Pamir: Land of the Aryan people]. Dushanbe, 1997. pp. 164. (in Russian).

The book consists of three articles dedicated to the issues of pre-Islamic culture and Ismaili doctrine. It attempts to shed some light on the religious and philosophical aspects of the Aryan people from both a historical and a cultural perspective.

648 —— 'Somoniën va junbishi ismoiliia' [The Sāmānids and the Ismaili Movement], in A. Muhammadkhojaev and M. Mahmadjonov, ed., *Falsafa dar ahdi Somoniën* [Philosophy during the Samanid Era]. Dushanbe: Donish, 1999, pp. 160–174. (in Tajik).

The Ismaili movement during the Sāmānid period, and especially during the reign of Naṣr I b. Aḥmad Sāmānī, acquired a religio-political and Iranian national character, both in terms of theoretical and political implications. Here it is considered a purely Iranian uprising against the rule of foreigners such as Arabs, Turks and Mongols.

649 —— 'The Sacred Lamp', in Sarfaroz Niyozov and Ramazon Nazariev, ed., *Nasir Khusraw: Yesterday, Today, Tomorrow*. (Proceedings of a conference held in Khārūgh, Tajikistan). Khujand: Noshir, 2005, pp. 656–670.

The Sacred Lamp talks about the emergence of fire as a miracle of divine provenance. The author maintains that this tradition or ritual existed for a thousand years before Zoroaster and is one of the many sacred traditions of the Zoroastrians.

The author also connects this to the text known as *Chirāgh-i Rawshan*, which is associated with Nāṣir-i Khusraw, and recited in religious ceremonies by the Ismaili community in Badakhshān.

650 —— *Razdelenie Badakhshana i sud'by ismailizma* [The Delimitation of Badakhshān and the Fate of Ismailism]. Dushanbe, 2008. pp. 125. (in Russian).

The work reveals the lesser-known aspects of the relationship between Russia and the Pamir region, and discusses the fate of the Pamiri peoples who were held hostage by the 'Great Game' of the 19th century that was played out between the Russian and the British empires in the Pamir-Hindu Kush region.

651 Shokhumorov, Saidanvar. 'Ismailizm: traditsii i sovremennost'' [Ismailism: Traditions and Modernity], *CAC*, 2 (2000), pp. 130–138. (in Russian).

The central subject of Ismaili doctrine throughout its history has been the doctrine of the imamate, characterised by unquestioning obedience to the Imam of the time who is regarded as the source of all religious, doctrinal and philosophical knowledge.

652 Shohzodamuhammad, Umed. 'The Tradition of Charaghrawshan – an Islamic Practice of the Ismailis of Central Asia', in Sarfaroz Niyozov and Ramazon Nazariev, ed., *Nasir Khusraw: Yesterday, Today, Tomorrow*. (Proceedings of a conference held in Khārūgh, Tajikistan). Khujand: Noshir, 2005. pp. 585–591.

Chirāgh Rawshan is a ritual tradition of the Ismailis of Central Asia and its origins and practices are still debated among scholars. Scholars such as A.E. Bertel's and A. Shokhumorov believed that *Chirāgh Rawshan* was inherited from *Mihrparasti* and Zoroastrianism. Another group of scholars such as Nāṣir al-Dīn Hunzaī and Azizullah Najib hold that this is a purely Islamic tradition and has little in common with pre-Islamic practices and doctrines.

653 —— ed. *Manobe'i sunnati charoghravshan* [The Source of the *Chirāgh Rawshan* Rituals]. Dushanbe: Merosi Ajam, 2009. pp. 137. (in Tajik).

The tradition of *Chirāgh Rawshan* is one of the most famous and the richest religious rituals practiced by the Ismaili community in Badakhshān of Tajikistan, Afghanistan, the Northern Areas of Pakistan and China. It is also referred to by different names by the inhabitants of these areas such as *Daʿwat, Daʿwat-i Pīr Shāh Nāṣir* and *Chirāgh Rawshan*.

654 —— Manzarsho Dilovarshoev and Sabohat Donaërova, ed. *Duʿoho va fotihahoi Ismoiliën* [*Duʿā*s and Prayers of the Ismailis]. Dushanbe: Paëmi oshno, 2015. pp. 80 (in Tajik).

A collection of verses of the Qurʾan, *duʿā*s (supplications) and prayers, which are recited by *khalīfa*s in the Ismaili community of Badakhshān during religious ceremonies.

655 Smirnov, Andreĭ V. 'Khristianskie motivy v religiozno-filosofskikh kontsepts̄iı̈akh sufizma i ismailizma' [Christian Motifs in the Religious and Philosophical Concepts of Sufism and Ismailism], *Vostok* (Moscow), 6 (1993), pp. 12–18. (in Russian).

Man's central place in the universe is the common denominator characterising the thought of medieval Christian and Muslim philosophers. A number of parallels are drawn between the Christian idea of God incarnated in a human being and the Ismaili concept of certain humans resembling the First Intellect.

656 —— 'Ismailizm' [Ismailism], *EES*, pp. 181–184. (in Russian).

According to the author Ismaili ethics are marked by the influence of Neoplatonic and, to a lesser extent, Platonic and Aristotelian ideas that entered into the Arabic-speaking world through translations from Greek and Latin. The dichotomy 'world of nature – peace of mind' is examined.

657 —— 'Khristianskie motivy v uzore islamskoĭ mysli: Ibn ʿArabī i al-Kirmānī' [Christian Motifs in the Pattern of Islamic Thought: Ibn Arabī and al-Kirmānī], *SSA*, 58 (2010), pp. 91–103. (in Russian).

One of the main features of this work is an anlysis of the relationship between man and God. Man is presented as being the microcosm, according to medieval philosophical constructs, structurally isomorphic to the world, i.e., the macrocosm.

658 —— 'Osnovnye cherty filosofskogo ucheniı̈a Khamīd ad-Dīna al-Kirmānī' [The Main Features of the Philosophical Teachings of Ḥamīd al-Dīn al-Kirmānī], *EIF*, vol. 4. Moscow: Izdatel'skaı̈a firma 'VL', 2013, pp. 204–218. (in Russian).

This article deals with the philosophical teachings of Ḥamīd al-Dīn al-Kirmānī, focusing in particular on issues such as human perfection,

God's attributes, origination (*ibdāʿ*), and the theory of knowledge and ethics.

659 Smirnov, A. 'O raskole shiitov i ismailitov v osobennosti' [On the Schism of the Shiʿis and in particular the Ismailis], *UZIKU*, 1 (1846), pp. 79–180. (in Russian).

This work seeks to establish the distinction between Twelver Shiʿis and Ismailis. However, besides the issue of the succession of Ismāʿīl b. Jaʿfar al-Ṣādiq, the author has not been able to identify any other major differences. However, Smirnov further sought to argue that the Shiʿis established a new, resourceful and radical organisation under the name of the Qarmaṭīs, and that this organisation quickly became a powerful political force, founding the Shiʿi Fatimid caliphate that stretched from the Atlantic Ocean to the Euphrates.

660 Smirnov, Nikolaĭ Aleksandrovich. *Musul'manskoe sektantstvo* [Muslim Sectarianism]. Moscow: "Bezbozhnik", 1930. pp. 56. (in Russian).

The Soviet scholar Smirnov viewed the emergence of Muslim groups as the result of social protest. His stance clearly echoes the opinion of pre-revolutionary Russian Orientalist scholars.

661 Snesarev, Andreĭ Evgen'evich (1865–1937). 'Religiia i obychai gortsev Zapadnogo Pamira' [Religion and Customs of the Mountain People of the Western Pamirs], *TV*, 89–93 (1904), pp. 89–93; also in Stanishevskiĭ, A.V. *Ismailizm na Pamire (1902–1931) Sbornik documentov* [Ismailism in the Pamirs (1902–1931), Collected Documents], compiled by A.V. Stanishevskiĭ. Tashkent: Institut Vostokovedeniia, 1932, pp. 57–86. (in Russian).

Notes on the religious beliefs and practices of the people of the Western Pamirs by a Russian and Soviet military officer who served in the region.

662 Stanishevskiĭ, Andreĭ Vladimirovich (1904–1993). *Ismailizm na Pamire (1902–1931), Sbornik documentov* [Ismailism in the Pamirs (1902–1931), Collected Documents], compiled by A.V. Stanishevskiĭ, Academiia Nauk USSR, Glavnoe Archivnoe Upravlenie pri-Sovete Ministrov Uzbekskoĭ SSR [The Main Archive, Directorate of the Council of Ministers of the Uzbek SSR: Institute of Oriental Studies]. Tashkent: Institut Vostokovedeniia, 1932, pp. 261. (in Russian).

This collection of articles 'Ismailism in Pamirs (1902–1931)' begins with an introduction by Stanishevskiĭ. One of the first articles, 'Religion and Customs of the Mountaineers of the Western Pamir', was written by a prominent Russian Orientalist, A.E. Snesariev. The next article, 'The Ismaili Denomination in Russian and Bukharan Central Asia', was written by another Russian scholar, Bobrinskoĭ, and it is followed by a series of documents on Pamiri Ismailism and a variety of Ismaili documents.

663 —— 'Sbornik arkhivnykh documentov i materialov po istorii Pamira i ismailizma' [Collected Archival Documents and Material on the History of the Pamirs and Ismailism], vol. 2 (1923), pp. 175–262 (Unpublished Report). (in Russian).

The second part of the report begins with the Regulation of the Ismaili Panjebhai movement compiled by Sayyid Munīr and with an explanation of the contemporary Ismaili Panjebhai dogma propounded by Sayyid Ḥaydar Shāh Mubārak Zāda which also includes several *farmans* of Aga Khan III.

664 Steinberg, Jonah. *Ismaʻili Modern: Globalization and Identity in a Muslim Community*. Chapel Hill, NC: North Caroline Press, 2011. pp. 256.

Informed by the richness of Ismaili history, theories of transnationalism and globalisation, and first-hand ethnographic field work in the Himalayan regions of Tajikistan and Pakistan as well as in Europe, this is an investigation of the development of the Ismaili Muslims' remarkable and expansive global structures in the 21st century. Led by a charismatic Europe-based hereditary Imam, Prince Karim Aga Khan IV, global Ismaili organisations make available an astonishing array of services – social, economic, political, and religious, to some three to five million faithful stretching from Afghanistan to England, from Pakistan to Tanzania.

665 Stėnli, Lėn-Pul'. *Musul'manskie dinastii* [Muslim Dynasties], tr. and introd. by V.V. Bartol'd. St Petersburg, 1899, pp. 55–73. (in Russian).

666 —— *Musul'manskie dinastii. Khronologicheskie i geneologicheskie tablit͡sy s istoricheskimi vvedenii͡ami* [Muslim Dynasties. Chronological and Geneological Tables with Historical Introductions]. Publisher: Book on Demand Ltd., 2013. pp. 364. (in Russian).

Chronological and genealogical tables with a historical introduction to the main events in Islamic history. This includes a history of the Fatimids in Egypt and the genealogy of the Fatimid imams, and the history of the Qarmaṭīs and their state in Bahrain.

667 Stroeva, Li͡udmila Vladimirovna (1910–1993). 'K istorii osnovanii͡a gosudarstva Il'khanov v Irane' [On the History of the Creation of the Īlkhānid State in Iran]. *Nauchnai͡a sessii͡a Leningradskogo gosudarstvennogo universiteta* [Academic Session of the Leningrad State University]. Leningrad, 1948, pp. 54–56. (in Russian).

668 —— 'Unichtozhenie mongolami gosudarstva ismailitov v Irane' [The Mongol Destruction of the Ismaili State in Iran], *UZLGU*, 4 (1954), pp. 192–214. (in Russian).

This article is in line with the Marxist approach to the study of religion, and argues that the causes of demise of the Ismaili state are to be found not simply in the treacherous policy of its ruling circles or the numerical superiority of the Mongol troops with their better military equipment. The main reason, according to the author, lies in the problems associated with the social ideals of popular uprisings aimed at recreating an irretrievable past, with unrealistic ideals of returning to a pre-class society of social and economic equality.

669 —— 'Ismaility v Irane' [Ismailis of Iran], in N.V. Pigulevskai͡a et al., *Istorii͡a Irana s drevneĭshikh vremen do kont͡sa XVIII veka*. Leningrad: Izdatel'stvo Leningradskogo Universiteta, 1958, pp. 151–152. (in Russian). Persian trans, 'Ismāʿīliya dar Īrān', in N.V. Pigulevskai͡a et al., *Taʾrīkh-i Īrān*, tr. Karīm Kishāvarz. Tehran: Payām, 1354 Sh./1975, pp. 276–278.

The Ismailis of Alamūt are portrayed here as a secret organisation whose members were bound to iron discipline, and an unconditional obligation to obey all orders from their spiritual leader. As the latter's authority increased, it is argued, their political objectives and religious dogma continued to be kept secret from the uninitiated.

670 —— 'Den' Voskresenii͡a iz mertvykh i ego sot͡sial'nai͡a sushchnost'. Iz istorii ismailitskogo gosudarstva v Irane XIIv.' [The Day of Resurrection and its Social Essence. On the History of the Ismaili State in 12th-Century Iran], *KSIV* (AN SSSR), 38 (1960), pp. 19–25. (in Russian).

The author argues that in proclaiming the doctrine of the Day of Resurrection, Ḥasan II *ʿalā dhikrihi al-salām* was promulgating a specific socio-political agenda which promoted social justice and material equality among the Ismailis.

671 —— 'Posledniĭ khorezmshakh i ismaility Alamuta' [The Last Khwārazm-Shāh and the Ismailis of Alamūt], in *Issledovanii͡a po istorii kul'tury narodov Vostoka. Sbornik v chest' akademika I.A. Orbeli* [The Study of the Cultural History of the Peoples of the East. Collected Articles in Honour of Academici͡an I.A. Orbeli]. Moscow and Leningrad, 1960, pp. 451–463. (in Russian).

Following Genghis Khan's defeat of the the last Khwārazm-Shāh, his son Jalāl al-Dīn (1220–1231), in his struggle against the Mongols, tried unsuccessfully to create a union of states between Transcaucasia and Asia Minor. Of these, a central role was played by Alamūt, the Ismaili state.

672 —— 'Dvizhenie ismailitov v Isfakhane v 1101–1107 gg.' [The Ismaili Movement in Iṣfahān 1101–1107], *VLGU*, 14 (1962), pp. 60–73. (in Russian).

The Ismaili state was created in 1090, with its centre in the Alamūt region, and encompassed a number of places, fortresses and castles between Iran and Syria. It arose due to the movement of artisans and mountain peasants, directed against the power of the Saljūqs and their feudal exploitation.

673 —— 'Ismaility Irana i Sirii v zarubezhnoĭ i sovetskoĭ istoriografii' [Soviet and Foreign Historiographical Literature on the Ismailis of Iran and Syria],

in *Mezhvuzovskai͡a nauchnai͡a konferent͡sii͡a po istoriografii i istochnikovedenii͡u istorii stran Azii i Afriki. Tezisy dokladov* [Inter-University Academic Conference on the Historiography and Study of Sources on the History of Asia and Africa. Reports]. Leningrad, 1963, pp. 46–51. (in Russian).

Stroeva shows that the Ismaili movement in Iran and Syria in the 5th–6th/11th–12th century was a popular undertaking of the working masses for social liberation under the leadership of Ḥasan-i Ṣabbāḥ and his associates.

674 —— 'K voprosu o sot͡sial'noĭ prirode ismailitskogo dvizhenii͡a v Irane XI-XIII vv.' [On the Problem of the Social Nature of the Ismaili Movement in Iran in the 11th–13th Centuries], *VLGU*, 20 (1963), pp. 46–51. (in Russian).

The Ismaili state is presented as the outcome of a revolt by artisans and poor mountain farmers directed against the power and feudal oppression of the Saljūqs.

675 —— 'Vosstanie ismailitov v Irane v kont͡se XI – nachale XII v.' [The Ismaili Rebellion in Iran at the end of the 11th – beginning of the 12th Century], in A.A. Zhelti͡akov, ed., *Issledovanii͡a po istorii stran Vostoka* [Studies on the History of the Countries of the East]. Leningrad, 1964, pp. 41–59. (in Russian).

Whilst in Egypt the religious reforms of Ṣalāḥ al-Dīn al-Ayyūbī were not opposed, in Syria he was confronted with extreme resistance by the Ismailis. While establishing their stronghold of Alamūt on the southern flanks of the Caspian mountains, as well as maintaining other Iranian fortresses in the second half of the 5th/11th century, the Nizārī Ismailis were successful in promoting their teachings in Syria, the cradle of the early Ismailis, skilfully using the support of the peasants for their cause.

676 —— 'Ismaility Irana i Sirii XI-XII vv. v zarubezhnoĭ i sovetskoĭ literature' [Soviet and Foreign Historiographical Literature on the Ismailis of Iran and Syria in the 11th–12th Centuries], in *Istoriografii͡a i istochnikovedenie istorii stran Azii* [Historiography and the Study of the Sources on the History of Asian Countries]. Leningrad, 1965, pp. 138–148. (in Russian).

The author puts forward her concept of the history of the Ismailis of Iran and Syria in the 5th–6th/11th–12th centuries. The Ismaili doctrine called *al-daʿwa al-jadīda* (the new preaching) is presented as a religious pretext for a broad popular movement proclaimed by Ḥasan-i Ṣabbāḥ.

677 —— 'Rashid-ad-din kak istochnik po istorii ismailitov Alamuta' [Rashīd al-Dīn's Work as a Source on the History of the Ismailis of Alamūt], *VISA*, 1965, pp. 123–142. (in Russian).

Publication of a section of Rashīd al-Dīn's *Jāmiʿ al-tawārīkh*. The work introduces much valuable material on the Ismailis of Alamūt such as the relationship between the Ismailis, on the one hand, and the various circles of the Persian nobility and the Saljūq sultans Muḥammad and Sanjar, on the other.

678 —— 'Vystuplenie ismailitov v Sirii na grani XI-XII vv. (1090-113 gg.)' [The Ismaili Uprising in Syria at the turn of 11th-12th Centuries (1090-1113)], *KSINA*, 86 (1965), pp. 189-195. (in Russian).

679 —— 'Vnutrennee polozhenie ismailitskogo gosudarstva v 20-50-kh gg. XII v.' [The Internal Situation in the Ismaili State 1120-1150], in *FISZAA. Tezisy nauchnoĭ konferentsii vostochnogo fakul'teta Leningradskogo gosudarstvennogo universiteta* [Philology and History of Asian and African Countries. Proceedings of the Conference of the Faculty of Oriental Studies of the State University of Leningrad]. Leningrad, 1965, pp. 84-86. (in Russian).

680 —— 'Gosudarstvo Ismailitov' [The Ismaili State], *SIE*, vol. 6, pp. 352-353. (in Russian).

681 —— 'Ismaility' [The Ismailis], *SIE*, vol. 6, pp. 353-356. (in Russian).

Two articles offering brief information on the Ismaili state based at Alamūt (Iran).

682 —— 'Shakhdiz - krepost' ismailitov' [The Ismaili Fortress of Shāhdiz], *IF* (1969), pp. 43-46. (in Russian).

683 —— '"Novyĭ prizyv" ismailitov kak ideologiiā narodnogo dvizheniiā v Irane v XI-XII vv.' [The Ismaili 'New Call' as the Ideology of the Popular Movement in Iran in the XI-XII Centuries], *Palestinskiĭ sbornik*, 21 (1970), pp. 199-213. (in Russian).

In 1090 following the establishment of Alamūt as a state independent of the Fatimids, Ḥasan-i Ṣabbāḥ proclaimed a new teaching (*daʿwat-i jadīda* - the 'new call') addressed to the masses and calling for an anti-Saljūq and anti-feudal struggle.

684 —— 'Izuchenie istorii ismailizma na Pamire i v Irane v sovetskoĭ istoriografii za 50 let' [The Study of the History of Ismailism in the Pamirs and Iran in Soviet Historiography during the last 50 Years], in *FISZAA, Kratkie tezisy nauchnoĭ konferentsii vostochnogo fakul'teta Leningradskogo gosudarstvennogo universiteta, 11-18 dekabriā 1972 g.* [Philology and History of Asian and African Countries. Proceedings of the Conference of the Faculty of Oriental Studies of the State University of Leningrad, 11-18 December 1972], 1972, pp. 85-88. (in Russian).

685 —— 'Provozglashenie "Dniā Voskresen'iā" (iz istorii gosudarstva ismailitov v Irane v XI-XII vv.)' [The Declaration of "The Day of Resurrection" (from

the history of Ismaili State in Iran in the 11th-12th centuries)], *IJHM* (1973), pp. 133–165. (in Russian).

This article/chapter examines historical sources relating to the concept of *qiyāma* and its declaration by Ḥasan II *ʿalā dhikrihi al-salām*, including an analysis of the genealogy of Ḥasan II.

686 —— *Gosudarstvo ismailitov v Irane v XI-XIII vv.* [The Ismaili State in Iran in the 11th–13th Centuries], Dissertatsii na soiskanie uchënoĭ stepeni doktora filosofskikh nauk [PhD Candidate for the Degree of Doctor of Philosophy]. Moscow, 1973. pp. 419. (in Russian).

This study highlights the socio-economic and political causes behind the Ismaili movement, with a particular focus on the Ismaili state in Iran, its territory and its history.

687 —— *Gosudarstvo ismailitov v Irane v XI-XIII vv.* [The Ismaili State in Iran in the 11th–13th Centuries]. Moscow: Nauka, 1978. pp. 274. (in Russian). Persian tr., *Tārīkh-i Ismāʿīliyān dar Īrān*, tr., Parwīn Munzawī. Tehran: Nashr-i Ishārah, 1371 Sh./1992. pp. 372.

688 —— 'Vozniknovenie nizaritskogo verouchenii͡a-eresi v islame' [The Emergence of the Nizārī Heretical Faith in Islam], in T.A. Stet͡skevich, ed., *Problemy izuchenii͡a i kritiki religiĭ Vostoka* [Problems in the Study and Criticism of the Religions of the East]. Leningrad: Muzeĭ istorii religii i ateizma, 1979, pp. 16–53.

689 Suponina, Elena V. *Religiozno-filosofskai͡a doktrina druzov* [The Druzes' Religio-Philosophical Doctrine], Dissertatsii na soiskanie uchënoĭ stepeni kandidata filosofskikh nauk [PhD Candidate for the Degree of Doctor of Philosophy]. Moscow, 1995. pp. 159. (in Russian).

The Druze movement dates back to the reign of al-Ḥākim at the beginning of the 5th/11th century. Despite the influence of the teachings of the Fatimid Ismailis on the development of the Druze doctrine, the movement pursued its own path diverging from certain Fatimid dogmatic principles.

T

690 Tadzhiddin, Mardonī. *Nasiri Khusrav i araboi͡azychnai͡a kul'tura* [Nāṣir-i Khusraw and Arabic-Speaking Culture]. Dushanbe: Payvand, 2005. pp. 142. (in Russian).

Undoubtedly, Nāṣir-i Khusraw was deeply familiar with the history and culture of the Arabs of both the pre-Islamic and the Islamic eras. His perfect knowledge of the Arabic language and literature vividly resonates in all his works and, particularly, in his poetry.

691 Taneeva-Salomatshoeva, Lola. 'The Metaphorical Interpretation of the Qur'anic Letters in *Khwan al-ikhwan* and its Impact on Sufi Poetry', in Sarfaroz Niyozov and Ramazon Nazariev, ed., *Nasir Khusraw: Yesterday, Today, Tomorrow*. (Proceedings of a conference held in Khārūgh, Tajikistan). Khujand: Noshir, 2005, pp. 131–134.

Ismaili rationalist thought, particularly Nāṣir-i Khusraw's, has interacted not only with Sufi traditions but also with the teachings of other Islamic theoretical schools.

692 —— 'The Contribution of A.E. Bertel's to Ismaili Studies', in Stanislav M. Prozorov and Hakim Elnazarov, ed., *Russian Scholars on Ismailism*. (Proceedings of a conference held in St Petersburg, Russia, in 2011). St Petersburg: Nestor-Istoriia̐, 2014, pp. 209–217.

This paper presents the outstanding contribution of A.E. Bertel's to the field of Ismaili studies, which is particularly visible in his analysis of the manuscripts which were found in the GBAO of Tajikistan during the expedition of the Academy of Sciences of the USSR (1959–1963).

693 Tavakkalov, Haidarmamad. 'Reciting Maddoh and Hakim Nasir Khusraw', in Sarfaroz Niyozov and Ramazon Nazariev, ed., *Nasir Khusraw: Yesterday, Today, Tomorrow*. (Proceedings of a conference held in Khārūgh, Tajikistan). Khujand: Noshir, 2005, pp. 580–585.

The author suggests that the *madīḥa-sarāyī* (singing of devotional poetry), which is known as *maddāḥ* or *qaṣīda* in different parts of Badakhshān, is an ancient traditional genre and part of the cultural heritage of the Badakhshānī people. Many such performances are associated with Nāṣir-i Khusraw and his legacy.

694 —— *An"anai madhiĭasaroi dar Badakhshon* [The Tradition of *Madhiya* Performance in Badakhshān], Dissertatsiia̐ na soiskanie uchënoĭ stepeni kandidata filologicheskikh nauk [PhD Candidate for the Degree of Doctor of Philosophy]. Dushanbe: Akademi Nauk, 2006. pp. 165. (in Tajik).

The thesis studies the *madhiya* tradition amongst the Badakhshānī Ismailis, and analyses its position in the spiritual life of the local people.

695 Tavurov, Kurbonnazar Soibnazarovich. *Filosofskie vozzreniia̐ Sayida Sukhraba Vali-i Badakhshani* [The Philosophical views of Sayyid Suhrāb Valī Badakhshānī], Dissertatsiia̐ na soiskanie uchënoĭ stepeni kandidata filosofskikh nauk [PhD Candidate for the Degree of Doctor of Philosophy]. Dushanbe: Akademi Nauk, 2018. pp. 146. (in Russian).

The aim of this study is to analyse the Nizārī Ismaili philosophy of Sayyid Suhrāb Valī and determine his role in the revival, preservation and development of Ismaili philosophy of the 9th/15th century. Studying the main philosophical treatise of Sayyid Suhrāb, *Sī va shish ṣaḥīfa*, and examining his philosophical views by revealing the connection between the philosophy of Sayyid Suhrāb and Ismaili philosophical teachings, Eastern Peripatetism and Sufism.

696 Terletskiĭ, N.S. 'Nekotorye svedeniia︠ ︡ob ostone Mushkilkusho (dolina r. Bartang) [Some Information about the Mushkilkusho Shrine (in the Bartang River Valley)], *EB*, Muzeia︠ ︡antropologii i ėtnografii im. Petra Velikogo (Kunstkamera), *RAN*, pp. 52–55. (in Russian). Available online at: http://www.kunstkamera.ru/lib/rubrikator/08/08_02/978-5-88431-211-1/ [Last accessed, 19 January 2019).

Since the arrival of Islam in Central Asia in general and in the Pamirs in particular, a significant role has been played by the tradition of visitation (*ziyāra*) to revered objects. In particular, the legends of Mushkilkusho, as well as many elements of *ziyāra* practice, it is argued display roots in eras prior to the emergence of Islam in the region.

697 Ṭūsī, Naṣīr al-Dīn [Nasiruddini Tūsī], *Saïr va suluk* [*Contemplation and Action*], transliterated from Persian to Tajik by Qimatshoh Qadamshoev, Dushanbe: Sino, 2015. pp. 39. (in Tajik).

Contemplation and Action is Naṣīr al-Dīn Ṭūsī's spiritual autobiography, in which he recounts details of his early education, his search for knowledge and his eventual conversion to the Ismaili faith.

698 —— *Matlub al-muʿminin va tavallo va tabarro* [*Desideratum of the Faithful and Solidarity and Dissociatiation*], transliterated from Persian to Tajik by Qimatshoh Qadamshoev. Dushanbe: Sino, 2015. pp. 26. (in Tajik).

In these treatises, Ṭūsī provides concise philosophical interpretations of key motifs in Nizārī Ismaili thought, with special reference to the existential condition of human beings, their primordial origin and nature, their earthly existence in relation to the Imam, and their destiny in the Hereafter.

U

699 Usmonov, Murodali Abdulloevich. *Ismailizm v Afghanistane: Istoriko-ėtnograficheskoe issledovanie* [Ismailism in Afghanistan: Historico-Ethnographic Studies], Dissertatsiia︠ ︡na soiskanie uchënoĭ stepeni kandidata istoricheskikh nauk [PhD Candidate for the Degree of Doctor of Philosophy]. Dushanbe: Akademi Nauk, 1996. pp. 160. (in Russian).

The aim of this study is to familiarise the reader with the history of the Ismaili community in Afghanistan and the role of its religious leaders in the preservation of its customs and traditions. The work also explores the relationship between the ethnicity and religious identity of the Ismailis in Afghanistan.

V

700 Vasil'tsov, Konstantin S. 'Mesta palomnichestva i pokloneniia Zapadnogo Pamira (po materialam polevykh issledovaniĭ 2008 g.' [Places of Pilgrimage and Worship in the Western Pamirs (on the basis of Field Research, 2008], *Iran-name*, 4 (2008), pp. 184–200. (in Russian).

The author investigates natural places of worship among the Ismailis of the Western Pamirs, as well as their mythological and folkloric themes. These places of worship are called variously *mazār* or *ziyārat-gāh* (Mazār-i Shāh Burhān, Mazār-i Sayyid Jalāl), and are the graves of the Ismaili preachers and *pīrs*. *Qadamgāh*, on the other hand, is the term primarily referring to the places of worship where it is believed the saints have left traces (Ḥaḍrat 'Alī, Zayn al-'Ābidīn).

—— 'Istoriia izgnaniia Ādama iz raia v ismailitskoĭ (nizaritskoĭ) traditsii' [The History of the Expulsion of Adam from Paradise in the Ismaili (Nizārī) Tradition], *Evraziĭskie prostory* (2008), pp. 89–93. (in Russian). Available online at: http://lib.kunstkamera.ru/files/lib/978-5-88431-173-2/978-5-88431-173-2_21.pdf [Last accessed, 20 March 2017].

An Ismaili interpretation of the story of Adam's expulsion from paradise.

701 —— *A'lām-i saghīr: k voprosy o simvolike traditsionnogo pamirskogo zhilishcha'* [Microcosms: On the Question of the Symbolism of the Traditional Pamiri House], *TSentral'naia Aziia: Traditsiia v usloviiakh peremen* [Central Asia: Tradition in a Changing Environment], 2 (2009), pp. 150–179. (in Russian).

The traditional Pamiri house (*chīd*), besides being a place for the activities of daily life, is also a ritual and symbolic space which reflects the specificity of the material and spiritual culture of the mountain peoples living in the Western Pamirs.

702 —— 'Kontseptsiia vremennykh tsiklov v ismailizme (po materialam traktata *Kalam-i Pir*)', [The Concept of the Cycle of Time in Ismailism (on the materials of the treatise *Kalām-i Pīr*)], *EIAK* (2009), pp. 370–374. (in Russian).

An analysis of the Ismaili concept of cyclical time in accordance with the Ismaili hierarchy.

703 —— 'Nekotorye voprosy izucheniia pamirskogo ismailizma' [Some Issues in the Study of Pamiri Ismailism], *EIAK* (2009), pp. 364–367. (in Russian).

An investigation into how places of pilgrimage and worship continue to play a very important role in the spiritual and religious life of the Pamiri Ismailis.

704 —— 'Iz istorii isma'ilitskogo prizyva v Badakhshane' [On the History of the Ismaili Call in Badakhshān], in M.E. Rezvan, ed.,*Tadzhiks: Istoriia, kul'tura,*

obshchestvo [Tajiks: History, Culture, Society, Festschrift in Honour of R.R. Rakhimov]. St Petersburg, 2014, pp. 191–210. (in Russian).

The Ismaili call in Badakhshān, which began with Nāṣir-i Khusraw's *daʿwa*, seems to have developed further, becoming even more active and ambitious, after the tragic events surrounding the capture of Alamūt by the Mongols.

705 Virani, Shafique. 'The Days of Creation in the Thought of Nasir Khusraw', in Sarfaroz Niyozov and Ramazon Nazariev, ed., *Nasir Khusraw: Yesterday, Today, Tomorrow*. (Proceedings of a conference held in Khārūgh, Tajikistan). Khujand: Noshir, 2005, pp. 74–83.

This is an exploration of Nāṣir-i Khusraw's spiritual hermeneutic of the tradition concerning the completion of creation in six days, with the seventh day or Sabbath having a particular sanctity. The Sabbath represents the cycle of the Lord of the Resurrction or *qāʾim-i qiyāma* through whom the divine unity and grandeur of God will be revealed and the purpose of creation fulfilled.

706 Voronovskiĭ, D.G. 'Bibliografiiā nauchnykh rabot A.A. Semënov' [Bibliography of the Scholarly Works of A.A. Semënov], *Sbornik Stateĭ po Istorii i Filologii Narodov Sredneĭ Azii* [Articles on the History and Philology of the Peoples of Central Asia], 17 [Special Issue] (1953), pp. 7–22. (in Russian).

A collection of articles on the history and philology of the peoples of Central Asia, devoted to the 80th anniversary of the birth of A.A. Semënov.

707 Vvedenskiĭ, B.A., ed. 'Nosir Khisrou' [Nāṣir-i Khusraw], *ES*, vol. 2, pp. 512–513. (in Russian).

Entry on the life and works of Nāṣir-i Khusraw.

W

708 Wahid, Sanawbar. 'The Recognition of Nasir Khusraw in German Orientalism', in Sarfaroz Niyozov and Ramazon Nazariev, ed., *Nasir Khusraw: Yesterday, Today, Tomorrow*. (Proceedings of a conference held in Khārūgh, Tajikistan). Khujand: Noshir, 2005, pp. 335–339.

Nāṣir-i Khusraw first became known to European readers through the translation of works such as the *Safar-nāma*, *Rawshanāʾī-nāma*, *Wajh-i dīn*, *Zād al-musāfirīn* and *Jāmiʿ al-ḥikmatayn* by German, Russian and English scholars, such as Hette and others. The intellectual aspects of Nāṣir-i Khusraw's work, such as pluralism and the possibility of dialogue between the followers of different faiths as well as his synthesis of ancient Greek philosophy and eastern wisdom held a unique position in their studies.

Y

709 Ya'qubov, Yusuf. 'Pages on the History of Nasir Khusraw's Motherland', in Sarfaroz Niyozov and Ramazon Nazariev, ed., *Nasir Khusraw: Yesterday, Today, Tomorrow*. (Proceedings of a conference held in Khārūgh, Tajikistan). Khujand: Noshir, 2005, pp. 228–240.

Taking an anthropological approach the author argues that Zoroastrian doctrinal traces can be linked to the culture present in Nāṣir-i Khusraw's homeland. The cultural heritage of Nāṣir-i Khusraw's time, according to Ya'qubov, was multi-dimensional and of a sophisticated level that still continues to have significance to this day.

710 Yayoi, Kawahara and Umed Mamadsherzodshoev. *Documents from Private Archives in Right-Bank Badakhshan*. Central Eurasian Research Series 10, Department of Islamic Area Studies, Center for Evolving Humanities, Graduate School of Humanities and Sociology. Tokyo: The University of Tokyo, 2015. pp. 102.

This work introduces the historical documents found and copied from private collections in the villages in the region on the right bank of the Panj River, the present-day GBAO, in the Republic of Tajikistan, during two expeditions. The work is divided into two volumes: (i) produces facsimiles of the documents from private collections in Right-bank Badakhshān, (ii) presents an introduction to the documents.

Z

711 Zakhoder, Boris Nikolaevich. 'Mukhammed Nakhshabi. K istorii karmatskogo dvizheniia v Srednei Azii v X v.' [Muḥammad al-Nakhshabī. Towards a History of the Qarmaṭī Movement in Central Asia in the 10th Century], *Uchënye zapiski MGU*, 41 (1940), pp. 96–112. (in Russian).

This article investigates Muḥammad Nakhshab (al-Nasafī)'s method of attracting new adepts to the Qarmaṭī form of Islam.

712 Zarubin, Ivan Ivanovich (1887–1964). 'Materialy i zametki po ètnografii gornykh tadzhikov. Dolina Bartanga' [Materials and Notes on the Ethnography of the Mountain Tajiks. Bartang Valley], *Sbornik Muzeia Antropologii i Ètnografii*, 1 (1917), pp. 97–148. (in Russian).

Collected materials about the Rūshānīs and their language, calendar of rituals and celebrations, weddings, funerals and memorial rites.

713 —— 'Dopolneniia k stat'e N.I. Veselovskiĭ, "Rol' strely v obriadakh i ee simvolicheskoe znachenie"' [Appendices to the article by N.I. Veselovskiĭ, 'The Role of the Arrow in the Rites and Its Symbolic Meaning'], *ZVORAO*,

25 (1921), pp. 91–96; republished in I.I. Zarubin. *Spisok narodnosteĭ Turkestanskogo Kraĭa* [List of the Ethnic Groups in the Turkestan Region], *RAN* (1925), pp. 1–25. (in Russian).

Adding to Veselovskiĭ's arguments, Zarubin enriches his findings by inserting hand-written observations on the life and rituals of the Pamiri Tajiks.

714 Zhukovskiĭ, V.A. 'Sekta "Li͡udeĭ istiny"' [The 'People of Truth' Sect], *ZVORAO*, 2 (1888), pp. 1–24. (in Russian).

The doctrines professed by the Ahl-i Ḥaqq are presented as being mainly syncretic. Despite sharing common features with the Nuṣayriyya ('Alawiyya), among the 'people of truth', the cult of ʿAlī is completely obscure. Characterised mainly by Sufi *darvīsh* ceremonies, the election of *pīr*s, food distribution, fraternal associations, etc., the adherents of the Ahl-i Ḥaqq were mainly members of the lower classes: nomads, inhabitants of rural areas, the urban poor and ordinary *darvīshes*.

715 —— 'Pesn' Nasiri-Khosrova', *Zapiski Vostochnogo Otdelenii͡a Imperatorskogo Russkogo Arkheologicheskogo Obshchestva*, 4 (1890), pp. 386–393. (in Russian).

In 1890 a Russian translation of Nāṣir-i Khusraw's poetry was published for the first time.

716 —— 'Batinity' [Bāṭinīs], *FES*, pp. 49–50. (in Russian).

Brief entry on the Bāṭinīs.

717 Zimmermann, Béatrice. *A Society in Transition: Ismāʿīlīs in the Tajik Pamirs*, Lizentiatsarbeit, Institut für Islamwissenschaft, Bern University, 2006. pp. 200.

This research addresses issues relative to the Ismaili faith and tradition under the atheist propaganda of the Soviet era. It also investigates developments since the collapse of the Soviet Union.

718 Zoolshoev, Muzaffar. 'A Short Survey of the 19th and 20th Centuries Literature on the Religious and Political History of Tajik Badakhshan', Unpublished Report for the IIS, 2010. pp. 107.

This survey of literature analyses the sources devoted to the history of small ethnic groups spread across the Pamir–Hindu-Kush region (also known as historic Badakhshān) of Central Asia. It includes sources on the region's history which cover the period from the end of the 19th to the first half of the 20th century.

719 —— 'The Soviet State and a Religious Movement: A Socio-Historical Study of the Ismāʿīlī Panjebhai Movement in Soviet Tajik Badakhshan (early 1920s late 1930s)', Unpublished Report for the IIS, 2015. pp. 203.

The work seeks to take a fresh look at the history of the Panjebhai religious movement as well as to attract greater scholarly attention to the study of Ismaili history in the rural areas of Central Asia. It examines not only the issues related to the emergence of the Panjebhai religious movement (which coincided with the rise of the Soviet state), but it also attempts to identify the major socio-historic, ideological, political and economic factors that formed the backdrop against which the movement emerged and developed in Soviet Tajik Badakhshān.

720 —— 'Farghāna', *EIS*, vol. 6, pp. 748–782.

Even though the article is about the history and religions of the Farghāna region, it contains several observations on the Ismailis and Qarmaṭīs during the Sāmānid era, including the periods when the regions of Badakhshān and Ferghāna were under the same ruling dynasty.

721 —— 'Forgotten Figures of Badakhshan – Sayyid Munir al-Din Badakhshani and Sayyid Haydar Shah Mubarakshahzada', in Dagikhudo Dagiev and Carole Faucher, ed., *Identity, History and Trans-Nationality in Central Asia: The Mountain Communities of Pamir*. London: Routledge, 2018, pp. 143–172.

This article includes the biographies of the two leading religious authorities of Badakhshān, whose names and contributions have been largely ignored by later religious authorities and expertise in the study of the history of Badakhshān. Sayyid Munīr and Sayyid Haydar Shāh were two actively religious state figures during the first decades of the twentieth century. However, due to political and ideological circumstances, their names remained obscure until the break-up of the USSR in 1991.

722 —— *Ancient and Early Medieval Kingdoms of the Pamir Region of Central Asia: Historical Shughnan and Its Lost Capital*. Forthcoming.

Although this work covers the ancient and early medieval history of Shughnān, it contains a short, but important description of life in Shughnān during the first centuries of Islam. At the same time, it provides solid references about the possible conquest of Shughnān and adjacent regions by the Arab armies.

References

Abaev V.I., and H.W. Bailey. 'Alans', *EIR*, vol. 1, pp. 801–803; an updated version is available online at http://www.iranicaonline.org/articles/alans-an-ancient-iranian-tribe-of-the-northern-scythian-saka-sarmatian-massagete-group-known-to-classical-writers-from [Last accessed, 17 May 2014].

Abibov, Amirbek. *Az tārīkh-i adabiët-i tojik dar Badakhshon*. Dushanbe, 1971.

Afsahzod, A. *Odamushshu'aro Rūdakī* [Adam of the Poet – Rūdakī]. 2nd ed., Dushanbe, 2008.

Alam, Muzaffar. 'The Pursuit of Persian: Language in Mughal Politics', *Modern Asian Studies*, 32, 2 (1998), pp. 317–349.

Alibhai, Fayaz S. 'An Architectural Manifestation of the Continuity between Tradition and Modernity', *The Middle East in London* (2009), p. 8.

Allworth, Edward A. *The Modern Uzbeks. From the Fourteenth Century to the Present*. Stanford. 1990.

Aminrazvi, Mehdi. 'Nāṣir-i Khusraw', *The Oxford Encyclopedia of Philosophy, Science, and Technology in Islam*, vol. 1, pp. 71–74.

Andreev, M.S. 'Bliny v pripamirskikh stranakh' [Oral Epic in the Pamir Countries], *TV*, 32 (1905), pp. 3–33.

—— *Tadzhiki Doliny Khuf (Verkhov'ia Amu Dar' ia)* [The Tajiks of the Khuf Valley (The Upper Reaches of the Amū Daryā)]. Stalinabad, Part. 1, 1953; Part. 2, 1958.

Ayīnī, Kamol, ed. and intr. *Nosiri Khusravi Qabodiënī Sarsukhan bo Gulchine az ash'or* [Nāṣir-i Khusraw Qubādiyānī. Preface, Selected Poems]. Stalinabad, 1957.

Babaev, Aktam. *Kreposti Drevnego Wakhana* [The Fortress of Ancient Wakhān]. Dushanbe, 1973.

Bābur, Ẓahīr al-Dīn Muḥammad. *The Baburnama: Memoirs of Babur, Prince and Emperor*, tr. W.M. Thackston, Washington, 1996.

Badakhshī, Mirzo Sangmuhammadi and Mirzo Fazlalibeki Surkhafsar. *Tārīkh-i Badakhshon* [The History of Badakhshān]. Dushanbe, 2007.

Badakhshī, Saidjalol. *Baḥr ul-akhbor: silsilai ḥikoiatho doir ba ḥaëti Noṣiri Khusraw va saëḥati u ba Badakhshonzamin* [Ocean of Tales: Sequence of Legends about the Life and the Journey of Nāṣir-i Khusraw in the Land of Badakhshān]. Khārūgh, 1992.

Baiza, Yahia. 'The Shiʿa Ismaʿili *Daʿwat* in Khurasan: From its Early Beginning to the Ghaznawid Era', *JSIS*, 8, 1 (2015), pp. 37–59.

Bartol'd, V.V. 'Badakhshan', *EI*, vol. 1, pp. 552–554. [Reprint in *EI2*, vol. 1, pp. 851–855].

—— *Four Studies on the History of Central Asia*, tr. V and T. Minorsky. vol. 1, Leiden, 1956; vol. 2, Leiden, 1958; vol. 3, Leiden, 1962.

Beal, Samuel. *Si-Yu-Ki. Buddhist Records of the Western World*. tr. from the Chinese of Hiuen Tsiang (A.D. 629). London, 1884; rpr. Munshiram Manoharlal, New Delhi, 2004.

Beben, Daniel. *The Legendary Biographies of Nāṣir-i Khusraw: Memory and Textualization in Early Modern Persian Ismāʿīlism*, PhD dissertation, Indiana University, 2015.

—— 'The Ismaili of Central Asia', *Oxford Research Encyclopedia of Asian History*, Available online at: https://oxfordre.com/asianhistory/view/10.1093/acrefore/9780190277727.001.0001/acrefore-9780190277727-e-316 [Last accessed, 11 June 2019].

Becker, Seymour. *Russia's Protectorates in Central Asia: Bukhara and Khiva, 1865–1924*. London, 2004.

Berg, Gabrielle van den. 'Keeping Religion Alive: Performing Pamiri Identity in Central Asia', *International Institute for Asian Studies*, 74 (2016), p. 37.

Bergne, Paul. *The Birth of Tajikistan: National Identity and the Origins of the Republic*. London, 2007.

Bertel's, Andreĭ E. *Nasir-i Khosrov i ismailizm* [Nāṣir-i Khusraw and Ismailism]. Moscow, 1959.

—— and Mamadvafo Bakaev. *Alfavitnyĭ katalog rukopiseĭ obnaruzhennykh v Gorno-Badakhshanskoĭ avtonomnoĭ oblasti ėkspedit͡sieĭ 1959–1963 gg.* [Alphabetical Catalogue of Manuscripts Discovered by the 1959–1963 Expedition to the GBAO], ed. Bobodzhan G. Ghafurov and A.M. Mirzoev. Moscow, 1967, pp. 78–119.

Bertel's, Evgeniĭ. 'Nasir Khusraw', *EI1*, pp. 869–870.

Biddulph, John. *Tribes of the Hindoo Khoosh*. Calcutta, 1880.

Bliss, Frank. *Social and Economic Change in the Pamirs (Gorno-Badakhshan, Tajikistan)*, tr. from German by Nicola Pacult and Sonia Guss. London, 2005.

Bobrinskoĭ, A.A. 'Sekta ismailʾi͡a v russkikh i bukharskikh predelakh Sredneĭ Azii' [The Ismaili Sect in Russian and Bukharan Central Asia], *EO*, 2 (1902), pp. 1–20; also published separately, Moscow, 1902.

Bogoutdinov, A.M., ed. *Istoriiā filosofii* [The History of Philosophy], vol. 1. Moscow, 1957.
—— *Ocherki po istorii tadzhikskoĭ filosofii* [Essays on the History of Tajik Philosophy]. Dushanbe, 1961.
Bosworth, C.E. 'Khurāsān', *EI2*, vol. 5, pp. 55–59.
—— 'Pamirs', *EI2*, vol. 8, p. 245.
—— 'Shughnān', *EI2*, vol. 9, pp. 495–496.
Bregel, Yuri. *An Historical Atlas of Central Asia*. Leiden, 2003.
Bretschneider, E. *Mediaeval Researches from Eastern Asiatic Sources: Fragments towards the Knowledge of the Geography and History of Central and Western Asia from the 13th to the 17th Century*, vol. 2. London, 1888.
Browne, Edward G. 'Nasir-i-Khusraw, Poet, Traveller, and Propagandist', *The Journal of the Royal Asiatic Society of Great Britain and Ireland* (Apr., 1905), pp. 313–352.
—— *A Literary History of Persia: from the Earliest Times until Firdawsi*. London, 1909.
Bubnova, M.A. *Gorno-Badakhshanskiiā Avtonomniiā Oblast' Zapadnyĭ Pamir (pamiātniki II tys. do n. ė. - XIX v.)* [Gorno-Badakhshan Autonomous Region of Western Pamir (monuments of the 2nd millennium BC –xix c.). Dushanbe, 1997.
Bushkov, Valentin and Tokhir Kalandarov. 'Ismaility Tadzhikistana: Traditsii i Sovremennost", *Central Asia and the Caucasus*, 6, 24 (2002), pp. 130–135. Available online at: http://www.ca-c.org/journal/2002/journal_rus/cac-06/15.busrus.shtml [Last accessed, 9 Nov. 2014].
Buzurg-Zoda, Lutfullo. *Iskatel' pravdy i spravedlivosti Nosir Khisroy* [Nāṣir-i Khusraw, the Seeker of Truth and Justice]. Stalinabad, 1953.
Cherkasov, A. Baron. 'Otchët', in N.A. Khalfin, ed., *Rossiiā i Bukharskiĭ ėmirat na Zapadnom Pamire (konets XIX – nachalo XX v.)*, [Russia and the Bukharan Emirate in the Western Pamir (late 19th and early 20th Centuries)]. Moscow, 1975, pp. 104–105.
Corbin, Henry. *History of Islamic Philosophy*, tr. L. Sherrard. London, 1993.
Crone, Patricia and Luke Treadwell. 'A New Text on Ismailism at the Samanid Court', in Patricia Crone, *The Iranian Reception of Islam: The Non-Traditionalist Strands*, Collected Studies in Three Volumes, vol. 2. Leiden, 2016, pp. 238–261.
Dadabaev, Timur. 'Religiosity and Soviet "Modernisation", in Central Asia: Locating Religious Traditions and Rituals in Recollections of Antireligious Policies in Uzbekistan', *Religion, State and Society*, 32, 4 (2014), pp. 328–353.
Daftary, Farhad. *The Ismāʿīlīs: Their History and Doctrines*. Cambridge, 1990; 2nd ed., Cambridge, 2007.
—— *The Assassin Legends: Myths of the Ismaʿilis*. London, 1994.
—— *A Short History of the Ismailis*. Edinburgh, 1998.

—— 'The Medieval Ismaʿīlīs of the Iranian Lands', in C. Hillenbrand, ed., *Studies in Honour of Clifford Edmund Bosworth, II: The Sultan's Turret: Studies in Persian and Turkish Culture*. Leiden, 2000, pp. 43–81.
—— *Ismaili Literature: A Bibliography of Sources and Studies*. London, 2004.
——, ed. *A Modern History of the Ismailis: Continuity and Change in a Muslim Community*. London, 2010.
—— *Historical Dictionary of the Ismailis*. Lanham, MD, 2012.
—— 'The Iranian School of Philosophical Ismailism', *Ishrāk* [Illumination], *EIF*, 4 (2013), pp. 13–24.
—— 'Wladimir Ivanow and Modern Ismaili Studies', in Stanislav M. Prozorov and Hakim Elnazarov, ed., *Russian Scholars on Ismailism*. St Petersburg, 2014, pp. 24–37.
——, ed. *Fifty Years in the East: The Memoirs of Wladimir Ivanow*. London, 2015.
—— 'Omm al-ketāb', *EIR*, Available online at: http://www.iranicaonline.org/articles/omm-al-ketab [Last accessed, 15 June 2020].
—— 'Assassins', *EIS*, vol. 3, pp. 911–914.
—— 'Sunni Perceptions of the Ismailis: Medieval Perspectives', in Orkhan Mir-Kasimov, ed., *Intellectual Interactions in the Islamic World: The Ismaili Thread*. London, 2020, pp. 13–26.
Dagiev, Dagikhudo. *Regime Transition in Central Asia: Stateness, Nationalism and Political Change in Tajikistan and Uzbekistan*. London, 2013.
—— 'Pamiri Ethnic Identity and Its Evolution in post-Soviet Tajikistan', in Dagikhudo Dagiev and Carole Faucher, ed., *Identity, History and Trans-Nationality in Central Asia: The Mountain Communities of Pamir*. London, 2018, pp. 23–44.
—— 'The Ismāʿīlī Hierarchy – Ḥudūd al-Dīn – in the Context of Central Asia', *JSIS*, 10, 3 (2019), pp. 343–370.
Daniel, Elton L. *The History of Iran*. London, 2001.
Davydov, A.S. *Ėtnicheskaia prinadlezhnost' korennogo naseleniia Gornogo Badakhshana (Pamir)* [Ethnicity of the Indigenous Population of Gorno-Badakhshān (Pamir)]. Dushanbe, 2005.
Dawlatshāh b. ʿAlāʾ al-Dawla. *Tadhkirat al-shuʿarā*, ed. Fāṭima ʿAlāqah. Tehran, 1385 Sh./2007.
Devonaqulov, Ali Quli and Nurmuhammad Amirshohiī, ed. *Nosiri Khusravi Qubodiënī* [Nāṣir-i Khusraw Qubādiyānī], *Wajhi din* [Wajh-i dīn]. Dushanbe, 2002.
D'iakov, A.M. *I͡Azyki sovetskogo Pamira. Kul'tura i pis'mennost' Vostoka* [Languages of the Soviet Pamirs. Culture and Script of the East], vol. 10. Moscow, 1931.
Dihkhoda. *Lughat-Nāma-i Dihkhudā*. Available online at: http://parsi.wiki/dehkhodaworddetail-cbe368c6fbcf43b68107af29bc35fb45-fa.html [last accessed, 21 December 2015].

Dinorshoev, Muso. *Nasir-i Khusraw i ego 'Zad al-musafirin'* [Nāṣir-i Khusraw and his *Zād al-Musāfirīn*], tr. from Tajik into Russian. Dushanbe, 2005.
Dodge, B., tr. *The Fihrist of al-Nadīm: A Tenth-Century Survey of Muslim Culture*, 2 vols. New York, 1970.
Dodikhudoev, Khaëlbek. *Mazhabi Ismoiliīa va mohiīati ijtimoii on. Rohhoi bartaraf namudani boqimondai din* [Ismaili Belief and its Social Aspects. Methods of Eliminating Traces of Religion]. Dushanbe, 1967.
—— *Filosofiīa krest'īanskogo bunta: O roli srednevekovogo ismailizma v razvitii svobodomysliīa na musul'manskom Vostoke* [The Philosophy of Peasant Revolt: The Role of Medieval Ismailism in the Development of Thought in the Muslim East]. Dushanbe, 1987.
—— *Filosofskiĭ ismailizm* [Philosophical Ismailism]. Dushanbe, 2014.
Dovudi, D. and L. Ilish. 'Manety Badakhshana v sobranii Tīubigenskogo universiteta FRG' [Badakhshānī Coins in the Collection by Tübingen University FRG], *Soobchshenie natsional'nogo muzeīa respubliki Tadzhikistana* [Communications of the National Museum of the Republic of Tajikistan], 8 (2009).
Dūghlāt, Mīrzā Muḥammad Ḥaydar. *Tārīkh-i Rashīdī*, ed. ʿAbbāsqulī Ghaffārī Fard. Tehran, 1383 Sh./2004.
Elias, Ney. 'Report of a Mission to Chinese Turkistan and Badakhshan 1885–1886', in M. Ewan, ed., *Britain and Russia in Central Asia, 1880–1907*, vol. 5. London, 2008.
Elisseeff, Vadime. *The Silk Roads: Highways of Culture and Commerce*. New York, 2001.
Ėl'chibekov, Kudratbek. 'Novye materialy po istorii Shugnana' [New Materials on the History of Shughnān], *IAN (TSSR)*, (1973), pp. 3–11.
—— 'Istoricheskie istochniki v Badakhshane' [Historical Sources in Badakhshān], *IAN (TSSR)*, (1975), pp. 27–31.
—— (A senior research associate at the Oriental Institute of Manuscript Studies Academy of Sciences of the Republic of Tajikistan.) Author interview. (2015).
—— *Ierarkhiīa Dukhovenstva v Ismailizme Badakhshana (na osnove rukopisi 'Sīlk-i gawhar-riz')* [The Religious Hierarchy of the Ismailis of Badakhshān (based on the manuscript of *Sīlk-i gawhar-rīz*)]. Dushanbe, 2016.
—— *Sīlk-i gawhar-rīz*, ed. Qudratbek Elchibekov (retyped version of a manuscript held in the collection of the ISCU, IIS, London).
Elnazarov, Hakim and Sultonbek Aksakolov. 'The Nizari Ismailis of Central Asia in Modern Times', in Farhad Daftary, ed., *A Modern History of the Ismailis: Continuity and Changes in a Muslim Community*. London, 2011, pp. 45–75.
Emadi, Hafizullah. 'Praxis of *Taqiyya*: Perserverance of Pashaye Ismāʿīlī Enclave, Nangarhar, Afghanistan', *Central Asian Survey*, 19, 2 (2000), pp. 253–264.

Emel'i͡anova, Nadezhda. *Darvaz—religioznai͡a i kul'turnai͡a zhizn' Tadzhikskogo-Afganskogo prigranich'i͡a* (po materialam polevykh issledovanii 2003-2006 gg.) [Darvāz—Religious and Cultural Life of the Tajik-Afghan Borders (based on field research)]. Moscow, 2007.

Ewans, Martin, ed. *Britain and Russia in Central Asia, 1880-1907*. London, 2008.

Fidā'ī Khurāsānī, Muḥammad b. Zayn al-'Abidīn Dīzābādī. *Kitāb-i hidāyat al-mu'minīn al-ṭālibīn*, ed. A.A. Semënov. Moscow, 1959.

Firdawsī, Abulqosim. *Shohnoma*, ed. Kamol Ayīnī and Zohir Ahrorī. 12 vols, Dushanbe, 2007-2010.

Foltz, Richard. *A History of the Tajiks: Iranians of the East*. London, 2019.

Frye, Richard N. *The Heritage of Persia*. London, 1976.

—— tr. with commentary, *Ibn Fadlan's Journey to Russia: A Tenth-Century Traveler from Baghdad to the Volga River*. Princeton, NJ, 2005.

Furūzanfar, Badī' al-Zamān. *Sukhan va sukhanwarān*. 4th ed., Tehran, 1369 Sh./1990.

Ghafurov, B. *Istorii͡a Tadzhikskogo Naroda v Kratkom Izlozhenii. S Drevneĭshikh vremien do velikoĭ Okti͡abrskoĭ Revoli͡utsii 1917* [A Summary History of the Tajik People. From Ancient Times to the Great October Revolution of 1917], vol. 1. Moscow, 1952.

—— *Tadjiki. Drevneyshai͡a, drevnai͡a i srednevekovai͡a istorii͡a*, *Kniga pervai͡a* [The Tajiks. Earliest, Ancient and Medieval Histories, Book One]. Dushanbe, 1989.

—— 'Aga khan', *Journal Bezbozhnik* [The Atheist], 10-11 (1940), pp. 8-9.

Ghani, M.A. *Pre-Mughal Persian in Hindustan*. Allahabad, 1941.

Ghubār, Mīr Ghulām Muḥammad. *Khurāsān*. Kabul, 1937.

Grenet, Frantz. 'Zoroastrianism in Central Asia', in Michael Stausberg and Yuhan Sohrab-Dinshaw Vevaina (with the assistance of Anna Tessmann), *The Wiley Blackwell Companion to Zoroastranism*. Oxford, 2015, pp. 129-147.

—— and Zhang Guangda. 'The Last Refuge of the Sogdian Religion: Dunhuang in the Ninth and Tenth Centuries,' *Bulletin of the Asia Institute*, 10 (1996 [1998]), pp. 175-1986.

Gulamadov, Shaftolu. *The Hagiography of Nāṣir-i Khusraw and the Ismā'īlīs of Badakhshān*, PhD dissertation, University of Toronto, 2018.

Ḥasan, Ibrāhīm Ḥasan. *Ta'rīkh al-dawla al-Fāṭimiyya fī'l-Maghrib wa-Miṣr wa-Sūriyā wa-bilād al-'Arab* [The History of the Fatimid State in the Maghreb, Egypt, Syria and the Arab lands]. Cairo, 1964.

Ḥasan-i Maḥmūd-i Kātib. *Dīvān-i Qā'imiyyāt*, introd. M.R. Shāf'ī Kadkanī, Persian ed. and English introd. Jalal Badakhchani. Tehran, 2011.

—— *Devoni Qoimiët* [*Dīvān-i Qā'imiyyāt*], ed. Jalal Badakhchani and Ato Mirkhoja. Dushanbe, 2015.

—— *Haft bāb*, ed. and tr. S.J. Badakhchani as *Spiritual Resurrection in Shi'i Islam: An Early Ismaili Treatise on the Doctrine of Qiyāmat*. mat. London, 2017.

Hodgson, Marshall. 'The Ismāʿīlī State', in J.A. Boyle, ed., *The Cambridge History of Iran*, vol. 5, *The Saljuq and Mongol Periods*. Cambridge, 1969, pp. 422–482.

Hojibekov, Ėl'bon [Khodzhibekov, Ėl'bon]. *Ismailitskie dukhovnye nastavniki (piry), ikh rol' v obshchestvennoĭ zhizni Shugnana (vtoraia polovina XIX – 30-e gody XX vv.)* [Ismaili Spiritual Mentors (*pīrs*) and their Role in the Social Life of Shughnan: the Second half of the 19th Century – 1930s]. Dushanbe, 2015.

Hunsberger, Alice C. *Nasir Khusraw, The Ruby of Badakhshan: A Portrait of the Persian Poet, Traveller and Philosopher*. London, 2000.

—— *Pearls of Persia: The Philosophical Poetry of Nāṣir-i Khusraw*. London, 2012.

Hyechʻo. *The Hye Chʼo Diary: Memoir of the Pilgrimage to the Five Regions of India*, ed. and tr. Han-Sung Yang and Yün-Hua Jan. Berkeley, CA, 1984.

Ibn al-Athīr, ʿAlī b. Muḥammad. *al-Kāmil fiʼl-taʼrīkh*, ed. C.J. Tornberg. Leiden, 1863; repr. Beirut, 1399/1979.

Iloliev, Abdulmamad. *The Ismāʿīlī-Sufi Sage of Pamir: Mubarak-i Wakhani and the Esoteric Tradition of the Pamir Muslims*. Amherst, 2008.

—— 'Pirship in Badakhshan: The Role and Significance of the Institute of the Religious Masters (*Pirs*) in Nineteenth and Twentieth Century Wakhan and Shughnan', *Journal of Shiʿa Islamic Studies*, 6, 2 (2013), pp. 155–175.

—— 'The Silk Road castles and temples: ancient Wakhan in legends and history', in Dagikhudo Dagiev and Carole Faucher, ed., *Identity, History and Trans-Nationality in Central Asia: The Mountain Communities of Pamir*. London, 2018, pp. 91–105.

Iṣfahanī, Ghiësud al-Din Alii [Ghiyāth al-Dīn ʿAlī Iṣfahānī], *Nujūm*, ed. Umed Shohzodamuhammad. Khārūgh, 1995.

Iskandarov, I. Bakhodur. *Vostochnaia Bukhara i Pamir v period presoedineniia Sredneĭ Azii k Rossii* [Eastern Bukhara and the Pamirs during the Annexation of Central Asia to Russia]. Stalinabad, 1960.

—— *Iz istorii dorevoluṯsionnogo Tadzhikistana* [On the History of Pre-Revolutionary Tajikistan]. Dushanbe, 1974.

Istoriia Pamira [The History of the Pamirs]. Available online at: http://www.pamir-spb.ru/istoriya.html [Last accessed, 16 April 2017].

Ivanow, Wladimir. 'Ismailitskie rukopisi Aziatskogo Muzeia. Sobranie I. Zarubina, 1916 g.' [Ismaili Manuscripts of the Asiatic Museum. I. Zarubin Collection, 1916], *Izvestiia Rossiĭskoĭ Akademii Nauk*, 6, 11 (1917), pp. 359–386.

—— *A Guide to Ismaili Literature*. London, 1933.

—— *Brief Survey of the Evolution of Ismailism*. Leiden, 1952.

—— 'The Organisation of the Fatimid Propaganda', *JBBRAS*, NS, 15 (1939), pp. 1–35; reprinted in Bryan S. Turner, ed., *Orientalism: Early Sources*, vol. 1, *Readings in Orientalism*. London, 2000, pp. 531–571.

Jackson, Williams. *Early Persian poetry, from the beginnings down to the time of Firdausi*. New York, 1920.

Jamal, Nadia Eboo. *Surviving the Mongols: The Continuity of Ismaili Tradition in Iran*. London, 2002.
Johanson, Lars and Christiane Bulut, ed. *Turkic-Iranian Contact Areas: Historical and Linguistic Aspects*. Wiesbaden, 2006.
Jonboboev, Sunatullo. 'Geography, Ethnicity and Cultural Heritage in Interplay in the Context of the Tajik Pamiri Idenity', in Dagikhudo Dagiev and Carole Faucher, ed., *Identity, History and Trans-Nationality in Central Asia: The Mountain Communities of Pamir*. London, 2018, pp. 11–22.
Khalīlī, Khalīl Allāh. *Yumgān*. Kabul, 1959.
Khan, Mir Baiz. 'Living Traditions of Nasir Khusraw: A Study of Ismāʿīlī practices in Afghan Badakhshān'. Unpublished Fieldwork Report for the IIS, 2004.
Kharîukov L.N. *Anglo-russkoe sopernichestvo v TSentralʾnoĭ Azii i ismailizm* [Anglo-Russian Rivalry in Central Asia and Ismailism]. Moscow, 1995.
Khayr-khʷāh-i Harātī, *Taṣnīfāt*, ed. W. Ivanow. Tehran, 1961.
al-Kirmānī, Ḥamīd al-Dīn. *Uspokoenie razuma* [*Rāḥat al-ʿaql*]. Vvedenie, perevod s arabskogo i kommentarii A.V. Smirnova [Intr., and tr., from Arabic with a commentary by A.V. Smirnov]. Moscow: Ladomir, 1995.
Kreutzmann, Hermann and Teiji Watanabe, ed. *Mapping Transition in the Pamirs: Changing Human-Environmental Landscapes*. Cham, NY, 2016.
Kuchāk [Gawhar Rīz]. *Sīlk-i gawhar-rīz*, ed. K. Ėlʾchibekov, Photostat version. Dushanbe, n.d.
Landolt, Hermann. 'Early Evidence for the Reception of Nāṣir-i Khusraw's Poetry in Sufism: ʿAyn al-Quḍāt's Letter on the Taʿlīmīs', in Omar Alí-de-Unzaga, ed., *Fortresses of the Intellect: Ismaili and other Islamic Studies in Honour of Farhad Daftary*. London, 2011, pp. 369–386.
Lashkarbekov, B., S. Yusufbekov and S. Khodjaniyazov. 'Ismailism and Central Asian Ismailis in Russian and Soviet Studies'. Unpublished Report for the IIS, 2000.
Le Strange, G. *The Lands of the Eastern Caliphate: Mesopotamia, Persia and Central Asia; from the Moslem Conquest to the time of Timur*. London, 1966.
Lenin, Vladimir. 'Novaiā Zhizn" [New Life], in *Lenin: Collected Works*, vol. 10. Moscow, 1965, pp. 83–87.
Lewisohn, L. 'Sufism and Ismāʿīlī Doctrine in the Persian Poetry of Nizārī Quhistānī (645–721/1247–1321)', *Iran, Journal of the British Institute of Persian Studies*, 41 (2003), pp. 229–251.
Lika, Eva-Maria. *Proof of Prophecy and the Refutation of the Ismāʿīliyya: The Kitāb Ithbāt Nubuwwat al-Nabī by the Zaydī al-Muʾayyad bi-llāh al-Hārūnī (d. 411/1020)*. Berlin, 2017.
Madelung, Wilferd and Paul E. Walker, ed. and tr. *An Ismaili Heresiography: The 'Bāb al-shayṭān' from Abū Tammām's Kitāb al-shajara*. Leiden, 1998.
—— 'Ismāʿīlīya'. *EI2*, vol. 4, pp. 198–206.
Mahmoodi-Bakhtiari, Behrooz. 'Planning the Persian Language in the Samanid Period', *Iran and the Caucasus*, 7, 1/2 (2003), pp. 251–260.

Maĭskiĭ, Petr Mikhaĭlovich. 'Sledy drevnikh verovaniĭ v pamirskom ismailizme' [The Traces of Ancient Beliefs in the Pamiri Ismailism], *Sovetskaia̐ etnografiia̐*, 3 (1935), pp. 48–58.

Mamadsherzodshoev, S. *Excerpt from a report by ISCU Khārūgh Unit* (4 September 2014).

Mastibekov, Otambek. *Leadership and Authority in Central Asia: the Ismaili Community in Tajikistan*. London, 2014.

Matveeva, A. 'The Perils of Emerging Statehood: Civil War and State Reconstruction in Tajikistan an Analytical Narrative on State-making', *Crisis States Research Centre* (2009), pp. 1–60.

Millward, James A. 'Positioning Xinjiang in Eurasian and Chinese History: Differing visions of the "Silk Road"', in Colin Mackerras and Michael Clark, ed., *China, Xinjian and Central Asia: History, Transition and Crossborder Interaction into the 21st Century*. London, 2009, pp. 55–74.

Mingaleeva, Mina, ed. *Pamir – Krysha Mira. Sbornik proizvedeniĭ o Pamire* [Pamir – the Roof of the World. A Collection of Essays about Pamir] (N/P, 2011). Available online at: http://www.skitalets.ru/books/pamir_mingaleeva/ [Last accessed, 11 June 2019].

Minorsky, V. *Ḥudūd al-'Ālam, 'The Regions of the World': A Persian Geography 372 AH – 982 AD*. London, 1937.

Mirzoev, A. *Abūabdullo Rūdakī* [Abū 'Abd Allāh Rūdakī]. Dushanbe, 1958.

Mirzozoda, S. 'Yagnabskiĭ yazyk-bogatstvo tadzhikskogo naroda, kotoroe neobkhodimo peredat' slediu̐shchim pokoleniia̐m' [The Yaghnāb language is the wealth of the Tajik people, which must be passed on to the future generations]. Available online at: http://sugdnews.com/2017/10/30/mirzozoda-yagnobskij-yazyk-bogatstvo-tadzhikskogo-naroda-kotoroe-neobkhodimo-peredat-sleduyushchim-pokoleniyam-3/ [Last accessed, 29 October 2020].

Mitha, Farouk. *Al-Ghazāli and the Ismailis: A Debate on Reason and Authority in Medieval Islam*. London, 2003.

Mohammad Poor, Daryoush. 'Extra-Ismaili Sources and a Shift of Paradigm in Nizārī Ismailism', in Orkhan Mir-Kasimov, ed., *Intellectual Interactions in the Islamic World: the Ismaili Thread*. London, 2020, pp. 219–245.

Monogarova, L.F. *Preobrazovaniia̐ v bytu i kul'ture pripamirskikh narodnosteĭ* [Transformations in the Life and Culture of the Pamiri Nationalities]. Moscow, 1972.

Moran, Neil K. *Kipling and Afghanistan: A Study of the Young Author as Journalist Writing on the Afghan Border Crisis of 1884–1885*. London, 2005.

Morgan, David. *Medieval Persia, 1040–1797*. London, 1988.

Muborakshohzoda, Sayyid Haĭdarshoh. *Tārīkh-i Mulk-i Shughnān* [The History of the land of Shughnān]. Khārūgh, 1992.

Mu'izzī, Maryam. *Ismā'īliyya-yi Badakhshān* [The Ismailis of Badakhshān]. Tehran, 1395 Sh./2017.

Mukhamadzoda, Kurbon (Ākhūnd Sulaymān) and Mukhabbat (Shāh Fitūr) Shokhzoda. *Istoriia͡ Badakhshana* [The History of Badakhshān], ed. B.I. Iskandarov. Moscow, 1973.

Nājī, Muḥammad Riza. *Farhang va tamadduni Islāmī dar qalamru-yi Sāmāniyān*. Tehran, 1342 Sh./1964.

Nāṣir-i Khusraw, Ḥakīm Abū Muʿīn. *Dīvān-i Ḥakīm Nāṣir-i Khusraw*, ed. Naṣr Allāh Taqavī et al. Tehran, 1304–1307 Sh./1925–1928; ed. Mujtabā Mīnuvī and Mahdī Muḥaqqiq. Tehran, 1353 Sh./1974.

—— *Kitāb-i jāmiʿ al-ḥikmatayn*, ed. Henry Corbin and M. Muʿīn. Tehran–Paris, 1953. English trans. as *Between Reason and Revelation: Twin Wisdoms Reconciled*, tr. Eric Ormsby. London, 2012; *Jome'-ul-hikmataïn* [Jāmiʿ al-ḥikmatayn], ed. K. Olimov, K. Askardaev and A. Sharipov. Dushanbe, 2011.

—— *Safar-namė: kniga puteshestviia͡*. tr. and intr. by E.Ė. Bertel's [Nāṣir-i Khusraw. *Safar-nāma*. Travelogue. tr. and intr. E.Ė. Bertel's]. Moscow-Leningrad, 1933; English trans. as *Nāser-e Khosraw's Book of Travels (Safarnāma)*, tr. Wheeler Thackston, Jr. Albany, NY, 1986.

—— *Zād al-musāfirīn*, ed. Muḥammad Badhl al-Raḥmān. Berlin, 1341/1923.

Nazarshoev, M. *Muborizi rohi haqiqat* [Fighter for Justice]. Dushanbe, 1993.

Niyozov, Sarfaroz. 'Shiʿa Ismaili Tradition in Central Asia: – Evolution, Continuities and Changes', *Central Asia and the Caucasus*, 24, 6 (2003), pp. 39–46. Available online at: http://www.ca-c.org/journal/eng-06-2003/05.niyprimen.shtml [last accessed, 7 May 2019].

—— and Ramazon Nazariev ed. *Nasir Khusraw: Yesterday, Today, Tomorrow*. (Proceedings of a conference held in Khārūgh, Tajikistan). Khujand, 2005.

Nizārī Quhistānī, Ḥakīm Saʿd al-Din b. Shams al-Dīn. *Dīvān*, ed. M. Muṣaffā. Tehran, 1371–1373 Sh./1992–1994.

Nourmamadchoev, Nourmamadcho. *The Ismāʿīlīs of Badakhshan: History, Politics and Religion from 1500 to 1750*, PhD dissertation, SOAS, University of London, 2015.

—— *Analytical Mapping of Persian Manuscripts from Badakhshan of Tajikistan: Revised version* (November, 2019).

—— *Analytical Mapping of Persian Manuscripts from Badakhshan of Afghanistan: Revised version* (November, 2019).

—— *Review of the Hand-List of Manuscripts from Badakhshan of Tajikistan* (20 January 2016).

al-Nuʿmān b. Muḥammad, al-Qāḍī Abū Ḥanīfa. *Ta'wīl al-daʿā'im*, ed. M.Ḥ. al-Aʿẓamī, 2 vols. Cairo, 1968–1972.

Nuʿmānī, Shibli. *Shiʿr al-ʿAjam ya tārīkh-i shiʿr va adabiyāt-i Īrān*, tr. Muḥammad Taqī Fakhr Dāʿī Gīlānī. 2nd ed., Tehran, 1365 Sh./1984.

Olufsen, O. *Through the Unknown Pamirs; the Second Danish Pamir Expedition, 1898–99*. London, 1904.

Pakhalina, T.N. *Pamirskie i͡azyki* [The Pamiri Languages]. Moscow, 1969.

Petrov, A.B. 'Badakhshan XIII–XIV vv. pod Vlast'i͡u Mongol'skikh Khanov' [Badakhshān 13th–14th Centuries under the Rule of the Mongol Khans], *ZVORAO*, 2 (2006), pp. 496–540.

Pirumshoev, Haĭdarsho S. 'The Pamirs and Badakhshan', in Chahryar Adle, Irfan Habib and Karl M. Baipakov, ed., *History of Civilizations of Central Asia*, vol. 5, *Development in Contrast: from the Sixteenth to the mid-Nineteenth Century*. Paris, 2003.

—— *Tārikh-i Darvoz* [The History of Darvāz]. Dushanbe, 2008.

Plekhanov, Georgi. *Selected Philosophical Works*. Moscow, 1976.

Plekhanov, Sergeĭ. *Raskrytai͡a ladon'*: *Aga Khan i ego Mi͡uridy* [An Open Hand: the Aga-Khan and His *Murīds*]. Moscow, 2008.

Pohl, Walter. 'Conceptions of Ethnicity in Early Medieval Studies', in Lester K. Little and Barbara H. Rosenwein, ed., *Debating the Middle Ages: Issues and Readings*. Oxford, 1998, pp. 13–24.

Polo, Marco. *The Book of Ser Marco Polo the Venetian, Concerning the Kingdoms of Marvels of the East*, ed. Sir Henry Yule. London, 1871; Russian ed., *Kniga Marco Polo* [The Book of Marco Polo]. Moscow, 1956.

Pospielovsky, Dimitry V. 'A History of Soviet Atheism in Theory, and Practice, and the Believer', vol. 1: *A History of Marxist-Leninist Atheism and Soviet Anti-Religious Policies*. New York, 1987.

Prozorov, Stanislav, ed. *Khrestomatii͡a po Islamu* [Readings on Islam]. Moscow, 1994.

—— and Hakim Elnazarov, ed. *Russian Scholars on Ismailism*. St Petersburg, 2014.

Qalandarov, Hokim. *Rudakī va Ismoilii͡a* [Rūdakī and the Ismailis]. Dushanbe, 2012.

Rashīd al-Dīn Ṭabīb, Faḍl Allāh b. ʿImād al-Dawla. *Jāmiʿ al-tawārīkh: qismat-i Ismāʿīliyān va Fāṭimiyān va Nizāriyān*, ed. Muḥammad Taqī Dānishpazhūh and Muḥammad Mudarrisī Zanjānī. Tehran, 1338 Sh./1959.

al-Rāzī, Abū Ḥātim. *Kitāb al-Iṣlāḥ*, ed. Ḥasan Mīnūchihr and Mahdī Muḥaqqiq, with an English introduction by Shin Nomoto. Tehran, 1377 Sh./1998.

Reis, Sidi Ali. *The Travels and Adventures of Turkish Sidi Ali Reis*, translated from the Turkish with notes by A. Vambery. repr., Lahore, 1975.

Sagadeev, A.V. and S.N. Grigorian, tr. *Iz istorii filosofii Sredneĭ Azii i Iran VII–XII vv*. [On the History of the Philosophy of Central Asia and Iran 7th–12th centuries]. Moscow, 1960.

Sameev, A. *Somoniën dar oinai tārīkh* [Sāmānids in the Mirror of History], vol. 2. Khujand, 1998.

Sampson, Gareth C. *The Defeat of Rome: Crassus, Carrhae and the Invasion of the East*. Barnsley, 2008.

Scott, D.A. 'Zoroastrian Traces along the Upper Amu Darya (Oxus)', *JRAS*, 2 (1984), pp. 217–228.

Semënov, A.A. 'Iz oblasti religioznykh verovaniĭ shugnanskikh ismailitov' [On the Realm of the Religious Belief of the Shugnani Ismailis], *MI*, 1 (1912).

Semënova, Lidiia̐. *Iz istorii Fatimidskogo Egipta. Ocherki i materialy* [On the History of Fatimid Egypt. Essays and Sources]. Moscow, 1974.

Serebrennikov, A. 'Ocherki Shugnana' [Essays on Shughnān], *Voennyĭ sbornik*, vol. 226 (1896), pp. 1–52.

—— 'Ocherk Pamira' [A Sketch of Pamir]. St Peterburg, 1900.

Sherzodshoev, S. 'Discovery of Documents in Badakhshan of Tajikistan' (Unpublished Report for the IIS, 2016).

—— *Report from the Khorog Office: Discovery of Historical Documents* (January, 2015).

Shokhumorov, Abusaid. *Pamir—strana Ariev* [Pamir: Land of the Aryan people]. Dushanbe, 1997.

—— 'Somoniën va junbishi ismoiliia̐' [The Sāmānids and the Ismaili Movement], in A. Muhammadkhojaev and M. Mahmadjonov, ed., *Falsafa dar ahdi Somoniën* [Philosophy during the Samanid Era]. Dushanbe, 1999.

—— *Razdelenie Badakhshana i sud'by Ismailizma* [The Delimitation of Badakhshān and the Fate of Ismailism]. Dushanbe, 2008.

al-Sijistānī, Abū Ya'qūb. *Ithbāt al-nubuwwāt*, ed. W. Madelung and P. Walker. Tehran, 1395/2016.

—— *Kitāb al-maqālīd al-malakūtiyya*, ed. I.K. Poonawala. Tunis, 2011.

Smirnov, N.A. *Ocherki Istorii Izucheniia̐ Islama v SSSR* [Essays Exploring the History of Islam in the USSR]. Moscow, 1954.

Stanishevskiĭ, A.V. *Ismailizm na Pamire* (1902–1931) [Ismailism in the Pamirs (1902–1931)]. Sbornik documentov [Collection of Documents], compiled by A.V. Stanishevskiĭ, Academiia̐ Nauk USSR, Glavnoe Archivnoe Upravlenie pri-Sovete Ministrov Uzbekskoĭ SSR: Institut Vostokovedeniia̐ [The Main Archive Directorate of the Council of Ministers of the Uzbek SSR: Institute of Oriental Studies].

—— *Sbornik Arkhivnykh Documentov po Istorii Pamira i Ismailizmu*, compiled by A.V. Stanishevskiĭ, TSentral'nyĭ Gosudarstvennyĭ Arkhiv Uzbekskoĭ SSR [Central State Archive of the Uzbek SSR]. Tashkent, 1933.

Stern, S.M. 'The Early Ismā'īlī Missionaries in North-West Persia and in Khurāsān and Transoxiana', *BSOAS*, 23 (1960), pp. 59–60; reprinted in his *Studies in Early Ismā'īlism*. Leiden, 1983, pp. 189–233.

Stroeva, Liudmila V. *Gosudarstvo Ismailitov v Irane v 11–13 vv.* [The Ismaili State in Iran in the 11th-13th Centuries]. Moscow, 1978.

—— 'Dvizhenie ismailitov v Isfakhane v 1101–1107 gg.' [The Ismaili Movement in Iṣfahān 1101–1107], *VLGU*, 14 (1962), pp. 60–73.

—— 'Ismailiti Irana i Sirii v zarubezhnoĭ i sovetskoĭ literature' [Soviet and Foreign Historiographical Literature on the Ismailis of Iran and Syria], in *Istoriografiia̐ i istochnikovedenie istorii stran Azii*. Leningrad, 1965, pp. 138–148.

Susumu, Najima N. Pir. 'Waiz and Imam: The Transformation of Socio-Religious Leadership among the Ismailis in Northern Pakistan', *Area Studies Working Paper Series*, 23. Tokyo, 2001.

Tadzhikskiĭ narod v period mezhdu dvukh revoliūtsiĭ (fevral'-oktiabr' 1917 goda) [The Tajik People between the Two Revolutions (February-October 1917]. Available online at: http://diplomba.ru/work/84575 [Last accessed, 11 June 2019].

Trakhtenberg, O.B. *Ocherki po istorii zapandno-evropeĭskoĭ srednevekovoĭ filosofii* [Essays on the History of Western European Medieval Philosophy]. Moscow, 1975.

Tsung, Linda. *Language, Power and Hierarchy: Multilingual Education in China*. London, 2014.

Tukhtametov, T.G. 'Antirusskie poiski inostrant͡sev v Bukhare i na Pamire. Politicheskie techeniia v emirate Bukhara' [The Anti-Russian Search for Foreigners in Bukhara and the Pamirs. Political Trends in the Emirate of Bukhara], *Voprosy istorii Tadzhikistana. Uchenye zapiski* [Questions on the History of Tajikistan. Scholarly Notes], vol. 26. Seriia obshchest. nauk, 4. Stalinabad, 1961, pp. 140–177.

Tūsī, Naṣīr al-Dīn Muḥammad b. Muḥammad. *Rawḍa-yi taslīm*, ed. and tr. S.J. Badakhchani, as *Paradise of Submission: A Medieval Treatise of Ismaili Thought*. London, 2005.

Vaset͡ski, G. *Ocherki po istorii filosofskoĭ i obshchestvenno-politicheskoĭ mysli narodov USSR* [Essays on the History of the Philosophical and Socio-Political Thought of the Peoples of the USSR], vol. 1. Moscow, 1955.

Virani, Shafique N. *The Ismailis in the Middle Ages: A History of Survival, A Search for Salvation*. New York, 2007.

Walker, Paul E. 'The Ismaili Daʿwa in the Reign of the Fatimid Caliph Al-Ḥākim', *Journal of the American Research Center in Egypt*, 30 (1993), pp. 161–182.

Wendtland, Antje. 'The Position of the Pamir Languages within East Iranian', *Orientalia Suecana*, 58 (2009), pp. 172–188.

Wink, André. *Early Medieval India and the Expansion of Islam Seventh to Eleventh Centuries*, vol. 1, 'Al-Hind: The Making of the Indo-Islamic World'. Delhi, 1990.

Wood, John. *A Journey to the Source of the River Oxus*. London, 1872.

Xin, Wu. 'Zoroastrians of Central Asia: evidence from Archaeology of Art', *FEZANA Journal* (Summer 2014).

Yaacov, Ro'i. *Islam in the Soviet Union: From the Second World War to Gorbachev*. New York, 2000.

Yaqubov, Yusufsho. *Davlati Kaëniën* [Kayyanian State]. Dushanbe, 2012.

—— and Dagikhudo Dagiev. 'A Badakhshāni origin for Zoroaster', in Dagikhudo Dagiev and Carole Faucher, ed., *Identity, History and Trans-Nationality in Central Asia: The Mountain Communities of Pamir*. London, 2018, pp. 79–90.

Yettmar, Karl. *Religii Hindukusha*, tr. into Russian from the German by K.D. Tsivina. Moscow, 1986.

Zakuev, A.K. *Filosofiia 'Brat'ev chistoty'* [The Philosophy of the 'Brethren of Purity']. Baku, 1961.

Zinoviev, Alexander. *Homo Sovieticus*. Boulder, CO, 1986.
Zoolshoev, Muzaffar. 'Forgotten Figures of Badakhshan – Sayyid Munir al-Din Badakhshani and Sayyid Haydar Shah Mubarakshahzada', in Dagikhudo Dagiev and Carole Faucher, ed., *Identity, History and Trans-Nationality in Central Asia: The Mountain Communities of Pamir*. London, 2018, pp. 143–172.
—— 'The Soviet State and a Religious Movement: A Socio-Historical Study of the Ismāʿīlī Panjebhai Movement in Soviet Tajik Badakhshan (early 1920s late 1930s)'. Unpublished Report for the IIS, 2015.
—— *Ancient and Early Medieval Kingdoms of the Pamir Region of Central Asia: Historical Shughnan and Its Lost Capital*. Forthcoming.
Zoroastrian Cemetery found in Xinjiang, Tashkurgan Tajik Autonomous County, Jirzankal, 2013. Available online at: http://www.kaogu.cn/en/News/New_discoveries/2013/1026/43277.html [Last accessed, 18 October 2020].

Index

Page numbers in *italics* refer to illustrations.

Abbasids 5–6, 85
'Abd al-Nabī b. Khwāja Ṣālīḥ-i Yamgī
    91–92, 133
    see also Gawhar-rīz
'Abd al-Raḥmān Khān, *amīr* of
    Afghanistan 46, 63–64, 158, 204
Abū Ḥātim al-Rāzī, early Ismaili *dāʿī* and
    author 9–10, 12, 110, 128, 152, 156,
    190, 211–212
Abū Saʿīd, Tīmūrid ruler 29, 41–42, 166
Abū Saʿīd al-Shaʿrānī, Ismaili *dāʿī* 7
Abu'l-Haytham, Ahmad b. al-Ḥasan
    al-Jurjānī, Ismaili author 18, 215,
    222–223
Abu'l-Maʿālī ʿAlī b. al-Asad, Ismaili *amīr* of
    Badakhshān 17, 42, 215
Achaemenids, ancient Persian dynasty 41
Afghanistan 2, 4, 7–8, 38, *40*, 46–47, 51–52,
    58, 63–64, 98, 106–107, 123, 130,
    133, 161–163, 188, 204, 208, 216,
    238, 240, 246
    19th century 117, 169
    amīrs of 46–47
    ancient history 64, 75, 88, 144, 181
    and British India 46–47, 63–64
    the early Ismaili *daʿwa* in 7–8, 15, 17,
    20, 23, 35, 69, 135, 161
    Islamic history 17, 38

Ismailis of 35, 39, 40, 52, 70, 75, 106,
    161–163, 165
    medieval era 45, 71
    Nāṣir-i Khusraw tradition 14, 15,
    35–36, 40, 90, 129
    northern border 46, 58, 63, 88, 98. 162,
    194, 258
    as part of Central Asia 1, 1 n.2, 8, 29,
    33, 40, 43, 52, 88
    and Soviet Union 66, 81–82, 90, 922,
    95, 111, 133, 159, 161
    and Tsarist Russian 46, 50, 52, 99
    and Zoroastrianism 87–88, 237
Aga Khan III, Sulṭān Muḥammad
    (Mahomed) Shāh, Ismaili imam
    51–52, 57, 66, 70, 74, 78, 109, 118,
    120, 192–193, 236, 240
Aga Khan IV, Shah Karim al-Husayni,
    current Ismaili imam 60–62,
    112–113, 151, 193, 199, 223, 225,
    233, 240
ahl al-bayt (people of the house) 98, 214
Ākhūnd Sulaymān, Qurbān
    Muḥammadzāda, Tajik author 82,
    99, 101
Alamūt, fortress and seat of the Ismaili
    state, in northern Persia 21–22,
    23–32, 34, 35–36, 74, 82–83, 94, 132,

139, 147–148, 152–153, 161, 167,
    174–176, 179–180, 202, 204, 214,
    217, 226, 241–243, 248
  contact with Central Asian Ismailis
    fall of 30–31
  after fall of 30–32, 34–36, 39, 148
  fortress of 30, 69, 175
  foundation of Nizārī Ismaili state 24,
    30, 69
  Nizārī scholarship 110
  post-Alamūt era 30–32, 34–36, 39, 148
  and Saljūqs 13
Alans, ancient nomadic people of Indo-
    Iranian origin 2
Alexander the Great 41–42
ʿAlī b. Abī Ṭālib, first Shiʿi imam and
    fourth caliph 150, 173, 220
ʿAlī Mardān Shāh, Ismaili *pīr* in
    Badakhshān 66
ʿAlī Shāh, local ruler of Badakhshān 39, 41
Alimadadshoev, Mamadhusayn 106–107
Alphabetical Catalogue of Manuscripts
    43 n.164, 91 n.76
Amū Daryā 2, 26, 49, 64n 79 n.39, 87,
    88 n.55, 122, 142, 179, 202
  see also Oxus
Anatolia 16
Andreev, Mikhail Stepanovich, Soviet
    scholar 64, 79, 80, 122, 232
*Anglo-Russkoie Sopernichestvo v T͡Sentralʹnoĭ
    Azii i Ismailizm* 109
anjuman (society; committee) 56, 165, 178
ʿaql-i kull (universal intellect) 93, 154, 231
Arabic 2–3, 6, 9 n.33, 23, 31 n.117, 97, 110,
    111 n.116, 147, 173, 187, 204, 232,
    238
  Ismaili works in 226
  language 211, 244
  literature 97 n.2
  and Persian 2, 6, 9
  terms 36, 147
  toponyms 2–4
  translation 111, 121, 173, 189
Arabs 12 n.45, 33, 237, 244
ʿārif (gnostic) 31, 180
Aryan 5, 88 n.67, 151, 236
asās 231
Avestan 88
ʿAyn al-Quḍāt Hamadānī, Sufi poet 22

Aynī, Kamol, Tajik scholar 63 n.1, 89, 128
āzādmard 14, 138
Azerbaijan 8
al-Azhar, mosque and university 110
ʿAzīz al-Dīn Nasafī, Sufi scholar 82 n.44, 97

Bāb dar bāyān-i dānistan-i ʿālam-i dīn 33
Bābā Farghānī 98
Bābā ʿUmar-i Yamgī 94
bāb-i bāṭin 34
Babis 53
Bābur, founder of the Mughal empire and
    dynasty 41–42
Bactria, Bactrians 2, 88, 102
Badakhchani, Jalal 24, 107 n.106, 108,
    167
Badakhshān 3–32, 33–63, 70–71, 75,
    79–82, 86–88, 90–103, 105–107,
    109–111, 114, 117–118, 120–121,
    129, 135–136, 140–142, 144–146,
    149–150, 157, 159–162, 166–169,
    171, 174, 181, 184–187, 189,
    191–192, 194–195, 199–201,
    214–215, 217, 225, 228–229,
    233–234, 236–238, 245, 247–251
  in 19th century 90, 169
  of Afghanistan 7 n.26, 17, 36, 40, 40, 47,
    52, 88, 90, 99, 105 n. 103, 106–107,
    123, 133, 161–162, 204
  division of 99, 111
  geography 4
  historical 4, 40, 40, 47
  meaning 3
  post-Soviet rule 102–104
  pre-Islamic history 102–104
  province of 8–9
  Soviet rule 63–66
  stories about 109
  of Tajikistan 36, 52, 61, 76, 88, 102,
    105–108, 238, 262, 264
  toponym 3–4
  Tsarist rule 54, 99, 104, 167
Badakhshī, Mīrzā Sang Muḥammad,
    author 27–28, 43 n.166, 98, 129
Baghdad 9 n.33, 26, 68–89
al-Baghdādī, Abū Manṣūr ʿAbd al-
    Qāhir b. Ṭāhir, Sunni jurist and
    heresiographer 69
Baghlān 3, 130

Bakaev, Muhammadvafo 43, 91, 95, 133, 140
Balkh 1, 3, 8, 14–17, 42
Baluchistān 8
al-Barbar (Berbers/North Africa) 12 n.45, 33
Bartang, district in Badakhshān 46, 53, 122, 189, 246, 249
Bartol'd, Vasiliĭ Vladimirovich, Russian orientalist 4 n.14, 28, 65, 134, 210, 228, 240
Basmachi, anti-Bolshevik group 54
bāṭin (inward, hidden or esoteric meaning of sacred texts) 34, 156, 200
Bāṭinī (adj., esoteric) 69
Bāṭinīs, Bāṭiniyya (the Esotericists) 69, 164, 201, 218, 250
Beben, Daniel 18, 22, 27 n.99, 42 n.161, 43 n.165, 87, 108–109, 135
Bengal 78, 175
Bertel's, Andreĭ Evgen'evich, Russian scholar 32, 43, 70, 74, *80*, 80–82, 91–92, 95, 104, 132, 139–141, 143, 149, 181, 210, 213, 237, 245
Bertel's, Evgeniĭ Ėduardovich, Russian scholar 70, 80–81, *81*, 94, 141, 208
Bobrinskoĭ, Alekseĭ A., Russian ethnographer and archaeologist 37, 51, 53, 66–67, 142–143, 181, 189, 196, 210, 228, 239
Bogoutdinov, Alautdin Mukhmudovich, Soviet scholar 70, 71 n.25, 72, 84, 143
Bolshevik 54–55
Bombay 57, 66, 78, 179, 181
Bosworth, C. Edmund 1 n.2, 4, 27
Braginskiĭ, E., Soviet scholar 70
Britain, British 40, 46–47, 52, 63, 64, 66, 70, 74, 109, 196
British empire 38, 51, 52, 63, 66, 70, 81, 99, 190, 196, 199, 237
Browne, E. G., British orientalist 144
Buddhism 88
Buddhist 3, 87
Bughrā Khān, Qarakhānid governor of Khurāsān 13
Bukhārā 2, 6, 8, 13, 38, 46–47, 49–51, 53–54, 66, 229
Būyid/s, Persian dynasty 6
Buzurg-zoda, Lutfullo, Tajik scholar 89, 145

Cairo 7, 15–16, 25, 110, 173, 215
Calcutta 78
Caspian 2, 16, 30, 242
Central Asia 1–62, 63–64, 66, 69–71, 75, 77–78, 87–88 n.65, 93–94, 102–104, 108–109, 113–115, 117–118, 122–123, 132, 135–136, 142, 145–146, 149, 154–155, 159–160, 165–166, 171, 179, 184, 187–189, 192, 194, 197, 199–200, 202, 205, 208, 213–214, 224–225, 227–229, 232, 237, 239, 246–251
Chaghatay state 29
chahār ʿanāṣir (the four elements) 93
Chahār-wilāyat 63
charāgh-i rawshan, ceremony, text 56, 171
Cherkasov, Baron A. 66
China, Chinese 1, 2 n.5, 3–4, 8, 25–26, 33, 36, 40, 46, 51–52, 58, 88, 99, 135, 188, 226–227, 238
Chingiz Khan 28–29
Chitral 36, 43, 51, 98, 129, 188
civil war 60, 225
Communist, government, party 37, 55, 58, 68, 70, 75, 90, 101, 109, 115, 145, 163, 190
Corbin, Henry 15, 32, 72, 146, 149, 204
Crusaders 69, 147

Daftary, Farhad 9–12, 15, 20, 25, 27 n.101, 28, 32–33, 69, 104, 115, 146–147, 149, 160, 169, 226
dāʿī (lit., summoner; missionary) 6–13, 15–17, 19–20, 23, 25, 27–28, 35–36, 38 n.148, 73, 79, 89, 93, 101, 126, 132, 139, 154, 156–157, 160–161, 171, 174, 187, 190, 198–199, 202, 215, 220, 223, 231, 233, 236
19th century 38
20th century 35
in Badakhshān 27–28, 94
Central Asia 6–7
early *dāʿī*s 10
hierarchy 34
Fatimid *dāʿī*s 13
in Khurāsān 8, 17
meaning 6
post-Alamūt 34
reform of 56–57
term 6

Dānish-nāma-yi jahān 42
Dar nadāmat-i rūz-i qiyāmat 97
Darvāz 29, 41, 45–47, 51, 99, 114, 129, 162, 192, 202
darvīsh (dervish) 27, 31, 101, 250
Dāstān-i dukhtar-i Shaykh Manṣūr-i Hallāj 97
dast-i qudrat, rank in the Ismaili hierarchy 34
Davlatbekov, N.D., historian 108, 150
daʿwa (mission) 7–15, 17–18, 20–21, 23, 25, 30–31, 35–36, 38–39, 44, 69, 73, 81, 94, 101, 104, 118, 130, 135–136, 154, 161, 168, 171, 174, 195, 200, 248
   19th century 39
   Alamūt 21, 83
   ar. *al-daʿwa al-jadīda* 83–84, 242
   ar. *al-daʿwa al-qadīma* 84
   early *daʿwa* 7–15
   Fatimid *daʿwa* 7, 33 n.130, 188, 236
   hierarchy 34
   post-Alamūt 30, 36
   and Soviet rule 63–66
   Soviet scholars views of 66, 71–72, 74, 86, 89, 110
Dawāzdah faṣl 33, 91
al-Daylam 33
D'iakov, A.M. 55 n.199
D'iakov, T.M. 54
Dinorshoev, M. 112, 146, 151
Dīvān-i qāʾimiyyāt 24, 167
Dīvān-i Shams-i Tabrīzī 94
Dodikhudoev, Khaëlbek 70–72, 108–110, 119, 153
Durrānī, Aḥmad Shāh, founder of the Durrānī dynasty and empire 44
Dushanbe, capital of Tajikistan 61, 82, 96, 114
Dvizhenie Ismailitov v Isfakhane v 1100– 1107 gg. 82, 241

East Asia 2
East Iranian languages 4
Eastern Pamir 46
Egypt 7, 12, 15–16, 26, 30, 33, 69, 92, 104, 146, 148, 154, 173–174, 191, 217, 228, 232–233, 240, 242
   Fatimid 7, 12, 16, 30, 69, 85, 174, 225, 232, 240, 258, 264

   Nāṣir-i Khusraw and 15–16
   in Soviet scholarship 85, 89
Ėl'chibekov, Kudratbek 108, 111, 158, 160
Elnazarov, Hakim 126, 148, 160–161, 169, 183, 189, 199, 210, 213–214, 218, 245
Emel'ianova, Nadezhda 114, 162
Europe 2, 8, 240

Faḍl ʿAlī Bek Surkhafsar, author 98
Farā-rūd 2
Farghāna 13, 55, 251
Farīd al-Dīn ʿAṭṭār, Persian mystic poet 96
Farīd al-Dīn ʿAṭṭār-i Tūnī 107
Fārighī 96
farmān (edict) 24, 39, 168, 240
Farrukh Shāh, Ismaili *pīr* in Shughnān 92, 100, 169
Farsi 4, 52, 102, 126
   see also Tajik language
Fatimid caliphate 7, 15, 147, 177, 239
Fatimids 7, 12, 17, 30, 33, 69, 85, 89, 144, 174, 232–233, 240, 243
Fayḍābād, capital of historical Badakhshān, present capital of Afghan Badkhshān 40, *40*, 98
feldsher 50
Fenin, Colonel V.V. 54
Fidāʾī Khurāsānī, Ismaili author 76, 188–189, 231
Filosofskiĭ Ismailism 109
Fire Temple 88
First World War 180

Gawhar-rīz, Ismaili author 91–92, 101
Ghafurov, Bobojon, Soviet scholar 70, 72–73, 74, *74*, 163
Ghārān 46, 51, 142, 168
al-Ghazālī, Abū Ḥamīd Muḥammad, Sunni theologian 22, 69
Ghaznavids, of Afghanistan and Khurāsān 13
Ghiyāthī 96
Ghūmaĭ 51
Ghund 46
Ghūr 7
Ghūrids, of Ghūr and Khurāsān 130
glasnost' 60
Gosudarstvo Ismailitov v Irane v 11–13vv. 82, 243–244

Index

Great Game, the 38, 51, 63, 237
Greater Khurāsān 1, 6, 8, 11, 39
    see also Transoxania, Mā warāʾ al-nahr
Greek philosophy 12, 67, 217, 248
Grigorian, S. 70
Gross, Jo-Ann 109, 166
Gulamadov, Shaftalou 28, 44, 108–109, 166
Gushāyish va rahāyish, of Nāṣir-i Khusraw 20, 134, 190, 203, 207, 209

Habibov, Amirbek, Tajik scholar 82
ḥadīth (lit., report; sayings of the Prophet) 6, 136, 153, 185, 200, 216
Ḥāfiẓ, Shams al-Dīn Muḥammad, Persian poet 80, 106
Haft bāb-i Bābā Sayyidnā 23–24, 107
al-Ḥākim, sixth Fatimid Imam-caliph 33, 225, 244
Hamadān, in Iran 7
Ḥasan-i Maḥmūd-i Kātib, Nizārī Ismaili author and poet 23–24, 107, 167
Ḥasan-i Ṣabbāḥ, Nizārī Ismaili leader and founder of Nizārī state 23, 35, 69, 83–84, 97, 107, 110, 132, 139, 176, 202, 217, 242–243
Ḥasan-i Ṣalāḥ-i Munshī, *see* Ḥasan-i Maḥmūd-i Kātib
Ḥaydar Shāh Mubārak Shāhzāda, Ismaili author 28, 99
Herat 1, 7–8, 73
Hijaz, the 16
Ḥikāyat-i qahqaha 94
al-Hind (the Indian sub-continent) 33
Hindu Kush 2, 28, 117, 142, 149, 164, 195–196, 201, 237, 250
Hojibekov, Elbon 108, 111, 167–168
Homo Sovieticus 58
Hüan tsʾang, Chinese Buddhist monk 3
ḥudūd al-dīn (*daʿwa* hierarchy) 32–36, 39, 91, 149
ḥujja (lit. proof; chief *dāʿī*) 17, 19, 33–36, 38 n.148, 94, 181, 199, 212, 215, 231
ḥujjat-i aʿẓam (rank in the *daʿwa* hierarchy of Badakhshān) 34
Hukūmat-e Shūravī 54, 58–59
Hunsberger, Alice 21, 109, 169–170
Hunza 36, 170

Ibn al-Haytham, medieval Muslim scientist 110
Ibn al-Nadīm, Abuʾl-Faraj Muḥammad b. Isḥaq, author 9, 11
Ibn Rizām 68
Ibn Sīnā, Persian philosopher and polymath 42, 96, 123–124, 151, 178, 217, 220–221
Ikhwān al-Ṣafāʾ (Brethren of Purity) 85, 119, 138, 160, 182, 210
Iloliev, Abdulmamad 21, 37, 108, 172–173
Imam 6 n.24, 24–27, 34–37, 44, 58, 66–67, 69, 83–85, 90, 94, 103–104, 112, 130, 138, 144–145, 150, 154, 159, 163–164, 167–168, 173–174, 177, 179, 187, 190, 208, 210–211, 213, 216, 221–223, 231–232, 237, 246
    Fatimid 9–11, 13, 17, 23, 33, 215, 240
    in Ismaili tradition 6
    modern era 55
    Nizārī 26–27, 30, 38, 94
    post-Alamūt 26, 30, 34–36, 39
    in Soviet scholarship 65, 71, 108
    in Western scholarship 117, 233
Imamate 6, 9–10, 13, 44, 72, 84, 86, 103, 113, 125, 164, 172, 174, 182, 187, 211, 225, 237
    of Badakhshān 39
    Fatimid 9–11, 13, 17, 23, 33, 215, 240
    in Ismaili tradition 6, 30, 39
    and Ismailis of Central Asia 1–2
    modern 33, 55
    Nizārī 26–27, 30, 38, 94
    in Soviet scholarship 65, 71, 108
    in Western scholarship 117, 233
India 7–8, 33, 39, 44, 46–47, 52, 54, 63, 66, 70, 78, 104, 163, 174, 181, 193, 228
Institute of Ismaili Studies, The 103, 105, 114, 218
Institute of Oriental Manuscripts 95, 214
Iran 1, 5–8, 10, 16–17, 19, 21, 23–24, 26–28, 30–31, 44, 69, 78, 80, 83, 93, 104, 110, 132, 135, 148, 152, 154, 163, 165, 167, 174–175, 181, 200, 202, 204, 216–217, 241–244
    eastern Iran 1, 9, 102
    geography 5–6
    history 1, 3

languages 4
Nizārī Ismailis and 6, 26–27
Iraq 8, 26, 97
Irshād al-ṭālibīn 27
Iṣfahān 7, 82, 241
al-Iṣfahānī, Ghiyāth al-Dīn ʿAlī b. Amīrān Sayyid al-Ḥusaynī, scholar and author 38, 42, 136, 174
ishān (rank in the *daʿwa* in Badakhshān) 34, 118, 187
Ishkāshimī, East Iranian language 4
Iskandarov, Bahodur, historian 45, 82, 99, 174, 204, 235
Ismāʿīl b. Jaʿfar al-Ṣādiq, Ismaili imam 6, 86, 138, 218–219, 239
Ismaili Special Collections Unit, ISCU 105–108
Istoriia Badakhshana 82, 204
Ithnāʿasharī, Ithnāʿashariyya, 6, 51, 141
   see also Twelver/s Twelver Shiʿi
Ivanow, Waldimir, Russian orientalist 15, 19, 32, 36, 38 n.148, 72, 78–79, 78, 92, 97, 115, 119–120, 148–149, 174–181, 213–214, 218, 221
Iz Istorii Fatimidskogo Egipta 85, 232

Jābir b. Ḥayyān, Abū Mūsā 110
Jaʿfar al-Ṣādiq, Shiʿi imam 6, 86, 138, 218–219, 239
Jalāl al-Dīn Ḥasan, Ismaili imam and lord of Alamūt 83
Jalāl al-Dīn Rūmī, Persian mystic and poet 77, 98, 185–186, 198, 201, 230
Jāmarj 51
Jāmiʿ al-ḥikmatayn, of Nāṣir-i Khusraw 17–18, 22, 32, 134, 206–207, 215, 248
al-janāḥ 34
Jang-nāma-yi Amīr-i Sīstān 97
Jārf 51
jazīra, pl. *jazāʾir* (lit., island/s) 33, 35, 236
Jaxartes 2
   see also Syr Daryā
Jerusalem 16
Jibāl 7
Jonboboev, Sunatullo 108, 148, 157, 182
Jurm 92
Juwaynī, ʿAṭāʾ Malik, Persian historian 30

K Voprosu O Soťsialʾnoĭ Prirode Ismailitskogo Dvizheniia v Irane v XI-XIII vv Kublai Khān 82, 165, 242
kāfir 12, 17, 31, 125
Kāfiristān 63
kalām (theology) 10, 156
Kandjut 51
Karān, archaeological site in Badakhshān 88
Kashf al-ḥaqāʾiq 97
Kashgar 51–52, 66
Kashmir 1
Kazakh 3
Kazakhstan 1–2, 61–62, 187, 205
Khādara 51
al-Khādim, Abū ʿAbd Allāh, early Ismaili *dāʿī* in Khurāsān 7, 9
Khalaf al-Ḥallāj, early Ismaili *dāʿī* in Rayy 7
Khalīlī 43, 187
khalīfa (deputy; rank in the Ismaili *daʿwa*) 20, 34–37, 57, 59, 113, 166, 196, 205, 235, 238
Khāmūsh, Sayyid Shāh (Sayyid Mīr Ḥasan Shāh) 27–28, 99–101, 129, 158
khān 98
khānaqāh (sufi convent) 31
Khariukov, L.N., Russian officer and author 49, 109, 188
Khatlān 98, 129
Kholm 3
Khrestomatiia po Islamu 108
Khrushchev, Nikita, leader of the USSR 75
Khujand 2
Khurāsān 1–2, 7–10, 11 n.42, 12–18, 24, 26, 28, 33, 35, 38, 69, 89, 93–94, 100, 130, 138, 216, 236
   see also Greater Khurāsān, Central Asia, Transoxania, Mā warāʾ al-nahr
Khuseĭnbaev, T., organiser of the *Ḥukumat-e Shūravī* 54
Khwān al-ikhwān, of Nāṣir-i Khusraw 20, 134, 138, 245
Khwārazm 8, 29
Khwārazmians 2
Khwārazm Shāh 29, 73, 241
Kievan Rusʾ 68
Kirmān 8
al-Kirmānī, Ḥamīd al-Dīn, Ismaili *dāʿī* and author 33, 110–111, 121, 147, 152, 163, 189, 238

kishwar (province, land) 41
Kitāb al-Fihrist, of Ibn al-Nadīm 9 n.33
Kitāb al-Iṣlāḥ, of Abū Ḥātim al-Rāzī 9 n.36, 10
Kitāb Hidāyat al-mu'minīn al-ṭālibīn, of Fidā'ī Khurāsānī 76
Kitāb al-Maḥṣūl, of al-Nasafī 9
Klimovich, L., Soviet scholar 70, 190
Kublai Khān 3
al-Kūfī, Abū ʿAbd Allāh Muḥammad b. ʿAlī b. Rizām, Sunni heresiographer 68
 see also Ibn Rizām
Kyrgyz 3-4, 46, 61-62
Kyrgyzstan 1-2, 50, 166

lāḥiq (rank in the *daʿwa*) 33-34
La'l-i Badakhshān 60
Leadership and Authority in Central Asia: the Ismaili Community in Tajikistan 113, 199
Luqmān al-Ḥakīm 97

Mā warā' al-nahr 2, 29
 see also Central Asia, Greater Khurāsān, Transoxania
ma'dhūn (lit. licentiate, a rank in the *daʿwa*, assistant to the *dāʿī*) 34-36
ma'dhūn-i akbar 34, 94
ma'dhūn-i aṣghar 34, 94
al-Mahdī, ʿAbd Allāh, first Fatimid Imam-caliph 7, 187
Maĭskiĭ, Petr Mikhaĭlovich 70, 194
Manuscript Analysis Project 107
Marco Polo, medieval Venetian merchant and traveller 3-4, 42, 147
Markaz al-adwār-i Fāyḍ-i Dakkanī 94
Marv 1, 15
al-Marvazī, al-Ḥusayn b. ʿAlī, Ismaili *dāʿī* in Khurāsān 7-8, 10, 73
Marxism 67, 86, 101, 150
Marxist 58, 67-68, 71-72, 74, 85, 90, 109, 128, 143, 145, 153-154, 158, 165, 174, 190, 194, 199, 206-207, 233, 240
Mashhād 99, 176
Mastibekov, Otambek 108-109, 113, 199
Mathnawī-yi Tārīkhī 100
Maymana 7
Māzandarān 17

mazār 44, 247
Maẓhar al-ajā'ib 107
Middle Ages 120, 155, 165, 193
Middle East 8, 30, 74, 165
mīr 28-30, 99, 129
Mīr Muḥammad ʿAlīm Khān, amīr of Bukhāra 54
Mīr Yārībeg Khān 43
Mir'at al-Muḥaqqiqīn 94
Mīrzā ʿIbādī Shidzī 96
Mīrzā Sang Muḥammad Badakhshī, author 27-28, 98
Mongols 28-29, 161, 237, 241, 248
Monogarova, Lidiia Fedorovna, Soviet scholar 86, 202
muʿallim 34-35, 94
muʿallim-i ṣādiq 34
al-Mu'ayyad fi'l-Dīn al-Shīrāzī, Ismaili *dāʿī* and author 16
Mubārak-i Wakhānī, author and poet 93, 96, 98, 107, 172-173, 201
Muḥabbat Khān, Afghan ruler of Shughnān 99
Muḥabbat Shāh-zāda, Tajik scholar (Shāh Fitūr) 82, 96, 98-99, 101, 158
Muḥammad, Prophet of Islam 69, 86, 125, 191
Muḥammad Ḥusayn, Tajik scholar 98
Muḥammad-Shāhīs, branch of Nizārī Ismailis 6, 26-27, 43
mulḥid (heretic) 17, 31
Mullā Tīmī 98
Multan 8, 178-179
Mu'min Shāh, ʿAlā' al-Dīn, Muḥammad-Shāhī imam 26
Mundjān 51
Murād Beg, ruler of Qunduz 45
Murghāb 50
murīd (disciple) 30, 36-37, 39, 55, 70, 118, 159, 163, 217
murshid 31
 see also pīr, shaykh
Mūsā al-Kāẓim, Ithnāʿasharī imam 6, 27
al-Mustaʿlī, Fatimid caliph 23
mustajīb 20, 34, 94
al-Mustanṣir bi'llāh, Fatimid imam-caliph 13, 17, 84, 94
al-Mustaẓhir, Abbasid caliph 69
mutaʿalim 34
Muʿtazila, school of theology 12

nafs-i kull (the Universal Soul) 93, 155, 231
al-Nakhshabī, *see* al-Nasafī
naqīb 33
al-Nasafī, Muḥammad b. Aḥmad, Ismaili *dāʿī* and author 8–12, 110, 147, 152, 163, 190
Nāṣir-i Khusraw, Ismaili *dāʿī*, author and poet 12–23, 28, 32–37, 40, 42, 56 n.204, 75–77, 80–81, 86, 90–91, 93–94, 97–98, 100–101, 110, 112, 114, 118–131, 134–147, 149–152, 155, 157–159, 162–164, 166, 168–173, 178–179, 181–188, 190–191, 194, 199–222, 227, 229–237, 244–245, 248–250
   conversion of 15, 89, 164, 222, 224
   and Ismailis of Badakhshān 18, 94
   legends of 21
   persecution 13–14, 17–18
   in poetry 13–14, 16, 19–20, 23, 81, 121–122, 137–138, 141, 152, 157, 164, 168, 179, 191, 194, 200, 245
   tomb of *16*, 44, 187
   tradition of 23, 36, 171
   travels of *16*, 129
   works 15, 18–23
Nāṣir-i Khusraw: Yesterday, Today, Tomorrow 114
Naṣr b. Aḥmad, Sāmānid *amīr* 9–11, 237
Naẓm-i Shughnānī 107
Neoplatonism 10
Nicholas II, last Russian Tsar 51–52, 99, 204
Nile 7
Nīshāpūr 1, 7, 9, 15, 73, 176
Niyozbekov, Davlat 108
Niẓām al-Mulk, Saljūq vizier 69, 132
Niẓāmiyya madrasa 69
Nizār, Nizārī imam 23
Nizārī Quhistānī, Ḥakīm Saʿd al-Dīn b. Shams al-Dīn, Nizārī Ismaili poet 25–26, 132, 147, 153, 180
North Africa 7, 10, 104, 173, 177, 198
North India 52
Nourmamadchoev, Nourmamadcho 108–109, 214
Nūḥ b. Manṣūr Sāmānī, Sāmānid *amīr*, Nūḥ I 11, 18, 96
al-Nuʿmān, al-Qāḍī Abū Ḥanīfa, Ismaili jurist and author 10, 33, 94 n.84

October Revolution 52, 68, 99, 186, 204
   see also Russian Revolution
Orient 25–26, 233
Oriental Studies 33, 53, 73, 82, 90–91, 96, 101, 133, 139–140, 142, 162, 170, 239, 243
Orientalist 64 n.3, 65, 71, 86, 97, 104, 108, 114, 117, 119, 141, 150, 177, 186, 189, 194, 197, 210, 214, 219, 221–222, 232, 239, 248
Osh 50–51
Oxus 2–3, 25–26, 64, 87 n.65
   see also Amū Darya

Pakhalina, T.N., Soviet scholar 4
Pakistan 1, 4, 30, 36, 40, 51–52, 78, 88, 123, 135, 163, 171–172, 188, 192–193, 238, 240
Palestine 16, 208
Pamir/s 3–12, 28, 36, 46–47, 49–57, 61, 63–66, 75–76, 79–81, 86, 88, 98, 100, 102, 104, 111, 117–122, 129, 133, 135, 139–140, 142, 144–146, 149–150, 157, 162, 164–168, 171–174, 179, 183–189, 191–192, 194–198, 200–202, 204–205, 214–215, 218, 224–228, 231, 234–237, 239–240, 243, 246–247, 250–251
   geography 53 n.191, 166
   languages 4 nn.14, 16,
   name 5
   peoples 5
   provinces 3
Pamir-Strana Ariev 5
Pand-nāma 96
Panj River 47, *49*, 51, 142–143, 150, 184–185, 249
panj tasbīḥ ʿAlī-i Zamān 56-7
Panjakent 2
Panjebhai movement 34, 54–57, 118, 165, 167, 196–197, 240, 250–251
Panjtanī 66
Pārshinev 92
Pashtunistān 63–64
perestroĭka 60
Persia, 1 n.2, 7, 26, 35, 39, 69, 134, 170, 175–176, 178, 180
   see also Iran

Piať filosofskikh traktatov na temu Āfāq va Anfus 82
pīr 19-20, 28, 31-32, 34-39, 44, 47, 49-50, 53, 55, 57-58, 66-67, 76, 90, 92, 100-101, 111, 113, 136, 159, 168, 179, 199, 230
see also shaykh, murshid, pīrship
Pīr Sabzalī Ramḍān ʿAlī 56
pīrship 32, 36-39, 172
Plekhanov, Sergeĭ 112, 217
Provisional Government 54
Prozorov, Stanislav Mikhaĭlovich 108, 126, 148, 160, 169, 183, 189, 199, 210, 213-214, 217, 245

qāʾim 6
see also Mahdī
qalandar 31
see also darvīsh
Qalandarov, H. 108, 113, 218, 220, 222-223
Qalandarov, T. 108, 183
Qalʿa-yi Khumb 46, 51
Qalmuq 99
Qarakhānid, Central Asian Turkic dynasty 13
Qārlūq 99
Qarmaṭīs 6, 11, 73, 113, 139, 144, 177, 201, 211, 216, 219, 222, 239-240, 251
qaṣīda-i Dhurriya 76, 231
Qāsim-Shāhīs, branch of the Nizārī Ismailis 26-27, 38 n.148, 215
Qaṭaghān 3, 63, 99, 129
Qayd-hā-yi tārīkhī 99
Qazwīn 24, 167
Qiṣṣa-yi Chihil-tanān 97
Qiṣṣa-yi Sargudhasht-i Bābā Sayyidnā 97
qiyāma (resurrection) 23-24, 244, 248
Qoqand 51
Qubād Khān 99, 158, 204
Qubādiyān 15, 123, 128
Quhistān 24-26, 31 n.122, 132, 147, 153, 167, 180, 225-226
Qumm 7
Qunduz 45
Qurʾan 6, 77, 92, 136-138, 153-155, 185-186, 191, 200, 203, 210-211, 216, 218, 221, 231, 234, 238, 245
exegesis of 20

Nāṣir-i Khusraw 77, 125, 136-138
and the *sharīʿa* 157, 186, 221
Sufism 198
taʾwīl of 154, 157, 170
verses in Ismaili works 77, 92, 136-139, 153
Qurbān Muḥammad-zāda 82
Qurbān Shāh Zuhūr Bekzāda 99

Rāḍī al-Dīn ʿAlī, Muḥammad-Shāhī imam 43
Rāfiḍī 17
Rāgh 98
Rāḥat al-ʿaql, of Ḥamīd al-Dīn al-Kirmānī 111, 121, 189
Rahmon, Emomali 61
Raqqāmī Khurāsānī 76, 231
Raskrytaia Ladon': Aga-Khan i Ego Miuridy 112, 217
Rawḍa-yi taslīm, of Naṣīr al-Dīn al-Ṭūsī 22, 34, 139, 167
Rawshanāʾī-nāma, of Nāṣir-i Khusraw 121, 149, 209, 232, 248
Rayy 7-8, 10
Razdelenie Badakhshana i sud'by Ismailizma 13 n.50, 110, 237
religious hierarchy, see daʿwa
risāla 107, 166
Risāla dar bāb-i haft ḥudūd-i dīn 33, 91
Rome 26
Rūdakī, Persian poet 9, 85, 113, 139, 143, 168-169, 182, 202, 218-219, 222-223
Rudaki Institute of Oriental Studies 33, 82, 101
Rūdakī va Ismoiliia 9 n.32, 113, 219
Rukn al-Dīn Khurshāh, Nizārī imam and last lord of Alamūt 30
Rūshān, Rūshānī 4-5, 45-47, 50-51, 56-57, 79, 91-92, 99, 114, 120, 142, 144, 167-168, 175, 184, 189, 202, 249
Russia, Russian 1, 4, 32, 37 n.141, 46-47, 49-53, 63-115, 121, 126-127, 139, 141-142, 147-150, 169, 173, 179, 183, 186, 189, 192, 194-199, 204, 208, 210, 213-214, 220-221, 228, 230, 237, 239, 245, 248, 250
and *amīr* of Bukhārā 47, 49, 54
and Afghanistan 40, 47, 63

army 65
and British 40, 196
and Central Asia 46 n.175, 47 n.176, 49, 52, 142
Empire 38, 50, 63, 64, 66, 68, 70
Imperial 75, 78
languages 53
scholars 65, 75, 94–95, 104, 160, 162, 181, 218
Tsarist 46, 65, 99, 104, 167
Russian empire 38, 51, 63–64, 66, 70
Russian Revolution 51–52, 54–57
Russo-British agreement 46

Sa'ādat-nāma, of Nāṣir-i Khusraw 94, 121, 149
Ṣad naṣīḥat 97
Sa'dī, Persian poet 98
Safar-nāma, of Nāṣir-i Khusraw 15–16, 80–81, 90, 94, 120–121, 131, 152, 183, 208, 248
Safar-nāma-yi mashriq 90
Ṣaffārids, local dynasty in Sīstān 6
Sagadeyev, A., Soviet scholar 70
Ṣaḥīfat al-nāẓirīn 38, 136
St Petersburg 46, 52, 95, 115
Saka, ancient Central Asian people 2, 102
Ṣāliḥ, Khwāja Muḥammad 44, 92
Saljūqs, Turkish dynasty 13–14, 73, 84, 112, 146, 241–242
Sāmānids, dynasty of Persian amīrs in Khurāsān and Transoxania 6, 8–10, 12–13, 15, 41, 222, 236
Samarqand 1, 6, 8, 13
al-Ṣaqāliba 33
Sarikūl, Sarikūlī 4–5, 51, 218
sayyid, descendant of the Prophet 19, 37, 166
Sayyid Farrukh Shāh, Ismaili pīr 92, 100, 169
Sayyid Mursal 92
Sayyid Yūsuf 'Alī Shāh, Ismaili pīr 66, 168–169
Scythians, ancient Central Asian people 2
see also Saka
Sebüktigin, Turkish amīr and founder of the Ghaznavid dynasty 11
Second World War 59, 70, 74

Semënov, Aleksandr Aleksandrovich, Russian scholar 34, 67, 70, 75–77, 91, 95, 99, 135, 141, 181, 188–189, 196, 210, 227–232, 248
Semënova, Lidii͡a, Soviet scholar 85, 232
Serebrennikov, A., Russian explorer 64
Shabistarī, Maḥmūd, Persian poet 98
Shāh Burhān 99, 101, 247
Shāh Fitūr 82, 96, 98–99, 101, 158
see also Muḥabbat Shāh-zāda
Shāh Kāshān 101
Shāh Malang 27–28, 99, 101
Shāh Partāwī 100
Shāh Vanjī, ruler of Shughnān 44, 158
al-Shahrastānī, Muḥammad b. 'Abd al-Karīm 22
Shākhdara 46, 53
Shams al-Dīn Muḥammad, Nizārī Ismaili imam 26, 106
Shamsherbek 98
shari'a (lit. way; Islamic religious law) 31, 76, 156–157, 170, 186, 200, 203, 221, 230
Shaybānids, Central Asian dynasty 43
Shaykh Zayd 24
Sherzodshoev, Shozodamamad 106–108
Sherzodshoev, Umed 108
Shi'a, Shi'ī 6–7, 9–10, 13, 17, 20, 30, 42, 53, 72, 86, 97, 110–111, 117, 130–131, 135–136, 142, 144, 147, 154, 159, 163, 213
Shish faṣl 20
see also Rawshanā'ī-nāma
Shokhumorov, Abusaid, Soviet scholar 5, 11, 42, 108, 110–111, 235
Shotemur, S. 54
Shughnān 27, 44–47, 50–51, 54–55, 76–77, 79, 91, 94, 98–100, 114, 120, 129, 135–136, 151, 158, 161, 166–169, 172, 191, 202, 204, 214–215, 218, 229–230, 232, 251
division of 29, 41
expeditions to 92, 111
Ismailis of 76, 229
province of 50, 98
and Rushān 4, 5, 45–47, 50, 51, 56, 57, 79, 99, 114, 142, 144, 167, 168, 175, 184, 189, 202, 249
Shughnī, dialect/language of Shughnān 4–5

Shuʿūbiyya 12
Sī va shish ṣaḥīfa 38, 245
Sih faṣl-i ʿAṭṭār 94
al-Sijistānī, Abū Yaʿqūb, Ismaili *dāʿī* and author 10, 12, 110, 147, 152, 163, 207
Silk Road 2, 8, 88
Sīlk-i gawhar-rīz 24, 37, 39, 44, 90–93, 101, 133, 159–160
al-Ṣīn, *see* China
Sind 7, 31
Sīstān, province in southeastern Iran 2, 7–8
Siyāsat-nāma, of Niẓām al-Mulk 69
Smirnov, Andreĭ Vadimovich 111, 121, 189, 210, 238–239
Smirnov, Nikolaĭ 68, 239
Sogdiana, Sogdians 2, 102
South Asia 2, 56, 193
   see also India, al-Hind, Pakistan
Soviet Union 57–58, 60, 65, 71, 101, 103, 109, 112, 115, 125, 140, 142, 163, 166, 187, 225, 250
Sovetskaīa Vlastʾ 54
Stroeva, Lîudmila V., Soviet scholar 70, 72, 74, 82–84, 217, 240, 242
Sufi/s 21, 31–32, 76, 95, 106, 136, 141, 164, 172–173, 179, 191, 198, 203, 214, 233, 229–230, 245, 250
Suhrāb Valī Badakhshānī, Sayyid Khwāja 91, 156, 245
al-Sulṭān al-ʿĀẓim 41
Sulṭān Ways Mīrzā, Tīmūrid governor of Badakhshān 43
Sunni Islam 42–43, 119, 144, 154–155
Syr Daryā 2
   see also Jaxartes
Syria 16, 26, 69, 83, 148, 154, 173, 217, 224, 241–242

Ṭabaristān 8
Tadzhiki 73, 79
   see also Tajik/s
Tadzhiki Doliny Khuf 79, 122
Tajik/s 4–5, 11, 30, 45, 49, 52, 57–58, 60, 65–66, 73, 76, 79–80, 88 n.69, 89, 98, 99, 108–109, 118–119, 121–122, 127, 129, 133, 143, 152, 155, 159, 162, 166, 190–192, 194, 199, 207, 211, 213, 223, 226–227
   of Badakhshān 4, 55

Cyrillic script 103, 148
history 50, 82, 138, 183
literature in 82, 138, 201
and Persian 149, 219
post-Soviet era 4 n.17, 102, 113, 149, 256
Soviet era 34, 58, 120, 224, 250–251, 266
Tajik language 55, 102–104, 113–114, 118–121, 126, 133, 138, 143, 149, 157–158, 171, 174, 181, 201, 219–223, 225, 234, 236
Tajikistan 1–2, 4–5, 15, 33, 36, 39–40, 52, 55, 57–58, 60–62, 71, 98, 101–103, 105–107, 113–114, 120–123, 126, 129, 135, 145–146, 161, 166, 169, 172, 179, 183, 188–189, 208, 215–216, 223–225, 240
border with 88
post-Soviet era 4 n.17, 102, 113, 149, 256
Soviet era 34, 58, 120, 224, 250–251, 266
taʿlīm (teaching; instruction) 22, 30, 69, 216
taqiyya (precautionary dissimulation of one's beliefs) 30–32, 36, 45, 136, 161, 175
Tārīkh-i Afghānistān 99, 204
Tārīkh-i Badakhshān, of Mīrzā Sang Muḥammad Badakhshī 27–28, 98
Tārīkh-i Mulk-i Shughnān, of Sayyid Ḥaydar Shāh Mubārak Shāhzāda 28, 99, 202
Tārīkh-i Shāhān-i Shughnān 100
ṭarīqa (lit. way, path; the mystical, spiritual path followed by Sufis) 101, 225, 230
Tirmiz 28
Tīmūr, Central Asian conqueror, founder of Tīmūrid dynasty 29
Tīmūrids 29, 41, 43–44, 214
thanāwiyyūn (dualists) 12
Ṭokhāristān 3
Trakhtenberg, O.B., Soviet scholar 70
Transoxania 2, 6, 11 n.42, 35
   see also Central Asia, Greater Khurāsān, Mā warāʾ al-nahr
Treasures of Badakhshān, The 82
troĭka 54
Tunisia 7

Tūrān 25–26
  see also Central Asia, Transoxania, Mā
    warā' al-nahr
Turbat 7
Turkestan 49–50, 50 n.182, 52, 54 n.195,
    55, 63–66
  see also Central Asia, Greater Khurāsān,
    Transoxania, Mā warā' al-nahr
Turkic, Turkicised 2–3, 13, 30, 41, 54 n.195,
    83, 110, 224
Turkmenistan 1
Turko-Iranian 3
Turks 14, 41, 69, 83, 237
Ṭūs 1
al-Ṭūsī, Khwāja Naṣīr al-Dīn Muḥammad,
    Shi'i scholar and polymath 22, 147
Twelver Shi'i 6, 15, 27, 31, 44, 100, 214, 239
  see also Ithnā'asharī, Shi'i, Shi'a

'ulamā' (scholars of Islamic sciences) 11,
    13, 125
Umayyad/s 5
Umm al-kitāb 94, 97, 110
umma (lit., community; the Islamic
    community) 79
Universal Intellect 76, 93, 126–127, 154,
    156, 163, 230
  see also 'aql-i kull
Universal Soul 76, 93, 125–127, 155–156,
    163–164, 171, 194, 230
  see also nafs-i kull
Uṣūl al-ādāb 97, 139
Uzbek 3–4, 29, 43, 45, 98, 142, 239
Uzbekistan 1–2, 118, 196–198
Uyghur 3, 52, 226

Vanj 46

Wajh-i dīn, of Nāṣir-i Khusraw 20, 75, 77,
    94, 100, 187, 231, 248
Wakhān 29, 41, 45–47, 50–51, 87, 99, 120,
    122, 142–143, 166, 168, 172, 189,
    202, 218

Wakhān corridor 88
Wakhī 4–5
waqf (endowment) 43–44
al-waṣī (legatee) 34
West Asia 2
Western Pamirs 66, 86, 104, 120, 150, 184,
    189, 202, 225, 239, 247
Written Heritage 33, 82, 101, 139, 199

Xinjiang 1, 29, 36, 88 n.69, 226–227
Xuanzang 3
al-yadd 34
Yaghnābis 102
Yāgīd 51
Yārid, local dynasty 43–44
Yumgān 16, 17, 20–21, 162, 166, 187,
    228
Yūsuf 'Alī Shāh, Ismaili pīr 49, 66,
    168–169
Yazghulām 46
Yemen 7
Yūsuf 'Alī Khān 99, 158

zabān-i 'ilm 34
Zād al-musāfirīn, of Nāṣir-i Khusraw 20,
    112, 121, 127–128, 134, 149, 152,
    200, 207, 248
Ẓafar-nāma 96
zakat (religious dues) 57, 67, 131
Zakuev, A.K., Soviet scholar 70, 85,
    210
al-Zanj 33
Zarubin, Ivan Ivanovich, Russian
    ethnographer and historian 94, 95,
    175, 186, 230, 249–250
Zilzila-nāma 94
Zingiria 51
Zoroaster, Prophet and eponymous
    founder of the Zoroastrian religion
    87 n.65, 88, 237
Zoroastrian, Zoroastrianism 5 n.18, 86–88,
    235, 237, 249
Zubdat al-ḥaqā'iq 22 n.82, 97

www.ingramcontent.com/pod-product-compliance
Lightning Source LLC
Chambersburg PA
CBHW051805230426
43672CB00012B/2633